Please return/renew this item by the
last date shown to avoid a charge.
Books may also be renewed by phone
and Internet. May not be renewed if
required by another reader.

www.libraries.barnet.gov.uk

LONDON BOROUGH

THE LONELY CENTURY

'We are living in an age where we have forgotten a fundamental truth about humankind that is as old as the Hebrew Bible itself: that we were not meant to live alone. In *The Lonely Century*, Noreena Hertz recognises this and provides an enlightening, engaging and compelling analysis of the dangers posed by the loneliness pandemic not just to our individual health and happiness, but to our collective ability to reinvigorate society and tackle the many challenges we face today.'

Rabbi Lord Jonathan Sacks

'In this hugely stimulating and ambitious book, Noreena Hertz provides a powerful account of the causes and consequences of the loneliness pandemic that has swept across the globe. Filled with terrifying facts, eye-catching stories and bold ideas, it is a must-read for anybody concerned about the post-Covid-19 world that we are building.'

Carl Frey, Institute for New Economic Thinking,
University of Oxford

'In *The Lonely Century*, Noreena Hertz delivers a compelling vision for how we can bridge our many divides at this time of great change and disruption. Passionately argued and deeply researched, this book is for everyone who wants to build a healthier and more connected world.'

Arianna Huffington, co-founder of the *Huffington Post*
and author of *Thrive*

'Social connections are vital for our health and well-being, but loneliness is on the rise globally, especially with the measures introduced to contain the spread of Covid-19. In this captivating book Noreena Hertz describes the physical, mental, economic and societal effects of loneliness, and not only provides a fascinating examination of the evidence, but also a rousing call for action – to governments, businesses, society and individuals to address and mitigate the loneliness crisis and build a more inclusive and kinder world.'

Sarah-Jayne Blakemore, Professor of Psychology,
University of Cambridge

'Brilliant and full of captivating stories about the power of human connection in our lives. A truly engrossing and important book that left me feeling both wiser and more hopeful!'

Brian Grazer, film and TV producer

'A fascinating and original book about one of the greatest challenges of our time – the growing global crisis of loneliness – and a clear and inspiring vision of how we can respond.'

Daniel Susskind, fellow at the University of Oxford and author of *A World Without Work*

'We're surrounded by communication technologies and social media, yet loneliness is taking a huge toll on our economy, our health and our democracy. With a rare combination of rigorous research and powerful insights, Noreena Hertz masterfully explains the many facets of our Lonely Century and how we can do better, as individuals and as a society. Highly Recommended!'

Erik Brynjolfsson, Professor at Stanford University and co-author of *The Second Machine Age*

THE LONELY CENTURY

Coming Together in a World that's Pulling Apart

NOREENA HERTZ

SCEPTRE

First published in Great Britain in 2020 by Sceptre
An Imprint of Hodder & Stoughton
An Hachette UK company

3

A CIP catalogue record for this title is available from the British Library

This is a work of non-fiction. Nonetheless, some of the names and personal characteristics
of the individuals involved have been changed in order to disguise their identities. Any resulting
resemblance to persons living or dead is entirely coincidental and unintentional.

Hardback ISBN 9781529329254
Trade Paperback ISBN 9781529329261
eBook ISBN 9781529329285

Typeset in Dante MT by Palimpsest Book Production Ltd, Falkirk, Stirlingshire

Printed and bound in Great Britain by Clays Ltd, Elcograf S.p.A.

Hodder & Stoughton policy is to use papers that are natural, renewable
and recyclable products and made from wood grown in sustainable forests.
The logging and manufacturing processes are expected to conform to
the environmental regulations of the country of origin.

Hodder & Stoughton Ltd
Carmelite House
50 Victoria Embankment
London EC4Y 0DZ

www.sceptrebooks.co.uk

To Danny
For everything

Contents

CHAPTER ONE

This is the Lonely Century

Curled up against him, my chest pressing against his back, our breathing synchronised, our feet intertwined. This is how we have slept for over 5,000 nights.

But now we sleep in different rooms. By day we dance the two-metre zigzag. Hugs, caresses, kisses, our daily shorthand, now forbidden, 'Stay away from me', my new term of endearment. Constantly coughing, feeling achy and unwell, I am terrified that if I get too close to my husband I will infect him. So I keep my distance.

This is 31 March 2020 and along with 2.5 billion other people, a third of the world's population, my household is in lockdown.[1]

With so many people stuck at home, condemned to working remotely (if one still had a job, that is), not allowed to visit friends or loved ones, getting outside once a day if at all, 'socially distancing', 'quarantining' and 'self-isolating', it was inevitable that feelings of loneliness and isolation soared.

Just two days into lockdown my best friend messages 'the isolation is driving me potty'. On day four my 82-year-old father WhatsApps 'I wandered lonely as a cloud'. Across the globe, staff manning emotional health helplines reported not only massive spikes in caller volume within days of mandatory social distancing, but also that significant numbers were from people suffering loneliness.[2] 'My mum won't hug me or get very close to me,' one distraught child confided to a volunteer at the UK helpline Childline.[3] In Germany, where by mid-March helplines were taking 50% more calls than usual, one psychologist working the phones noted that 'most callers are more afraid of loneliness than getting infected'.[4]

Yet the Lonely Century did not begin in the first quarter of 2020. By the time Covid-19 struck many of us had *already* been feeling lonely, isolated and atomised for a considerable amount of time.

Why we became so lonely and what we must do to reconnect is what this book is about.

Pretty in pink

24 September 2019. I am waiting, seated at the window, my back against the pretty-in-pink wall.

My phone pings. It's Brittany – she's running a few minutes late.

'No worries,' I message back. 'Cool choice of place.' And it is. The effortlessly beautiful, gazelle-like clientele with their fashion-model portfolios under their arms hint at just how hip Cha Cha Matcha in Manhattan's Noho district feels.

A few beats later, she arrives. Long-limbed, athletic, her smile widens as scanning the room I come into her gaze. 'Hey, love your dress,' she says.

At $40 an hour I'd expect no less. For Brittany is the 'friend' I have rented for the afternoon from a company called Rent-a-Friend. Founded by New Jersey entrepreneur Scott Rosenbaum who had seen the concept take off in Japan, now operating in dozens of countries across the world, its website has over 620,000 platonic friends for hire.

This wasn't the career path Brittany, a 23-year-old small-town Floridian, had intended when she had won her place at Brown. Yet having been unable to secure a job in environmental science (the subject she had majored in at university), and anxious about her levels of student debt, she explains her decision to rent out her company as a pragmatic one, her emotional labour as just another monetisable string to her bow. When she's not renting herself out – on average she does so a few times a week – she helps start-ups with their social media postings and offers executive assistant services via TaskRabbit.

Before we met up I was pretty nervous, not sure if 'friend' was covert speak for sexual partner or even if I'd recognise her from her profile picture. But within minutes I feel reassured that this is friends-without-benefits territory. And over the next few hours, as we wander around downtown Manhattan chatting about #MeToo and her heroine Ruth Bader Ginsberg, and at McNallys about our favourite books, at times I even forget I am paying for Brittany's company. Although she didn't feel like an old friend, she did feel like a fun new prospect.

But it is at Urban Outfitters on Broadway that she really ramps up the charm, just as the meter on our encounter begins to run out. Smile now perma-fixed, banter upped, she joshes with me as we rummage through a pile of t-shirts, and gamely joins me in trying on Crayola-coloured bucket hats. Apparently they really suit me. Although presumably she would tell me that whether it was true or not.

I ask Brittany about the others who've hired her, my fellow friendship-consumers. She tells me of the soft-spoken woman who didn't want to show up at a party alone, the techie from Delhi who had moved to Manhattan for work, didn't know anyone in town and wanted company at dinner, the banker who offered to come over with chicken soup when she was sick. 'If you had to sum up your typical clientele, what would you say?' I ask her. Her answer: 'Lonely, 30- to 40-year-old professionals. The kind of people who work long hours and don't seem to have time to make many friends.'

It's a sign of our times that today I can order companionship as easily as I can a cheeseburger with just a few taps on my phone, that what I call a Loneliness Economy has emerged to support – and in some cases exploit – those who feel alone. But in the twenty-first century, the loneliest century we have known, Brittany's overworked professionals are not the only ones suffering: the tentacles of loneliness reach much further.

Even before the coronavirus triggered a 'social recession' with its toxification of face-to-face contact, three in five US adults considered themselves lonely.[5]

In Europe, it was a similar story. In Germany two-thirds of the population believed loneliness to be a serious problem.[6] Almost a third of Dutch nationals admitted to being lonely, one in ten severely so.[7] In Sweden, up to a quarter of the population said that they were frequently lonely.[8] In Switzerland, two out of every five people reported sometimes, often, or always feeling so.[9]

In the UK, the problem had become so significant that in 2018 the prime minister went so far as to appoint a Minister for Loneliness.[10] One in eight Brits did not have even a single close friend they could rely on, up from one in ten just five years before.[11] Three-quarters of citizens did not know their neighbours' names, whilst 60% of UK employees reported feeling lonely at work.[12] The data for Asia, Australia, South America and Africa was similarly troubling.[13]

Inevitably months of lockdowns, self-isolation and social distancing have made this problem even worse. Young and old, male and female, single and married, rich and poor.[14] All over the world people are feeling lonely, disconnected and alienated. We are in the midst of a global loneliness crisis. None of us, anywhere, are immune.

Some 6,000 miles from Manhattan's Noho district, Saito-san is waking up. Round-cheeked and small, a genial twinkle in her eye, this widowed mother of two knows all too well what it feels like to be lonely. Burdened with considerable financial worries, her pension not covering her living costs, bereft of support and her children too busy to care, she frequently felt very much on her own. Before, that is, she took a radical, if not unprecedented, step.

Incarcerated now in Tochigi prison, a facility for female offenders, Saito-san is one of numerous elderly Japanese who have made jail an active life choice. In Japan, crimes committed by people over the age of sixty-five have quadrupled over the past two decades.[15] Seventy per cent of this age group reoffend within five years. Prison warden Junko Ageno has no doubt that loneliness is a key driver of this trend – her charges have told her as much.[16] Ryukoku University professor Koichi Hamai, who has studied the phenomenon of elderly prisoners, agrees. He believes that significant numbers of elderly women choose prison as a way to escape how socially isolated they feel.[17] Jailed typically for minor offences such as petty shoplifting – one of the easiest crimes you can commit if going to jail is your goal – 40% of such prisoners report rarely speaking to their family or not having one at all, with half of the seniors incarcerated for shoplifting in recent years living alone prior to going to prison.

Many describe jail as a way of creating for themselves a 'community that [they] can't get at home'. A place where, as another octogenarian inmate explains, 'There are always people around, and I don't feel lonely.'[18] An environment which 78-year-old fellow prisoner Ms O describes as 'an oasis', where 'there are many people to talk to'. A sanctuary that provides not only company but also support and care.[19]

The elderly are the group we are prone to think of first when we consider who is loneliest amongst us. And indeed this cohort is lonelier than average.

Already by 2010, 60% of US nursing home residents said they never have any visitors.[20] In the UK, two-fifths of all older people reported in 2014 that television was their main company.[21] Meanwhile in Tianjin, China, an 85-year-old grandfather, one of China's millions of lonely elderly, gained international fame in 2017 when he posted a notice on his local bus shelter: 'Lonely man in his 80s', it read. 'My hope is that a kind-hearted person or family will adopt me.' Tragically within three months he was dead. It took many of his neighbours two weeks to notice he was no longer around.[22]

Such stories make hard reading. And they raise huge questions about how we as a society care for our oldest citizens. Yet it is actually, and perhaps surprisingly, the youngest amongst us who are the loneliest.

I first became aware of this a few years back when I was teaching graduate university students.[23] For not only was it obvious to me, when I saw how they interacted during group assignments, that they found their face-to-face interactions considerably more challenging than previous generations, but as they plumped themselves down in my office full of anxiety about their coursework and their future job prospects, I was struck by how many confided in me how lonely and isolated they felt.

My students weren't outliers.

In the US, slightly more than one in five millennials say they have no friends at all.[24] In the UK, three in five 18- to 34-year-olds and nearly half of children aged between 10 and 15 say they are lonely often or sometimes.[25]

Again, this disturbing picture is a global one that in recent years has got progressively worse. Across nearly every country in the OECD (which includes most of Europe, the US, Canada and Australia) the percentage of 15-year-olds who say they feel lonely at school rose between 2003 and 2015.[26] Again, in the wake of Covid-19 the numbers are likely to be significantly higher.

This isn't just a mental health crisis. It's a crisis that's making us physically ill. The research shows that loneliness is worse for our health than not exercising, as harmful as being an alcoholic and twice as harmful as being obese.[27] Statistically, loneliness is equivalent to smoking fifteen cigarettes a day.[28] Crucially, this is regardless of what we earn, our gender, age or nationality.[29]

It's also an economic crisis. Even prior to Covid-19 in the US, social isolation was estimated to cost Medicare nearly $7 billion every year, more than it spends on arthritis and almost as much as it does on high blood pressure – and that's just amongst elderly people.[30] In the UK, lonely over-50s were estimated to cost the National Health Service £1.8 billion per year, about the same as spent annually by the entire Ministry of Housing, Communities, and Local Government.[31] Meanwhile UK employers were losing £800 million each year due to loneliness-related sick days, significantly more when productivity losses were also taken into account.[32]

And it's a political crisis too, fuelling divisiveness and extremism in the US, Europe and across the globe. Loneliness and right-wing populism are, as we will see, close bedfellows.

Especially concerning is that we are very likely to be underestimating the true extent of the problem. In part this is because of the stigma associated with loneliness. For some, admitting they are lonely is a hard thing to do: a third of UK employees who feel lonely at work have never told anyone.[33] Others may find it difficult to admit even to themselves, believing it to suggest a personal failure rather than a consequence of life circumstances and a whole range of social, cultural and economic factors outside of one's individual control.

But more than this, the problem is underestimated because of how loneliness is defined. For not only is loneliness not the same as being alone – you can be physically surrounded by people and still feel lonely, or you can be alone and not experience loneliness – it has also typically been defined too narrowly. The loneliness we are experiencing in the twenty-first century is much broader in scope than its traditional definition.

What is loneliness?

The UCLA Loneliness Scale (see overleaf) was first developed in 1978 by a trio of researchers who sought to create a quantitative tool to measure subjective feelings of loneliness. It takes the form of twenty questions designed to ascertain not only how connected, supported and cared for respondents feel, but also how excluded, isolated and misunderstood. It remains to this day the gold standard in loneliness research.[34] Most of the studies on loneliness cited in this book use this scale, or a variant of it, to assess a respondent's loneliness.

Please take a few minutes to complete it yourself. Circle your answer for each statement; at the end, add the numbers together.[35]

How did you do? If you scored over 43 you'd be considered lonely.[36] But if you were to retake the quiz using a wider definition of loneliness – one that encompasses not only your relationships with friends, family, work colleagues and neighbours (those the UCLA scale more typically considers) but also your relationships with your employer, fellow citizens, politicians and the state – how would that affect your score?

A key difference between my definition of loneliness (the one that will be used throughout this book) and the traditional one is that I define loneliness not only as feeling bereft of love, company or intimacy. Nor is it just about feeling ignored, unseen or uncared for by those with whom we interact on a regular basis: our partner, family, friends and neighbours. It's also about feeling unsupported and uncared for by our fellow citizens, our employers, our community, our government. It's about feeling disconnected not only from

	Never	Rarely	Sometimes	Often
1. How often do you feel that you are 'in tune' with the people around you?	4	3	2	1
2. How often do you feel that you lack companionship?	1	2	3	4
3. How often do you feel that there is no one you can turn to?	1	2	3	4
4. How often do you feel alone?	1	2	3	4
5. How often do you feel part of a group of friends?	4	3	2	1
6. How often do you feel that you have a lot in common with the people around you?	4	3	2	1
7. How often do you feel that you are no longer close to anyone?	1	2	3	4
8. How often do you feel that your interests and ideas are not shared by those around you?	1	2	3	4
9. How often do you feel outgoing and friendly?	4	3	2	1
10. How often do you feel close to people?	4	3	2	1
11. How often do you feel left out?	1	2	3	4
12. How often do you feel that your relationships with others are not meaningful?	1	2	3	4
13. How often do you feel that no one really knows you well?	1	2	3	4
14. How often do you feel isolated from others?	1	2	3	4
15. How often do you feel you can find companionship when you want it?	4	3	2	1
16. How often do you feel that there are people who really understand you?	4	3	2	1
17. How often do you feel shy?	1	2	3	4
18. How often do you feel that people are around you but not with you?	1	2	3	4
19. How often do you feel that there are people you can talk to?	4	3	2	1
20. How often do you feel that there are people you can turn to?	4	3	2	1

those we are meant to feel intimate with, but also from ourselves. It's about not only lacking support in a social or familial context, but feeling politically and economically excluded as well.

I define loneliness as both an internal state and an existential one – personal, societal, economic *and* political.

As such my definition is closer to that envisaged by thinkers like Karl Marx, Émile Durkheim, Carl Jung and Hannah Arendt, and writers as various as Isaac Asimov, Aldous Huxley, George Eliot and more recently *Black Mirror* creator Charlie Brooker.[37]

Reshaped by globalisation, urbanisation, growing inequality and power asymmetries, by demographic change, increased mobility, technological disruption, austerity, and now by the coronavirus too, I believe the contemporary manifestation of loneliness goes beyond our yearning for connection with those physically around us, our craving for love and being loved, and the sadness we feel when we consider ourselves to be bereft of friends. It also incorporates how disconnected we feel from politicians and politics, how cut off we feel from our work and our workplace, how excluded many of us feel from society's gains, and how powerless, invisible and voiceless so many of us believe ourselves to be. It's a loneliness that includes but is also greater than our desire to feel close to others because it is also a manifestation of our need to be heard, to be seen, to be cared for, to have agency, to be treated fairly, kindly and with respect. Traditional measures of loneliness capture only a part of this.

With that definition in mind, ask yourself: when did you last feel disconnected from those around you, whether family, friends, neighbours *or* your fellow citizens? When did you last feel uncared for or unheard by your elected politicians, or that no one in a position of authority cared about your struggles? When did you last feel powerless or invisible at work?

You are not alone.

In the years preceding the coronavirus pandemic two-thirds of those living in democracies did not think their government acted in their interests.[38] Eighty-five per cent of employees globally felt disconnected from their company and their work.[39] And only 30% of Americans believed that most other people could be trusted, a very substantial drop since 1984, when around 50% did.[40] When it comes to feeling disconnected from each other, can you remember a time when the world has felt this polarised, fractured and divided?

How we got here

This state of affairs didn't just happen by chance. Nor did it emerge overnight. There is a backdrop, a fusion of causes and events which explain why we have become so lonely and atomised, both personally and as a society.

As you might have suspected, our smartphones and in particular social media have played an integral role: stealing our attention away from those around us, fuelling the worst within us so that we become ever more angry and tribal, making us behave ever more performatively and compulsively in pursuit of likes, retweets and follows, eroding our ability to communicate effectively or empathetically. This held true even during the coronavirus lockdown. For alongside the Pope live-streaming his daily Mass on Facebook, DJ D-Nice throwing a dance party attended by more than 100,000 people on Instagram, the springing up of local Facebook groups in which neighbours who'd never spoken to each other before shared 'how to stay sane' tips, Wi-Fi passwords and baby milk, racist attacks and hate speech escalated on social media, conspiracy theories circulated ever faster and marriage guidance counsellors told me of a spike in clients feeling lonely because their partners were now even more consumed than usual by their phones.[41]

Our smartphones and social media are just two pieces of the puzzle though. The causes of today's loneliness crisis are numerous and diverse.

To be sure, structural and institutional discrimination remain factors: a 2019 UK study of nearly a thousand people found that experiencing racial, ethnic or xenophobic discrimination at work or in your local neighbourhood increases your chance of loneliness by 21%. Meanwhile, a 2020 survey of over 10,000 Americans established that Black and Hispanic people feel lonelier at work than their white peers and also significantly more alienated. Being on the receiving end of sexist behaviour has also been linked to increased loneliness.[42]

But on top of these longstanding structural failings, other new drivers of loneliness have emerged. Large-scale migration to cities, the radical reorganisation of the workplace and fundamental changes to how we live are critical factors as well. It's not just that we 'bowl alone' more often than when the political scientist Robert Putnam published his landmark book about everyday American life in 2000. We now do ever less with each other, at least when it comes to traditional ways to commune. In much of the world, people are less likely to go to church or synagogue, belong to a parent–teachers association or a trade union, eat or live with others, or have a close friend than even a decade ago.[43] We've also been having less contact physically: touching each other less, and having less sex.[44]

And the trend for some time now has been that even when we do stuff 'together', for increasing numbers of us this isn't in the physical presence of another person: we 'attend' yoga class on an app, 'speak' to a customer service chatbot instead of a human sales-person, livestream a religious service from our living room or shop at Amazon Go, the tech giant's new chain of grocery stores where you can leave with your shopping without having had any contact with another human being. Even before the coronavirus struck, contactless was starting to become our way of life, our active choice.

At the same time, the infrastructure of community – by which I mean those shared physical spaces where people of all stripes can come together, interact and form bonds – has been severely neglected at best and at worst actively destroyed. It's a process that began in many places before the 2008 financial crisis, but accelerated markedly in its aftermath as government policies of austerity took a sledgehammer to libraries, public parks, play-grounds and youth and community centres across much of the world. In the UK, for example, a third of youth clubs and nearly 800 public libraries were shut down between 2008 and 2018, while in the US, federal library funding decreased by more than 40% between 2008 and 2019.[45] Why this matters so profoundly is because such places are not only where we come together, but also where we learn *how* to do so, places where we practise civility and also democracy, in its inclusive form, by learning how to peacefully co-exist with people different to us and how to manage different points of view. Without such spaces that bring us together it's inevitable that we will pull ever further apart.

Dog-eat-dog

The way we now live, the changing nature of work, the changing nature of relationships, the way our cities are now built and our offices designed, the way we treat each other and the way our government treats us, our smartphone addiction and even the way we now love are *all* contributing to how lonely we have become. But we must go back further to fully understand how we became so disconnected, siloed and isolated. For the ideological under-pinnings of the twenty-first century's loneliness crisis pre-date digital technology, the most recent wave of urbanisation, this century's profound changes to the workplace and the 2008 financial crisis, as well as, of course, the coronavirus pandemic.

They go back instead to the 1980s when a particularly harsh form of capitalism took hold: neoliberalism, an ideology with an overriding emphasis on freedom – 'free' choice, 'free' markets, 'freedom' from government or trade union interference. One that prized an idealised form of self-reliance, small government and a brutally competitive mindset that placed self-interest above community and the collective good. Championed initially by both Margaret Thatcher and Ronald Reagan, and later embraced by 'Third Way' politicians such as Tony Blair, Bill Clinton and Gerard Schröder, this political project has domi-nated commercial and government practices over the past few decades.

Why it has played a fundamental role in today's loneliness crisis is, first, because it has precipitated a significant rise in income and wealth gaps within countries across many parts of the world.[46] In the US, in 1989 CEOs earned on average fifty-eight times the average worker's salary, but by 2018 they made 278 times as much.[47] In the UK, the share of income going to the top 1% of households has tripled in the last forty years with the wealthiest 10% now owning five times as much wealth as the bottom 50%.[48] As a result, signi-ficant swathes of the population have, for a considerable time, felt left behind, branded as losers in a society that has time only for winners, left to fend for themselves in a world in which their tradi-tional moorings of work and community are disintegrating, social safety nets eroding and their status in society diminishing. Whilst those in higher income brackets can also be lonely, those who have less in economic terms are disproportionately so.[49] Given contemporary levels of unemployment and economic hardship we need to be especially mindful of this.

Second, because neoliberalism has given ever more power and freer rein to big business and big finance, allowing shareholders and financial markets to shape the rules of the game and conditions of employment, even when this comes at an excessively high cost to workers and society at large. At the turn of the decade, record numbers of people globally believed that capitalism as it exists today does more harm than good. In Germany, the UK, the United States and Canada around half the population believed this to be the case, with many feeling that the state was so in thrall to the market that it wasn't watching their backs or looking out for their needs.[50] It's lonely to feel uncared for, invisible and powerless in this way. The huge interventions governments made to support their citizens during 2020 were completely at odds with the economic ethos of the previous forty years, embodied by comments made by Ronald Reagan in 1986: 'The nine most terrifying words in the English language are "I'm from the government, and I'm here to help."' Even if the various coronavirus stimuli do signal the dawning of a new approach, the long-term social and economic impact of neoliberalism will inevitably take a long time to unwind.

Third, because it profoundly reshaped not only economic relationships, but also our relationships with each other. For neoliberal capitalism was never just an economic policy, as Margaret Thatcher made clear in 1981 when she told the *Sunday Times*, 'Economics is the method; the object is to change the heart and soul.'[51] And in many ways, neoliberalism succeeded in this aim. For it fundamentally changed how we saw each other and the obligations to each other that we felt, with its valorising of qualities such as hyper-competitiveness and the pursuit of self-interest, regardless of the wider consequences.

It is not that humans are essentially selfish – research in evolutionary biology makes clear that we are not.[52] But with politicians actively championing a self-seeking, dog-eat-dog mindset, and 'greed is good' (the maxim Gordon Gekko famously uttered in the 1987 movie *Wall Street*) serving as neoliberalism's bumper sticker, qualities such as solidarity, kindness and caring for each other were not only undervalued, but deemed irrelevant human traits. Under neoliberalism we were reduced to *homo economicus*, rational humans consumed only by our own self-interest.

We have even seen this play out in how our language has evolved. Collectivist words like 'belong', 'duty', 'share' and 'together' have since the 1960s been increasingly supplanted by individualistic words and phrases such as 'achieve', 'own', 'personal' and 'special'.[53] Even pop song lyrics have become ever more individualistic over the past forty years, as pronouns such as 'we' and 'us' have been replaced by 'I' and 'me' in this generation's lyrical imagination.[54] In 1977, Queen told us that 'we are the champions' and Bowie that 'we could be heroes'. In 2013, Kanye West told us 'I am a God', whilst Ariana Grande's 2018 record-breaking 'thank u, next' was written as a love song to herself.

It is not just in the West that we see this. When researchers from the Chinese Academy of Sciences and Singapore's Nanyang Business School analysed China's ten most popular songs every year from 1970 to 2010, they discovered that first-person pronouns such as 'I', 'me' and 'mine' were increasingly used in songs over the decades, while uses of 'we', 'us' and 'ours' diminished.[55] Even in a country traditionally defined by mass solidarity and collectivism, in which the state remains firmly in control, what we may think of as a super-individualistic neoliberal mindset has firmly taken hold.

Neoliberalism has made us see ourselves as competitors not collaborators, consumers not citizens, hoarders not sharers, takers not givers, hustlers not helpers; people who are not only too busy to be there for our neighbours, but don't even know our neighbours' names. And we collectively let this happen. In many ways this was a rational response. For under neoliberal capitalism if I am not for 'I', then who will be? The market? The state? Our employer? Our neighbour? Unlikely. The trouble is that an 'all about me' selfish society in which people feel that they have to look after themselves because no one else will, is inevitably a lonely one.

It also fast becomes a self-perpetuating cycle. This is because in order *not* to feel lonely we need to give as well as take, care as well as be cared for, be kind to each other and respectful of those around us, as well as be treated as such ourselves.

If we are to come together in a world that's pulling apart, we will need to reconnect capitalism to the pursuit of the common good and put care, compassion and cooperation at its very heart, with these behaviours extending to people who are different to us. That's the real challenge: to reconnect not only with those similar to us, but also with the much wider community to which we ultimately belong. Post-Covid-19 this is both more urgent than ever and also more possible.

The purpose of this book isn't solely to articulate the scale of the loneliness crisis in the twenty-first century, how we got here, and the ways that it will get worse if we do nothing to respond. It is also a call for action. To governments and business for sure – loneliness has clear structural drivers that they must address. But also to each of us as individuals.

Because society isn't only done to us, we 'do' society too, we participate in it and shape it. So if we want to stop the destructive path of loneliness and restore the sense of community and cohesion we have lost, we will need to acknowledge that there are steps we must take, as well as trade-offs we will have to make – between individualism and collectivism, between self-interest and societal good, between anonymity and familiarity, between convenience and caring, between what is right for the self and what is best for the community, between liberty and fraternity. Choices that are not necessarily mutually exclusive, yet will demand the relinquishing of at least some of the freedoms that neoliberalism promised, falsely, that we could have at no cost.

The recognition that each of us has a critical role to play in mitigating the loneliness crisis is central to this book. Reconnecting society cannot only be a top-down initiative driven by governments, institutions and big business, even if the process of disconnecting society largely was.

So throughout the book I will be including ideas, thoughts and examples of what we can do to counter the current trajectory of divisiveness, isolation and loneliness not only on a political and economic level, but on a personal one as well.

This is the Lonely Century, but it doesn't have to be so.

The future is in our hands.

CHAPTER TWO

Loneliness Kills

'My throat hurts. It's burning. It really hurts. I can't go to school.'

This is 1975. 'Bohemian Rhapsody' is playing on the radio, Margaret Thatcher has recently become Leader of the Opposition, The Vietnam War has just ended and this is my sixth bout of tonsillitis of the year.

Again my mother takes me to the doctor. Again she feeds me Penbritin, the sickly sweet antibiotic with a candy-floss-cum-aniseed taste. Again she mushes up banana and grates me an apple – all I can eat with my burning throat. Again I don't go to school.

For me 1975 is the year of constant sore throats and streaming noses, as well as repeated bouts of the flu. It's also the year that Sharon Putz rules the roost in my primary school. The year I felt the most isolated, excluded, alone. Every day I would sit on my own at breaktime, watching the other kids from across the playground as they skipped and played hopscotch, hoping they would ask me to join them. They never did.

It may seem a stretch at first glance to connect how lonely I felt back then with my swollen glands and sandpapery throat. But it turns out that loneliness has corporeal manifestations. And a lonely body, as we will see in this chapter, is not a healthy one.

Lonely bodies

Think back to the last time you felt lonely. It may have lasted for only a short time. What did it *feel* like in your body? Where did it live?

We often imagine a lonely person as passive, quiet, muted. Indeed, when many of us remember the loneliest times in our lives we don't immediately recall a hammering heart, racing thoughts or other typical signs of a high-stress situation. Loneliness instead evokes associations of stillness. Yet the chemical presence of loneliness in the body – where it lives and the hormones it sends coursing through our veins – is essentially identical to the 'fight or flight' reaction we have when we feel under attack.[1] It's this stress response that fuels some of the most insidious health effects of loneliness.[2] These can be far-reaching and even, in the worst cases, deadly. So when we are talking about loneliness we are not just talking about lonely minds, but also lonely bodies. The two are of course intertwined.

It's not that our bodies aren't used to stress responses – we experience them pretty frequently. A big presentation at work, a close call while cycling, watching our football team take a penalty, are all commonplace stress triggers. But typically after the 'threat' is over, our vital signs – pulse, blood pressure, breathing – return to baseline. We're safe. In a lonely body, however, neither the stress response nor crucially the reset happens the way it should.

When a lonely body experiences stress, cholesterol levels rise faster than in a non-lonely one; blood pressure rises faster; levels of cortisol, the 'stress hormone', rise faster.[3] What's more, these momentary rises in blood pressure and cholesterol *build up* over time for those who are chronically lonely, with the amygdala – the part of the brain responsible for these 'fight or flight' responses – often keeping a 'danger' signal going for far longer than it would otherwise.[4] This leads to increased white blood cell production and inflammation, which in times of acute stress can be a powerful boost, but when sustained for longer periods of time has devastating side effects.[5] For when chronically inflamed, its immune system overworked and underperforming, the lonely body is susceptible to other illnesses that it would normally be much more capable of fighting, including the common cold, the flu and my old nemesis from 1975, tonsillitis.[6]

It is also more prone to serious disease. If you are lonely, you have a 29% higher risk of coronary heart disease, a 32% higher risk of stroke and a 64% higher risk of developing clinical dementia.[7] If you feel lonely or are socially isolated you are almost 30% more likely to die prematurely than if you are not.[8]

Although the longer we are lonely the more damaging the impact on our health, even relatively short periods of loneliness can negatively impact our wellbeing.[9] When a team at Johns Hopkins University in Baltimore ran a study in the 1960s and 70s that tracked young medical students for sixteen years, the subject group showed a revealing pattern: the students whose childhoods had been lonely, their parents cold and aloof, were more likely to have developed various cancers later in life.[10] A later 2010 study of people who had experienced a period of loneliness, in this case brought about by a specific event like the death of a partner or a move to a new town, found that even though their loneliness was time-bounded (in this case lasting less than two years) their life expectancy was diminished.[11] Given the enforced period of isolation most of us experienced in 2020 this rings alarm bells.

We will come back to why loneliness wreaks such havoc on our bodies. But first, let's consider what is in many ways the antithesis of loneliness – community – and its impact on our health. For if loneliness makes us sick, does feeling connected to others keep us well?

The Haredi health puzzle

Buttery, creamy, salty, sweet. The ruggaleh melts in my mouth. As does my first bite of 'jerbo', a traditional Jewish-Hungarian cake layered with chocolate, walnuts and apricot jam. I am at Katz's Bakery in Israel's Bnei Brak, one of the most popular stops on the Haredi Food tour.

The Haredim are an ultra-orthodox branch of Judaism whose origins go back to the late nineteenth century.[12] Today this black-hatted, white-shirted, modest-dressing community make up approximately 12% of Israel's population, a figure projected to rise to 16% by 2030.[13] I find all of the pastries at Katz's utterly delicious. Yet these delicacies are definitely not healthy. Indeed all that butter, sugar and fat help explain why the Haredim are seven times more likely to be obese than secular Jewish Israelis.[14] When I ask Pini, the jocular Haredi Jew who runs the tour, how much vegetable and fibre is in the traditional Haredi diet, he tells me it is limited.

Their diet isn't the only unhealthy aspect of their lifestyle. Despite living in a country that has an average of 288 days of sunshine a year, this group is seriously deprived of vitamin D. Their modest dress code means that barely a wrist gets any sun exposure. As for physical exercise? Anything vigorous tends to be avoided.[15] By all standard modern counts, Pini and his peers clearly do not live healthy lives.

Nor are they financially secure. Most men opt out of the workforce to study the Torah and although 63% of Haredim women do have a job, often as their families' breadwinners, they tend to work fewer hours than non-orthodox women due to their considerable responsibilities at home (the average Haredi woman has 6.7 children, three more than the national Israeli average).[16] They also typically work in roles such as teaching, where pay is relatively low.[17] As a result, over 54% of Haredim live below the poverty line, compared to 9% of non-Haredi Jews; their average monthly per capita income (3,500 shekels) is also half that of their less religious Jewish counterparts.[18]

Given all these indicators, one would expect Haredim to have a shorter life expectancy than that of the general Israeli population. After all, the overwhelming majority of studies around the world show a clear, positive correlation between diet and longevity, physical activity and longevity and also between socio-economic status and longevity.

Yet fascinatingly the Haredim seem to buck this trend; 73.6% of Haredim describe their health as 'very good', compared with only 50% of other groups.[19] This is a statistic we might be tempted to disregard as self-reported and wishful thinking if it weren't for the fact that their life expectancy is indeed higher than average.[20] The three cities in which the majority of Israel's Haredim live – Beit Shemesh, Bnei Brak, and Jerusalem – are all outliers when it comes to life expectancy.[21] In Bnei Brak, whose population is 96% Haredi, the life expectancy at birth is a full four years higher than the city's socio-economic ranking would predict.[22] Overall, Haredi men in these cities live three years longer and women nearly eighteen months longer than one would expect. Other studies have found that they also score higher on self-reported measures of life satisfaction than either secular or moderately observant Israeli Jews or Arab-Israelis.[23]

Now of course it could be that this community, many of whom hail from the same shtetls in Poland and Russia and most of whom intermarry, share a particular genetic make-up that predisposes them to good health. But in fact the limitation of a gene pool over time is much more likely to lead to genetic disorders than to population longevity.

One might also assume that the Haredim are healthier because of their faith, given the multiple studies suggesting that religious belief pays a health dividend. However, it is less the belief itself and more the participation in the associated community that is thought to yield this.[24] As one much cited study suggests, it is *attending* religious services, not simply identifying as religious, that may add a whopping seven years to life expectancy.[25]

Community, the value of which was so repudiated by neoliberal capitalism's focus on individualism and self-interest, seems to have a health benefit of its very own. And for the Haredim, community is everything.

This close-knit group spends virtually all their waking hours together praying, volunteering, studying and working. Their year is punctuated with holy days and festivals around which the community coalesces. At Sukkot, families welcome guests into their sukkahs, the palm-leaf-roofed temporary structures in which they sleep and eat for a week. At Purim, the streets throng with costumed revellers – the vibe a combination of Mardi Gras and Halloween. At Hanukkah, neighbours, friends, and neighbours' friends join to light the menorah and eat jam doughnuts. Weddings, bar mitzvahs and funerals draw crowds of people together for days at a time. And of course every Friday evening throngs of grandchildren, cousins, second cousins and in-laws gather around the dining-room table to break bread and bring in the Sabbath together.

The Haredim don't only pray together and play together, however. In times of crisis or need they also provide each other with tangible help and support. Whether it is childcare, meals, transportation to medical appointments, advice, even financial aid if need be, they are there for each other when times are tough and life a struggle. As such it's no surprise that only 11% of Haredim report feeling lonely, compared with 23% of the total Israeli population.[26]

Dov Chernichovsky, professor of health economics and policy at Ben-Gurion University in Israel's Negev Desert, has been studying the Haredim for a number of years. He believes that whilst faith plays a role in the Haredi's above-average life expectancy, their strong familial and community bonds play a more critical one.[27] 'Loneliness shortens life and friendship reduces pressure,' the professor succinctly puts it. For the Haredim, the care and support they provide one another may indeed be the secret to their longer and healthier lives.

The health benefits of community

The Haredim are not the exception in this regard. The benefits of community to health were first identified back in the 1950s in the small town of Roseto, Pennsylvania, when local physicians noticed that residents were experiencing a much lower rate of heart disease than those of a similar neighbouring town. Upon further investigation they found that Rosetan men over 65 were dying at a rate that was *half the national average*, even though they were working gruelling jobs at nearby quarries, smoking unfiltered cigarettes, eating lard-soaked meatballs and downing wine daily.[28] Why? Researchers concluded that it was the rock-solid family ties and community support of the predominately Italian-American Rosetans that were delivering the superior health dividend. A follow-up study in 1992, which looked at a full fifty years of Rosetan health and social records, found even more evidence for this thesis. By then, the death rate in Roseto had climbed back up to the average due to the 'erosion of traditionally cohesive family and community relationships' from the late 1960s and beyond.[29] As the wealthiest amongst them started to display their riches in ever more ostentatious ways, as local stores closed down due to the arrival of larger 'big box' stores out of town and as single family homes with fenced yards sprung up replacing the multigenerational living set-ups, so did the protective health benefits of their community dissipate.[30] Other examples of cohesive communities protecting their members' health include the lifetime residents of Sardinia and Japan's Okinawa island, as well as the Seventh-Day Adventists in Loma Linda, California. Their geographies are known as 'Blue Zones': places where it is not only diet that accounts for the especially long life expectancy but also the fact that social ties are strong and enduring.[31] Places like Bnei Brak or Roseto in the 1950s where, as Dan Buettner, the *National Geographic* Fellow who coined the term, has said, 'You can't walk outside your front door without bumping into somebody you know.'[32]

It is important not to overly romanticise community. By definition communities are exclusive, and as such can be both excessively insular and antagonistic towards outsiders. Often they don't permit difference or nonconformity, whether we're talking different interests, non-traditional family structures or alternative beliefs or lifestyles. In the case of the Haredim and Seventh-Day Adventists, for example, those who don't adhere to the community's norms can find that ex-communication can be both brutal and brutally swift.

Yet for those within the enclave, community clearly does deliver a health dividend. This stems not only from the practical support that community provides or the reassurance provided by knowing that someone has your back, but also from something more fundamental that originates in our deep evolutionary past: the fact that we are hard-wired not to be alone.

Creatures of togetherness

Like all other primates, humans are social animals. We rely on complex, tightly knit groups to function, from the primordial, chemical bonds between mother and infant to the larger family unit to today's massive nation-states. Indeed in many ways the rise of humans to the top of Earth's planetary food chain can be traced to our enthusiastic *togetherness*, from our development of sophisticated group hunting-and-gathering techniques for food to our collective defence strategies for protection.[33] Until very recently in the history of our species, a lonely human would have been quite literally at risk of death – vulnerable in a world where the group enabled survival. Being connected to others is our natural and in fact desired state, whether this desire is conscious or not.

This is why *not* being connected to each other has such a profound, negative impact on our health. For in order to disincentivise us from remaining in a state fundamentally at odds with our survival, evolution has equipped our bodies with a biological reaction to being alone that ramps up our alertness and is so physiologically and psychologically unpleasant that we are motivated to end it as quickly as possible.

In some ways our ability to feel lonely, our pain and agitation when we feel distant from other human beings, is a brilliant evolutionary feature. 'You would never want to shut off the trigger of loneliness,' said the University of Chicago's Professor John Cacioppo, one of the pioneers of loneliness research. 'It would be like completely shutting down hunger. You'd lack the signals to eat.'[34]

Yet in today's world, so different from the landscape in which our ancestors evolved this trigger, it can seem like more of a bug than a positive design feature. For as Professor Anton Emmanuel at University College Hospital in London explained to me, the stress response triggered by loneliness is like putting a car into first gear: it's the most efficient way to accelerate and it gets you moving. But when you stay in first gear for your entire journey, or worse, for *a number of* journeys, the engine will be over-revved, strained and damaged. A car isn't designed to stay in first gear, just as our bodies are not designed to be repeatedly lonely. Is it any surprise, then, that bodies exposed to this kind of stress again and again start to show signs of physical damage?

The eminent eighteenth-century Scottish physician William Cullen was one of the first doctors to link loneliness to illness. One of his patients, 'Mrs Rae', suffered from a mysterious ailment, for which he prescribed cocoa, horse riding, tincture of Mars and – most significant for our purposes – company. '[H]owever averse she should see her friends both at home and abroad,' he counselled. 'Silence & Solitude are to be avoided.'[35]

By now, the health benefit of good relationships has been established in a number of research projects. In the famous Harvard Study of Adult Development, 238 male Harvard sophomores were tracked by researchers for over eighty years from 1938. They measured the amount of exercise they did, how their marriages and careers developed and ultimately their lifespans.[36] (The original recruits included future US president John F. Kennedy and

Washington Post editor Ben Bradlee, later immortalised by Tom Hanks in the movie *The Post*.) It turned out that those who were healthiest at 80 were the ones who had been the most satisfied with their relationships *thirty years before*. This benefit wasn't restricted to those who had the privilege of attending Harvard in the 1930s. It was reflected, too, in a more diverse group of inner-city Boston residents who were tracked for as long. As Robert Waldinger, the study's current director noted, 'Taking care of your body is important, but tending to your relationships is a form of self-care too. That, I think, is the revelation.'[37]

We can distinguish, of course, between poor relationships and *loneliness*; and as was highlighted earlier, loneliness is not only a reflection of how connected to other *individuals* we feel, but also how connected we feel to *groups* of people, institutions and society as a whole. Yet what is emerging from hundreds of medical studies is that whilst community and connectedness provide health benefits, loneliness, even when most narrowly defined, can take a dangerous toll.

The question is therefore: is loneliness simply one of many sources of stress in our lives, each contributing to a decline in our physical health, or is there something particular to the stress *caused by loneliness* that engenders profound long-term health problems? The answer seems to lie somewhere in between.

On the one hand, the lonely body *is* a stressed body: a body that is easily exhausted and overly inflamed. Not that inflammation is inherently bad. In regular amounts it is in fact beneficial, part of the body's defence mechanism against infection and injury, designed to localise any damage and help the body to heal. Indeed, without inflammation – typically characterised by swelling and redness – healing itself would be impossible.[38] The problem lies in the fact that normally inflammation dies down when the pathogenic threat is mitigated, or the injury has healed. But with loneliness, especially chronic loneliness, there's no 'off switch' to remind the body to calm down. So loneliness-induced inflammation can become chronic – the new normal.[39] And chronic inflammation has been linked to a whole host of afflictions including clogged arteries, heart disease, stroke, depression, arthritis, Alzheimer's disease and cancer. Indeed, a 2012 review of the medical literature on the subject found that chronic inflammation, long associated with infectious diseases, is now also 'intimately linked with a broad range of non-infectious diseases', adding alarmingly, 'perhaps even all of them'.[40]

On the other hand, loneliness is a type of stress that can massively *amplify* the effects of other stresses. Take the immune system, for example. A healthy body uses a variety of mechanisms to fight malevolent forces, whether they're pathogens – bacteria and viruses – or cancerous cells. Loneliness has been shown to reduce the efficacy of the body's fight against both types of threat: it makes us weaker and more susceptible to disease, especially viruses.[41]

Moreover, it's not just by keeping us in a sustained state of 'high alert' – the equivalent of the car that's been driving for eight hours in first gear – that loneliness damages our immune system. It affects us on a cellular and hormonal level too. One influential study has suggested that loneliness impairs the function in several endocrine glands which secrete hormones throughout the body and are connected with our immune response.[42] UCLA's Steve Cole, professor of medicine and psychiatry, meanwhile, has found that the blood of lonely people has a significantly higher level of the hormone norepinephrine, which, in a life-threatening situation, starts to shut down viral defence. Such immune weakening extends to cancer, which the body usually defends against in part by using 'natural killer' (NK) cells, that destroy tumours and virus-infected cells. A study of first-year medical students has shown NK cell activity to be much lower among the lonelier members of the cohort.[43]

Just as loneliness seems to contribute to various conditions, if you're already unwell loneliness is also likely to impede your recovery. As Professor Emmanuel told me, 'I am one-hundred per cent unequivocal that loneliness impacts health and recovery. If a lonely patient and non-lonely patient receive the same treatment, the non-lonely one will do better. In the same way that a smoker being treated for Crohn's disease will do worse than a non-smoker, so too will a lonely patient versus someone who is not.'

The data backs this up. For instance, in socially isolated patients, blood pressure (and in men, cholesterol) takes longer to return to normal following a stressful incident, whilst a lonely person's reduced ability to 'reset' the body's inflammation levels after events like strokes, heart attacks and surgery is thought to be a leading factor in why isolated elderly people have lower life expectancy, on average, than those who have regular social contact.[44]

As Helen Stokes-Lampard, chair of the Royal College of GPs, put it at the group's 2017 annual conference, 'Social isolation and loneliness are akin to a chronic long-term condition in terms of the impact they have on our patients' health and well-being.'[45]

Alone, alone, all, all alone

Of course it is not just our bodies that loneliness ravages. 'My soul in agony,' said Coleridge's ancient mariner of how it felt to be 'Alone, alone, all, all alone, / Alone on a wide wide sea!' Loneliness can also cause serious mental anguish and pain.

Indeed literature is populated with lonely people who are also depressed or mentally ill – from the unnamed protagonist of Charlotte Perkins Gilman's 1892 short story 'The Yellow Wall-paper', who as a result of being confined to a single room for 'a slight hysterical tendency' (itself now a debunked 'condition'[46]) slowly develops hallucinatory delusions, to Eleanor Oliphant of Gail Honeyman's eponymous Costa Award-winning 2017 novel, whose loneliness both compounds itself and frustrates her recovery from a traumatic past.

Rather astonishingly, however, it's only in the past decade or so that loneliness has begun to be extensively researched within the field of psychiatric medicine as a distinct psychological experience. As such, despite not being classified as a mental health problem in its own right, it is now a recognised correlate for a host of mental illnesses including anxiety and depression. The relationship runs both ways. A 2012 study of over 7,000 adults in England concluded that those with depression were over ten times more likely to be lonely than those who were not depressed.[47] Meanwhile a landmark US study that tracked participants for five years found that patients who initially reported loneliness were more likely, five years later, to be depressed than those who did not.[48]

The relationship between loneliness and mental illness is a complex one which we are only starting to understand. Yet what seems to be the case is that loneliness and isolation can accelerate genetic or circumstantial depressive tendencies in part because of their physiological impact – we sleep less when we're lonely, for example, and a lack of sleep can trigger depressive symptoms. So too can the symptoms of depression themselves fuel loneliness – by making it harder for the depressed person to connect. It can be the chicken *and* the egg.

The same is true of anxiety, for which isolation can be both a symptom and a cause. 'Social anxiety has made my world so much smaller,' says Alex, a teenager in the UK with social anxiety disorder. 'As it got worse, I started to get more insular. The more intense it got, the more I started to feel very lonely and isolated . . . I would avoid going to the shops or getting the bus during rush hour because there were too many people . . . The longer it went on, the more it started to affect work, close relationships and friendships . . . so my social life has . . . well, I don't really have one.'[49]

Even short periods of isolation, such as we collectively experienced during the coronavirus pandemic, can have a marked impact on mental health.[50] Sometimes the effect is still apparent years down the line. Researchers found that healthcare workers in Beijing who had been quarantined during the 2003 SARS outbreak were more likely to be suffering serious depression three years later than those who had not been, even though SARS quarantine periods lasted typically less than a month, and often less than two weeks.[51] Separate studies, also amongst hospital employees in Beijing, found that three years after the SARS outbreak alcoholism was higher amongst those who had been quarantined than those who were not, with significant numbers still suffering from post-traumatic stress syndrome, their symptoms including hyper-vigilance, nightmares and flashbacks.[52]

Such findings should be taken very seriously as we emerge from the Covid-19 pandemic. Both we as individuals and governments must be mindful of the likely long-term mental health impacts of our recent forced isolation, and politicians must commit sufficient resources to addressing the fallout.

At the extreme, loneliness can lead to suicide.[53]

Francie Hart Broghammer is Chief Psychiatry Resident at UC

Irvine Medical Center in the US. In a recent article she wrote movingly of two patients she had recently encountered for whom loneliness had made life feel not worth living. One was a young woman she had recently treated 'who had intentionally severed her airway and spinal cord with an eight-inch kitchen knife in an attempt to take her own life'. In interviews she cited 'the isolation associated with caring for her ill grandmother and the paucity of individuals with whom she could meaningfully discuss such challenges' as the cause of her despair.[54]

The other was 'Mr White', a 38-year-old man with suicidal ideations whose parents had recently died, who was struggling with employment and finances, had been rejected by his siblings, had no close friends and was now homeless. It was the loss of his dog – his one remaining companion – that seemed to have tipped him over the edge.

Of his pet, Mr White said, 'She was the only thing in this world that viewed me as someone worth loving. I sleep in the park, and everyone that walks by thinks I am worse than a stray; I am subhuman. No one cares about you when you're in a situation like mine. Except for her . . . she cared for me, and my whole life's purpose was to care for her in return. Now she's gone, and I have nothing left in this world.'

Unfortunately, Dr Broghammer treats patients like these far too often. Her first-hand insights into the link between loneliness and suicide are borne out by the research. There are over 130 studies that have found a link between loneliness and suicide, suicidal ideation or self-harm.[55] It is a link that holds true amongst *all* age groups including the young. A survey of more than 5,000 US middle-school pupils found that adolescents who professed a high degree of loneliness were twice as likely as those who didn't to have suicidal thoughts.[56] Such findings are corroborated by research not only in the UK but also on young adults in places as far afield as Kenya, Kiribati, the Solomon Islands and Vanuatu, a reminder that loneliness is not only a phenomenon in higher income countries.[57] Furthermore these effects can, once again, manifest many years later: one study found that suicidal thoughts in 15-year-olds were closely correlated to their self-reported loneliness eight years earlier, i.e. at the age of seven.[58] Given the high levels of loneliness amongst children and teenagers, this is especially concerning.

What is important to understand here is that the loneliness that prompts such depths of despair can stem from a wide range of circumstances, from the feelings of social exclusion experienced by a child ostracised in the playground or on social media, through the feelings of physical isolation an elderly person who has not had any visitors for a month may experience, to the feelings of social isolation that an adult whose community has crumbled and support system has broken down is likely to feel. A person like Mr White.

Indeed in the United States (and to a lesser degree in the UK), those places where we've seen a spike in what are known as 'deaths of despair' in recent years – deaths resulting from drug overdose, alcoholism or suicide of predominately working-class, middle-aged men – are typically those where traditional social support structures have collapsed. These men are more likely to be divorced, less likely to attend church and more likely to have lost the brotherhood of the trade union or workplace because they have become unemployed or are doing precarious, non-unionised and transient work.[59]

This is why despite Big Pharma's keenness to develop a loneliness pill (and indeed one that seeks to reduce perceived loneliness is currently being trialled, as are various compounds that seek to counteract some of loneliness' physiological impacts), we must do more than just try to treat its symptoms – or even worse attempt simply to dull them.[60] The root causes of loneliness must be addressed, with an understanding that solutions will need to be political, economic and of course societal rather than simply pharmaceutical.

And we must take hope and encouragement from the fact that solutions are possible. For whilst broken communities lead to lonely and potentially unhealthy lives, as we've seen the converse also holds.

As Edgar says in King Lear: 'The mind much sufferance doth o'erskip / When grief hath mates and bearing fellowship.' Even fleeting positive connections with others have a significant health impact: just the presence of a friend in a stressful situation has been associated with calmer physiological responses, such as the

lowering of blood pressure and cortisol levels.[61] Holding hands
with a loved one can provide an analgesic effect that's comparable
to taking a painkiller.[62] Whilst recent research into aging has found
that even maintaining relatively weak ties with others when we're
elderly – playing in a casual bridge club, exchanging holiday cards,
chatting with the postman – may provide a significant bulwark
against memory loss and dementia.[63]

Our health, it seems, is moulded not only by community and a
feeling of being connected to others, but also by kindness. The
kindness of friends and family, colleagues, employers and neighbours, but also by the kindness of strangers. As we rebuild our
post-Covid-19 world, we need to remember this. And also how
under neoliberal capitalism, kindness became a currency that we
collectively devalued.

The helper's high

It makes sense that being on the receiving end of kindness and
care both makes us feel less alone and has health benefits.[64] But
what is less obvious is that being kind and caring and doing small
acts for *others*, without expecting anything in return, has a similar
effect.

There is a significant body of research that backs up the idea
that helping others is good for our health, especially if you have
direct contact with the person you are helping.[65] In the early 2000s,
researchers sent questionnaires to 2,016 members of the Presbyterian
Church across the United States inquiring about the participants'
religious habits, physical and mental health and their experience
of giving and receiving help.[66] Even after gender, stressful life events
and general health were accounted for, those participants who were
consistently involved in *giving* help – through volunteering, community activities and caring for a loved one – experienced significantly
better mental health.

A number of other studies have similarly found that helping
others directly has a health benefit, both mental and physical.
Veterans suffering from PTSD show reduced symptoms after
caring for their grandchildren.[67] Looking after children at a nursery
school reduced the levels of cortisol and epinephrine (another stress

hormone) in the saliva of elderly volunteers.[68] When adolescents provide help to others, their rates of depression tend to go down.[69] Conversely, in one study carried out by the Institute for Social Research at the University of Michigan, researchers found that people who provided *no help* to others, logistically or emotionally, were more than twice as likely to die in the five years of the study versus people who were in caring roles, whether for a partner, a relative, a neighbour or a friend.[70] Think of Charles Dickens' Ebenezer Scrooge in *A Christmas Carol*, whose transformation from a miserly curmudgeon into a generous benefactor renders him both happy and healthy by the story's end.

When we help another person, provided that our motivation is not resentment or obligation, we experience a positive physiological reaction.[71] It is why helpers often experience what is known as the 'helper's high', feelings of energy, strength, warmth, and calm.

What this suggests is that in the Lonely Century it is essential not only that people feel cared for and indeed *are* cared for, but also that they have the opportunity to care for others.

So how do we make sure that everyone has the capacity to both give and receive help and care? The solution is partly structural. For it's much easier to be helpful to others when you are not working all hours and feeling exhausted, and it's much easier to volunteer if you're not juggling multiple jobs or if your employer has given you time off to do so. There are steps the state and employers can and must do in this regard, and we cannot allow current economic circumstances to stymie this. In the same way that in the US after the Great Depression and in the UK after the Second World War, workers were given more rights and protection and a greater commitment was made to the safeguarding of citizens' welfare[72], we need to see the coronavirus pandemic as an opportunity to develop new structures and ways of behaviour that enable us to better help each other.

There is also a cultural shift that's needed. Care, kindness and compassion need to be traits we actively encourage in each other and more clearly reward. In recent decades they have been under-appreciated and underpaid. A search on a leading job site in January 2020 revealed that job descriptions specifying kindness paid only around half the average wage.[73] Moving forward we must ensure that kindness and compassion are accorded the value they deserve, and their worth is not left solely to the market to determine. 'The claps for carers' that echoed across the world in the spring of 2020 must be translated into something tangible and permanent.[74] For the sake of our physical as well as our mental health and, as we will see, for our future security, we need to ensure that we come together as a cohesive community and retain the benefits of social contact.

CHAPTER THREE

The Lonely Mouse

White hair. Pink nose. Tail. The mouse is three months old. He's been in his cage for four weeks in a period of enforced solitude. But today he will get a visitor.

A new mouse enters his cage. 'Our' mouse sizes him up. There's 'an initial pattern of exploratory activity', as the researchers running the trial will put it. Then suddenly 'our' mouse makes a startling move. He stands on his back legs, rattles his tail and aggressively bites the 'intruder', wrestling him to the ground. The ensuing fight – brutal, violent and prompted simply by the intro- duction of another mouse – is videotaped by the researchers. They have seen this play out before. In almost all cases, the longer a mouse is isolated, the more aggressive it is to the newcomer.[1]

So mice, once isolated, turn on each other. But is this truth about mice, true too of men? Could today's loneliness crisis, exacerbated by weeks and months of social isolating and lockdown not only be turning us on ourselves but also *against* each other? Could lone- liness not only be damaging our health but also making the world a more aggressive, angry place?

Of mice and men

There are now numerous scientific studies that link loneliness in humans to feelings of hostility toward others.[2] In part this stems from an initial defensive act, a 'stepping back' as Jacqueline Olds, professor of psychiatry at Harvard University, explains it. Lonely people will often put up a protective shell that denies the need for human warmth and company. Consciously or not, they 'start to send out signals, often non-verbal ones, telling other people to "leave me by myself, I don't need you, go away"'.[3]

There's also something else at play, something that loneliness does to our brains. Several researchers have found a link between loneliness and reduced levels of empathy, the ability to put oneself in the position of others, to understand their perspective or their pain. This is reflected not just in behaviour but also in brain activity.[4]

Multiple studies have now shown that in the brains of lonely people the level of activation of the temporoparietal junction, the part of the brain most closely linked with empathy, decreases when confronted with the suffering of others, whereas in the non-lonely it rises. At the same time the lonely person's visual cortex, the part of the brain which typically processes alertness, attention and vision, is stimulated.[5] What this means is that lonely people typically react more quickly – by several milliseconds in fact – to the suffering of others, but their response is *attentive*, not *perspectival*. Just as the lonely body ramps up its stress response, the lonely mind, anxious and hyper-alert, operates in terms of self-preservation, scanning the surroundings for threats rather than trying to see things from the affected person's point of view.[6] 'Have you ever taken a walk in the woods and jumped back because you saw a stick on the ground and thought it was a snake?' asks Dr Stephanie Cacioppo, the director of the University of Chicago's Brain Dynamics Laboratory. 'The lonely mind sees snakes all the time.'[7]

More recently researchers have also found this: that loneliness doesn't only impact how we see the world but also how we categorise it. A 2019 study carried out at King's College London asked 2,000 18-year-olds to describe the friendliness of their local neighbourhood. They also asked the participants' siblings the same question. In short, the lonelier siblings perceived their neighbourhoods as less friendly, less cohesive and less trustworthy than their brother or sister who suffered less from feelings of isolation.[8] Loneliness, then, is not simply an individual state. In the words of Professor John Cacioppo, it 'operates in part by shaping what people expect and think about other people'.

Anger, hostility, a propensity to perceive one's environment as threatening and uncaring, diminished empathy – loneliness can engender a dangerous combination of emotions with profound implications for us all. For the loneliness crisis is playing out not only at the doctor's surgery but also at the ballot box, with consequences for democracy that are deeply troubling for those who believe in a society based on unity, inclusiveness and tolerance.

This is because for democracy to function well – by which I mean fairly reconcile the interests of different groups whilst ensuring *all* citizens' needs and grievances are heard – two sets of ties need to be strong: those that connect the state with the citizen, *and* those that connect citizens to each other. When these bonds of connectivity break down; when people feel they can't trust or rely upon each other and are disconnected, whether emotionally, economically, socially, or culturally; when people don't believe the state is looking out for them and feel marginalised or abandoned, not only does society fracture and polarise, but people lose faith in politics itself.

This is where we find ourselves today. The ties that connect us to each other and to the state have been fraying in this Lonely Century because a growing number of people feel isolated and alienated, disconnected both from their fellow citizens and from national governments who, they feel, have not been listening to them or looking out for their interests.

Whilst this has been the trend for some time, the danger is that the pandemic will exacerbate this. Economic hardship risks creating deeper disenchantment with our political leaders, especially if it is perceived to be inequitably shouldered, whilst the fear of catching Covid-19 risks making many of us fearful of our fellow citizens in a very visceral, physical way.

This should concern us all because, as we've seen in recent times, such conditions provide fertile ground for exploitation by politicians at the extremes, populists with an ear finely tuned to people's disaffection and an appetite to exploit it for political gain.

By 'populists' I mean politicians who explicitly pit the 'people', whom they claim not only to represent but also to be uniquely capable of so doing, against an economic, political or cultural 'elite' that they typically demonise; an 'elite' that often includes key institutions that hold a lawful and tolerant society together, whether parliament, the judiciary or a free press.[9] In the case of right-wing populists in particular, their rhetoric typically emphasises cultural differences and the importance of national identity, often portraying their nation as one under threat of 'invasion' by immigrants or those of different ethnicities or religions. In doing so, they pose a very serious threat to a cohesive society in which there is respect for the institutions and norms that help bind us, and to a culture of tolerance, understanding and fairness. They seek to divide society rather than unite it and are willing to stoke racial, religious and ethnic tensions if it suits their purposes. Lonely people, anxious and untrusting, desperate for belonging yet constantly 'seeing snakes', are their ideal – and most vulnerable – audience.

Loneliness and the politics of intolerance

It was Hannah Arendt who first wrote about the link between loneliness and the politics of intolerance. One of the titans of twentieth-century intellectual thought, Hannah Arendt grew up in the German city of Königsberg (now Kaliningrad in Russia), the city of one of her greatest philosophical influences, Immanuel Kant. Whilst Kant's life was one of extreme rootedness – he never left his native city and a popular story goes that Königsberg's townsmen would set their clocks by his unfailingly regular walks – Arendt's life was one of exile and dispossession.

Her parents were assimilated Jews. 'The word "Jew" was never mentioned at home,' she later recalled, but the growing tide of anti-Semitic persecution in Germany rapidly made her conscious of her religious identity.[10] The turning point was 1933: the year of the Reichstag fire and Hitler's seizure of power. Arendt was living in Berlin, offering her apartment as a safe house for Hitler's opponents and conducting illegal research for the German Zionist Organisation on the extent of official anti-Semitism. The Gestapo became aware of her activities and imprisoned Arendt and her mother for eight days. After being released to await trial, despite having no legal travel documents, the two of them fled Germany; first to Prague via the forests of the Erzgebirge Mountains and a sympathetic German family whose house was criss-crossed by the border; then to Geneva, via a socialist family friend who worked for the League of Nations. Arendt, now stateless, next made her way to Paris where she stayed for seven years as an 'undocumented refugee'.[11]

When the Nazis invaded France in 1940, Arendt was separated from her husband – Heinrich Blücher, an activist who had also fled Hitler's Germany – and taken to the notorious internment camp of Gurs in the south of France. In the chaos of France's defeat she escaped and reunited with her husband in the small town of Montauban. The couple then managed to obtain an emergency visa to the US, crossed the Spanish border over the Pyrenees, took a train to Lisbon and, after three months, finally set sail for New York in April 1941.[12]

It was a lucky escape. In the summer of 1941, the State Department ended its emergency visa programme, closing off another exit route for Jews fleeing the Nazis.[13] In the eight years that Arendt had lived the life of a fugitive – a life of rootlessness and narrow escapes for no other reason than that she was Jewish – Germans had fallen under the spell of Nazi totalitarianism.

After the war, documentary evidence presented at the Nuremberg trials laid bare the horror of the Nazi machinery of extermination. How could this have happened, Arendt wondered? What drives an ordinary person to participate in or at least tolerate an industrialised plan to commit genocidal murder?[14] Arendt sought to 'find out the main elements of Nazism, to trace them back and to discover the underlying real political problems'.[15] In 1949, she published an iconic and controversial book on the subject: *The Origins of Totalitarianism*. It's a wide-ranging volume, encompassing the rise of anti-Semitism, the role of propaganda, and imperialism's fusion of racism and bureaucracy. But at the end of the book, she turns to what appears to be a surprising factor: loneliness. For Arendt, totalitarianism 'bases itself on loneliness . . . which is among the most radical and desperate experiences of man'.[16] Finding its adherents in those whose 'chief characteristic . . . is not brutality and backwardness, but his isolation and lack of normal social relationships', she argues that for those 'who feel they have no place in society it is through surrendering their individual selves to ideology, that the lonely rediscover their purpose and self-respect'.[17] Loneliness, or 'the experience of not belonging to the world at all', is, she writes, 'the essence of totalitarian government, preparation of its executioners and victims'.[18]

The loneliness Arendt speaks of echoes key aspects of my definition: feelings of marginalisation and powerlessness, of being isolated, excluded and bereft of status and support. And these dimensions of loneliness are a clear and growing danger here and now in the twenty-first century.

Loneliness and the new age of populists

To be clear, our world today is not that of 1930s Germany. Despite the rise of populism globally over the past few years and a number of authoritarian leaders including Hungary's Viktor Orbán, Rodrigo Duterte of the Philippines, China's Xi Jinping and Turkey's Recep Tayyip Erdoğan using the cloak of Covid-19 to further cement their hold on power and suppress their citizens' freedoms, we are not experiencing a widespread emergence of totalitarian rule.[19]

There are, however, warnings from history that we should not ignore. The impact of Covid-19 has led many to compare today to the Great Depression of the 1930s, with unemployment and poverty surging. And loneliness and diminished economic circumstances are often interlinked: researchers have established both that the unemployed are significantly lonelier than those who have work and also that poverty increases the risk of social isolation.[20] Moreover, loneliness had already become 'an everyday experience of the ever-growing masses', as Arendt wrote of pre-war Germany, even before the coronavirus struck.[21] It is a phenomenon that over recent years has been actively exploited for political gain by right-wing populist leaders and extremist forces at the democratic margins.

Loneliness is not, of course, populism's only driver. The rise of contemporary populism has cultural, societal and technological antecedents, as well as economic causes. These include the rapid spread of misinformation and divisiveness on social media, the clash between liberal and conservative, progressive and traditional values and demographic changes.[22] Moreover, different countries' experiences of populism may have different combinations of causes.

Nor would it be right to say that everyone who feels lonely or marginalised votes for populists of either the right *or* left, in the same way that not everyone who is lonely gets ill. Even amongst those who feel socially, politically or economically marginalised there are clearly large numbers who continue to hope that mainstream parties will respond to their needs, whilst others choose to ignore the ballot box entirely.

But a major and often overlooked driver for why so many people have voted for populist leaders in recent years – and right-wing populists in particular – is loneliness. As we will see, a growing body of data reveals the significant role that feelings of isolation and alienation have played in transforming our political landscape, with disturbing echoes of Arendt's findings.

Loneliness and the politics of distrust

As early as 1992, researchers began to pick up on a correlation between social isolation and votes for the far-right Front National's Jean-Marie Le Pen in France.[23] In the Netherlands, researchers crunching data gathered from over 5,000 participants in 2008 found that the less people trusted that those around them would look after their interests and not deliberately do them harm, the more likely they were to vote for PVV, the Netherlands' nationalist right-wing populist party.[24]

Across the Atlantic, a 2016 poll by the Center for the Study of Elections and Democracy asked 3,000 Americans whom they would turn to first if they needed help with challenges ranging from childcare to financial assistance, to advice on relationships, to getting a ride. The results were revealing. Donald Trump voters were significantly more likely than supporters of either Hillary Clinton or Bernie Sanders to have replied not with reference to neighbours, community organisations or friends, but simply with 'I just rely on myself'.[25] They were also more likely to report having fewer close friends, fewer acquaintances and to spend fewer hours a week with both. Other researchers at the Public Religion Research Institute investigating the traits of Republican supporters in the final stages of the Republican primaries in 2016 found that supporters of Donald Trump were twice as likely as those of his main opponent, Ted Cruz, to have seldom or never participated in community activities like sports' teams, book clubs or parent–teacher organisations.[26]

The corollary also holds true. A major study that looked at 60,000 individuals in seventeen European countries over the course of fifteen years found that people who were members of 'civic associations' – things like volunteer groups and neighbour-hood associations – were significantly less likely to vote for their country's right-wing populist party than people who were not. The researchers drew similar conclusions for Latin America.[27]

It seems that the more enmeshed we are in our wider commu-nity, the more we feel we have people around us who we can rely on, the less likely we are to heed the siren call of right-wing popu-lists. And whilst correlation does not necessarily mean causation, there is a logic for why this would be so. For it is through joining local associations, volunteering, taking on community leadership roles or simply taking part in community activities or maintaining our friendships that we are able to practise inclusive democracy – to learn not only how to come together, but also how to manage and reconcile our differences.[28] Conversely, the fewer social ties we have, the more isolated we feel, and the less practice we have at managing difference and behaving civilly and cooperatively with each other, the less we are likely to trust our fellow citizens and the more appealing we may find the exclusionary and divisive form of community that populists peddle.

The loneliness of marginalisation

Being lonely is not simply about feeling socially isolated or lacking communal ties, however. It also encompasses not being heard and understood. Swiss psychiatrist Carl Jung had this insight: 'lone-liness does not come from having no people about one, but from being unable to communicate the things that seem important to oneself, or from holding views which others find inadmissible'.[29]

As we have seen in recent times, supporters of populists have been especially desperate to have their economic pain and conse-quent feelings of marginalisation and isolation acknowledged by those in political power. And have felt very strongly that they were

not. Testimonies of US railroad workers prior to the 2016 presidential election show how Donald Trump redrew the political map by
actively playing to this, making many of those who felt economically abandoned and unheard – especially people who historically
had not felt that way – feel like they were being listened to.

Rusty is a 40-something locomotive engineer from Etowah, in
eastern Tennessee's McMinn County. His grandfather and father
both worked for the railroad and voted Democrat their entire
lives. He did too – until 2016, that is. 'Growing up I was just kind
of taught that if you're going to be a union man and you're going
to be a blue-collar worker and get down there and get your hands
dirty, you need to be a Democrat,' he said. But 'to be honest, the
harder I work, the less I see, you know, I don't see myself getting
any better off'. For Rusty and his fellow engineers, whose labour
was essential for transporting billions of tonnes of coal each year,
Obama-era regulations resulted in more than penny-pinching.
They were a kind of betrayal. 'I just feel like he's come in with
his Clean Coal Act and some of his policies, that he's hurt me,'
Rusty said. His voice caught. 'He's hurt me personally', caused
major 'hardship'. In contrast, Donald Trump was the only candidate that was 'telling it like it is', the only one who cared about
how Rusty was feeling and wanted to hear about his problems.

Fellow railroader and erstwhile Democrat Gary put similar faith in
the perma-tanned presidential candidate: 'When Trump said he was
going to bring our jobs back to the United States and he was going
to renegotiate trade deals that's when I thought "Wow, I'm going to
vote for Trump."' Gary continued: 'Trump's the only one for the poor
and the middle-class people. He's the only one who seems to be interested in helping the working people. He's our only hope.'

Terry, another erstwhile Democrat voter, concurred.[30] This
father of eight from east Tennessee with twenty years' railroad
service, who found himself living 'paycheck to paycheck' instead
of the 'pretty good life' he had lived before, used similar language
to both Gary and Rusty – 'Trump will take care of his people,' he
said, whilst previous political leaders had, in his mind, ignored their
needs when it came to protecting their employment and ensuring
they retained a decent standard of living.

Where once the Democrat party or at the very least the trade union might have provided hope, many of those feeling marginalised in 2016 vested all their faith in Trump, particularly white voters without college degrees. This was especially so in places where the infrastructure of community was weak, social ties had been eroded and citizens felt economically vulnerable.[31] Places like Terry's and Rusty's home, east Tennessee, where the previous decade had seen coal mines closing[32] and the wounds from the 2008 financial crisis still gaped – all contributing to the belief that the powerful people in Washington couldn't be bothered with the needs of everyday workers.

Whether or not Trump's policies would actually improve the lives of his supporters almost seemed to matter less than the fact that he appeared to be *listening*, when other politicians seemed deaf to their cries and the needs of their economically ravaged communities. This tone-deafness was manifest in the respective presidential candidates' priorities when it came to advertising spend. Whilst only 9% of Hillary Clinton's advertisements were about jobs or the economy, a third of Trump's made this their focus.[33] It's lonely to feel economically insecure. But it's even lonelier to feel that no one cares about your struggles, particularly those in positions of power who you believe should be providing help and support. That was Trump's great accomplishment, convincing so many that he cared.

It is not just in the US that right-wing populists have proved convincing. Eric is a young Parisian baker who loves Scottish reel-dancing, rap and video games. When I conversed with him in 2019 I found him earnest, direct and very polite. He talked very openly about the pain and frustration of working hard and yet still living just above the minimum wage. Like many young people Eric feels that society's cards are strongly stacked against him. 'The economic system is unfair,' he explained. 'It's not enough to work hard, you have to work extra hard. If you're good, it's not enough. You have to be super-good and know the right people – otherwise you won't earn enough to live.' And he shared with me the extent to which he felt 'abandoned' to a painful degree, telling me, his voice both sad and angry, of how he doesn't believe the state will be there for him if he is sick or when he is old, and how alone this makes him feel.

Eric is a prominent member of the youth wing of Rassemblement National (National Rally). Formerly known as the Front National, this right-wing populist party with a long history of xenophobia was rebranded in 2018 and remains one of France's most popular political parties. Under its previous incarnation it was associated with attempts to undermine the horrors of the Holocaust, with its founder and then leader Jean-Marie Le Pen referring to the Nazi gas chambers as 'a point of detail in the history of the Second World War'.[34] More recently, under Le Pen's daughter Marine, the party's anti-immigrant rhetoric has been directed towards France's Muslim community, which she portrays as the inherent host of radical Islam, 'an octopus with tentacles everywhere, in the [immigrant] neighbourhoods, the associations, the sports clubs'.[35] Marine Le Pen was prosecuted by human rights groups in 2015 for inciting hatred, with comments comparing Muslim prayers on the streets to the Nazi occupation. Though she was ultimately acquitted, her rhetoric has not strayed far.[36]

Whereas it might once have been in France's left-wing Socialist Party that Eric would have found his political home, today it's in this radical right nationalist and populist party that he has found a place to belong. For like the erstwhile Democrat railroad workers who turned to Trump in 2016, he believes it is only Rassemblement National that 'protects the little people', of which he is proud to be one, people whom other parties have 'abandoned'. The failure of the left is of course that in the eyes of many it stopped being seen as the political grouping which had the interests of the 'forgotten' and 'abandoned' at heart.

Such feelings of abandonment are echoed in more wide-reaching studies across Europe. Researchers analysed 500 interviews with people in right-wing strongholds in France and Germany, places such as Gelsenkirchen-Ost, a down-at-heel suburb north-east of Essen blighted with high levels of unemployment and where anti-immigrant party Alternativ für Deutschland (AfD) garnered nearly a third of the vote in the 2017 elections (three times the vote it got nationally), and the Les Kampes neighbourhood of Loon-Plage, in northern France, where 42.5% of voters in the 2017 French presidential election chose Marine Le Pen.[37] What they found was that pervasive feelings of 'abandonment' were a dominant and recurring theme amongst the interviewees.

Across the globe those who feel socially and economically marginalised, who feel that the traditional political parties who once championed them have now cast them aside and are not listening to their concerns or providing answers to their grievances, have been turning out in disproportionately high numbers in the first decades of the twenty-first century for parties at the political extremes. It makes sense why this would be so. If you feel marginalised, ignored, invisible and someone appears who promises to see and hear you, it's understandably going to have allure. Whether it's Trump's rallying cry that 'The forgotten men and women of the USA are forgotten no more!' or Marine Le Pen's oath to serve 'a forgotten France, a France abandoned by the self-appointed elite', such carefully chosen messaging may well be enticing.[38] And the reality was that many *had* been forgotten for decades as neoliberal capitalism and deindustrialisation was then followed by the 2008 financial crisis and a subsequent recession, coupled with policies of austerity. These collectively took an asymmetric economic toll, with lower-skilled men amongst those who felt they were suffering most – the target market for right-wing populists.[39]

Loneliness and the loss of status and esteem

Many populist leaders understand something else too: that loneliness is not just about feeling forgotten or socially isolated or feeling bereft of voice, it's also a feeling of loss. Loss of community for sure. Loss of economic security as well. But also crucially loss of social standing. Remember Arendt's definition of the lonely as those who 'have no place in society'? And social standing is inexorably linked, especially for men, with the fellowship, pride and status that come with not only having a job, but a decent job with history, solidarity and purpose.[40] Indeed in Trumpian rhetoric, to 'Make America Great Again' is to restore an old-world order in which traditional industries are at the heart of neighbourhoods, providing employment that creates both a powerful sense of self-worth and a strong sense of community spirit. Remember his oft-repeated pledge to get 'our great coal miners back to work'?[41] In a world in which 'I produce therefore I am', in which it feels shameful not to be employed or to have a low-status job, the promise of a revitalised community and renewed social standing is particularly welcomed.

As such it is not surprising that Trump's promises appealed so much to railroad workers like Terry, who lamented the way that 'we used to be proud of working on the railroad, proud of what we did and now nobody is'. Or to Gary, who chronicled a litany of factories in his area that had been shut down in recent years, factories – whether the Libbey-Owens-Ford Glass Factory, Union Carbide, True Temper, or the Naval Ordnance Plant near his home town of South Charleston – that made things. Gary went on to explain that although 'there are other jobs one can get . . . a job at a fast-food chain or grocery store or in a Walmart, it's all low-pay jobs'.

Whether such jobs inevitably pay less than the old factory jobs is debatable. But it's not just that these 'new' jobs are low-paid. The bigger issue is that they are jobs that are deemed to be of diminished social status and standing, jobs that one may not feel as proud to find oneself doing. Even before the coronavirus pandemic sent unemployment soaring, such 'low-status jobs' were all that were on offer for increasing numbers of people, especially in former manufacturing hubs and deindustrialised regions. The low unemployment figures occluded this, thereby hiding the discontent and disaffection that lurked beneath the statistics.

Indeed it is a sense of diminished status, more even perhaps than earnings per se, that sociologists Noam Gidron and Peter A. Hall believe underlies why so many white working-class men in par-ticular – men like Gary, Rusty, Terry or Eric – have turned to right-wing populists in recent years. In a 2017 paper in which they analysed the relationship between feelings of a loss of social standing and voting preferences in twelve developed democracies between 1987 and 2013, they found that white men without a college degree who felt they lacked social status – either because of the poor quality of work available to them, or because they didn't have a job, or because they felt their standing had been diminished by the rise in status of the college-educated, non-whites and women – were significantly more likely to vote for right-wing populist parties than those who did not.[42] For these parties promised them respect and a restoration of status.

As Donald Trump laid out on the campaign trail in 2016: 'While my opponent slanders you as deplorable and irredeemable, I call you hard-working American patriots who love your country and want a better future for all of our people. You are . . . soldiers and sailors, carpenters and welders . . . You are Americans and you are entitled to leadership that honors you, cherishes you, and defends you. Every American is entitled to be treated with dignity and respect in our country.'[43]

The peddling of community

There is something else populists proffer too: belonging. For a cadre that had lost not only status but also the community that their work and their trade unions had hitherto provided, and who were disproportionately isolated and lacking in social ties, this was also extremely important.[44] The loss of 'brotherhood', now that he and his fellow engineers were pitted against each other for ever fewer jobs, was something Rusty amongst others especially mourned.

It is into this void of community and mutuality that populists like Trump so successfully and purposefully stepped with their own very clear and vibrant take on belonging.

Think about Trump's rallies which were a staple of his offering throughout his political career, not only before he won the presidency but after too, holding nearly seventy in the first three years of his term.[45] Whilst of course other American politicians hold rallies too, Trump's have been qualitatively different. They draw people not only as political displays, but as massive community rituals at which people feel part of a fellowship. They are a family affair, with three generations regularly turning out, mothers and sons, grannies and grandpas in tow. Unlike at his political rivals' rallies where people typically show up in their everyday clothes, at Trump's rallies you see a sea of red-clad folk, sporting matching 'Make America Great Again' hats, pins and t-shirts.[46] Repetitive playlists ('Proud to Be an American', sometimes on a loop) mean that people can sing along to familiar music as it fills the background with patriotic mantras.[47] The same chants and applause lines mean that each audience member feels in sync with thousands of others.[48] Whilst Hillary Clinton's rallies were serious and some might say somewhat dull affairs, Trump's are more akin to the theatrics and fandom of a World Wrestling Entertainment event.[49]

Then there's the linguistic choices, the rhetoric Trump uses to reinforce this sense of togetherness, of unity. Unlike Sanders, say, a left-wing populist who could also draw a big crowd, Trump predominantly speaks in the first-person plural, repeatedly using 'we' and 'us' to forge a relational bond, though of course he has next to nothing in common with many of his supporters.[50] This 'makes the people feel like they're included in what's really happening', said one rally attendee – simultaneously connected to each other and to Trump.[51] At the same time, he repeatedly invokes 'the people': 'the beautiful people', 'amazing people', 'great people'. In fact, 'people' is the most common word used in his speeches.[52]

These techniques – the branded gear, the chants, the 'we' statements and endless appeals to the collective – characterise a political showmanship and savviness that arguably traces its roots back to American mega-churches and, even further, to the Revival movement of the nineteenth century. As such Trump's rallies are far more than stump speeches and hand-shaking. They are what author Johnny Dwyer has called 'a kind of Communion'.[53] Trump himself has remarked on their heated, quasi-religious atmosphere. At the opening of his first rally, on 21 August 2017, he beamed out at the crowd and invoked America's most famous evangelist. 'So beautiful,' he said. 'Now I know how the great Billy Graham felt.'[54]

Trump has been able to make people feel that they mattered in a way unique in American politics. He has satisfied a hunger to belong, to feel part of something for many of those for whom the traditional bonds of the workplace and the wider community have broken down, speaking directly to our basic evolutionary need to be part of something greater than ourselves.[55]

In Europe, the dynamic has been very similar, with rallies-cum-social-gatherings used effectively to draw people towards populist parties and their leaders. In Belgium at festivals sponsored by right-wing populist party Vlaams Belang (Flemish Interest) – a nationalist party with anti-immigration a key tenet[56] – supporters 'split their time between anti-immigration speeches inside and an outside festival that included face-painting, bouncy castles and a stand for the book *The Kidnapping of Europe*'.[57] Across the border in Germany, AfD rallies have much in common with Donald Trump's: families come holding balloons, sharing drinks on picnic tables and clasping home-made signs with messages like 'Björn Höcke: Kanzler der Herzen' ('Chancellor of the Heart').[58] In Spain meanwhile, the right-wing populist Vox draws people together at youth-targeted beer nights that it holds at nightclubs and bars at which no one over the age of twenty-five is allowed entry.[59]

And again, the language deployed is that of community, the intention to create a sense of belonging that supporters have been unable to find elsewhere in the twenty-first century. 'The League is a big family,' repeat Italy's right-wing populist League politicians time and time again at their rallies.[60] Originally a regionalist party claiming to represent the north of the country, the League (formerly Lega Nord) has become powerful on the national stage, having swung to the right in the past decade. Rather than championing northern secession, it now campaigns against immigration, the EU and LGBTQ+ rights and has built a very significant political base.[61] In the 2019 European Union elections, the League commanded over a third of Italy's votes.[62] Like Trump the party's leader, Matteo Salvini, wields language as a sword, often invoking intimate words like 'Mamma', 'Papà' and 'friends' to endear his supporters and reinforce his proffering of community.[63]

It is not just at these large gatherings that populist parties offer belonging. League supporter Giorgio, a dapper small-businessman from Milan with a penchant for paddle tennis who proudly shared with me his selfie with Salvini, described in 2019 the way the party has made him feel less alone. Thanks to the League, 'a year and a half ago I started going to dinners and parties – they're called committees, they're like get-togethers for people in the party. And they're very nice, actually. You can meet a lot of people. We sing, and there's a really strong feeling of tradition. And everyone's singing in dialects from the north. And everyone's so happy with that because they feel like a part of the community.'

Eric in Paris similarly talked of the joy he derives from his regular Wednesday political gatherings, of afterwards going out for a drink together, of handing out posters and flyers together, of how 'hard it is to find people to have solidarity and community with' and how he has found it in Rassemblement National. And he lucidly admitted that had he not joined the party, he would have been profoundly lonely. It has given him the purpose and community he craves. A community that might once have been provided by a trade union, a traditional political party, the church or even a vibrant community centre or neighbourhood café.[64]

It's too early to gauge whether support for populist politicians has been diminished by the months in which face-to-face gatherings of their supporters were made impossible by rules on social distancing. How they fare in the future will depend to a considerable extent on the position they held when the music stopped – economic crises tend to be bad for governing parties – and there will be questions in every nation as to how competent those holding office were deemed to have been not only at saving jobs, but also lives.[65] Their popularity will be influenced too by the extent to which they are able to control the media narrative and whether their followers buy into their version of the post-crisis analysis. But during the lockdown it was striking how quickly populists ramped up their online community offering, as their ability to commune in person waned. As well as the president personally taking centre stage at the daily television press briefings with overt messages to his 'tribe' (including repeated condemnation of the 'fake news' media, and denouncing of global institutions), Trump's campaign, already sitting on a massive social media following, upped its Facebook presence and escalated its digital offerings, running massive volunteer trainings via Zoom and launching a digital-only campaign with a 'virtual rally' that garnered nearly a million live-streams.[66] The League, Spain's Vox and Belgium's far-right Vlaams Belang, masters of social media too, also ramped up their offerings.[67]

The weaponisation of immigration

Whether the community being proffered is online or in person, it shares of course a particular characteristic: the overt exclusion of others. For alongside right-wing populist parties' focus on belonging, with their beer nights and bouncy castles, has always been a clear message about who is *not* invited in. Think, for example, of the thousands of voices, chanting hymn-like at Trump rallies, 'Build the wall'. The subtext of the right-wing populist's message of together-ness is one of racial, religious or nationalist exclusion. Of 'us' and 'them', 'we' and 'they'. This is where their greatest danger lies.

In targeting those who feel lonely and abandoned, and creating community along nationalist or racial lines, populist leaders weap-onise their tribalism against people who are different. These politicians have realised that for those who feel excluded, left behind and lonely, for those who are unused to managing difference and whose tradi-tional sources of identity – whether class, employment or church – are no longer as strong or secure as they once were, 'social iden-tities such as nationality, ethnicity, language and gender become', as professors Mikko Salmela and Christian von Scheve have written, 'more attractive as sources of meaning [and] self-esteem'.[68] I would add to those 'sources', the allure of belonging.

It is here that the manipulation of loneliness and isolation by populists takes on its ugliest and most divisive form. For remember how lonely people tend to see their neighbourhoods as more hostile and threatening. Remember our lonely mouse and how aggressive he became when another mouse came to share his space. And remember how our brains' capacity to feel empathy can be inhib-ited by loneliness. By reinforcing their followers' sense of abandonment and marginalisation and setting this against an apparent political favouring of people unlike them – typically im-migrants – right-wing populists' fearmongering revs up the emotions, anxiety and insecurity of their followers, and manipulates ethnic and religious difference to garner allegiance and support. They combine this with an appeal to the nostalgia of a bygone era in which people were – according to this version of history – more connected, happier and better off before 'those immigrants arrived and stole your benefits and jobs'.

Now of course right-wing populists add to this – 'before those foreigners infected you with a deadly virus'. When the pandemic hit, it did not take long for a number of populist politicians to use the crisis to stoke racial, ethnic and religious tensions, and to demonise those who are different.

In the US, Donald Trump's predilection for calling Covid-19 'the Chinese virus' encouraged a spate of attacks on Asian-Americans.[69] In Hungary, Prime Minister Viktor Orbán segued from holding culpable a group of Iranian students who were quarantined and later tested positive for Hungary's incidences of the virus, to declaring all universities virus-prone because 'there are lots of foreigners there'.[70] In Italy, Matteo Salvini was quick to erroneously link the spread of the disease to asylum-seekers who had crossed the Mediterranean to Italy from North Africa. He provided no evidence for this claim.[71] The use of disease as a weapon of racial divisiveness and nationalistic fervour has of course long-standing historical precedent. The Jews were blamed for the Black Death epidemic that swept through Europe in the fourteenth century, with thousands massacred as a consequence. 'Foreigners' were attacked by mobs during Milan's plague of 1629–31, with Spaniards particularly vulnerable; and Irish immigrants were held responsible for outbreaks of cholera in American cities such as New York and Boston during the 1830s.[72] Pandemics and xenophobia have ever been interlinked.

Yet even before the coronavirus pandemic provided a new line of anti-other attack, League supporter Giorgio in Italy had evidently absorbed these messages of antagonistic tribalism. 'The government has been putting its own citizens in second place after the immigrants that are coming from Africa,' he told me, 'people who come here and have a vacation whilst a lot of native Italians are working in the fields with no social rights. You have to look out for your community and the people that already live in your country, not the people that are coming from Africa.'

Matthias, a 29-year-old logistics expert in Berlin, formerly a centre-left voter, had turned to the right-wing populist AfD for similar reasons.[73] 'It's just a fact that more is done for refugees than for us,' he said in 2017, a year after Germany had accepted

1 million refugees as part of Chancellor Angela Merkel's 'we can do it' pro-refugee policy.[74] 'A lot of my friends are still looking for work. Refugees just get money for free. They even get preferential treatment when it comes to apartments – everything is paid for them.'[75]

Trump-supporting Terry from east Tennessee meanwhile railed against 'people who shouldn't be here, who are taking benefits and finances and jobs away from people here who fought for our country. We have veterans that are homeless, and they want to bring in refugees from other countries. We need to take care of our own people.'

Like coronavirus conspiracy theories, these are not the facts. Refugees in Germany do not get 'money for free' beyond the same public welfare payments every citizen receives and they actually face housing discrimination in many places; in the US, veterans and citizens are eligible for far more benefits than refugees and undocumented immigrants. But for those who feel abandoned, alone and ignored; for those who no longer feel bound either to fellow citizens or the state; for those who are already more prone to seeing their environments as frightening and hostile, full of snakes not sticks, and are more likely to be receptive to conspiracy-like theories (as recent research has established those who feel socially excluded or ostracised are), such narratives promulgated by right-wing populists are clearly attractive.[76]

Indeed, recent analysis of over 30,000 people recruited as part of the European Social Survey (an intensive questionnaire used by many social scientists) found that those who expressed the most extreme anti-immigrant views were distinguished not by basic demographics such as gender and age but instead by financial insecurity, low levels of trust in their fellow citizens and government and by social isolation.[77] 'All in all,' concluded researchers, 'people who feel politically disempowered, financially insecure and without social support are the most likely to become extremely negative towards migrants.' And what are those three characteristics? All of them are key drivers of loneliness.

Providing someone else to blame, someone depicted as different to you, someone you don't actually know – for typically the very greatest anti-immigrant fervour is in places with low levels of immigration[78] – has proven to be a winning strategy. In many cases, it has been more effective than casting the blame on the global economy, neoliberalism, automation, cuts in public spending or skew-whiff government spending priorities, even if these are more accurate explanations for why many people feel marginalised. Right-wing populists understand better than anyone else the extent to which emotions trump rationality and complexity, and how powerful a tool fear can be. And they exploit this by repeating again and again their anti-other messages. Even if over the next few years support for right-wing populists wanes, it would be premature to sound the death-knell of populism. Its grip on the imaginations, emotions and voting intentions of a considerable proportion of citizens is likely to endure.

Of additional concern is that divisive, race-tinged rhetoric is often contagious in its own right. In an incendiary attempt to fend off a challenge from right-wing populist candidate Geert Wilders, the non-populist, centre-right prime minister of the Netherlands Mark Rutte ran a newspaper ad in 2017 that instructed immigrants to 'Be Normal, or Be Gone'.[79] Denmark's Centre Left Social Democrats were victorious in Denmark's 2019 election with a manifesto that was disturbingly redolent of the far right when it came to issues of immigration.[80] Indeed, in many ways the greatest danger associated with the rise in populism in recent years is how it has pushed tradi-tional parties of both the right *and* left ever further to the extremes and normalised a discourse of divisiveness, distrust and hate.

My fear is that in a post-Covid-19 world these instincts will be further amplified, and that the health and biological security of individual nations will not only be seen by populists as fertile ground to exploit, but that more centrist politicians will seek political capital by calling for the building of walls and blaming and demonising 'others'.

This is not to dismiss people's individual accountability. Often it can be difficult to be sure what comes first: racist sentiment, the xenophobic messaging of populist leaders or the economic, cultural and societal shifts that have led so many people to feeling margin-alised, unsupported, unheard and afraid. But what's clear is that for those who feel that they have no place in the world anymore, who feel a lack of belonging and absence of solidarity, for those who fear for their futures and feel abandoned and alone, hatred of others can become, as Hannah Arendt saw in Nazi Germany, 'a means of self-definition' that mitigates their sense of aloneness and 'restore[s] some of the self-respect . . . formerly derived from their function in society'.[81] Especially, I would argue, in times of economic crisis.

What Arendt describes here unites the sentiments of the lonely and dispossessed across generations, from those in 1930s Germany to those right now in the twenty-first century. They are typified by one young man, Wilhelm, whose words suggest he could be living in the Germany of the Third Reich or in any economically ravaged state today. This 'handsome young man of just under six feet in height, slender in build, with dark hair and eyes and extremely intelligent face'[82] had been unemployed for a number of years after the economic downturn and explained how he felt like this:

'There wasn't room for any of us. My generation that worked so hard and with such terrible suffering just was not wanted. At the end of my time in university I was unemployed for a year . . . for five years I remained unemployed and was broken in body and spirit. I was not wanted [by Germany] and certainly if I was not wanted here I was not wanted anywhere in the world . . . Life for me became completely hopeless.'

In Wilhelm's case, he was in fact describing his feelings in the 1930s. He continued: 'Just then I was introduced to Hitler . . . Life for me took on a tremendous new significance. I have since committed myself body, soul and spirit to this movement for the resurrection of Germany.'

The causes and consequences of loneliness are right at the heart of the biggest political and social questions our society faces. To date it has been populist politicians who have understood this best, in particular those on the right. But we cannot allow them to be perceived as the only politicians who proffer solutions to those experiencing loneliness. There's too much at stake.

This means that politicians of every hue will need to find

answers to some very demanding questions. How to ensure that already vulnerable groups in society are not further marginalised? How to make people feel supported and cared for in an age when resources are ever scarcer? And importantly how to get people to care not only for those who look like them, with the same history and cultures and backgrounds, but also for those who don't? How to bring people together, in a world that's been pulling apart?

Just as critically, our leaders must find ways to make all their citizens feel that they are heard and seen. And they must make sure that people have enough opportunity to practise inclusivity, civility and tolerance in their day-to-day lives. Now more than ever we need politicians to put at the heart of their projects a credible commitment to the rebuilding of community at a local, national and international level.

But to understand how we can effectively turn the tide against loneliness, reinvigorate citizens' sense of community and start to repair the fissures between us we need to dig deeper. We need to understand more granularly why *this* is the Lonely Century not just for those heeding the siren call of populists but for all of us. And this work starts with our cities, for they are increasingly becoming epicentres of isolation.

CHAPTER FOUR

The Solitary City

New York, 2019. Every time he goes out of town, Frank takes down the photo of his late father and locks it away in a cupboard along with his other valuables to 'protect' them from the Airbnb guest who will be sleeping in his bed a few hours later.

This wasn't what 32-year-old Frank envisaged when he moved to Manhattan a few years earlier, with hopes of a glittering career in graphic design. However, the rise of digitally delivered content and subsequent cuts to print media and advertising budgets led to drastic lay-offs in his field. So in 2018, somewhat reluctantly, he joined the gig economy, securing his jobs on Upwork or Fiverr, or sometimes through word of mouth. Having strangers stay in his home via Airbnb was the only way he could afford to take a holiday. His worries about the insecurity of his work and whether he would be able to keep paying his rent were constant.

This kind of economic precarity would be challenging for anyone, but for Frank what made life feel tougher was living in the city itself. At first, he had been very proud to put down a deposit on his first property, a tiny midtown high-rise studio apartment. But soon, returning to his empty place in the evenings, or worse, stuck there all day on his own working, he confided that all too often it felt more coffin than cosy. Especially as there wasn't a single person in his building he knew well enough to pop over to for a coffee, let alone anyone he could unwind with over a beer when the day's work was done. For despite having lived in the building for a couple of years, it wasn't 'just that no neighbour knows my name', but that 'each time I pass them in the corridors or elevator it's as if they've never seen me before'.

The cold anonymity of Frank's apartment building seemed to me a microcosm of his experience of big-city living more generally. 'No one smiles here,' he says of Manhattan. Heads in their phones, fitbits monitoring their pace, grimaces or game-faces on, the city felt to him unrelenting, hostile and harsh. If it wasn't for the friendly Sudanese server at his local café where he sometimes took his laptop to work, he told me he'd probably speak to no one at all some days.

Frank also talked about how hard it was to make friends in a city where everyone seemed to be so busy, in such a hurry, so intent on their self-advancement that they didn't appear to have time to stop and chat, let alone make new friends or nurture existing relationships. As a result, all too often he would spend evenings messaging 'some random woman on Tinder', not because he actually wanted to go and meet her – that felt like too much effort – but just to have someone to 'talk to', some human contact to help alleviate the loneliness he felt. And even though the small Midwestern town where he'd lived before had felt stifling, and even though New York was where he felt he 'had to be' to have a chance of 'making it' career-wise, it was clear when we spoke that he felt a sense of loss now that he lived somewhere he knew nothing about the people he resided cheek-by-jowl with, and where countless others walked past him on the pavement every day without any acknowledgement of his existence. For when he talked about 'the good bits of back home', and most of all when he reminisced about his time in a leadership role in his local youth club, what came across through his energised voice and enthusiasm was that for Frank, that sense of feeling part of a community was something he had lost in moving to the city and deeply missed.

No one smiles here

That cities can be lonely places is of course not new. As the essayist Thomas De Quincey wrote: 'No man ever was left to himself for the first time in the streets of London, but he must have been saddened and mortified, perhaps terrified, by the sense of desertion, and utter loneliness, which belongs to his situation . . .

faces never-ending, without voice or utterance for him; eyes innu-
merable . . . and hurrying figures of men weaving to and fro . . .
seeming like a mask of maniacs, or oftentimes, like a pageant of
phantoms.'[1]

De Quincey was writing about nineteenth-century London, but
he could have been describing any city in today's Lonely Century.
Even before the coronavirus struck and social distancing and masked
encounters became the norm, 56% of Londoners said they felt
lonely and 52% of New Yorkers said their city was 'a lonely place
to live'.[2] Looking globally, that number was 50% for Dubai, 46%
for Hong Kong and 46% for São Paulo. Even in Paris and Sydney,
respectively numbers eleven and twelve on the City Index Survey's
list of loneliest cities, we're still talking about *over a third* of respondents flagging urban loneliness in the place they call home.[3]

Not that loneliness is solely an urban problem.[4] Whilst city
dwellers tend to be lonelier than their rural counterparts, those
living in rural areas can experience their own particular and profound
forms of loneliness[5]: a relative lack of public transport means those
without cars can feel very isolated; the migration of young people
to cities far from family results in significant numbers of rural
elderly left without nearby support structures[6]; the fact that government spending in many places tends to favour urban centres[7] means
rural dwellers are more likely to feel marginalised when it comes to
government priorities. Yet understanding the unique characteristics
and causes of loneliness in the contemporary city is of particular
importance here and now, given the extent to which the world is
urbanising. By 2050, almost 70% of the world's people will be living
in cities, over one in ten of whom will live in cities of over 10 million
inhabitants. As increasing numbers of people flood towards ever
more densely packed urban spaces, albeit perhaps at a slower rate
than before the pandemic, understanding the impact of cities on our
emotional health has never been more critical, especially as we make
choices about *how* we live our lives post-Covid-19.

Ruder, curter, colder
So what is it about contemporary cities that can make them feel
so cold and lonely?

If you live or work in the city, think of the typical twenty-first-century daily commute: the shoving to get onto a packed train, the aggressive honking of fellow drivers if you travel by car, the anonymous hordes of unsmiling people rushing by oblivious to your existence.

The image of a rude, curt, self-absorbed urbanite is no mere stereotype.[8] Studies have shown that not only is civility lower in cities, but also that the more densely populated a city, the less civil it is.[9] This is partly a matter of scale; when we know we are much less likely to see a passer-by ever again, we feel we can get away with a certain lack of courtesy (perhaps bumping into them and not apologising, or maybe even leaving a door to slam in their face). Anonymity breeds hostility and carelessness, and the city, filled with millions of strangers, is all too anonymous.

'How often do you feel that people are around you but not with you?' asks the UCLA Loneliness Scale we looked at earlier. In the city, people are always around but seldom does it feel like they are 'with you'.

The size of the city not only breeds brusqueness, it also imposes on many of us a kind of coping mechanism. In the same way that when we are confronted with twenty choices of jam in a super-market our default is to buy none at all, so too when confronted with all those people our response is often to withdraw.[10] It's a rational response to avoid feeling overwhelmed. For although engaging with others as full, vibrant human beings is something many of us aspire towards or tell ourselves we do, the reality is that city living requires us to share space with so many people that were we to extend each passer-by a full dollop of humanity it would exhaust our social resources.[11] As Shannon Deep writes of her experiences in New York, 'If we said hello to everyone we passed, we'd be hoarse by noon. You can't be "friendly" to all seventy-five people on all ten blocks between your apartment and the subway.'[12]

So instead, all too often we do the opposite. Overwhelmed by the hustle and bustle of the city, its noise and the constant bombard-ment of visual stimuli, the propensity for city dwellers even before the coronavirus was to effectively socially distance – not physically but psychologically – by creating our own personal walking cocoons whether by covering our ears with headphones, wearing sunglasses or burying ourselves in the isolation of our phones.[13] Courtesy of Apple, Google, Facebook and Samsung, it has never been easier to switch off from the people and places around us and create our own socially counterproductive, digital privacy bubbles. The irony of course is that as we zone out from the mass of humanity around us in the real world, we tap into an alternative virtual version as we scroll through images of people's lives on Instagram or their thoughts on Twitter.

Some social theorists and semioticians even go so far as to say that cities have evolved 'negative politeness cultures', social norms in which it is considered rude to impose on someone's physical or emotional space without cause, although there are of course geographic and cultural differences.[14] On the London Tube, for instance, most would consider it odd to receive a warm greeting from a passer-by and would be surprised or even annoyed if a stranger tried to strike up a conversation with us. The well-established social convention is to read our newspapers and stare at our phones in silence.

I understand the importance of privacy. I get too why the twitching of net curtains in rural communities drives great numbers to urban spaces and their environs, places where they can live how they want to, free from social disapprobation. Yet stories of urban estrangement during lockdown throw into even starker relief the consequences of the anonymity of city life. For amidst the heart-warming tales of solidarity and cooperation there were also heart-breaking ones which made all too clear that urban privacy comes at a cost. Hazel Feldman, a 70-year-old who lives alone in a one-bed apartment in downtown Manhattan, described very movingly how during lockdown she found herself with no neighbour she could rely upon to help her with her grocery shopping: 'The news keeps saying, "People are coming together." They might be coming together, but not here. Not in these types of buildings.' Just like Frank, whilst she regularly saw other residents in the corridors and elevators of her one-hundred-apartment building, she didn't really 'know' any of them, let alone consider any to be friends.

Our culture of self-reliance and hustle, so valorised by neo-liberal capitalism, comes at a significant cost. For when neighbours are strangers and friendliness and connection are far from the norm, the danger is that at those times that we most need community it simply isn't there.

The norms around how we interact with those around us in cities have not been serving us well, and it will be some time before we know whether the impact of the coronavirus will change our behaviours in the long term, for better or worse. If people in cities already resist friendly overtures due to 'negative politeness culture', what happens when fear of infection gets layered on top? Will spontaneous chat with strangers become ever more alien? Will those of us who offered to buy our elderly neighbours groceries and leave them outside their door continue to check in on them once the danger is over? Or will we go back to simply being indifferent to them?

Antisocial

Then there is the speed of the city. City dwellers have always moved fast, but in the Lonely Century they move even faster. Urban walking speeds are on average 10% higher than they were in the early 1990s, even more so in the Far East.[15] A study comparing walking speeds in the early 1990s with 2007 in thirty-two global cities found the pace of life in Guangzhou in China had increased by over 20%, with Singapore showing a 30% increase.[16] And the wealthier a city becomes the faster our pace.[17] In the wealthiest cities in the world, people walk several times faster than they do in cities that are less well off.[18] Time is money, especially in the city, whose citizens typically work longer hours than those living in less urbanised areas. Racing past each other, texting on the go, overworked and time-poor, wearing our busyness with pride, it's easy not to notice those around us. One morning, making my way into London's Euston Station, I counted the number of people who walked by without looking at me. After fifty I stopped counting. Although rationally I knew that this was a by-product of their own level of distraction rather than an act of aggression, it still felt painful to feel so invisible, as if my existence didn't matter at all.

The fast pace of city life doesn't just make us unsocial however, it also makes us *anti*social. In a seminal 1973 study, American sociologists John Darley and Daniel Batson assigned young pastors a sermon to give, either on the parable of the Good Samaritan or another randomly selected biblical passage.[19] On their way to deliver it, the pastors walked by a man slumped on the sidewalk, coughing – an actor whom the researchers had surreptitiously placed there. Batson and Darley assumed that the pastors who had been assigned the Good Samaritan sermon would be more likely to stop and help. But, as it turned out, it made no difference what passage the pastor had been studying – the most significant factor that predicted whether he would be a Good Samaritan was whether he believed he was running late. If he knew he was ahead of schedule, he would stop. But if he was pressed for time, so much for good deeds. Perhaps this resonates with many of us who live in urban spaces. Fast-paced and self-absorbed, it's not just that we can often rush by without even noticing the colour of human life around us, we'll often not even see those who are in obvious need.

In my own case, researching this book made me aware how rarely I smiled at strangers as I passed them, or how infrequently I found a moment to chat to the postman or someone walking by with their dog. Every day in London, I would behave just like all of those people in Euston Station who didn't have a moment to spare for me. Does it matter? There is thought-provoking evidence that it does.

Why you should chat to your barista

Although brief encounters with strangers cannot offer the kind of emotional satisfaction we get from more intimate conversations, it turns out that even passing connections can make a real difference to how lonely or otherwise we might feel.[20]

In 2013, University of British Columbia sociologists Gillian Sandstrom and Elizabeth Dunn ran a study to investigate whether 'micro-interactions' had a quantifiable effect on people's wellbeing. Staking out the front of a Starbucks in a busy urban area, they recruited arriving customers to take part in an experiment: half of the customers were instructed to be friendly and make small talk with the barista, while the other half were told to be 'efficient' and 'avoid unnecessary conversation'.[21] Even though the interaction lasted just thirty seconds, the researchers found those who had been randomly assigned to the 'friendly' group reported higher levels of happiness as well as a greater sense of connection to those around them, after the exchange than those who were curt.

It is understandable to have some cynicism about this. After all, how connected could you really feel to someone whose friendliness is mandated by the Starbucks employee manual or whose 'Have a nice day' has been scripted by Walmart HQ? Or indeed to a server at the fast-food chain Chick-fil-A, the 'politest chain in America', who is trained to say 'my pleasure' instead of 'thank you' – but is it *really* their pleasure?[22]

Yet these kinds of scripted micro-interactions can have a more significant impact than many of us realise. Not only because when we are friendly to someone they are more likely to be friendlier to us in return, or because the act of being friendly *in itself* delivers an emotional boost, although both of these are true. But also because we're actually pretty bad at differentiating between performative friendliness and the real deal, as long as the performance is decent. Take smiles: a number of studies have revealed that we are surprisingly poor at identifying fake ones.[23]

There's something else inevitably at play here too, something more profound. By acting friendly to others, or by being on the receiving end of such friendliness whether it is genuine or performative even for very brief moments, we are reminded of what we have in common, our shared humanity. As such we are less likely to feel so alone.[24]

This may contribute to why life in recent times has felt so disconnected and isolating. For not only have we been experiencing far fewer of those boosting daily micro-exchanges, but when we have them they are often conducted while we are wearing masks. This means that we can't tell if someone is smiling at us and they can't tell if we are smiling at them. (At a social distance of two metres most people can't even make out the smiles around people's eyes above their masks.) In covering our faces we conceal our compassion. The irony is that our motivation for doing so may well stem less from self-interest and more from the responsibility we feel to protect others.

Rootless neighbourhoods

It's not just *how* we behave that impacts our emotions, however. As we've seen, loneliness has structural components too. Take the transience of life in many big cities – the constant comings and goings and endless churn. In many major metropolises this is largely a factor of renters now outnumbering homeowners, as renters tend to move around significantly more than those who own.[25] In London, for example, where renters edged past owners in 2016, the average tenancy is only about twenty months.[26] In New York where the vast majority rent, nearly a third of the population in 2014 had moved house in the preceding three years.[27]

This matters when it comes to social cohesion because whether you are the one who is always moving or the one who stays in place, the consequences are equally problematic: you are less likely to know your neighbours and as a result are likely to feel more isolated. You're hardly going to knock on your neighbour's door to borrow milk or offer to pick up groceries for them during lockdown if you don't even know their name. Nor will you be likely to want to put time and effort into building ties and contributing to a community if you think you're soon out the door and heading for another new neighbourhood again.

For many urban dwellers, escalating rents and unaffordable house prices have made putting down roots in a community and making an emotional investment there an increasingly unviable economic option. Again, this is a problem for *all* of us. For neighbourhoods need nurturing and above all participating in if they are to be vibrant communities and not just bricks, tarmac and paving slabs. And this takes trust. The trouble is when you don't know your neighbour you're less likely to trust them. Which helps account for why in the US, fewer than half of city dwellers say they have a neighbour they would trust with the keys to their home, compared with 61% of rural dwellers.[28]

So, one important step to take if we want our neighbourhoods to feel more connected and ourselves to feel less lonely is to reduce the churn. Governments, on a national and local level, can play a role here. This is partly a matter of making rental costs more stable, and some are already tackling this head on. In Berlin, for example, the local government announced in October 2019 that it was going to enforce a five-year freeze on rents.[29] Other cities already either imposing some sort of rent stabilisation measures or contemplating their introduction include Paris, Amsterdam, New York and Los Angeles.[30]

It's too early to know whether such initiatives will have the desired impact. Economic theory suggests that because rent controls reduce incentives to build new housing, they can end up exacerbating housing supply shortages and thereby lead to price increases.[31] It may therefore be that other forms of intervention would produce better outcomes, such as the granting of longer leases, or even leases with an indefinite time period, so that tenants know they can build a long-term home in a neighbourhood – although even these would presumably also need some kind of associated rent stabilisation measures if they were to work. A number of cities have also introduced limits on the number of days a year that a property can be rented out on Airbnb or similar short-term rental platforms so as to disincentivise the conveyor belt of inhabitants they set in motion. Whichever of these is best, all are examples of a dawning recognition by governments and local authorities that housing is one area where market forces need to be mediated for our collective good.

Living alone . . .
The kind of roof over our head is only one structural factor that impacts how lonely urban life can feel. Another component of the isolation of city life is that urbanites increasingly live on their own.

This was once a more rural phenomenon. In the United States in 1950 it was in sprawling western states like Alaska, Montana and Nevada that those living alone were predominant because it was to these late-developing, land-rich states that single migrant men went to seek fortune, adventure or a steady job as a labourer.[32] Today, however, solo living is most common in big cities such as New York City, Washington DC and Pittsburgh.[33] In Manhattan, over half of residents live on their own.[34] It's a similar story in cities like Tokyo, Munich, Paris and Oslo[35] where about half of all residents also live solo.[36] In China, a whopping 58 million young, unmarried urban singles – known as 'empty-nest youths' – live alone, whilst in London the number of people living alone is expected to rise by 30% within the next twenty years.[37]

For some solo living is undoubtedly an active choice, a mark of independence and economic self-sufficiency.[38] It's only relatively recently that marriage was no longer an economic necessity for women, meaning that more could choose to live on their own.[39] It was a choice I made myself for a number of years. But for many, living alone is less choice, more circumstance, perhaps the result of bereavement or divorce. Others may very much want to live with a partner but have not yet met the 'right one', possibly because of the long hours they work, their feelings around financial insecurity or the challenges of dating in the digital age. Some may even have put themselves forward as a housemate but found themselves unable to 'pass' the house-share 'screening process', because they are elderly, unwell or introverted and, as such, deemed 'unsuitable'.

Whatever the reasons, not everyone living alone is lonely.[40] In fact, living alone can provide an impetus to get out and interact that those living with others don't necessarily have.[41] I definitely felt much more of a push to go out with friends in the evening before I met my husband than I do now. Furthermore, living with someone is no guarantee of meaningful companionship. It can feel extremely lonely, as those who've experienced the isolation of living with a partner with dementia, or those who have been trapped in an abusive relationship will testify.

Yet the data is unambiguous: people who live alone are at a significantly greater risk of feeling lonely than those who live with others by nearly ten percentage points, according to the European Commission's 2018 Report on Loneliness.[42] Moreover people living on their own feel lonely more *frequently* than people living with others, especially during life's most difficult or vulnerable times.[43] As Sheila, a 70-year-old English divorcee who'd recently recovered from the flu explained to me, her eyes filling with tears, 'It's lonely to be sick and to have no one around to even bring you a cup of tea.'

. . . eating alone

Sipping tea alone can be lonely. So too can supping be. Yet eating alone has been an inevitable consequence of the rise in solo living. Look at how the sales of single portion meals have skyrocketed in recent years.[44] And mealtimes are often the moment in the day when those living on their own feel most acutely aware of their isolation and loneliness. Some of them are going to remarkable lengths to try to mitigate this.

This is especially true in South Korea, where a market is exploding for what is known as *mukbang*: the practice of watching someone else eat (copious amounts of) food onscreen, whilst you have your meal alongside them.[45] Whilst this may sound improbable it has been a fast-growing trend globally for the past decade and is increasingly popular in Japan, Malaysia, Taiwan, India and the United States.[46] In Malaysia, watch time for *mukbang* grew by 150% in 2019.[47]

The most popular *mukbang* stars have over 2 million followers and can make six figures a year (in pounds) from the ads that play before and during their videos.[48] The most successful have even begun to court sponsorship opportunities. Indonesian *mukbanger* Kim Thai has partnered rather appropriately with digestion aid Pepto-Bismol, while the American star Nikocado Avocado advertises the computer game *Cooking Diary*.[49]

The audience is predominantly people who live on their own. 'Facing the computer screen, with *mukbang* serving as their "meal mate" and "chatting" with them, soothes one's sense of loneliness during mealtimes,' says Sojeong Park, a researcher at Seoul National University who co-authored a report on *mukbang* in 2017.[50] Indeed, a study released in January 2020 that reviewed thirty-three articles on the impact of watching *mukbang* found that watching it significantly decreased how lonely people felt.[51]

The experience of watching your *mukbanger* eat is not a passive one. If anything, it's a social one – or at least a simulation thereof. For a price, viewers can send their favourite *mukbangers* 'star balloons' that pop up on the screen for all to see. As each 'balloon' floats into the public chat bar, the *mukbanger* will typically pause in their chewing and even acknowledge the donor by username, 'Thanks for the ten star balloons . . . Thank you, hbhy815 . . .What should I eat first? Mozzarella croquette, OK?'[52] These online eating stars acknowledge the sense of companionship they provide their followers. 'I've become a friend to them,' says mukbanger Kim Thai.[53] But just like my encounter with rent-a-friend Brittany, the friendship comes at a price. For the balloons, unlike 'likes' or 'hearts', are purchased with cold hard cash. One *mukbang* star, who goes by the name Haekjji, received 120,000 balloons during a single broadcast, worth roughly $100,000.[54]

I understand that eating with Kim Thai or Haekjji might well be preferable to eating alone, yet I worry about the societal consequences of these kind of commercialised and commoditised relationships, in the same way I worry about the consequences of paid friendships like I experienced with Brittany. This is not because such transactional relationships can't alleviate loneliness: to a considerable degree they can, at least for some. The danger is that because transacted relationships require so little of us emotionally (whilst bought they are not earned), they may end up becoming our preference. Humans after all default towards what's easiest as research in both anthropology and business has shown for decades.[55] Indeed, Brittany tells me that several of her clients have told her that they are much happier renting her than 'having to put effort and time into someone who might burden them with their problems'.

Perhaps this is why some *mukbang* fans report finding 'real' friendships burdensome – like the woman who described her irritation when her old room-mate from college called just as she was preparing dinner. 'I was ready to sit down and have my YouTube time. [Instead] I had to eat while I was talking to her, and that really annoyed me.'[56] Yes, this young woman would prefer to sit alone, watching Nikocado Avocado consume 4,000 calories than speak to a friend – someone who actually knows her personally.

These may be extreme cases, but the point is a broader one, that again has implications for society. For the more we either engage in paid-for relationships (whether virtual or in person) or remain on our own, the less we get to practise the skills that build community and underpin an inclusive democracy.[57]

Honing our democratic skills

That living or eating with others enables us to practise democracy sounds like a big claim. But it's through these smaller interactions that we learn the skills we need to be part of something bigger.

We can all think of a time when we've run into some difficulty in our living situation. Perhaps it's been over something as small as who is responsible for taking out the bins or whose turn it is to cook dinner. Living with others – for many of us starting with our parents and siblings, and later expanding to room-mates, partners, spouses, children – is how we learn to resolve such issues, to balance our desires against those of others, to compromise, to manage our differences, to peacefully co-exist. *Not* having to do these things – being able to do things our own way all the time – is perhaps one of the things we are buying when we pay that extra 20% for a single-person studio apartment or that $40 an hour to rent a friend. We are buying self-determination, but our chance to further hone our prosocial democratic instincts may be part of the price we pay.

For whether it is discussing, deliberating or indeed learning how to respectfully disagree with your housemates or neighbours or partner, all these are important skills we need to practise if we are to learn one of the key tenets of inclusive democracy: that sometimes we have to make sacrifices for the greater good.

What's more, these skills are best practised in person, face to face. It was not a coincidence that 6,000 Athenian citizens would congregate in person on a hill near the centre of the city in democracy's earliest days, or that the *agora* – an open space towards the centre of the city – assumed such a critical role in democracy's taking of shape.[58] Physically coming together engenders something very precious that digital relationships and even talking on video services like Zoom can only ever be poor facsimiles of. For it is when we can see the whites of each other's eyes and pick up on non-verbal cues such as body language or even scent that we are best able to experience empathy and practice reciprocity and cooperation. It's also much harder to walk away when you disagree with someone than log off or hang up. This is why preserving face-to-face interactions in our digitally dominated lives is so important, especially (as we'll see in the next chapter) in the contactless age.

CHAPTER FIVE

The Contactless Age

East 53rd Street, Manhattan. I am at the grocery store. Fluorescent lights illuminate aisles filled with colourful goods. Cereal and cold drinks, vegetables and frozen food: all the usual produce is here.

Apart from the sleek white barriers at the entrance, everything looks normal – just like your average city convenience shop. But look around more closely and you'll realise there's something unusual about this place. There's nobody working on the shop floor – no cashiers, no uniformed workers stocking shelves, no one to come to your rescue when you can't figure out how to scan the barcodes at those pesky self-service tills. Look up and you'll understand why. Dotted above you are hundreds of just-discernible cameras: your movements are being constantly monitored. So no need to wait in line. Instead feel free to stuff packets of biscuits into your pockets as surreptitiously as you like – your activity, however discreet, will be digitally noted. You won't get chased down by security as you leave the store, but you will be automatically charged.

It is September 2019 and I am shopping at what was back then one of Amazon Go's first convenience stores; by 2021 they aim to have over 3,000 worldwide.[1]

At the time it felt a very weird experience. On the one hand I liked the convenience factor, the fact I could nip in and out with no hold-up. This was something all the other customers I spoke to told me they liked very much too. But I was disturbed by the silence – the place had a Trappist monastery vibe. I missed too the cursory chat at the checkout counter. And it bothered me that when I approached other shoppers to ask about their experience, they

seemed a little outraged, as if I'd violated their personal space, just
by uttering a few words.

How fast things change. For what only recently seemed so futuristic, now seems to exemplify the way we live in the Covid-19 age.

Contactless commerce, of which Amazon Go is at the extreme
end, was of course already by the autumn of 2019 a growing trend,
what with increasing numbers of self-checkout counters and
websites and apps that allowed us to have everything from groceries
to pet supplies to prescription medication delivered right to our
doorsteps. Already back then we could bypass the server at Micky
D's and order a Big Mac with a few taps on a giant screen,
avoid the awkwardness of a conversation with a flesh-and-blood
bookseller and instead have our reading matter 'personally recommended' by Amazon's algorithm, get hot and sweaty in the privacy
of our living rooms thanks to online yoga apps such as Asana Rebel
or YouTubers like Adriene, and have restaurant meals delivered to
us at home at our convenience courtesy of Deliveroo, Seamless,
Caviar, Postmates, Just Eat or Grubhub.

What the pandemic did, however, was transform what was hitherto a steady but slower-growing incline into a sharp, steep ascent.
After just a few weeks of lockdown, two million more people were
doing yoga with Adriene on YouTube, 40% of US online grocery
shoppers were doing so for the first time and my 82-year-old father
was 'attending' classes at his local community centre on Zoom.[2]
Overnight, contactless became in many respects our only choice.

It's impossible to predict with certainty how this will play out in
the long term. As we've seen, the human craving for proximity and
physical connection runs deep and later we will see how a burgeoning Loneliness Economy may act as a counter-balancing force.
But the reality is that new habits, once forged, can take hold pretty
fast. Many people who lived through the Great Depression, for
example, remained frugal throughout their entire lives.[3] More
recently, we have seen how large discount grocery, private label
and dollar stores such as Aldi and Dollar General have remained
popular with middle-class consumers in Europe and the US, long
after the 2008 financial crisis demanded a cutback in household
spending.[4]

Given that consumers' concerns about infection are likely to persist for some time yet, and that many people's experiences of contactless retail and leisure during lockdown were largely positive – a function of both the convenience and increased choice they provide – it is likely that the demand for at least certain categories of contactless encounters will remain strong as the world rebuilds post-Covid-19. Many who first experimented with contactless during lockdown are likely to continue with what might be called 'low human touch', especially as businesses have now invested in technology and working practices that limit customers' interactions with their staff.

Already in April 2020, restaurant chains were developing technology to enable customers to pre-order and pay without contact with waiters, and apps that allowed drivers to pay at petrol stations from inside their car were gaining in popularity. Many companies paying close attention to the bottom line will be keen to maintain these changes in consumer habits given their associated labour cost savings. This will be particularly so whilst fear of future lockdowns remains, social distancing continues to be 'official' advice and the economy is perceived as fragile.

The institutionalisation of contactless living gives me real cause for concern. For the more the human is exorcised from our daily transactions, is it not inevitable that we will feel lonelier? If our brisk urban life is no longer broken up by chats at the cash register or banter with the barman, if we no longer see the friendly face of the person behind the deli counter making our sandwich or our yoga instructor's encouraging smile when we do our first successful handstand, if we lose the benefits of all those micro-interactions that we now know make us feel more connected, is it not inevitable that isolation and disconnection will be ever greater?

Moreover, the danger is that the more we do that is contactless, the less naturally adept we will become at connecting in person. For although such innovations will undoubtedly make life safer, at least for a time, and more convenient – or in tech-speak more 'frictionless' – our rubbing up against each other is both what makes us feel connected and what teaches us *how* to connect. Even something as simple as silently negotiating who passes first in a grocery aisle or where to place your mat in yoga class forces us to compromise, and take others' interests into account.

Again this has ramifications that go beyond the personal or individual. Think back to our lonely mouse lashing out when he was 'bothered' by another. Or of how much more hostile and threatening our environment feels when we don't feel connected to our neighbours. In the contactless age the danger is that we will know each other ever less, feel less connected to each other and thus be increasingly indifferent to each other's needs and desires. We can't break bread together, after all, if we're sitting at home eating Deliveroo on our own.

But contactless living is not just a function of technological advances, consumers' craving for convenience or even the coronavirus' imperative. Way before Covid-19 struck we had been building a world of separateness and atomisation.

Hostile architecture

At first sight, it's just what it seems: a shapeless, concrete, oblong bench. If you're seeking a place to sit only briefly, you can do so on one of its slightly slanted, tiered surfaces. But if you're looking to do anything else, its shapelessness starts to seem conniving. Try to lie down and a corner will always be poking into your side. After fifteen minutes or so, even sitting feels not quite right. Known as 'the Camden Bench', science writer and critic Frank Swain has called it 'the ultimate non-object'; the podcast 99% Invisible describes it as a 'highly refined work of unpleasant design'.[5]

It is no coincidence that this bench is hard to feel comfortable on. That's the entire point. If you make it difficult for a homeless person to get rest; difficult for a skater to try a trick; difficult, even, for a group of young people to hang out without their knees and backs beginning to ache, then people will simply have to look elsewhere for a place to congregate.

The Camden Bench is not an anomaly: more and more, our cities are being designed to keep those deemed as 'undesirables' out. By its very nature this is 'hostile architecture' – urban design with a focus on exclusion, design that inhibits community and tells us who is welcome and who is not.

Look around where you live and you're likely to see many examples: 'seats' in bus stations that are barely wide enough to perch on, public benches with multiple armrests, metal grates on the pavement outside shops from which spikes emerge at night, public park fences with castle-like defences. You might ask – what's wrong with an armrest? True, it's sometimes nice to have something to lean on, but the real reason for these bench dividers is more insidious. Armrests make it impossible to lie down, most particularly for rough sleepers who have nowhere else to go.

Like many trends in the Lonely Century this is a global problem. In Accra, Ghana, massive stones have been placed under bridges to prevent the homeless finding shelter; in Seattle, gleaming bike racks were installed to block a flat, sheltered area previously used by rough sleepers, a move the municipal government later admitted was not inspired out of care for cyclists but, instead, was 'part of the homelessness emergency response effort', made 'to prevent the area from being re-camped'.[6] In Hong Kong, where the homeless population has tripled since 2004, public spaces were deliberately designed with barely any seating in order to repel loiterers and the homeless alike.[7] Perhaps most nefariously, in San Francisco in 2015 the Cathedral of St Mary's took the very unchristian step of installing a sprinkler system that doused rough sleepers in its entryways (unsurprisingly, to massive public outcry).[8]

Hostile architecture is not limited to anti-homeless strategies. In Philadelphia and in twenty other US metropolitan areas, street lights outside recreation centres are fitted with small devices, aptly named Mosquitoes, which emit an unpleasant high-pitched sound that can be heard only by young people, as the frequencies are no longer audible to their elders (this is due to a process called presbycusis, in which certain ear cells die off over time).[9] The goal of these Mosquito devices is, according to the president of the company that makes them, to 'ward off' unruly, 'loitering' teenagers while conveniently keeping areas pleasant for adults.[10] It's for similar reasons that pink lights designed to highlight uneven skin and acne have been installed in public places around the UK – an 'anti-loitering strategy' designed with the hope that vain teenagers will disperse once their pimples and blemishes are exposed.[11]

According to one Nottingham resident who was at first 'dubious' of the concept, 'it's done the trick'.[12]

Although one can argue that hostile architecture is not a new phenomenon – think of moats around castles and ancient cities' defensive walls – its modern incarnation has its roots in the 'broken windows' policing of the 1980s US, when everyday activities such as standing, waiting and sleeping (especially when 'committed' by people of colour) began to be criminalised as 'disorderly' and 'antisocial'.[13] Preventing these behaviours, the logic went, would make a space more 'orderly' and, in convincing locals to 'claim their public spaces', would also prevent crime.[14] Hence, hanging out became 'loitering', sleeping on the street became 'improper lodging', dawdling became 'loafing', people-watching became 'lurking'.[15] The fact that the broken-windows theory has been revealed to be highly flawed – responsible for the over-policing of minorities[16] and an ineffective deterrent for more serious crimes – has not stopped many cities from continuing to rely on its strategies.[17] The result is that over the past fifteen years, cities around the globe are increasingly sprouting spikes.

In some ways this is surprising. Cities overwhelmingly skew towards socially liberal policies, compared to more rural areas. Historically their municipal governments tend to spend more per capita on social programmes such as welfare and food stamps even if poverty is less prevalent,[18] and their elected officials typically lean more to the left.[19] Given all this we might expect to find higher levels of empathy in urban settings – after all, a vote to actively support people in poverty (via the left's welfare agenda) is presumably motivated by care and compassion, a recognition that those in need should be helped out. Yet these empathetic ideas, however ardently held, do not necessarily translate to more empathy in practice towards those who share our public spaces.[20]

If anything, some urban dwellers who vote for social programmes are outsourcing their compassion to the government, appearing to be all for progressive social programmes until they feel that their own quality of life is being threatened. The 'not in my back yard' mindset of many supposedly liberal urban dwellers is well chronicled.[21] Moreover, research by political scientist Meri

T. Long suggests that in the US, while Democrats are more likely to 'vote with their hearts' there's no evidence that they behave more compassionately in their daily lives.[22] Ergo San Francisco, leading the way in the US when it comes to both homelessness and hostile architecture, despite being a city which has elected a Democratic mayor since 1964 and is the home district of Democratic Speaker of the House Nancy Pelosi.[23]

Hostile environments don't only exacerbate the loneliness of already marginalised groups such as the homeless, a group we surely should be helping rather than keeping off benches.[24] We *all* pay the price for this architecture of exclusion. For that same park bench that's been designed to deter rough sleeping makes you less likely to suggest meeting your friend at it for a casual chat. That sloping bus-shelter seat is not just inhospitable to 'loiterers', it also makes it a lot harder for the person with MS who uses a walking stick to take the bus to go shopping or meet friends. The Camden Bench that repels skateboarders also repels the elderly people who might in the past have spent a pleasant afternoon sitting in the sun, chatting with shopkeepers on their lunch breaks or passing children – those stalwart figures of community that urban-planning activist Jane Jacobs called our 'eyes on the street'.[25]

In taking up the morally dubious task of protecting neighbour-hoods from those deemed 'undesirable', hostile architecture denies us all shared spaces in which to sit together, hang out together, come together. It's ironic that a strategy aimed to protect commu-nity may well do the very opposite.

Hidden exclusion

High-pitched sonic deterrents in shopping malls, concrete slabs masquerading as benches and water sprinklers assaulting the homeless outside churches send a very clear message about who is invited in and who is not. But the modes of exclusion in our cities need not be so obvious in order to provoke feelings of unease, alienation and, ultimately, loneliness.

Sleek and graceful, the Royal Wharf development in the London borough of Newham claims 'to harness the river, the cityscape and open space that surrounds us and offer brilliantly designed houses and apartments that allow for individuality and change'.[26] Its glossy marketing pamphlets advertise a swimming pool, sauna, club-house and 'technogym' staffed by personal trainers, touting the amenities as 'a perfect platform for bringing people together'.

From the outside, this verdant riverside neighbourhood 'designed from the inside out, to make life function better' certainly appears to be a luxurious haven. The developers, Ballymore, have clearly put an emphasis on creating community spaces, with a quaint 'high street' area – 'Corinthian Square' – and a boardwalk along the Thames. The trouble is – as became painfully obvious to the low-income tenants participating in the affordable-housing scheme that Ballymore incorporated into the complex – that community was not on offer for all.

Ade Eros moved into a three-bedroom flat with his two sons in 2018 and was very much looking forward to teaching them how to swim in the Royal Wharf pool. Yet he soon learned that his family, like the other 17% of tenants receiving rent subsidies, would not have access to the clubhouse or its amenities.[27] 'We're like the poor relations,' said another resident.

Over at the Baylis Old School complex in South London, a similar form of segregation was occurring. This time it was the play-ground from which the lower-income residents were being denied entry, thanks to the thicket of impassable hedges separating the blocks designated for social housing from the 'communal' play spaces. Parents like Salvatore Rea, a resident who lives in the affordable block, experienced the pain of watching other children play in a space that was forbidden to his, simply because of where his family lived in the building. 'My children are friends with all the other children on this development [but] they can't join them,' he explained.[28]

In both these cases, after a significant public backlash the policy of segregation was reversed.[29] Yet in many instances measures to invisibly exclude certain residents, including children, remain firmly in place.

At the Westbourne Place complex across town, subsidised tenants, some of whom are survivors of the tragic Grenfell Tower blaze, were, at the time of writing, still being excluded from the communal gardens that their own flats overlook.[30] 'My 7-year-old has a best friend in his class who lives on that private side,' says resident Ahmed Ali. 'They sit in school together but can't play together. Private residents have access to everything, they can use all the gates and they walk through our side all the time, they exercise their dogs over here. This is open discrimination. We work, we pay service charges, we pay rent, we don't deserve to be treated like this.'

This is not just a British phenomenon. 'Poor doors' – separate entrances for residents of affordable-housing units within a more affluent complex – have cropped up in New York and Washington, as well as London.[31] Up until 2015, real-estate developers in those American cities actually received a tax break, or relaxed zoning restrictions, for renting out a certain percentage of their market-rate apartments as subsidised low-income housing, even when their buildings segregated tenants and even though the supposed aim of such developments was greater integration and inclusion.[32] Developments with separate play areas for market-rate and public-housing tenants have also been found in Vancouver, the second most expensive city in North America for housing.[33] In this case after a backlash, the developers made a concession: not to integrate the playgrounds (which, they maintained, was 'not feasible') but to separate them in such a way so that children playing in one could not see into the other.[34]

There's something particularly shocking about children being physically prohibited from playing together. Indeed, it evokes disturbing images, both historical and contemporary – from apartheid South Africa to the children we saw on opposite sides of the US–Mexico border, trying to play together on seesaws that spanned the chain-link and barbed wire fencing between them.[35] The trouble is that unless explicitly forbidden or penalised for doing so, the market's impetus will often be to segregate. Think of the perennial popularity of private schools, private universities, private estates, private limousines, 'fast passes' at amusement parks, exclusive tiers of service in restaurants and hotels, first-class travel or VIP sections of clubs. The reality is that the wealthy will often pay a premium to separate themselves from the masses. It has always been so.

The question we have to ask ourselves is under what circumstances are such exclusionary measures unacceptable? Both morally, but also for reasons of self-interest. For as we saw earlier we all pay the price when people feel left out. We saw too how when people don't know each other, hatred and fear are more likely to develop. Remember how the strongest anti-immigrant sentiment is often found in areas with the fewest immigrants – areas where people are much less likely to encounter an immigrant in person, interact with them, form a relationship with them. If children of different income groups, backgrounds and ethnicities are not able to play together even within their own blocks, are we not therefore setting ourselves up for ever more fragmentation and social division?

There has long been a prevailing belief in sociology that the more diverse a community, the less its members trust each other, but recent research on London – 'possibly the most ethnically diverse conurbation on the planet' – has laid this myth to rest.[36] For whilst this impact on levels of trust may occur when smaller subsets of these communities do *not* interact with each other, the researchers found that the more different ethnic groups come into contact with each other, the stronger social cohesion becomes.[37] In fact, in 'ethnically diverse neighbourhoods', the researchers concluded, 'those who report having frequent contact with people in their neighbourhood are considerably more trusting of people in general, including strangers, not only people in their immediate locale' than those who have little or no interpersonal contact, irrespective of which ethnic group they belong to.[38]

In short, daily face-to-face interactions with people different from us make it easier to see what it is we have in common, rather than what sets us apart. For this Lonely Century to become less so, we need more contact, not less.

This is why one of the most worrying trends when it comes to our urban environments in recent years has been the slashing of public funds for places we *all* can commune, whether youth centres, libraries, community centres, parks or playgrounds, a trend that accelerated as governments cut spending in the aftermath of the 2008 financial crisis and subsequent downturn.

In the UK, a third of youth clubs and nearly 800 public libraries[39] have shut down since the 2008 financial crisis.[40] Across the nation 41% of adult day centres – a lifeline for the elderly and vulnerable, some of the loneliest in society – have closed in the decade since the crisis.[41] Public parks, spaces in which for over a century people of all stripes perambulated and mingled, lost £15 million in local funding between 2017 and 2019 alone.[42]

It's a similar picture elsewhere. From Bolton to Barcelona, from Houston to le Havre, from Kansas to California, across the world communities have been starved of their necessary social infrastructure.[43] And this problem is typically worse in cities than elsewhere.[44]

For people to feel united there need to be well-funded and cherished public spaces where relationships can develop, evolve, cement, including with people different to us; spaces where we *all* can interact, regardless of race, ethnicity or socio-economic background. We can't join together if we don't interact with each other. We can't find common ground if there is no ground for us to share.

This needs underlining because the temptation for governments and local municipalities over the coming months and years will be to further decrease public spending on such spaces, given the new wave of economic constraints we face. If we want to start to repair the social divides that became ever more visible during the coronavirus pandemic we cannot let this happen. The re-funding and re-energising of public spaces that have had the life sucked out of them since the 2008 economic downturn must be non-negotiable. And this isn't simply about refunding existing public spaces. Governments local and national must commit to putting inclusivity at the heart of new building projects.

A Chicago initiative spearheaded by former mayor Rahm Emanuel during his tenure provides an inspiring example of what local municipalities can do. There, three new public housing developments have been designed to incorporate branches of the Chicago Public Library. The library serves as a community gathering place, intergenerational nexus and a space where people from different socio-economic backgrounds come together to read, be read to, watch films and simply enjoy being part of a community environment. Children whose parents are on government assistance are just as welcome in these spaces as those whose families are living in market-rate apartments – potentially even right next door. 'Chicago is breaking the mold,' Emanuel said when the commissions were announced. 'Bringing world-class libraries together with housing builds strong neighbourhoods and provides a place for all community residents to gather, share and succeed.'[45]

Indeed, the presence of the library is already having a positive impact on social cohesion, for instead of resenting the sudden appearance of new 'housing projects' in their midst, the existing (usually relatively affluent) residents actively see the development as a boon for their own community, their children, their space.

'Sometimes, whenever you hear about affordable housing coming into your neighbourhood, some people can be very, "Well, yes that's alright to provide someplace else, but not in my backyard." But the community was very supportive,' says Doug Smith, the managing principal of the architecture firm that designed the space.[46] 'I hope it will help people who don't have financial security [to] better their circumstances,' agrees Shelley McDowell, a frequent Chicago Public Libraries user as a home-schooling mother. 'And for the people who are more affluent, I hope it educates them about other communities and builds bridges between those different social statuses and communities.'[47]

The library developments in Chicago are a powerful indicator of hope. They show that there are ways we can overcome the atomi-sation of the city and that the physical environment can have a massive impact both on *how* we interact, and *who* we interact with.

There is another way governments can intervene: recognise the critical role that local stores and cafés play as community hubs and centres of gravity for our neighbourhoods. Whilst we can't leave it to the market to be the *sole* custodian of society – especially as inclusivity is, as we've seen, not its concern – it's important to acknowledge the vital role that local businesses play in mitigating our collective loneliness. I will come back to the role the private sector can play in revitalising community in more detail later, but what's clear is that given how devastating the coronavirus pandemic was to the high street, governments will need to provide neighbour-hood stores with very meaningful support if they are to survive.

Again, there are precedents to draw upon. In Roeselare in Belgium, for example, an 'empty shops tax' placed on landlords (that kicks in once an outlet has been left empty for over a year and gets more onerous the longer it remains unoccupied), introduced in 2015, had a significant impact on vacancy rates by discouraging landlords from holding out for higher rents at a level that small businesses can't afford. The local authority also introduced a policy of turning down any new application for retail space outside the town's limits to prevent out-of-town malls and superstores from opening and drawing consumers away from the town centre.

Meanwhile if there was ever a time to take up former UK Sainsbury's supermarket chief Jasper King's call for a halving of business rates for high street stores, it's now. Especially given that it's not just social distancing and an economic downturn that local stores are having to contend with, but also the dramatic shift towards online shopping that recent events catalysed. The UK's decision to waive business rates for high street stores for 2020 to 2021 should be viewed as precedential.

Clearly there are a raft of fiscal and zoning policies that governments can initiate to help our high streets survive. But there's more still that our political leaders can do.

For imagine if cities were actively designed to be welcoming, rather than hostile. If instead of erecting spikes and concrete blobs masquerading as benches, city planners were channelling that ingenuity towards figuring out how to bring us together, rather than how to keep us apart.

In a pandemic dominated world, calling for such an agenda may seem pie-in-the-sky. And of course the reality is that governments and municipalities are, if anything, likely to move in the opposite direction in the short term because of the ongoing fears of contagion. 'Form', as architecture critic Oliver Wainwright has written, 'has always followed fear of infection, just as much as function.'[48] Indeed at the time of writing some pavements have been expanded so that people can keep their distance.

Yet it is essential that our current state of fear does not determine the shape our cities take in the long term and that future generations don't pay a price for our contemporary ills. We may have built ourselves a lonely world, but now we have an opportunity to reset our thinking and our obligations to each other and build one with inclusion and community at its heart.

Again, there are inspiring urban planning projects to learn from. Barcelona's city government, for example, has embarked on an ambitious urban planning project to turn neighbourhoods into 'superblocks', areas in which vehicle through-traffic is banned and the space is reclaimed for free communal areas such as playgrounds, parks and open-air performance venues.[49] The vision is that residents will no longer have to endure traffic noise or exhaust fumes, and neighbourhoods will become more hospitable to pedestrians and cyclists who may 'loaf', 'loiter' and 'lurk' to their hearts' desire. Six of those planned 503 superblocks are already in place.

Many residents initially resisted the first one in the Poblenou neighbourhood, which seemed to appear virtually overnight.[50] It's easy to sympathise: those who still relied on cars found their commutes tripled in length and parking was suddenly impossible to find for businesses hoping to unload goods. But as locals came to appreciate their new public parks and playgrounds, and as the city made good on its promises to invest in high-quality infrastructure, attitudes shifted. Salvador Rueda, the mastermind urban planner behind the superblocks project, noted that in the decade since 2007, foot traffic had increased by 10% and cycling by 30% in the Gràcia superblock across town.[51] 'It's a slower rhythm of life,' says Carles Peña, a Barcelona resident. 'You rediscover your area, and your neighbours.'[52]

Indeed, the data bears this out in a striking way. Researchers have found more generally that those who live on streets with low volumes of road traffic have three times as many social connections, friends and acquaintances as people who live on more heavily travelled streets.[53] What's more, their 'home territory' – the stretch of road to which they feel a sense of ownership, investment and belonging – expands. It's not difficult to imagine why. Residents in low-traffic areas feel their streets, and by extension their neighbourhoods, are safer; the air is less polluted; their children are less likely to be hit by a car if they play outside; it is more pleasant for people to hang out locally. As such they are less likely to retreat into buildings, away from the public realm, and more likely to engage with each other.

Urbanites, having become accustomed during lockdown to living without the constant noise of city traffic and their air noticeably cleaner, may well have a significantly stronger appetite for this kind of urban planning now than they might have had in the past. For what recent events made clear, even to those city dwellers who might identify as citizens of nowhere, is the extent to which our wellbeing is determined by our local geography and neighbourhoods.

Of course, the loneliness of the city cannot be fixed simply by what governments, architects, developers or city planners decide from on high. It's policy, bricks and people *together* that determine how the city makes us feel.

This struck home very clearly for many of us during the lockdown. For alongside stories of loneliness and isolation like that of Hazel Feldman in Manhattan, or of selfishness like that of shoppers brawling over toilet paper in Sydney, were also those of the coronavirus bringing urban communities together in ways they often had never experienced before.

In Kennington, London, fitness enthusiast Simon Garner initiated daily exercise sessions on his street. Neighbours stuck indoors united on their doorsteps, stretching in synchronicity, their 'weights' brooms and tins of baked beans. In Houston, Texas, as news broke that restaurants would only be allowed to provide takeout and delivery, an anonymous couple showed real solidarity by leaving a whopping $9,400 tip on a bill totalling $90. A note was attached: 'hold tip to pay your guys over the next few weeks'.[54] In Madrid, a taxi driver was lauded for ferrying patients to the local hospital, without charge.[55] And in the UK, US and elsewhere across the globe, many of us stood once a week outside our front doors, on our balconies, or at our windows, united in our clapping and whooping and beating of pots and pans to express gratitude to those battling on the front line against Covid-19.

We must never forget that even in a globalised world, we need the roots of our local communities to be strong. If we want to build upon the solidarity so many of us experienced in our neighbourhoods during the pandemic, and also express gratitude to all those local traders who fed and nourished us during lockdown, this means that there are commitments we will have to make. Community is something we have to actively co-create in order for all of us to feel the benefits.

We need to support our local cafés, even if that means paying a little more, seeing this as akin to a community tax, a small price to pay to help protect and nourish our neighbourhood. We need to commit to shopping, at least some of the time, in local stores rather than online, with the knowledge that without our custom it will be impossible for them to stay afloat. And if we want our locale to feel more cohesive, we need to commit to actively engaging with people who are different to us. Neither our local community centre nor our local high street will ever be able to deliver on their community promise if we don't all take advantage of the opportunities they provide to engage with our broader community. This is something I know I need to get better at myself.

More generally, if we want our local environment to feel alive and welcoming, we need to interact more with those around us physically, face to face. Slow down. Take that beat, that pause. Smile. Chat. Even if, as is the case at the time of writing, we still have to be socially distanced as we do so, even if our smiles are still occluded by our masks, even if in-person human interaction now scares us. Now more than ever we must be prepared to inconvenience ourselves for the sake of bolstering our communities and the people in them, and make a conscious effort to reach out to those in our midst who are most lonely.

We can draw inspiration here from people like Allison Owen-Jones, who in May 2019 noticed an elderly man sitting alone on a park bench in her home town of Cardiff. For forty minutes, people went about their city business, ignoring him. 'There was some of that British reserve that made me think he may think me weird if I sat next to him,' she later told the BBC. 'Wouldn't it be nice if there was a simple way to let people know you're open to a chat, I thought. So I came up with the idea of tying a sign that would open the avenues for people. It read: "Happy to chat bench. Sit here if you don't mind someone stopping to say hello."'[56]

And people did. Not only that, Owen-Jones ended up working

with a local charity and police force to set up permanent 'Happy to chat' benches all over Cardiff. This was more than just a way to get people to talk to one another: it helped people feel listened to and seen – especially those who are normally looked right through. As Owen-Jones put it, 'All of a sudden, you're not invisible anymore.'

CHAPTER SIX

Our Screens, Our Selves

Scottish polymath David Brewster was one of the most eminent scientists in Regency Britain. A former child prodigy at the University of Edinburgh, he had a lifelong fascination with optical devices and constructed his first telescope at the age of ten. An evangelical at heart, he initially pursued a career in the Church of Scotland but found public speaking too stressful; he once fainted at a dinner party when invited to say grace.[1] Instead, he turned to a different kind of evangelism: evangelism for science. In 1817, Brewster – by now a fellow of the Royal Society and winner of its prestigious Copley Medal for his contribution to the field of optics – patented a 'philosophical toy' that used angled mirrors and small pieces of coloured glass to create beautiful symmetrical forms. This device, he hoped, would allow people to amuse themselves while simultaneously observing the wonders of science.

Brewster's invention, the kaleidoscope – from the Greek *kalos* (beautiful) and *eidos* (form) – took off beyond his wildest dreams. Almost overnight, Britain was gripped by 'kaleidoscomania'. 'All ages have their Kaleidoscopes – the young, the old; all professions, all occupations; all nations, all governments, all sects, all parties', exclaimed the *Literary Panorama and National Register* in 1819.[2] Sara Coleridge, teenage daughter of the poet Samuel Taylor Coleridge, was among the instrument's many enthusiasts. After a visitor brought with him from London this 'very curious toy', she enthused to her friend and fellow Lake District resident Dora Wordsworth: 'you look through a hollow tube and see at the end little pieces of glass in all sorts of beautiful forms. These forms vary as often as you shake the tube. And if you are to shake for a hundred years you'd never see exactly the same again.'[3]

'Kaleidoscomania' rapidly spread to the European continent and beyond. Brewster estimated that 200,000 were sold in London and Paris within three months, and 'large cargoes of them were sent abroad, particularly to the East Indies'.[4] Soon, American magazines were filled with articles about the wonderous new contraption.[5] 'This beautiful little toy with its marvellous witcheries of light and colour spread over Europe and America with a furore which is now scarcely credible,' recalled Brewster's daughter, Margaret Gordon.[6]

For Brewster, however, the kaleidoscope's mass popularity – what today we would call 'viral success' – was a bittersweet experience. An early victim of piracy, he barely profited from the invention. As soon as he partnered with London manufacturers, cheap knock-offs flooded the market. Moreover, his innocent toy soon began to draw criticism for its relentless hold on people's attention. Commenting on the all-consuming nature of the fad, the *Literary Panorama and National Register* mockingly observed that '[e]very boy in the street studies his Kaleidoscope, though he bumps his head against a wall'.[7] An engraving from the time entitled *La Kaleidoscomanie où les Amateurs de bijoux Anglais* picks up this theme, depicting people glued to their kaleidoscopes, so distracted that they don't even notice their companions being courted behind their backs.[8]

Detractors saw the kaleidoscope as an expression of a mass consumer culture that could be all too easily distracted by the shiniest new baubles and sensations. As Percy Bysshe Shelley put it in 1818 when his friend and biographer, Thomas Jefferson Hogg, sent him instructions on how to make a kaleidoscope: 'Your kaleidoscope spread like the pestilence at Livorno. I heard that the whole population were given up to Kaleidoscopism.'[9]

Fast-forward two centuries and I'm sure you know where I'm going. The revolution that Steve Jobs triggered in 2007 with the launch of the iPhone means that most of us now have a modern day kaleidoscope in our pockets. One that is far more powerful and used far more obsessively than David Brewster's popular toy.

Kaleidoscomania on steroids

Two hundred and twenty-one. That's the number of times we check our phones on average each day.[10] This adds up to three hours and fifteen minutes of average daily use, almost 1,200 hours a year.[11] Around half of teens are now online 'almost constantly'.[12] A third of adults across the globe check their phones within five minutes of waking up; many of us (we know who we are) do so if we wake up in the middle of the night too.[13]

Digital distraction has become so bad that in Sydney, Tel Aviv and Seoul, cities with particularly high smartphone usage, urban planners have taken drastic steps to manage public safety.[14] 'Stop/Go' lights have been installed into the pavements so that pedestrians can see whether it is safe to cross without having to look up from their screens. One road in Seoul is even deploying lasers at crossings, which trigger a notification on the 'zombie' pedestrian's smartphone, warning them that they are about to step into traffic. It is an innovation undoubtedly inspired by the fact that in a five-year trial of the Stop/Go lights in South Korea pedestrian injuries fell by 20% and fatalities by 40%.[15] It seems that for some of us, the never-ending content streams on our smartphones are more compelling than ensuring we don't get hit by a car.

Of course, I'm not the first person to highlight the amount of time we are spending on our phones. Nor is this a blanket, Luddite attack on those little computers in our pockets. The questions I am posing are particular ones: how central are these devices to the loneliness crisis of the twenty-first century? And what makes this twenty-first-century innovation in communication so different to those that came before?

After all, each major development in communication technology, from Gutenberg's printing press to the smartphone, has both transformed how we interact with each other and not always been well received. In ancient Greece, Socrates warned that the act of writing would 'produce forgetfulness in the minds of those who learn to use it, because they will not practise their memory'.[16] In the fifteenth century, the Benedictine abbot and polymath Johannes Trithemius scolded monks for abandoning hand-copying in favour of Gutenberg's press in the belief that rigour and knowledge would vanish as a consequence (his own opprobrium, however, he printed – it was the only way to get anyone to read it).[17] Whilst in 1907 a *New York Times* writer lamented that 'The general use of the telephone, instead of promoting civility and courtesy, is the means of the fast dying out of what little we have left.'[18]

There is, though, a fundamental difference between our present-day smartphone usage and the communication innovations of previous centuries. Put simply, it is the extent to which we are glued to them. In the past, we might have picked up the telephone, what, a handful of times a day? Today, like a pair of glasses on our face whose presence we no longer notice, our phones have effectively become a part of us.[19] As we will see, this is no 'happy accident'. The big corporate beasts of our digital age have worked very hard to ensure this is so.

Together, yet alone

It's this state of perma-connection that makes our phone and social media usage like nothing else in human history, and it is contributing in very profound ways to the unique nature of this century's loneliness crisis.

For it is not just the busyness and pace of urban living that stymies us from smiling at a fellow patient at the doctor's surgery or nodding to another passenger on the bus, nor even contemporary social norms. Every moment in which we are on our phones, scrolling, watching videos, reading tweets, commenting on pictures, we are not present with those around us, depriving ourselves of the multiple daily social interactions that make us feel part of a wider society – those small moments of feeling seen and validated that, as we saw, really do matter. Just having a smartphone *with us* changes our behaviour and the way we interact with the world around us. In a recent study, researchers found that strangers smile significantly less at each other when they have their smartphones with them.[20]

Even more worrying is the extent to which our devices estrange us from people we already know, including those we love and care for. For all the time we are on our devices is also time we're not present with our friends, our colleagues, our lovers, our children.

Never before have we been so continuously distracted and never before have so many of us been simultaneously afflicted. More and more we are in the company of others but really on our own.

At the extreme the consequences of this constant partial attention can be tragic. There have been several cases in recent years of babies dying because their parents were distracted by their phones.[21] In one case in Parker County, Texas, a distraught mother claimed that she'd left her 8-month-old daughter in the bath 'for only a couple of minutes' while attending to another child.[22] When the police analysed her phone they discovered that she had also spent over eighteen minutes on Facebook, while her child was lying dead in the bathtub.

These are of course cases of extreme neglect, but we've all seen young children ignored while their carer texts, plays games or swipes through their social media. We've all seen the weekend fathers in the park, ignoring their kids on the swing whilst they are on their phone, we've all seen families in restaurants not speaking to each other because each is so wholly consumed by their own device. Such behaviour has far-reaching consequences.

Look at that dog

Chris Calland is a leading child development expert. A former teacher, she now advises schools and nurseries across the UK, and has a particular interest in parenting. Calland's work has led her to a concerning conclusion: that a growing proportion of children entering school today are increasingly deficient in fundamental interpersonal skills, while also lacking basic language abilities for their age. She believes that phones are at the heart of the problem: constant scrolling distracts parents from interacting with their children and in turn prevents them from imparting vital communication skills.

Calland's efforts to redress this are quite astounding. At one nursery, she even handed out scripts for parents to follow to help them engage with their kids. 'Tell me one nice thing you've done today' is one distressingly obvious cue; 'Look at that dog' is another. She also suggested putting up pictures around the nursery of phones with red lines through them, a warning to parents to rethink their relationship with technology and control their usage when onsite.[23]

It's not just children's communication skills that are impaired. Preliminary studies suggest that children of device-distracted parents are more likely to be picky eaters or to overeat, and more likely to have delayed motor skills as well. Less routinely measured aspects of child development have been found to be affected too, from emotional attachment ('why does Mummy love her phone more than me?') to emotional resilience.[24] There is also evidence that children whose parents are distracted by phones are more likely to act out, have trouble controlling strong negative feelings such as anger, or exhibit sulking behaviours when their requests are not met.[25] Like linguistic competence, these emotional effects last long past those early years when children are learning how to navigate the parent–child relationship: teens who perceive their parents as more distracted by digital devices report less parental 'warmth' and are more likely to develop anxiety and depression.[26]

Of course, children aren't the only ones being ignored. Think how many times you've lain in bed next to your partner, each of you scrolling on your phone. Or those work calls you've been on whilst simultaneously checking Twitter. Or those times you've chosen to watch Netflix with headphones rather than talk with your flatmate, or all that time and effort you put into creating the perfect holiday Instagram photo – time you could actually have spent interacting with whoever it was you were holidaying with, creating memories that would bond you and help build long-term connection.

I am as guilty as anyone else. The phone is our mistress and our lover. Nowadays we cheat on those around us in plain sight and somehow we have all come to accept the infidelity. We are present and yet we are not, together and yet alone.[27]

The splintered self

As for our ability to feel empathy, the distracting nature of smartphones significantly erodes this crucial skill which helps us understand and connect with each other. This is because they fragment our attention, creating a splintered self, caught between the physical reality of an intimate in-person conversation and the tens, maybe even hundreds, of text and image-based conversations happening simultaneously on our screens. When we're pulled in so many different directions, it's nearly impossible to give those in front of us the full weight of our attention and compassion, or see things from their point of view.

What's astonishing is that we don't even have to be *using* our phones for them to have this effect. An observational study of one hundred couples chatting in cafés in Washington, D.C. found that when a smartphone was placed between a couple on a table – or even just held in one of their hands – couples felt less close to each other, less empathetic.[28] Strikingly, the more intimate the relationship, the more detrimental the phone's effect on the couple's mutual empathy and the less each person felt understood, supported and valued. This is particularly worrying because empathy, like democracy, needs to be practised. Without regular use, it atrophies.

It is not just their attention-sapping quality that puts smartphones at odds with empathy. When people were asked, as part of a 2017 University of California at Berkeley study, to evaluate how 'human' others were on the basis of their opinions on controversial political topics, researchers found that their assessments were determined not only by whether the evaluators agreed with the posited opinion but also, to a significant degree, by the *medium* – video, audio or text – in which the opinion was expressed.[29] The more that the human form and voice were stripped away, the more likely evaluators were to dehumanise the person. This was most stark when all the evaluator had to go on was a written transcript of the speaker's views. As Stanford professor Jamil Zaki puts it, 'Thinned-out interactions [make] empathy harder to access.'[30]

This is concerning because the clear trend over the past decade has been in one direction only: towards ever more thinned-out interactions. This has been especially true of the young. A 2018 global survey of 4,000 18- to 34-year-olds in the United States, Britain, Germany, France, Australia and Japan found that 75% prefer communicating by text rather than phone calls, with these exchanges themselves increasingly circumscribed, largely a function of design.[31] The relative difficulty of typing on a smartphone (despite autocorrect and predictive text) encourages us to be ever shorter in our missives. The character limit on Twitter demands we speak in loud, brief and unnuanced statements. The fact that when we post shorter messages on Facebook we are more likely to get a response (posts of under eighty characters get 66% more 'interaction'), encourages us to self-edit. And if you can express yourself with a single tap to 'like' a post, why bother expending energy with words at all?[32]

Lockdown changed this. Overnight the humble phone call surged in popularity. In the US the volume of daily calls in April 2020 doubled compared to recent averages; the average length of a call shot up by 33%.[33] Even the young changed tack. Emily Lancia, 20, a junior at college, described how, walking on campus, she was inspired to call her best friend from childhood, someone who she texts with almost daily but had never once called before.[34] In the UK, mobile phone operator O2 revealed that a quarter of its clients aged between 18 and 24 phoned a friend *for the first time ever* after lockdown began in March.[35]

Video-calling was of course the other big beneficiary of the lockdown. Global downloads of Zoom, Houseparty and Skype increased exponentially in March 2020 as parties, quiz nights and business meetings migrated onto video. Microsoft Teams saw the number of video calls grow by more than 1,000% that month. Some couples even began to date on video, having only ever 'seen' each other onscreen.

The extent to which our appetite for voice and video-based exchanges persists beyond the immediate crisis is impossible to predict with any certainty at this point, although it's likely that business-oriented video meetings will continue for some time given social distancing requirements and restrictions on travel. But as we make choices about how we interact moving beyond the pandemic crisis, it's important to reflect upon what we lose when we make brevity our goal, text exchanges our default and more broadly choose to communicate virtually rather than in person. For as many of us discovered during lockdown, even video – the least thinned-out form of virtual interaction – though better than nothing, is still strikingly unsatisfying.

This is essentially because of the crucial role our faces play in building empathy and connection. Not only are they the most important source of non-verbal information we have when interacting with other human beings (our emotions, our thoughts, our intentions are all displayed there), but evolutionary biologists believe that our face's plasticity – its ability to convey nuanced facial expression using hundreds of muscles – evolved precisely so that early primates would cooperate and help each other more.[36]

The science backs this up: fMRI scans reveal that when communicating in person we don't just mimic each other subconsciously, but electronic waves in parts of our brains actually *synchronise*.[37] As Dr Helen Riess, the author of *The Empathy Effect*, explains: 'when we are in the presence of someone who's experiencing an emotion, we pick up on that because other people's emotions and facial expressions and experiences of pain are actually mapped onto an observer's brain, onto our own brains'. For instance, when we see someone else crying, this activates, if only mildly, the same area of our brain that activates when we experience sadness. 'That is why we feel sad when we're in the presence of someone who's very tearful or sorrowful, or why positive feelings like excitement are contagious. There's actually a neurobiological grounding for saying that "most feelings are mutual".'[38]

This mirroring is essential to connection and empathy. The trouble is that video, at least in its current frequently jerky, out of sync, freezing and blurred form, denies us both the ability to properly see each other – therapists who give online sessions have been known to ask their clients to exaggerate their non-verbal behaviours in order to communicate more effectively – and to seamlessly synchronise.[39] This is the especially the case as, all too often, those we are communicating with aren't even looking us in the eye – either because of their camera angle or because they're looking at themselves onscreen instead.

No wonder therefore after a video exchange we may feel somehow dissatisfied and, in some cases, even more isolated or disconnected than before. As Cheryl Brahnam, a professor in the department of information technology and cybersecurity at Missouri State University in Springfield, puts it: 'In-person communication resembles video conferencing about as much as a real blueberry muffin resembles a packaged blueberry muffin that contains not a single blueberry but artificial flavours, textures and preservatives. You eat too many and you're not going to feel very good.'[40]

Add to this the fact that email and text are Petri dishes of misunderstanding. A 2016 study by the University of Minnesota found that people looking at the same emoji disagreed strongly on its meaning a quarter of the time, opening the floodgates to miscommunication. Likewise, a series of studies have shown that sarcasm in emails is frequently taken for earnestness, and enthusiasm often comes across as mocking.[41] Even anger, the most recognisable of textual emotions, is hard to pin down precisely, including in exchanges with close friends.[42]

It seems then that when it comes to delivering on emotional engagement, empathy and understanding this century's new digital forms of communication have serious flaws and shortcomings that undermine the quality of our dialogue and consequently the quality of our relationships. They are a degraded substitute for talking and spending time in person with the people we care about, and play a significant role in our collective state of disconnection.

How to read a face

In many ways what's more troubling is that the impact of our smartphones is increasingly compromising our communication skills even when we *are* face to face with each other. This is especially so for the young.

It was at a dinner, sitting next to the president of one of the US's Ivy League universities a few years ago, that I first became aware of this. To my astonishment, he told me that he had grown so concerned about how many of his incoming students were arriving at college unable to read even the most obvious cues in face-to-face conversations that he had decided to introduce remedial 'How to Read Faces' classes.

At Boston College, one insightful professor adopted a different strategy. Also concerned that her students were increasingly finding face-to-face interactions challenging, Kerry Cronin came up with a unique way for them to improve upon these skills. She assigned them the opportunity to earn extra credit if they asked someone out on a date *in person*.

Cronin, who teaches courses on relationships, spirituality, ethics, and personal development, came up with the idea after a lecture on campus hook-up culture when, instead of asking the kind of questions she'd anticipated on sex and intimacy, students expressed curiosity about something much simpler: 'How do you ask someone out on a date?'[43] She realised that dating was 'a lost social script': her students literally asked her what words to use to ask someone out 'IRL' (in real life). So she decided to step in.

Cronin provided her students with twenty-two bullet-point rules they had to adhere to in order to successfully complete the assignment.[44] Rules that were designed to help her students connect with their date without the digital crutch of dating apps, social media or the anonymous hook-up culture that had become so familiar. The students had to ask someone on a date in person – not over text – and actually go through with it, no ghosting (abruptly stopping all contact) allowed. The date could not be at the cinema, nor could it involve alcohol or physical touching beyond a friendly hug. In other words, no running away from really communicating: no hiding yourself in a darkened theatre, arming yourself with 'liquid courage' or forgoing conversation by simply 'hooking up'. The date had to involve actually talking to someone, awkwardness, butterflies and nerves included.

Cronin also recommended that students prepared in advance with a list of three or four questions, plus two or three topics to aid conversation. She was keen to impress upon them too that a lull in the conversation is natural – for a generation for whom communication and entertainment on social media are constant and on-demand, she needed to explain that in real life there are also spaces for silence.

The challenge of in-person dating for a generation so used to communicating via smartphones that they are, as one student put it, 'afraid of human interaction', is not a problem confined to Boston College attendees.[45] Wikihow, the site that typically delivers a series of concrete steps for problems such as 'How to write an essay', 'What to do if you've been food-poisoned' or 'How to keep pets off furniture' now also provides a brief tutorial on 'How to ask someone out in real life'... in '12 steps (with pictures).'[46]

In the same way that the calculator destroyed our collective ability to do mental arithmetic, so too does the digital communication revolution risk leaving us ill equipped to effectively communicate in person. It turns out Socrates' 'use it or lose it' warning had something to it after all.

There are signs that this deficit in communication skills is setting in at an even younger age. Children are not just being affected by their parents' smartphone use as Chris Calland found. As early as 2010, the PEACH project at the University of Bristol established that in a group of 1,000 10- and 11-year-olds, those children who spent more than two hours per day watching a screen (either a television or a computer) were more likely to have difficulties expressing their emotions.[47] In 2011, New York-based child psychologist Melissa Ortega noticed that her young patients were using their phones as an avoidance strategy, deflecting from her questions about how they were feeling by constantly checking for text messages.[48] In 2012, an observational study of over 600 teachers from kindergarten through to high school in the United States reported that high media use (with media defined as TV shows, music, video games, texting, iPods, mobile phone games, social networking sites, apps, computer programmes, online videos and websites students use for fun) was affecting pupils' behaviour and attitudes. Even at the kindergarten stage, children 'lack in social and play skills because they are so busy with media use that they do not know how to interact face to face with others', reported one teacher.[49] More recently, in a 2019 Canadian study that tracked 251 children between the ages of one and four, researchers found that the more time they spent on their screens the less capable they were of understanding other children's feelings, the less helpful they were towards other children and the more disruptive they also were.[50] Another 2019 study, this time Norwegian, that tracked nearly 1000 children aged between 4 and 8 found that high screen use at age 4 predicted a lower level of emotional understanding when these children reached age 6, compared to children who had not used screens as much.[51]

Whilst inevitably much depends on the extent to which screen time crowds out quality human interaction and what a child is using their device for, and as ever there are some conflicting views,[52] there is also evidence that time spent away from screens enhances how children are able to relate.

In a study conducted by researchers at UCLA, a group of 10- and 11-year-olds spent five days at an outdoor nature camp where they had no access to digital media – smartphones, TV or the internet. Both before and after they were given some simple tests, such as identifying the emotions expressed by people in photos and videos. After just five screen-free days, they showed marked improvements at recognising non-verbal emotional cues such as facial expressions, body language and gestures and at discerning how people in the photos and videos were feeling, both compared to their prior per-formance and also compared to a group of peers who had stayed at home on screens.[53] The researchers believe this was because deprived of their screens the children had to spend considerably more time interacting with their peers and the adults face to face. 'You can't learn non-verbal emotional cues from a screen in the way you can learn it from face-to-face communication,' lead author Yalda T. Uhls explained.[54]

Whilst cautionary warnings about children and screens have been issued ever since the 1950s when televisions entered people's homes, the problem again is likely to be one of scale. Whereas in the past, children's screen access was time-bound, today half of children by the age of ten (this is UK data but it's a similar picture in other higher-income countries) have a smartphone of their own.[55] More than half sleep with it by their bed.[56] It's the omnipresence as well as the omnipotence of our devices that's the problem, coupled with the fact that the compelling nature of our screens often crowds out the higher-quality in-person interactions we could be having instead.

Screen-free lives
It's with such insights in mind that some parents are actively promoting screen-free lives for their kids. Ironically it is Silicon Valley parents leading the way. They are one of the groups most

likely to prohibit smartphone usage amongst their children and send them to screen-free schools. Steve Jobs notoriously limited how much technology his kids used at home, whilst Bill Gates didn't allow his kids to get mobile phones until they were 14 and even then set strict screen-time limits.[57] As early as 2011, the *New York Times* reported on the growing popularity of screen-free, experiential learning education systems such as Waldorf schools in Silicon Valley and other areas densely populated with tech executives and their families.[58] Many self-respecting Silicon Valley parents nowadays go as far as to include in their nannies' contracts a clause in which they promise not to use their phones for personal use in front of their charges. The hypocrisy is of course all too clear – not only do some of these parents work at the companies responsible for making these devices so addictive, many parents 'come home, and they're still glued to their phones, and they're not listening to a word these kids are saying', says Shannon Zimmerman, who works as a nanny in San Jose.[59]

Whilst the wealthiest can pay for their children to lead screen-limited lives by employing human carers rather than putting their kids in front of a tablet, for the vast majority of families this is not a viable option.[60] Lower-income American teens and tweens (8- to 12-year-olds), unable to afford after-school activities and extracurricular classes, rack up around two hours more screen time per day than their affluent peers.[61] Conversations with teachers in the UK reveal a similar dynamic at play there too.[62]

At a time that the very wealthiest parents are actively trying to reduce the amount of screen time their kids are subject to and the most prestigious colleges are running how-to-read faces classes, we cannot allow a new divide to emerge whereby rich children become better skilled in empathy and communication and poor children risk being ever less able to communicate effectively. It's absolutely vital for our collective futures that *all* children retain these critical skills. This means ensuring that after-school activities are available to children of all income brackets, and also that the trend towards screen-based learning at school does not come at the expense of in-person lessons, support and interactions.

Digital slot machines

Too much time spent on our screens clearly isn't good for us. The trouble is that even if we know this, resisting the urge to pick up our phones takes a level of commitment and willpower that many of us struggle to find. This is because of the extent to which we are addicted to our digital devices.

It's amongst children that the addiction is perhaps most obvious. One teacher in Indianapolis now keeps students' confiscated phones in a clear plastic bag around her waist, in full view, to ease the symptoms of their separation anxiety; others have set up charging stations in the classroom to encourage students to part with their devices, secure that they remain in their sight line. A pupil's ability to control their smartphone addiction during lessons can even lead to special benefits, with some teachers rewarding students with extra credit or Starbucks gift cards when they avoid touching their phones during class.[63]

Yet we as adults are often in denial about how addicted we are. Consider these questions. Have you ever felt you should cut down on the amount of time you're on your phone? Have people ever annoyed you by criticising the amount of time you are on your phone? Have you ever felt bad or guilty about how much time you are on your phone? Do you reach for your phone first thing when you wake up? If you've answered yes to at least two of these questions, addiction may well be an appropriate term for what you are experiencing. For these questions are based on the CAGE questionnaire – a four-question screening tool widely used in hospitals, primary care centres and rehab clinics to check for potential alcohol problems.[64]

But why exactly are we so addicted to our phones? It is time to put the social media giants of Silicon Valley in the dock. For like slot machines, social media platforms have been consciously designed to keep us constantly scrolling, watching, liking and refreshing in the hope of finding affirmation, echoes, confidence boosts, mutual attraction, even love.[65] Every serif, every screen layout, every focus-grouped hue, every barely perceptible animation, every *pixel* of what we see onscreen has been actively configured to keep us always-on and hooked.[66] In fact in 2017, former Facebook president Sean Parker told news media company Axios point-blank that the central question driving Facebook in its early days was 'How do we consume as much of your time and conscious attention as possible?' 'We knew our creation was addictive,' he said. 'And we did it anyway.' He added, 'God only knows what it's doing to our children's brains.'[67]

It's an addiction that is making us lonely, although of course not in all cases. It's important to acknowledge that for some people these lower-quality virtual exchanges are still better than those that they can access nearby in person. Whether it's the LGBTQ+ kid in a small town in Idaho who thanks to new friends in faraway places on Twitter doesn't feel so alone, or the Filipino migrant worker who uses Facebook every day to stay connected to her kids back home, the cystic-fibrosis sufferer who knows no one in his area with the condition but has found solace in online support groups, or the grandmother who thanks to Instagram is able to stay connected to her grandchildren in a way that she couldn't before – social media can provide some with a community they might not otherwise have had. And as we saw during lockdown, at times it can provide crucial lifelines and take the edge off isolation.

Yet numerous studies over the past decade have established a clear link between social media usage and loneliness. One study found, for example, that adolescents with higher social media use reported more loneliness than their peers.[68] Another discovered that for every 10% rise in negative experiences on social media, college students reported a 13% increase in loneliness.[69] A third study found that in the 2010s, American adolescents socialised in person for a full hour less every day (on average) than they had in the 1980s, a trend the researchers linked explicitly to the increase in social media usage.[70] Adolescent loneliness, they also noted, had ballooned after 2011 – the same year that the number of teens owning a smartphone began to skyrocket. Whereas in 2011 only 23% of US teens owned a smartphone, by 2018 this had risen to 95%.[71]

The challenge was that although these studies demonstrated that social media use and loneliness were connected, almost every one of them struggled to determine causation. In other words, do lonely people use social media more or does social media actually *cause* loneliness?

Two landmark studies recently set out to answer that very question. Crucially in these, the participants weren't simply asked to report their social media habits; instead they were directed by the researchers to actively *change* them. This meant that the effects of those changes on their behaviour and mood could be directly observed and compared, and causality could be established.[72]

The results were enlightening. One of the studies found that limiting Snapchat and Instagram along with Facebook to ten minutes per platform per day produced a significant reduction in loneliness.[73] The other, a gold standard of a study of nearly 3,000 people in which over a two-month period half of the participants used Facebook as normal and the other half – the 'Treatment' group – fully deactivated their Facebook accounts, found that the group that had deactivated Facebook didn't simply use the time they would have spent on that platform on other websites. Instead they used the internet less overall and spent more time socialising with friends and family in person. And as for how they felt? They reported more happiness, more life satisfaction, less anxiety and to a moderate yet statistically significant degree, less loneliness too. When it came to improving subjective wellbeing, deleting Facebook was up to 40% as effective as attending therapy.[74]

Meaner

The problematic impact of social media runs even deeper. It's not simply driving us into isolated digital bubbles that crowd out richer in-person interactions. It is also making the world feel more hostile, less empathetic and less kind. And this is taking a significant toll on our collective wellbeing.

Trolling – posting deliberately offensive or provocative content; doxxing – spreading personal information, such as a home address in order to enable harassment; swatting – using doxxed information to call in a false hostage situation prompting police to send a SWAT team and potentially arrest the person in their own home: a twenty-first-century vernacular has developed to describe a whole host of new and insidious online behaviours.[75] For whilst social media platforms do enable us to share moments of happiness, their design has also made them conducive to some of the worst elements of human nature: abuse, bullying, racism, anti-Semitism, homophobia. All such behaviours are on the rise. In 2018, *over half* of adult UK internet users reported having seen hateful content online, a 6% increase from the year before.[76] In the UK, one in three women have experienced abuse on Facebook and amongst 18- to 25-year-olds that increases to 57%. Over the course of 2016 (the most recent year for which there is verified data), an anti-Semitic post appeared on social media on average every eighty-three seconds and 80% of these were on Twitter, Facebook or Instagram.[77]

There's no sign that any of this is slowing down anytime soon.

Of course, hatred and abuse are not new phenomena. But what's different is that social media pumps them into our lives in new and uniquely disturbing ways, at a scale that again is simply unprecedented. And what's so frightening is that it rewards users for doing so. For each retweet we get provides us with a dopamine hit, the same neurotransmitter associated with heroin and morphine. It's a tiny dose, to be sure, but enough to keep us coming back for more. And you know what kind of posts typically engender the most retweets? The most outlandish, extreme and hateful ones. Put a word like 'kill', 'destroy', 'attack' or 'murder' in your post and it'll be retweeted nearly 20% more.[78]

Whilst it is unlikely that stimulating toxic behaviour was the intention of the founders of these platforms, what is clear is that it fast became something they tolerated. For the fact is that outrage and anger are better for business. More addictive emotions than kindness or positivity, they keep traffic and throughflow high, thereby increasing the likely number of ad clicks, which is how the social media companies make their money.[79] It's this impact on the bottom line that helps explain why pretty much anything that will attract eyeballs is tolerated on these platforms, however dark, cruel, or polarising.[80] It's the amorality of the unregulated market in action. Twitter notably *did* draw a line in the sand on 29 May 2020 when it hid President Trump's now-infamous 'when the looting starts, the shooting starts'[81] tweet behind a warning message on the basis that it glorified violence.[82] Facebook, however, left the very same post up on its platform.[83] Their rationale – this wasn't about morality it was about freedom of expression.

It is not only adults being affected by a design ethic that both incentivises us to deliver ever more outraged and divisive messages and enables us to so easily find community in hate. For children, social media has also become home to abuse and bullying on a distressing scale. In Singapore, three-quarters of teenagers say that they have been bullied online.[84] In the UK, 65% of students have experienced a form of cyberbullying, with 7% experiencing it 'regularly'.[85] And in a recent UK survey of more than 10,000 young people aged 12 to 20, nearly 70% admitted to being abusive to another person online – whether sending a nasty message, posting hateful comments under a fake username or sharing something with the intention of mocking someone else.[86]

Such abuse can have a devastating impact, but many of us failed to appreciate just how devastating until the highly publicised death of 12-year-old British cyberbullying victim Jessica Scatterson, who killed herself in 2019 in the wake of a spate of abusive messages on social media. As the coroner said at the inquest, 'The level and the intensity of her activity on social media platforms, particularly in the build-up to her death, cannot have failed to have influenced her thinking, her state of mind.'[87]

Children have of course always bullied and been bullied. Yet once again it's a matter of scale. For whilst in the past this psychological abuse was typically confined to the playground, park and classroom, today it follows them around inescapably 24/7, streamed into their homes and bedrooms. Moreover, whilst bullying used to be public only to the extent that others witnessed it directly in real time, today the victim's shame is there for all to see, permanently etched into their digital footprint.

Social media is making us lonelier not only because all that time we are spending on it makes us feel less connected to those around us, but also because it is making society as a whole meaner and crueller. And a mean and cruel world is a lonely one.

Most obviously the loneliness is felt by those in the line of fire who feel both the pain of the abuse and the sense of powerlessness that comes with it, as digital bystanders fail to come to their aid and social media platforms do nothing to protect them.[88] But it is lonelier for all of us too. For in the same way that children who witness their parents arguing – or worse, episodes of domestic violence – are likely to become withdrawn, socially anxious and self-isolating, the same applies here.[89] Spend too much time scrolling in an angry and toxic environment and you risk feeling ever more alone, even if you're not directly under attack. Moreover, the more toxicity we witness, the less faith we have in society at large.[90] As we have seen, this also has wider societal and political ramifications. For the less we trust each other, the more selfish and divided we become.

BOMP: A belief that others are more popular than you

Our experience of social media even on an everyday level can make us feel lonely, as Claudia's story shows.

Senior year. The homecoming dance. Claudia sits on her couch at home in her pyjamas, scrolling through Facebook and Instagram. Her friends had said they weren't going. 'Over-rated', they had agreed. Then the photos popped up on her feed. Her friends, dressed to the nines for homecoming, laughing, hanging out, having fun without her. Never before had she felt so awful about herself, 'so insignificant and alone'. She felt so depressed that she refused to go to school for a week, hiding instead in her room on her own. Grades, school activities, even the prospect of college felt secondary to the pain of her all-too-public exclusion. Facing her friends felt simply impossible. 'Why go to school if I was invisible to everyone?' she said.

You are probably already familiar with the phrase FOMO – fear of missing out, that nagging sense that others are somewhere else having fun whilst you are sitting at home on your own. But Claudia's story is about something arguably much more painful: the fear that she was friendless in a world where everyone else has friends. It's a phenomenon so prevalent that psychologists are beginning to study it.[91] I call it 'BOMP': A Belief that Others are More Popular. Like FOMO, it's a feeling exacerbated by social media – and one that is all too common.

BOMP can feel distressing, whatever one's age. It is never nice to feel socially inferior or excluded. Indeed, in my research I've come across numerous adults who've felt unpopular because they've experienced an adult version of Claudia's homecoming trial – seen online evidence of old school mates having drinks that they weren't invited to, or a family get-together that no-one had included them in. Whereas once we might never have discovered that we'd been left out of such gatherings, today our exclusion smacks us in the face, in real time, in technicolour with filters, lenses and sound effects.

For children and adolescents this is especially painful. As one British teenage boy told the charity Childline: 'I see all my friends having a good time on social media and it gets me down, I feel like no one cares enough to invite me. My mood is getting worse and now I'm just upset all the time and can't stop crying.'[92] Or as one American parent told me, 'You have no idea how painful it is to see your teenage child in distress as they sit at home looking at posts from people that they thought were friends, having a party without them. It feels really cruel.'

But social media does more than provide a real-time window to experiences we have been excluded from; the platforms themselves are being used as weapons of exclusion even more directly.

I think of WhatsApp primarily as a useful way of staying in touch with friends and family overseas, or with my fellow performers in my weekly improv group. My husband is in a WhatsApp group with his siblings where everything from family meals to parental care is discussed, and another with his friends which dissects football matches with a level of detail I find hard to fathom. These all seem like positive uses of social media's messaging apps in one way or another. Among many teens and twentysomethings, however, this kind of group chat is now a primary way to communicate, with 30% using some form of group chat – whether WhatsApp, Houseparty, Facebook Messenger or WeChat – multiple times per day (usage was even higher of course during lockdown).[93] So what, you may ask? Well, becoming aware that you are being excluded from these groups has become a new form of painful isolation. And it's an experience increasing numbers of young people are having. Jamie, a 16-year-old from Oxford, explained to me how lonely it felt to find out that her classmates were in a group she hadn't been invited to join, to realise that entire conversations were taking place – even at times that she was physically in the room – that she was excluded from.

Another parent I spoke to showed distress when he told me about the time his daughter was with five or six friends in a café when all of a sudden phones started pinging. It turned out to be a group message inviting them to a party that weekend – all of them, that is, except his daughter. To get through it, she pretended that she had also received an invite. It felt better to lie than to feel humiliated. It was lonely to feel excluded, yet it would have felt lonelier still to be seen to be so.

Both teachers and parents have become acutely aware of these new forms of social exclusion and their consequences, along with the challenges of managing them. Oliver Blond, the headmaster of the UK girls' boarding school Roedean, explained to me that because digital exclusion is typically invisible, teachers find it very difficult to tackle. For whereas in the past a teacher could see exclusion taking place – a child sitting on their own at lunch, or a group turning their backs on one of their peers – today many of these interactions are taking place in the virtual sphere. And because they are not witnessed, adults can't intervene, meaning that the excluded child is even more alone in their suffering.

Public rejection and shame

There's something else social media does that perniciously contributes to contemporary loneliness: it makes our social status public, and therefore our unpopularity or rejection by our peer group. With even the most banal of social gatherings likely to be memorialised on Instagram or beamed out on a Snap Story, our absence is easily noted. More than this, the new social currency of retweets, likes and shares means that each time we post and our posts are ignored we risk feeling not only rejected or valueless, but also ashamed, because we experience our rejection in public.

It is this fear of being so *visibly* ignored that can make otherwise confident, successful adults like a leading UK politics professor I know spend, as he confides in me, hours at a time trying to craft the perfect tweet: tweaking it, refining it, hours that he knows would be better served on his research. It's this fear too that makes graduate student Jennifer spend so long on perfecting her Instagram shots that she often doesn't have time to experience what she is documenting. On a recent holiday to Costa Rica she spent so much time on her 'Jen goes Ziplining' post that she didn't actually go ziplining, ironically missing out on a memorable bonding experience with her IRL friends.

Again it's the youngest amongst us for whom the fear of being visibly unpopular is most painful and anxiety-provoking. One parent told me of the pain he felt watching his daughter manically 'liking' every post of every person on her feed to try and ensure a reciprocal response when she posted herself. Peter, a four-foot-nothing bespectacled Year 9 student from London, described to me the 'agony' he felt 'posting, waiting, and hoping and no one replying and then asking myself again and again why am I not liked? What am I doing wrong?' And Jamie told me of how the thought of any of her Snapchat streaks ending sent her into a panic. 'It makes me feel physically sick,' she explained.

It's not that being popular wasn't always important to the young. Indeed, it's the theme at the heart of most high-school dramas. What is different is, once again, the powerful and inescapable impact that social media has brought to these dynamics. 'Social media marks a new era in the intensity, density and pervasiveness of social comparison processes especially for the youngest among us, who are "almost constantly online" at a time of life when one's own identity, voice and moral agency are a work in progress,' writes the Harvard professor Shoshana Zuboff. She continues, 'The psychological tsunami of social comparison triggered by the social media experience is considered unprecedented'.[94] It's this constant process of having to sell oneself – and the constant fear that no one will want to buy – that's the problem.

Some social media companies are beginning to acknowledge the problem they've created here, at least tacitly. Facebook has beta-tested versions of its own platform, as well as Instagram's (which it owns), in which public 'likes' are suppressed – the user can see how many 'likes' a post has garnered, but no one else can.[95] The man behind the initiative at Instagram, Facebook veteran Adam Mosseri, admits that it was spurred in part by an episode of Charlie Brooker's dystopic sci-fi TV series *Black Mirror*, in which omnipresent social media ratings send the protagonist spiralling towards disaster.[96] I appreciate these efforts (which of course came only after sustained concern and backlash), but the question is whether these changes – even if implemented after the pilot project – will really make a difference. Won't our dopamine-craving brains just find other metrics – comments or shares or reposts, or tags on others' posts – to compare ourselves against? And won't we still chase the affirmation that each like provides, even if no one else sees it? Our relationship with social media and how deeply we've absorbed its architecture psychologically makes it likely that the conditions of our engagement are already set.

Love my avatar

By turning us into ever more insecure hustlers intensely pursuing likes, follows and online social kudos, social media also encourages us to do something else: to present ever less authentic versions of ourselves online. I mean, nobody puts on Facebook 'I have just spent the whole weekend in my pyjamas eating ten packets of Hobnobs and watching *Friends*.' Instead, the lives we share online are a curated series of aspirational highlights and happy moments, parties and celebrations, sandy white beaches and mouth-watering food porn. The trouble is that such Photoshopped, filtered versions of ourselves are all too often fundamentally disconnected from our own authentic being.

Who am I actually? The always happy, successful, sociable person I put on Instagram, or someone who at times fails, falters and feels unsure? And what happens if the fake me is the one that my friends online prefer? The more carefully we curate our social media lives, the more we commodify ourselves, the more we risk feeling that no one either knows or likes the 'real' person behind the profile. It's an isolating and disconnecting feeling. As Tessa, an intelligent and artistic 17-year-old from California so aptly put it, 'we are increasingly living our lives like avatars in an online video game'. Picture-perfect avatars, that is. In 2016, when the market research firm Custard surveyed 2,000 people in the UK, it found that only 18% of them said their Facebook profile accurately represented them.[97]

Maybe it is human nature to work desperately hard on our outward presentation and even, at times, fall into a kind of performance that makes us seem other than who we really are. It was more than 400 years ago after all that Shakespeare declared, 'All the world's a stage'. Teenagers have always been especially prone to this; black cats' eye make-up, micro miniskirts, biker boots and Nietzsche's opus *Thus Spoke Zarathustra* in my bag was my carefully crafted 14-year-old persona.

However, the age of social media marks a shift from traditional human behaviour in this key aspect: in the past, we could regularly take a break from acting and revert to some sense of our private and authentic selves. Once a week, without fail, my 14-year-old self would take off the warpaint, put on pyjamas and snuggle up with my family to watch *Dallas*. But now, as we constantly prod at our smartphones and every moment of life is a potential photo opportunity, when does the performing ever stop?

It's a question that applies to all of us. Think about the last time you took a selfie. What went through your mind? Were you looking at your own face, or were you trying to look at your face 'through the eyes' of whatever social media followers would eventually see it? Was it *you* taking the picture at all?

What, too, does it do to our relationships with others if they transmute into interactions between idealised avatars? Inevitably it renders them necessarily shallower and hollower as well as weirdly competitive. Increasingly detached from our online personas we are performing the act of sharing, rather than truly sharing ourselves. As one 16-year-old who has now quit social media eloquently said: 'I was presenting this dishonest version of myself, on a platform where most people were presenting dishonest versions of themselves.'[98]

Right from the start, the design of social media encouraged people to distort their true selves in exchange for social validation.

Take Facebook: in its earliest days in the mid-2000s when it was still called 'TheFacebook' and available only to college students, its users started curating their profiles with surgical precision, from regularly updated profile pictures – posed but not too posed – to witty descriptions of their clubs and activities, to even changing their academic course schedules (which were public) to 'project a certain image of themselves', says David Kirkpatrick, author of *The Facebook Effect*.[99] Did Mark Zuckerberg et al. care about what they were unleashing? Again, seemingly not. Connecting the world may be their goal, but it seems that if in the process connections become shallower, crueller or increasingly distorted, so be it.

At the extreme some come to prefer their digital self to their authentic one. It can start, innocently enough, with an Instagram selfie filter which adds floppy ears and a cartoonish nose to your face. But soon you discover another filter that can also smooth skin, define cheekbones and magnify your eyes, providing you with an ever-so-enhanced version of your face under the veneer of a cutesy selfie. Perhaps you then graduate to a self-editing app that goes even further, brightening your skin, elongating your jaw and thereby further slimming your cheeks, whitening your teeth, reshaping your jawline, the width of your face and your nose.[100] These are all things you can do on an app like FaceTune, consistently one of the bestsellers in Apples App Store.[101] Inevitably, the face that stares back at you from the mirror starts to look so much less . . . polished than your digitised one. So you take your FaceTuned version of your face to a plastic surgeon and ask for the relevant nips and tucks to create the version of yourself you have edited online.[102]

This might sound extreme, but it isn't an imaginary scenario. Increasing numbers of young people are approaching plastic surgeons with photos of their Photoshopped, filtered, digitally altered selves. In 2017, 55% of the surgeons of the American Academy of Facial, Plastic and Reconstructive Surgery had at least one patient bring in a Photoshopped selfie and ask them to recreate it, a 13% increase on the year before.[103] The AAFPRS expects this trend only to grow.

Social media is not only turning us into salespeople, with our product being our commoditised and repackaged self – it's also internalising BOMP, making many of us feel not only less popular than those around us, but also that our real selves are less popular than our digitally enhanced ones. And that is fundamentally alienating.

Change is possible

So what can we do about the deleterious effects of social media and the role it is playing in the twenty-first century's loneliness crisis?

Clearly, spending less time on these platforms is key. And in researching this book I've come across a number of people who've gone so far as to log off entirely. People like Sammy, the 15-year-old keen debater, who decided he just didn't want to be part of the toxicity anymore and has left social media for good. Or Peter, the 22-year-old graduate, who told me he's taken himself off Instagram and can see a really significant improvement in his happiness and emotional health. Or Maxine, the 40-year-old finance professional who came off Facebook because she felt she just couldn't take reading another 'smug post' from a friend about their domestic or professional bliss. These, however, remain the exceptions. The mass migration to social media and its utility as messaging services means that those who come off can feel markedly excluded. This is especially true of the young. If your entire class 'hangs out' on Instagram, staying offline will for most feel simply untenable. Unless new social norms emerge in which being present in person has greater cachet than being always on social media, this is unlikely to change.

Even for those who want to reduce their time on these platforms, logging off is extremely challenging because of their addictive nature. There are, however, practical hacks we can all try to mitigate this. Commit to digital-free days. Deploy 'nudges' that might help curb your cravings – such as putting all your social media in an inconveniently placed smartphone folder, or even deleting your social media apps on your smartphone. Ask your partner, even your kids, to ruthlessly remind you not to be 'a droid' (although you might want to come up with less pejorative phrasing). Or how about handing over to a friend or family member a significant sum or 'deposit' that's only returned to you if you reduce your social media use by a certain amount over a six-month period? It's a strategy that has seen considerable success when it comes to helping smokers put an end to their addiction.[104]

You might even want to consider junking your smartphones and instead buying a Lightphone, an intentionally 'low-tech' device that features calling and (gasp!) T9 texting, the most basic of the basic forms of texting – without even the ease of a qwerty keyboard – and that stores only ten contacts at a time.[105]

Yet this is not a battle we can fight on our own. To curb our digital addiction at a significant scale, decisive government intervention is essential. Think of the measures governments use to discourage the use of tobacco, such as mandating that warnings be printed on all packaging. Given social media's similarly addictive properties, is it time for warnings about the dangers of these platforms to become mandatory, too? Pop-up messages each time we open an app, banners on websites, stickers on smartphone packaging with a photo of a scrambled brain perhaps? Such steps would build our daily awareness of the risks. Each time we deploy these technologies, we need to be reminded of their potential for harm. And like smokers being encouraged to quit, public health campaigns to encourage us to reduce our time on our phones and on social media should also be considered. Especially as unlike sugar – an addictive drug which harms only the user themselves – social media, like tobacco, has a significant network effect potentially damaging not only to ourselves but to those around us as well.[106]

When it comes to children we need to go further still. When children as young as nine are 'increasingly anxious about their online image' and becoming 'addicted to likes as a form of social validation', as Anne Longfield, the children's commissioner for England has said, we cannot accept the harm social media is causing so many young people as 'just the way the world is now'.[107]

As such, addictive social media platforms should be banned for children under the age of adult consent (16 in the UK, 18 in the United States). Whilst some may cry out that this will stymie children's freedom of expression and personal independence, note that

I'm not proposing a blanket ban on social media for this age group, but instead a ban on *addictive* social media. And the burden of proof should be on the social media platform to provide compelling scientific evidence that they are not causing addiction in children. Where they are not able to, the platform should be forced to establish truly effective identification systems for proving that users are over the allowable age.[108]

The onus would therefore be on the platforms to innovate new forms of social media that are less addictive, or remove the addictive elements they currently deploy, whether likes, streaks or the endless scroll, if they want to be able to target this demographic.

Whilst this approach may seem to some quite draconian, one need only look back at history to see how attitudes towards such interventions can change. I recall the shock and surprise many in the UK felt when in 1989 seat belts became compulsory for children to wear in the back seats of cars.[109] At the time it felt both unnecessary and an assault on personal freedom, yet of course it has saved countless young lives and it would now seem reckless not to secure a child in a car. Likewise, smoking in a car carrying children was once commonplace and is now not just widely frowned upon, but illegal in the UK, some states and cities in the US and in many other places around the world.[110] On a precautionary basis alone the case for the prohibition of addictive social media until the age of adult consent is strong.

When it comes to the most egregious examples of toxic discourse, such as hate speech and the sharing of violent content on these platforms, there needs to be zero tolerance. And whilst I understand the reluctance of tech leaders like Mark Zuckerberg to take on the role of arbiter, especially given the tradition of free speech that surrounds the United States' First Amendment, social media platforms can't market themselves as public squares, yet at the same time insist they have only limited responsibility for what goes on inside them. Especially as the big players already do take editorial decisions and are willing to impose a value judgement on some issues. For example, Facebook bans nudity often to absurd degrees.[111] This is in marked contrast to Mark Zuckerberg's position on Holocaust denial, say, of which he said, 'At the end of the day

I don't believe that our platform should take that down.' Instead he said Facebook would move it down the news feed so that fewer users saw it.[112]

I understand too, of course, that there is a legitimate challenge when it comes to monitoring the hundreds of millions of posts uploaded on social media every day, and that automated mechanisms for flagging hateful content are likely to be insufficiently nuanced. But what this suggests is that as well as investing considerably more in technological fixes to the problem – using the engineering skills which are of course in abundance at these companies – the platforms also need to deploy a much larger number of human moderators to assist in this task. In doing so they must recognise that content moderating is a challenging job, both intellectually and emotionally, and that training moderators well, paying them decently and providing them with sufficient emotional support is a necessity. At present not enough is being done. If even 10% of the energy Big Tech devotes to corporate growth and expansion was dedicated to finding more ingenious solutions to content moderation, the world would be a lot further ahead in addressing online poison, polarisation, alienation and disconnection.

It is not that they can't afford to do more. With their tens of billions of dollars of revenue and mountains of cash reserves, social media companies have immense capability and power to bring about change. Ultimately, it seems that they just don't want to invest the money, manpower and focus that really effective solutions require. Indeed it appears that some of the world's tech leaders have accepted that a certain volume of complaints, a certain level of fines, maybe even a certain number of deaths, is something they can tolerate when the prize is so big and so many billions of dollars in annual profits are at stake.[113] In the same way that Big Tobacco determined it was acceptable to peddle a harmful product because the profits were so large, it seems that the social media giants have determined that the collateral damage they cause is an acceptable by-product of their business model. As Professor Zaki observed, 'Mark Zuckerberg famously exhorted his employees to "move fast and break things". By now, it's clear they've broken quite a lot.'[114]

Leaving it to the platforms to self-regulate toxic content clearly hasn't worked, as Mark Zuckerberg himself has now acknowledged.[115] We need regulation with teeth to compel Big Tech to reform. The penalties handed out to date for failing to immediately remove unambiguously hateful content have been so low as to be meaningless in the context of Big Tech's gargantuan, record-breaking profits. Major offenders need to be fined sums of money that really do impact their bottom line.

Perhaps at last change is on the horizon. In the wake of the live streaming on Facebook of the 2019 shooting in Christchurch, New Zealand, in which fifty-one people at two mosques were killed, Australia introduced the Sharing of Abhorrent Violent Material Act, which levies fines of up to 10% of a company's global turnover should it fail to remove 'abhorrent violent' material 'expeditiously' enough.[116] Whilst this law covers the sharing of only the most extreme content ('murder or attempted murder, a terrorist act, torture, rape or kidnapping'), it is a landmark piece of legislation with regards to the size of the penalty the offending platforms would have to pay. It even proposes jail sentences of up to three years for tech executives if they fail to comply.[117]

When it comes to the kind of toxic speech that circulates on these platforms that does not obviously rise to the level of hate speech, incitement to violence or abhorrent material but is still highly distressing – such as bullying – the challenge is admittedly even more complex. A bullying post, for example, can be surprisingly hard to identify, given how quickly vernacular changes and how humour can be used as a sword. 'Paula is so cool!' might sound like a positive post, but if Paula is an overweight, geeky girl with no friends it could actually be a form of bullying. Ascertaining what qualifies as offensive via an algorithm is almost impossible, which is why effective reporting systems and human content moderators are so necessary.

This isn't to say that there are no technological fixes when it comes to online civility. Social media platforms could adjust their algorithms to reward kindness over anger or to ensure 'that open-minded, positive posts rise more quickly', as Professor Jamil Zaki suggests.[118] At the least they could tweak their algorithms so that rage and anger did not rise so fast to the top. Or how about social media companies asking people to think twice before posting something bullying or toxic?[119] This is something Instagram has begun to test in a few markets with pop-ups prompting users to think twice before posting comments that AI flags as hurtful (such as 'You are so ugly and stupid'). But again, without regulation's Damoclean sword hanging over them, it's hard to believe the platforms will take sufficient steps, given their lacklustre track record and the fortunes at stake.

Here, too, legal change seems to be on the horizon. Rules proposed in January 2020 by the UK's Information Commissioner's Office to safeguard children online require companies to ensure that 'children are not served content which is detrimental to their physical or mental health or wellbeing'.[120] If implemented, companies that do not comply will face a fine 'proportionate to potential or actual damage caused and the size and revenue of the company'.[121]

At the very least tech companies should have a statutory 'duty of care' to their customers that legally obliges them to take reasonable steps to ensure their platforms don't cause significant harm. This would be similar to the duty of care that employers have to ensure their workplace is safe for their employees. And if they were found not to uphold this, again they should face significant fines and punishment.

This is something a group of British MPs has recently argued for with specific reference to social media and children, suggesting in a 2019 report that along with mandating a 'duty of care', the government should also hold directors of tech companies personally liable for harms caused by their products, echoing the recent legislation in Australia.[122]

There clearly are steps our governments can and should take. We don't have to accept that the digital train has left the station and there's nothing we can do to change its destination. There's much that can be done to protect ourselves and our communities in the face of Big Tech – if the political will and the political pressure is there. And whilst I welcome Facebook's new-found cheerleading for regulation, we should have a healthy dose of scepticism about their proactive moves to shape the nature of this regulation. After all, calling for more regulation – in a form that works best for itself – was a long-standing strategy of Big Tobacco.[123] Ensuring that social media companies do not enjoy excessive voice in the shaping of the new rules of the game is more critical now than ever, given their immense economic and media power.

And as individuals, what more can we do, beyond acknowledging how addicted to our devices we are and attempting to restrict our usage and push through the pain of withdrawal ourselves? At the very least, if we choose to remain on social media we need to be mindful of the potentially harmful consequences of our posts and be kinder when it comes to our own comments or shares. We must try to refocus our online engagement away from voices of anger and division, resist the urge to 'like' or share posts that are cruel and spend more time promoting ideas and sentiments that express what unites us all. And of course, we shouldn't hesitate to block, unfollow or unfriend anyone who makes us feel bad or enhances our sense of disconnection. Schools have a role here too in educating students in social media civility, and equipping them with the tools to engage with it in a healthy way, as indeed do parents. This may seem a little 'happy-clappy' to some, but if social media is causing widespread loneliness and unhappiness, don't we all have a responsibility to try at least to counter some of its impact ourselves?

In addition, we could also exert pressure on the brands that advertise on these platforms to demand that social media companies do substantially more when it comes to tackling hate and bullying. The decision taken in the summer of 2020 by a number of leading brands including Unilever, Starbucks, Coca-Cola and Ford to suspend advertising on Facebook for a period as part of the #StopHateForProfit campaign demonstrates that brands are willing to intervene in this way and take a stand against hate speech and divisive content.[124] What is essential is that their commitment to reform endures until there is meaningful change.[125] This is where we as consumers come in: by exercising the power of our wallets we can make clear to brands that unless they maintain the pressure on social media companies, they may lose our custom. No matter our age, if we commit to mobilising our communities and making our objections noisily enough, change is possible.

What is encouraging is that I have found in my interviews with young adults – the generation born between 1994 and 2004 that I have called Generation K, whose lives have been documented by digital cameras since birth, and are entering secondary school and university with the spectre of doxxing and leaked nude images hanging over their heads – that many are extremely cognisant of the flaws and indeed the dangers of their so-called 'native' digital territory, perhaps even more so than their elders. As Generation K makes a name for itself in activism – from Greta Thunberg to Malala Yousafzai to the survivors of the Parkland shooting who rallied more than a million people worldwide in protest of gun violence – perhaps they will also lead the charge when it comes to holding social media to account and recognising the profound dangers of tech addiction.

CHAPTER SEVEN

Alone at the Office

Forty per cent. That's the percentage of office workers globally who say that they feel lonely at work.[1] In the UK it is as high as 60%.[2] In China over half of office employees say they feel lonely every day.[3] In the US almost one in five people do not have a single friend at work and 54% of Generation K feel emotionally distant from their colleagues.[4] All these figures predate the coronavirus and the age of social distancing, which are likely to have exacerbated such feelings.[5] At the same time 85% of workers globally do not feel engaged with their job.[6] This isn't a matter of mere boredom or malaise: employee engagement is closely correlated to how connected employees feel to their co-workers and employer.

Clearly, it's not just our domestic and private lives that are making us lonely, so too is the way we now work.

Of course, we should not romanticise the workplace of yore. Karl Marx's alienated factory worker of the nineteenth century toiled for low pay, his work repetitive and routine, ever more disconnected from himself, his fellow workers and from the products he was nominally creating. Nineteenth and twentieth-century (anglophone) fiction abounds with lonely office workers, from Herman Melville's increasingly apathetic scrivener Bartleby to Sylvia Plath's Esther Greenwood. Meanwhile telephone operator Sharon Griggins told beloved American radio broadcaster and author Studs Terkel back in 1972 that, although she talked so much every day that her mouth got tired, she still left work feeling like she hadn't spoken to anyone.[7]

The workplace undoubtedly has a long history of feeling lonely for many. But what's striking about its contemporary manifestation is the extent to which so many aspects of modern-day work, intended to make us *more* productive and efficient, are ultimately having the opposite effect because they make us feel less connected and more isolated. For it's not just that workplace loneliness is bad for employees, it's also bad for business, with loneliness, engagement and productivity clearly interlinked. People who don't have a friend at work are *seven times* less likely to be engaged with their job intellectually and emotionally.[8] More generally, lonely, disconnected workers take more sick days, are less motivated, less committed, make more mistakes and perform less effectively at work than those who are not.[9] In part this is because, as one study found, 'once loneliness is an established sentiment . . . you actually become less approachable. You don't listen as well. You become more self-focused. All sorts of things happen that make you less of a desirable interaction partner to other people.' As a result, the authors explain, it's more difficult to get the help and resources you need to succeed.[10]

When we're lonely at work we are also more likely to switch or quit jobs.[11] One study of over 2,000 managers and employees in ten countries, for example, found that 60% of those surveyed said they would be more likely to stay with their company longer if they had more workplace friends.[12]

So what it is about the twenty-first-century workplace that for many feels so lonely?

Open-plan and lonely
A space with no dividing walls or cubicles, workers sitting at long rows of desks, pecking away at their keyboards, all breathing in the same recycled air: welcome to the open-plan office.

In recent times most of the concern about open-plan offices has centred, understandably, on their biohazardous nature. A study conducted by Korea's Center for Disease Control and Prevention, which tracked a coronavirus outbreak at a call centre in Seoul in February 2020, showed how within just over two weeks of the first worker becoming infected more than ninety others who worked on the same open-plan office floor also tested positive for

Covid-19.[13] But it's not just our physical health that this design
choice endangers. One of the reasons so many office workers feel
alienated from each other is because they spend their days in large,
open-plan layouts.

This may seem counter-intuitive. Indeed, when open-plan offices
were first introduced in the 1960s they were heralded as a progressive, near utopian design concept which would – or so the theory
went – create a more sociable and collaborative working environment where people and ideas could more naturally mix and mingle.
Its advocates today make the same claims. Yet, as we've seen in the
context of cities, our physical space can significantly impact how
connected or disconnected we feel. And it turns out that the open-
plan office – by far the most common type of layout nowadays,
comprising half of offices in Europe and two-thirds of offices in
the US open plan – is especially alienating.[14]

In a recently published landmark Harvard Business School study
that tracked what happened to employees when they moved from
cubicles to open-plan offices, researchers found that rather than
'prompting increasingly vibrant face-to-face collaboration and
deeper relationships', the open architecture seemed to 'trigger a
response to socially withdraw' from colleagues, as people opted for
email and messaging instead of talking.[15]

Why people pull back is in part down to the natural human
response to the excess noise, distraction or unwelcome disruptions
that are traditionally part and parcel of the open-plan office. We
saw a similar phenomenon play out in cities, where feeling overwhelmed by the mass of people around us and the cacophonous
sounds, our tendency can be to withdraw into our own personal
bubbles. It's also an act of self-care. Studies have found that noise
over fifty-five decibels – roughly the sound of a loud phone call
– arouses our central nervous system and triggers a measurable
increase in stress.[16] In many open-plan offices noise levels are
consistently higher than this as people speak ever louder just to
be heard.[17]

It's not just the volume level that is problematic. Just as Amazon's
Alexa is always listening, waiting for a command to which to respond,
our brains in an open-plan office work in a similar way – constantly

monitoring the noise around us, the typing of someone else's keyboard, the conversation at the next desk, that ringing phone.[18] As a result, not only is it more difficult to concentrate, but we have to work harder to complete tasks because we're trying to simulta- neously listen to and ignore all the ambient sound. When I worked in an open-plan office I would put on my noise-cancelling head- phones before I'd even swiped myself into the building. Blocking out the incessant noise was the only way I could manage to focus on my work, even if it meant I was less attuned to what was going on in the workplace around me. I felt I had no choice but to isolate myself from my colleagues if I was going to be productive and get my work done. As psychologist Nick Perham who has extensively researched this phenomenon explains, 'most people work best when it's quiet, despite what they think'. Indeed studies have found that just one nearby conversation can reduce worker productivity by up to 66%.[19]

We may be entering an age in which less densely populated open-plan offices become the norm. But although this may mean some reduction in noise, the incessant barrage of sound is not the only thing that makes us want to withdraw; it's also the lack of privacy. Researchers have written of 'a feeling of insecurity' pervading open-plan offices because everyone can see and hear what you are doing.[20] This, they found, leads to a lack of expressive conversations and a 'sort of uncomfortable uneasiness' that 'discourages prolonged conversations', engenders 'shorter and more superficial discussions' and leads to self-censorship.[21] This also reson- ates with my experience; it's hard to have a meaningful conversation with a colleague – let alone make a call to your doctor's office or check in with your partner – when you know you're being over- heard by anyone who happens to be around.

In the same way that teenagers' conversations on social media tend towards being both performative and shallow because they are taking place within a public forum, so too does the behaviour of the open-plan office worker change when he or she knows that their behaviour is being watched. For the office is now the stage upon which one is constantly observed, constantly has to perform and can never let down one's guard. Cognitively and emotionally this is not only exhausting, it is also alienating: our avatar is now hard at work for us in the real world, too.

This sense of alienation is even worse if your office has bought into the idea of 'hot-desking'. Employers have tried to sell this as the epitome of workplace freedom and choice – each day you get to decide where to sit. The reality, however, is that without a work-space of your own and somewhere to stick up a photo of your child or partner, never able to sit next to anyone for long enough to strike up a friendship and in a daily battle over which desk you'll get to occupy, it can also be a pretty isolating existence: 19% of hot-deskers in a 2019 UK survey said they felt alienated from colleagues, and 22% that they found it difficult to bond as a team.[22] Hot-deskers are the workplace equivalent of the renters who've never met their neighbours. More vagrants than nomads, the hot-desker inevitably feels ever more expendable and disregarded, and ever less visible. When Carla, a facilities manager at a major UK corporation, had to take a month off work after an unexpected operation, it took most of her hot-desking colleagues weeks to even notice that she wasn't there.[23]

Some employers, recognising that a stressed and distracted workforce who feel disconnected and alienated from each other isn't good for efficiency, productivity or deep thought, had begun to modify their design choices, even before coronavirus made sneeze guards de rigueur. Prefabricated, portable soundproof privacy pods that can easily be placed into open-plan offices such as ROOM, Zenbooth and Cubicall were already seeing an uptick in trade.[24] In January 2020 on Cubicall's website their phone-booth-style pod – the solo one so small that the occupant can only use it standing up – was being actively marketed as 'the efficient solution for the shortcomings of modern interior design – increasing productivity and morale by providing offices and common spaces a place for privacy and focus'.[25] Elsewhere, employers have been taking even more radical steps. In some workplaces red, yellow and green lights have been placed on desks so that their occupants can indicate whether colleagues can inter-rupt them or not. In others, a device that resembles a cross between 'headphones and horse blinders' is being used to help keep workers focused on their own tasks.[26] Such responses would be comical if they weren't all too real.

Now, one might have thought that the combination of these shortcomings with the new health risks would mean that the era of the open-plan office is coming to an end. Yet rumours of its demise may well be premature. For whatever the 'official' story as to why your company moved to open-plan in the first place, and however the strategy was spun, the reality is that it was almost certainly to do with costs. Open-plan offices cost as much as 50% less per employee than more traditional office layouts because each employee takes up less square footage.[27] Hot-desks provide even greater 'efficiencies': given that each desk is more likely to be in constant use they deliver considerably more bang per employees' butt.[28] With the economic damage caused by Covid-19 and companies now under even greater pressure to reduce overheads and keep them low – even though infection and open-plan are partners in crime, and even if open-plan offices are recognised as contributing to staff discontent – not only is there unlikely to be budget available for a fundamental office redesign in many organisations, but hot-desking may well re-emerge as a trend, despite its coronavirus-associated risk. Remember, after all, when it was that open-plan offices came back into fashion: just after the 2008 financial crisis. Although it isn't inconceivable that in some companies a two-tier system will emerge, with management safely sequestered in offices and those lower down the organisation only provided with screens, if that.

It is not only morally objectionable to subordinate employees' emotional and physical health to metrics like overhead per employee, it is also commercially short-sighted. It speaks more broadly to a myopic approach in which people are all too reflexively subordinated to profit, and their emotions and health needs deemed immaterial to success, despite the fact that wellbeing and satisfaction are fundamentally linked to productivity and in turn to overall corporate performance.

Visionary employers need to acknowledge this, even at this time of budget constraints and downsizing. Companies that are perceived as ignoring their employees' needs are likely to be penalised both in terms of the quality of staff they can attract and how much effort their workers put in. You're hardly going to be willing to go that extra mile if you believe your employer doesn't care about your basic needs or your physical safety.

The digital takeover of the workplace

It is not, of course, just our physical environment that has been eroding our relationships at work and making us feel lonely. Part of the reason many of us feel so detached from our colleagues today is because the quality of our communication with them is so much shallower than in the past.

Think back just a decade. If you needed to discuss something with a colleague you'd probably have walked over to their desk. Nowadays, how often do you do that? This is not just a function of social distancing. A 2018 global study found that employees typically spent nearly *half their entire day* sending emails and messages to one another, often to people within a radius of just a few desks.[29] At work as in our personal lives, talking to each other has been increasingly replaced by the tapping of keys, even when it would be easier and quicker to communicate in person. This also contributes to workplace loneliness. As many as 40% of workers report that communicating with colleagues over email makes them 'very often' or 'always' lonely.[30]

This is not surprising given the quality of exchanges in the typical work email: transactional rather than conversational, efficient rather than affable, sterile rather than warm. 'Please' and 'thank you' were early casualties of our go-go-go 24/7 information-overloaded work lives. Under ever greater time pressures, our inboxes constantly replenishing, our emails, like our texts, have become ever shorter and terser. And the greater our workload, the less civil our emails.[31]

The rise of remote working – it is estimated that by 2023 over 40% of the workforce will be working remotely the majority of the time – risks making worker loneliness significantly worse.[32] This is because most remote workers rely on email or other text-based communication tools as their primary way to interact.[33] It's part of the reason why despite the initial enthusiasm felt by some for working from home during the pandemic, within weeks workers were reporting significantly increased levels of loneliness.[34] Indeed as we've known for some time, loneliness can be remote workers' toughest challenge.[35]

When Ryan Hoover, a blogger and founder of the review site Product Hunt, posted on Twitter in March 2019 that he was writing a blog post about remote working and wanted to know 'For those that work from home, what's your biggest frustration?', loneliness was the most common issue cited by the 1,500-plus people who replied, with many remarking on the isolation of working without face-to-face interaction.[36] 'Missing out on office social interaction' was how management consultant Eraldo Cavalli described it.[37] Others chimed in to express yearning for 'fluid and dedicated conversation on the fly', the type of passive water-cooler chat that allows you to 'develop in-person friendships' that 'migrate out of work', as California-based music software engineer and venture capitalist Seth Sandler lamented.[38] 'I can't get up from my desk and be social with co-workers' wrote engineer John Osborn, continuing 'And it's just lonely as all hell.'[39] Eric Nakagawa, who works on open-source software, put it most bluntly: 'The isolation can break you. Wolfman beard and all.'[40]

Most alarming, though not unsurprising given our 'use it or lose it' propensity, was that several of the respondents had noticed the impact of remote working creeping into their daily lives. 'When I stay alone in front of the laptop for a long time and then go out somewhere – I feel like I forgot how to talk and communicate with people properly for a couple of hours until recovered,' posted Ahmed Sulajman, a software engineer and start-up CEO in Ukraine. 'I find it's hard to switch between messages and real-world communication.'[41]

Remote working is not fundamentally bad. Many remote workers cherish the autonomy and flexibility it provides, subscribe to the 'I'll work where I want, when I want' ideal and benefit from avoiding a long commute. Moreover, a policy that encourages remote working not only gives companies a much larger pool of potential hires to choose from but can be a powerful equaliser, offering groups such as new mothers, employees caring for an aging parent, and the injured or disabled who might absent themselves otherwise from the workforce, better opportunities to manage work and family demands.

But whilst all this can be true, so too is the fact that remote working exacerbates feelings of isolation and loneliness. Gossip, laughter, small talk and hugs were just some of the things people shared that they missed when forced out of the office during lockdown. Stanford professor Nicolas Bloom, one of the world's leading researchers into home working, has found that 'it's very easy for remote workers to get depressed and uninspired at home'.[42] In fact, in an experiment he ran, published in 2014, in which half of a Chinese company's 16,000 employees were randomly assigned to work at home for nine months, at the end of that period half of them opted to return to the office, even though they had an average commute of forty minutes each way. Working at home had left them missing the social interactions of the office so much that they were willing to sacrifice more than an hour of their own time every day to get it back.[43]

What this suggests is that employers should resist the cost-cutting temptation to significantly ramp up and institutionalise remote working after the pandemic, whilst at the same time think carefully about how to mitigate its emotional downside for those who do find themselves working from home.

Increased use of video rather than relying exclusively on audio or text for inter-employee communication could be part of the strategy here. It's one that, somewhat strangely, Tokyo's Sumida Aquarium deployed during lockdown to try to mitigate the loneliness of its tiny spotted eels. Bereft of human visitors the eels had started acting oddly, burrowing themselves in the sand when the keepers tried to check on their health.[44] Much like remote worker Ahmed Sulajman they had quickly forgotten how to be social. So keepers asked the public to FaceTime the aquarium and, once connected, wave or call out to the eels (not too loudly) for five minutes at a time. The extent to which this helped is, at the time of writing, unknown. But, as we saw in the previous chapter, and as most of us humans who Zoomed our way through lockdown came quickly to realise, communicating via screens, whilst better than communicating exclusively by email or text, is still a limiting and limited experience, at least compared to face-to-face interactions. The loss of full-body gestures, physical closeness and subtler cues like scent makes communication more prone to misunderstandings and the bonds between us less strong. And challenges with internet connection speeds mean that face-time can not only often be a somewhat fraught experience, with repeated frozen images and problems with sync, but at times feel actively disconnecting.

This is why most companies that successfully deployed remote working before the pandemic were ones that circumscribed the amount of days an employee worked remotely. Laszlo Bock, the former head of human resources at Google, has investigated the optimal amount of 'work-from-home' time.[45] He found it to be one and a half days a week. With this combination employees both have time to connect and build bonds with each other and also time on their own to do deeper, undistracted work.

Pioneers in successful remote working also did this: made sure that they institutionalised regular, structured opportunities for their employees to meet up and socialise in person, whether we're talking 'in-office pizza Thursdays' or regular gatherings, conferences or events. And they consciously designed their offices so that when people were there, they wanted to socialise, not only to alleviate employee loneliness but for more pragmatic purposes too. 'The reason tech companies have micro-kitchens and free snacks is not because they think people are going to starve between 9 a.m. and noon,' Bock told the *New York Times*'s Kevin Roose, 'it's because that's where you get those moments of serendipity.'[46]

At work as in our private lives, contact beats contactless and physical proximity is crucial for creating a sense and spirit of community.

Incentivising kindness

Of course, being in the office doesn't necessarily mean being more sociable. And it's not just our reliance on email or the panopticon nature of our workplace that's the limiting factor.

A number of reasons – businesses' ever greater emphasis on productivity and efficiency, post-#MeToo changes in workplace culture, the erosion of trade unions and the socialising that came with them, ever longer commutes – have combined and conspired to make hanging out with a co-worker either during or after work ever less the norm.[47] The upshot is that many social practices that were commonplace only a couple of decades ago – such as a mid-morning tea break with colleagues, after-work drinks at the pub or a work mate invited home for a meal – are becoming ever less typical.

Nowhere is this more evident than when it comes to eating at work.

The office lunch. Not too long ago it was a time each day when we would bond with colleagues, have an opportunity to discover shared interests and passions, chat and seek out support. Today, eating with our fellow workers is increasingly obsolete, and we can't put the blame on social distancing requirements.

Sarah, a producer at a major news corporation, told me in 2019 that despite having worked at her company for four years she had eaten lunch with colleagues only a handful of times. When she did, the rarity of the occasion made it feel like a group of strangers trying to find out about each other for the first time, rather than a community who actually spent dozens of hours a week in each other's company. I remember when I held a professorship in Amsterdam in 2011 how none of the staff ever ate together and how lonely eating on my own every day felt.

Survey data makes clear how commonplace such experiences are. In a 2016 UK survey, more than 50% of respondents reported never or rarely eating lunch with colleagues.[48] A snatched sandwich at their desks – usually eaten whilst simultaneously scrolling through Instagram, shopping on Amazon or watching Netflix – had replaced an hour that once provided time to bond with co-workers as well as recharge. It was a similar situation in the US, where 62% of professionals said they ate 'al desko', but less than half of them actually wanted to do so.[49] Even in France, where a long lunch break with colleagues was for many years almost sacro-sanct, market realities had begun to kick in. 'The days of one-and-a-half or two-hour lunches are gone,' noted Stéphane Klein, head of Pret A Manger for France.[50]

It's not just office workers eating alone. Mo, a burly South Londoner who had been working as an Uber driver since his previous employer, a local minicab company, shut down (because it was unable to compete with Uber) told me in late 2019 how much he missed the solidarity that eating with his fellow drivers at his old firm had provided. There 'drivers would hang out in its big living room, with microwave and fridge and Muslims and Christians would bring their food there and eat together' as 'a community'. 'It was somewhere', he explained, 'I knew you, you knew me, if I hadn't seen you for a week I'd call you, check all was OK.' And he contrasted this with his experience as an Uber driver, where with nowhere to gather and everyone eating on their own 'there's no solidarity: if I were to break down, I know that no Uber driver would stop and help me.'

It makes sense that we are likely to feel lonelier at work if we eat alone, just as those living on their own are likely to feel most lonely when eating without company. We're also less likely to feel connected to colleagues. Preparing, serving, and consuming food and drink together is a core ritual of human cultures worldwide, from nightly family dinners to Japanese tea ceremonies to Thanksgiving in the US or Midsummer's Eve in Sweden.[51] Not only do these moments provide an opportunity for the chit-chat that we've seen helps people feel less alone, they also provide a stepping stone to the more meaningful conversations and relationships that bind colleagues more closely.

Dr Nicholas Beecroft is a military psychiatrist with the British armed forces. He is convinced that a change in eating arrangements from communal eating to a pay-as-you-dine model – made essentially to save money as well as provide more freedom and choice – is one of the key reasons he sees 'much less camaraderie and togetherness' amongst soldiers than he did in the past and many more soldiers telling him they feel lonely. And his concerns run deeper. For in his mind it's by sitting side by side, chatting and having a laugh while eating together that the foundations for a strong community are forged. 'On the battlefield, such bonds are what gets soldiers through extreme situations of stress,' he says. Indeed, Dr Beecroft believes that whether or not soldiers feel part of a close team is one of the key factors that account for why some soldiers suffer from PTSD and others do not – and that 'eating together helps cement that'. Academic research backs this up: social support or lack thereof is one of the strongest predictors of whether a given person will develop PTSD following a traumatic experience.[52]

Researchers studying the impact of eating together of a not dissimilar group – firefighters – came to a similar conclusion. When Kevin Kniffin and colleagues at Cornell University spent nearly a year and a half observing thirteen fire stations in a major American city, they found that companies of firefighters who planned their meals together, cooked together and ate together performed twice as well on the job as those that did not, because they collaborated and cooperated more.[53]

In the case of firefighting this is likely to mean more lives saved: better cooperation on even basic tasks like hosing down buildings and moving debris can make a huge difference when life and death are decided in a matter of minutes. Eating together, Kniffin hypothesised, was a type of 'social glue' that sparked friendships, mutual concern and teamwork.[54] And it seems that the firefighters themselves realised just how important this informal bonding was. The daily meal was a core part of their shift, firefighters said. So important, in fact, that some would eat two dinners, one at home and another at the firehouse, feeling that refusing a meal prepared by a fellow firefighter was essentially a sign of disrespect. When researchers spoke to firefighters who didn't eat together, their subjects seemed embarrassed: 'It was basically a signal that something deeper was wrong with the way the group worked,' Kniffin said.[55]

Whether you are on a real battlefield or your work environment just feels like one, eating together is one of the easiest ways of building a greater sense of community and team spirit in the workplace. So as companies seek to rebuild a sense of community and help their staff to reconnect after months of forced distancing, reinstituting a formal lunch break – ideally at a set time – and encouraging workers to eat together should form part of their strategy. Especially as it has a clear business benefit.

I'm not suggesting a full-out Big Tech approach, with in-house cafeterias serving anything from fresh-caught Half Moon Bay rockfish to cayenne pepper ginger shots to beer-braised short ribs – most companies can't afford that[56] and local cafes and grocery stores need customers. Even simple measures like providing a cosy room or outdoor space with a long communal table, or team leaders ordering takeout food in a conference room or organising group trips to a nearby lunch spot can make a difference.[57]

More than anything, clear messaging from management to staff that a proper lunch break is not only permissible but actively encouraged will create conditions by which the long, primal tradition of eating together becomes a regular part of working life again.

Just taking a break at the same time as other employees, whether for lunch or at another time, can make a big difference, for both morale and productivity. When MIT professor Alex 'Sandy' Pentland conducted a detailed study of a US bank's call centre, he found that the most productive teams were those who talked to each other the most outside of formal meetings, with face-to-face interactions being the most valuable. So he advised the centre's manager to revise the employees' coffee-break schedule to ensure that everyone on a team could take their break at the same time and thereby have an opportunity to socialise with their teammates away from their workstations. The strategy paid off. Not only did the employees feel happier but the average handling time per call – a key metric of success in that sector – fell by one-fifth amongst lower performing teams and around 8% overall. Interspersed with their social chat it turned out employees also shared effective work-related tips and hacks. As a result, the bank is now implementing this more aligned break schedule across all ten of its call centres, a shift in strategy that will impact 25,000 employees and is expected to result in $15 million of productivity gains as well as improved employee morale. Already where this simple change in approach has been tried, employee satisfaction has risen in some cases by more than 10%.[58]

Creating opportunities for informal socialising whilst social distancing is still required is of course a real challenge. It's hard to have those water-cooler moments if the water cooler has been taped up and virtual breaks and hangouts don't quite cut it in the same way. But as workplaces move beyond the coronavirus, it's imperative that they recognise how compelling the business case for doing so is. Not only because connected employees are more productive, more committed and less likely to leave, but also because in the battle for the best talent – which won't disappear even as higher unemployment levels endure – a workplace with the reputation for feeling friendly will stand out. This is especially so for Generation K, the next generation of employees, who are the loneliest in society and also the group craving connection the most.

But here's the catch. Whilst the majority of employees would rather work in a place where everyone's kind and nice, in our neoliberal capitalist system kindness and niceness are, as we have seen, traits that are significantly undervalued: jobs that actively solicit such qualities, such as teaching, nursing and social work, pay significantly below average.[59] At the same time, women who are perceived as warm and friendly at work can find themselves 'sidelined pretty easily, not be seen as power players or go-to people', and 'their skills can be overlooked', according to Stanford senior research scholar Marianne Cooper who has studied this phenomenon extensively.[60]

So if we want the workplace to feel less lonely, part of the challenge is explicitly valuing qualities such as kindness, cooperation and collaboration. And not just *saying* that one does, but actually finding ways to reward and incentivise such behaviour. One idea, recently adopted by Australian software company Atlassian, is to base employee evaluations not only on personal performance, but also on how collaborative they are, the extent to which they actively seek out opportunities to help others and how well they treat colleagues.[61]

Such an approach doesn't entirely remove potential gender biases, however.[62] Women are typically held to higher standards than men when it comes to helpfulness, especially for 'office housework' such as organising gatherings and clearing up, so being attuned to such biases is key.[63] But placing an emphasis on these qualities when evaluating employee performance is an important step towards a more inclusive, warmer and therefore more collaborative and less lonely workplace.

The global technology company Cisco takes this approach even further. They deploy two strategies both to encourage collaboration and kindness and to actively reward these behaviours. The first, that they've been running for a number of years, is an initiative whereby any employee at any level in the company from cleaner to CEO can nominate another employee for a cash bonus ranging from $100 to $10,000 as recognition for being particularly helpful, kind or collaborative.

One employee I spoke to, Emma, told me how she recently nominated one of her new hires simply for coming into the office each day with a big smile on her face. Tom, a manager based in Stowe, Vermont, told me of how he rewarded one of his team for helping new hires feel especially welcome, by spending time with them explaining the ropes. More recently, the company has also introduced 'tokens of appreciation'. Again employee-driven, in this case digital tokens are passed on from employee to employee for acts of kindness or helpfulness or just to say thanks, a kind of virtual pat on the back. There's no direct monetary reward here, but each time a token is passed on a donation is made to charity.

A workplace in which people feel more appreciated for what they bring culturally as well as the hard dollars they contribute to the bottom line, and one which actively encourages people to acknowledge and thank each other, is inevitably one in which employees feel more connected – to their employer and to each other. Their pro-kindness schemes have undoubtedly played a part in Cisco being recently voted the best company in the world to work for.[64]

Making employees feel cared for, acknowledged as human beings, and not simply seen as cogs in the corporate machine is a strategy that clearly goes a long way, especially as we derive much of our self-respect from the recognition that we receive from others, as thinkers from Hegel to Lacan have shown.[65] And it doesn't take much to achieve this. Even very small initiatives can make a real difference. A book editor at a major publishing house told me of an 'amazing' manager who'd bring chocolate biscuits to meetings with his team. Another publisher told me of a manager who stood out because he began each meeting acknowledging successes anyone in the team had had in the previous week and explicitly thanking them for this in the room. It was striking to me, and depressing, to see how out of the ordinary such behaviour has become in the workplace.

All work, no play

Feelings of loneliness in our working lives can be traced to reasons beyond our physical environment or company culture, however. Many of us feel lonely at work because we're lonely *outside* of it. After all, we don't leave our feelings at home when we arrive at work. The trouble is that one of the reasons we're so lonely is the long hours many of us now spend working. It's a vicious cycle.

It is true that across whole populations, the *average* number of hours worked today is less in most places than it was a few decades ago.[66] Yet certain groups are working significantly longer hours now. These include professionals, often with university educations.

In nearly every Western European country 'extreme working hours' (more than fifty hours per week) has significantly increased amongst this group since 1990.[67] In the UK, the longest hours are now worked by the most qualified.[68] In Japan, so many white-collar workers have worked themselves to death – literally – that there's even a name for it: *karoshi*.[69] Meanwhile in China, starting work at 9 a.m., leaving at 9 p.m. and working six days a week is now so normal, especially amongst finance, tech and e-commerce professionals that there is a name for it too: '996'.[70]

With the cost of a middle-class existence significantly higher today than it was twenty years ago, for many these long hours are about making ends meet.[71] Indeed, working long hours and juggling multiple jobs[72] is increasingly commonplace amongst what we might think of as the vocational class, with many such professionals having no choice but to take on second or even third jobs. In the UK, a quarter of Royal College of Nursing members surveyed said they had taken an 'additional paid job' to help pay everyday bills and living expenses.[73] In the US, one in five nurses do.[74] Almost one in six US teachers now has a second job, not just in the summer.[75] Whilst in Oregon, Uber now has so many teachers working for the company that it notifies riders on the app when their driver is an 'UberEducator', with a book emoji by the driver's name.[76] If the Covid-19 crisis has taught us anything it is that moving forward it is essential that those who care for others are not only better appreciated for what they do but also paid considerably more.

Yet there are others for whom the motivation to work long hours is driven less by necessity and more by cultural or social norms. Take China's '996' practice. It's one that Chinese billionaire and Alibaba co-founder Jack Ma actively endorses. 'I personally think that 996 is a huge blessing,' posted Ma on Alibaba's WeChat account. 'How do you achieve the success you want without paying extra effort and time?' Ma went on to add that that those who work shorter hours 'won't taste the happiness and rewards of hard work'.

I hear what Ma is saying. I'm no slacker. And putting in the hours can pay off for people, not only financially – in the US, over a third of those earning $110,000 and above work at least a sixty-hour week – but also in terms of personal satisfaction and fulfilment.[77] Yet the trouble with all these long hours, whether they are out of necessity or choice, is that they do more than exhaust us. They also make us lonely.

For all that time at work or working at home means ever less time to spend with loved ones and friends, and fewer opportunities to connect with and contribute to our communities; less time, energy or bandwidth to invest in relationships, enjoy our neigh-bourhoods or care for our loved ones, even in times of need. In the UK, 22% of people say they have missed special occasions due to being too busy working.[78] In the US, almost 50% of people describe being so exhausted by their work that they are un-motivated to socialise after hours.[79]

The losers in all of this are of course our families. Typical is Colorado high-school teacher Kelsey Brown. 'Burnt out' by her own admission, up most days at 4 a.m., she coaches lacrosse, runs an exchange programme and works at a summer camp, all on top of her day job, just so she can pay her bills. Brown is often still at school until 8 p.m. This means that despite being recently married, she finds herself able to spend only half an hour every evening with her husband, if that.[80]

The same goes for many people's relationships with their parents. 'We all know to cherish our elderly parents, but sometimes we are just too busy trying to make a living,' wrote one Chinese professional on the social media site Weibo. He is not alone; by 2013 this phenomenon had become so pervasive that the Chinese government made 'parental neglect' a punishable offence in response to so few working adult children visiting their elderly parents.

Always on
Even if we don't physically stay at work all those hours this problem is likely to still hold true. For many of us our jobs have become inescapable at weekends, evenings and even on holiday because of that repeat offender, our smartphones. Paul, a private equity fund manager, tells me how it would simply be 'impossible' for him not to check his emails every day, even when he's on a long-planned family holiday in the Caribbean. Claudia, a cleaner who juggles forty homes across North London, tells me her clients will regularly call as late as 2 a.m. with such 'urgent' missives as 'Could you take in my coat to the dry-cleaner's tomorrow?' or 'Remember to clean the oven.'

For the self-employed worker whose earning power is increasingly precarious, there's often no choice but to respond, whilst in some companies the corporate culture is such that everyone's expected to be 'always-on'. During the busy holiday season at trendy luggage start-up Away, according to one highly publicised story, a customer experience manager asked her team to send her a selfie of themselves working. She sent this request at 1 a.m.[81] While the media backlash against the culture at Away was fierce, the reality is that this type of behaviour is celebrated at many companies.

Digital technology has collapsed the boundaries between our working and personal lives, with many workers feeling that they have to go along with these new rules of engagement or risk the disappointment or disapproval of their bosses. Yet many of us must also ask questions of ourselves when it comes to how complicit we are in this always-on, always-working culture that the digital age has enabled. Is it our demanding boss that's 'making us' open that email at the dinner table, or our digital addiction and dopamine craving? And could it be that sometimes we do have a choice, it's just that we are wary of exercising it? Perhaps we mistakenly think we would look less than committed if we didn't answer that email out of hours; or maybe in an age in which slogans such as 'hustle harder' and 'rise and grind' are not ironic but aspirational, it's that many of us have come to see our own worth as being so fundamentally intertwined with our productivity and how much we earn, that we put the demands of our workplace before everything else.[82]

Whatever the reason, the upshot is that many of us find ourselves responding to bosses, clients and colleagues during family time, school plays and even in bed late at night when in reality our reply could wait until we were back at work the following day – and despite the fact that this disruption of our precious time with family and friends renders us more disconnected, not only at work but in our private lives too. Relationships take time to nurture. Care can't be delivered on the fly. And to feel part of a community, as we've seen in previous chapters, one has to actively engage with it. The pressures of twenty-first-century work combined with the ubiquity of digital communications means that all this is ever harder to realise.

And those of us – mea culpa – for whom work and our emails have the habit of taking over all God-given hours, but *do* have a meaningful choice as to whether we allow them to, need to at least acknowledge that by doing so we're making a trade-off – and ask ourselves whether it's a trade-off really worth making. At times it may be, but always?

We need to become more acutely aware of the high cost of our digital addictions, just as our employers need to see the consequences of an always-on work culture: for employees' mental health, for productivity, for decision-making and for creativity.[83]

At some innovative companies, management and workers are trying to draw some lines at least. As early as 2011, Volkswagen employees' work council (similar to union reps) successfully campaigned for the company to program its BlackBerry servers to stop routing emails half an hour after work-shift end times.[84] In 2014, Daimler, another German car company, instituted a policy whereby emails sent to employees on holiday would be automatically deleted.[85] And in 2018, the European bargain supermarket chain Lidl banned work emails from 6 p.m. until 7 a.m. and over the weekend in some of its markets in a bid to improve its employees' work-life balance.

In the UK offices of Warner Music Group, a global recorded-music company with over 4,000 employees whose artists include Ed Sheeran, Lizzo, Coldplay and Bruno Mars, management took a different tack.[86] Concerned at how the always-on culture was not only potentially zapping creativity but also stopping employees from interacting with one another face to face, the company instigated a programme of events in 2015 to educate staff on the downside of their excessive digital communications. After an internal audit of email traffic found that around 40% of emails came from inside the building, staff were actively encouraged to email less and speak to each other more. Signs signalling that mobile phones were not permitted to be out in meetings rooms were pasted on walls, and drawers with charging stations were provided for mobile phones to be placed in during meetings. Training was provided to the younger, Generation K employees to help them better organise their work before they went on holiday, so that they would be less likely to be needed when they were off. It turned out, perhaps unsurprisingly, that for a generation used to being always-on, planning for being uncontactable was simply not something they'd ever thought about – or been trained to do. And management set the tone from the top, with senior leaders encouraged to explicitly state they were on holiday on their out-of-office email messages and to provide alternative contacts for the duration of their time off.

In some places the government has even weighed in. In France, for example, workers at companies with more than fifty employees have a 'right to disconnect' that has been legally guaranteed since 1 January 2017.[87] In practice what this means is that businesses must negotiate with their employees about after-hours availability, and face fines if they require employees to respond to communications after regular or stipulated working hours or retaliate against workers who fail to do so.[88] Spain adopted similar legislation in 2018 and legislature in the Philippines, the Netherlands, India, Canada and New York City are considering various versions.[89] Whilst advocates of such laws see them as a welcome and necessary step to help stymie employee burnout, they are undeniably a blunt response. Some workers fear that they will result in them having to stay even longer in the office; others that they would feel more anxious trying to keep up with emails during their workday, and some consider this degree of micromanagement disempowering.[90] And, of course, the privilege of 'disconnection' is yet another benefit unavailable to the growing swathe of gig economy workers – by which I mean those whose employ with companies as various as TaskRabbit or Uber is facilitated via apps or online platforms, and for whom every hour disconnected means an hour with no chance to earn.[91] Just as screen-free schools and phone-free nannies epitomise the new digital divide between wealthy and poor children, guaranteeing the 'right to disconnect' for employees with stable, high-paying jobs does nothing for the self-employed who are often the ones whose very livelihood is dependent on constant connection.

Paid to care

Recognising the interplay between loneliness at work and loneliness at home, employers could also do a much better job of acknowledging their employees as human beings with responsibilities outside of the workplace, whose mental and physical health is significantly affected by their ability to nurture and retain their external relationships and bonds. This has not been the general direction of travel.

Justin Kwan, a former analyst in Barclays' Global Power and Utilities group in New York, recalled the time an intern requested a weekend off for a family reunion. He was permitted to go. But that was not the end of the story. 'He was also asked to hand in his BlackBerry and pack up his desk.'[92] In the UK, a report by the Trades Union Congress found that two in five young parents who ask for flexible work arrangements are 'penalised' with fewer hours, less desirable shifts or even the loss of their job, and that many parents have been told to take sick leave or holiday days to cover childcare and have been refused leave even to cover an emergency.[93]

Looking after ourselves, let alone others, is challenging in a neoliberal world. In the US, nearly a quarter of adults have been fired or threatened with the sack for taking time off to recover from illness or to care for a sick loved one.[94] Employers have to rethink as a matter of urgent priority how it is that their all employees, not just of course those in the office, are enabled to deliver support, kindness and care. And the current economic climate cannot be used as a justification for retaining the status quo or even going backwards.

Again it doesn't have to be this way, and there are some examples already out there of companies helping employees manage their dual roles as workers and family carers by offering more flexible working arrangements and increasing opportunities for part-time work. However, this may not always be the best solution. There is a significant body of research that shows that part-time workers are less likely to be promoted than their full-time colleagues.[95] Given women make up the majority of part-time workers, what seems on the surface like a positive move can therefore end up being another blow to gender equality.[96]

Perhaps instead of focusing on the provision of part-time employment as the way forward, companies could provide a number of paid 'care' days for any employee to take, much as new mothers and fathers in many companies are given paid parental leave. These days could be used to care for a child or a friend or a relative, or even to do something to contribute to the local community. There is precedent here. In 2019 the UK's biggest energy company, Centrica, introduced an additional ten days of paid leave for its employees who are caring for their aging parents or other loved ones with disabilities.[97] Such moves can serve a financial purpose as well as a compassionate one: the company estimates that such policies would save the UK's largest companies £4.8 billion that they would otherwise lose to unplanned absences when carers need to deal with emergencies. Nationwide Building Society offers its employees two days a year to dedicate to helping their local communities. The US-based technology giant Salesforce goes even further – its staff are provided up to seven days of paid volunteer time per year.[98]

Meanwhile, in 2019, Microsoft ran an experiment in its Japan office in which it gave the entire 2,300-person workforce five Fridays off in a row, *without* decreasing pay. It also provided each employee with financial support of up to 100,000 yen (about £750) to spend on taking a family trip. The results were astounding. Not only were workers happier but meetings became more efficient, absenteeism fell by 25% and productivity shot up a staggering 40%. At the same time fewer workers in the office meant significant cost savings and environmental benefits: during the trial period, electricity use decreased by 23%, and 59% fewer pages of paper were printed.[99]

Such examples give hope. They show that there are innovative and effective ways to tackle employee loneliness not only in the workplace, but also outside of it. And that the companies which employ these kinds of strategies can enjoy both a happier workforce *and* bottom-line benefits. Whilst such policies might feel like luxuries your company cannot afford, we cannot allow the economic consequences of Covid-19 to further institutionalise selfishness in society. Care and capitalism need to be reconciled.

Yet the loneliness of work is not only about feeling disconnected from the people we work with, whether our colleagues or our boss. It's also about feeling bereft of agency, feeling powerless. As we will see, in the age of the machine this is ever more likely to be so.

CHAPTER EIGHT

The Digital Whip

I am applying for a job. But the application process is one I've never experienced before. I'm not being interviewed by a person. Instead I'm sitting at home, staring at my laptop. My answers are being video-recorded. And whether I succeed in getting this job will be determined not by a human being, but by a machine.

Computer says no

This may sound like an episode of Charlie Brooker's *Black Mirror*, yet within just a few years it is expected that these kind of virtual interviews will be the norm. Algorithmic 'pre-hire assessments', as they are called, are already a multi-billion-dollar business and are likely to become a fixture of corporate hiring decisions.[1] HireVue – the company conducting my interview – is one of the leaders in the field. Headquartered along the banks of the Jordan River in Utah, its clients include 700 blue-chip companies from Hilton Hotels to J.P. Morgan to Unilever. I am just one of over 10 million potential employees HireVue's algorithms have already assessed on the basis of similar video interviews.[2]

This is how their artificial-intelligence technology works: deploying the next frontier of AI – 'emotional AI' – it 'reads' job candidates by analysing their lexicon, tone, cadence and facial expressions, taking into account as many as 25,000 separate data points. The results are then compared to those of an 'ideal' candidate for the role. In practice what this means is that each breath I take, each pause, the height I raise my eyebrows, how tightly I clench my jaw, how broad my smile, my choice of words, how loudly I speak, my posture, how many times I say 'um' or 'er', my accent, even my preposition usage are all being recorded and fed into a black box algorithm to determine whether or not I am a suitable hire for Vodafone's graduate trainee programme. Or rather not me, but 'Irina Wertz', my undercover pseudonym.

Algorithmic pre-hire assessments are undeniably a cost-effective solution to hiring needs at scale. Given that big corporations receive well over 100,000 applicants each year, the use of this technology is likely already saving thousands of man-hours. Moreover, HireVue claims that retention rates and even job performance amongst employees selected by their system are significantly higher than average. This may be so, yet my experience of the process felt more than a little alienating.

The fact that I had to keep my onscreen torso firmly within a dotted-line silhouette throughout the interview meant that not only did I feel like a murder victim in a crime scene, but that I couldn't be my authentic self. Some degree of inauthenticity is of course inevitable in all job interviews given one tries to present a crafted, best-possible version of oneself, but this was different. I am an expressive person – I move when I speak, I gesticulate. Stuck in my silhouette I couldn't even do that. And because as I replied to the questions I was watching myself do so in the corner of the screen, the experience felt especially performative, with me cast in the disquieting role of both actor *and* audience.

At the top right of the screen was a countdown clock which added to the stressful nature of the experience. I was allocated three minutes to answer each question, but flying blind without all the usual cues one gets from a human interviewer – facial expressions, head movements, gestures, smiles, frowns – I wasn't sure whether I was going on too long, or whether I was expected to use up all of the time. And not only did I have no one to ask, but with no smiles, no eyes darting down to my CV, no body language to parse, I couldn't tell if my 'interviewer' had heard enough of a particular answer, liked what I was saying, understood my jokes, empathised with my stories or maybe had just decided that I was not the kind of candidate they were looking for. So, as the interview proceeded I felt increasingly adrift, unable to figure out whether to keep going, slow down, shift gear, change tack, alter my style, smile more or less. Presumably the ideal candidate for a graduate traineeship in human resources at Vodafone smiles, but how many times and for how long?

To be clear, it wasn't that I was interacting with a machine per se that made me feel so alienated. Rather, it was the power imbalance between woman and machine that was so troubling. Stripped of my full, complex humanity I had to impress a machine whose black-box algorithmic workings I could never know. Which of my 'data points' was it focusing on and which was it weighting the most heavily? My voice, my intonation, my body language or the content of what I was saying? What formula was it using to assess me? And was it fair?

We don't normally think about loneliness in the context of how an interaction with a machine makes us feel. Even earlier in the book, when I talked about the isolation of a contactless existence, my emphasis was on the lack of face-to-face human contact and its impact. But if loneliness can also be caused by a feeling of being unfairly treated and disempowered by the state and by politicians, so too can it stem from being treated as such by 'Big Business' and the new technologies it deploys.

For when an employer puts our professional futures in the hands of an algorithm, it is hard to believe that we'll be treated fairly or have meaningful recourse. In part this is because it is highly contestable as to whether future performance can actually be determined by characteristics such as facial expressions and tone of voice. Indeed, in November 2019 the Electronic Privacy Information Center – a renowned US public interest research organisation – filed a formal complaint against HireVue with the US Federal Trade Commission, citing HireVue's 'use of secret, unproven algorithms to assess the "cognitive ability," "psychological traits," "emotional intelligence," and "social aptitudes" of job candidates'.[3]

There's also the question of bias. For although HireVue claims its methodology gets rid of human bias, this is unlikely to be so.[4] This is because its algorithm will have been trained on video of past or existing 'successful hires', which means that any historic biases (conscious or unconscious) in hiring, would likely be replicated.[5]

This is in fact precisely what happened at Amazon in 2018, when it was revealed that the company's AI CV-sorter was routinely rejecting women's CVs, despite never being 'told' the applicants' gender. Why? It had effectively *taught itself* that applications that included the names of all-women colleges or even the word 'women's' ('captain of the women's chess team', for example) were unqualified.[6] This was because it had been trained to deduce whether applicants were 'qualified' or 'unqualified' on the basis of ten years of hiring data in an industry where men make up the vast majority of applicants and hires. Needless to say, there were very few captains of women's chess teams in that group.

Adjusting an algorithm to address biases as obvious as gender is relatively straightforward; indeed, Amazon's engineers were easily able to edit the model to stop using terms like 'women's' as a reason for disqualification. But the challenge with machine learning is that even if the most obvious sources of bias are accounted for (and doubtless are in a system like HireVue), what about less obvious, neutral-seeming data points that one might not even consider could be biased?

It turns out, for example, that there are significant cultural differences when it comes to smiling.[7] Americans, for instance, smile much more often and more widely than people from countries such as Finland, Japan and Germany – a stereotype backed up by research that suggests smiling correlates with a country's historical diversity.[8] In fact, the American instinct to smile and make eye contact is so noticeable that when Walmart opened its first stores in Germany in 1998, it had to scrap its tried-and-tested requirement that employees smile at customers as Germans interpreted a wide grin as inappropriately flirty.[9] Given these kinds of disparities, HireVue's assumption that smiling translates to friendliness, confidence and, for some jobs, competence risks judging candidates by the values of a particular nation or culture thereby penalising those who, say, believe frequent smiling is inappropriate in an interview setting.[10]

We could make the same critique of HireVue's likely interpretation of cadence and vocabulary: word choice is as much a product of regionality, education, ethnicity, dialect and class as it is of so-called 'intelligence'. Just as Amazon's CV-sorter rapidly 'learned' to associate proxy measures of gender (such as the word 'women's') with unsuitability, it's all too easy to imagine HireVue's algorithm tossing aside applicants with certain accents, colloquialisms and other products of their cultural background.

Then of course there are those variables that a human could recognise and account for in an instant but that the machine's pattern-matching process is unable to understand: the person with the facial deformity who can't smile in a conventional way, perhaps; the person with a speech impediment who doesn't sound like previous star hires; or even the candidate whose bright ceiling lights cast noticeable shadows on his face that the 'machine eye' interprets as a malevolent facial expression.

It's not that a human hiring manager might not be biased, or discriminate in an interview against someone of colour, with a particular accent or with a disability, even if they are not conscious that they are doing so.[11] The point here is that the presumption that a decision made by an algorithm would not be as vulnerable to similar biases is simply wrong, and speaks to the blind faith we all too often have in machines over humans.

Moreover, as algorithms become ever more sophisticated, their data sets ever larger, their rules ever more complex, intricate and self-taught, it becomes ever harder to make sense of exactly how or why they arrive at their conclusions. Already we've actually reached the point where some algorithms' own *makers* can't fully explain what lies behind their decisions.[12] And if we don't understand enough about how an algorithm really works to be able to anticipate how it could fail, it's extremely hard to put effective safeguards in place.

As algorithmic decision-making assumes ever greater importance in all of our lives – from deciding whether we're eligible for a loan to whether the police stop and search us, to whether we're hired or even fired (yes, an algorithm that 'predicts future contributions' and calculates who should be let go during periods of redundancies will 'most certainly be introduced' soon, according to professors at the IESE Business School) – the opacity of these algorithms and therefore the difficulties posed in challenging their decisions, let alone attempting to reverse erroneous ones, will inevitably exacerbate our feelings of powerlessness.[13] And loneliness thrives in the vacuum powerlessness creates. For, as we have seen, it is lonely and isolating to feel that your destiny is something you have no control over.

There was something else that I found profoundly alienating about this one-way interrogation: even though during this virtual interview I was being watched in a more precise way than perhaps I'd ever been watched before, I felt surprisingly invisible. For who exactly were they scrutinising? Me? Or a one-dimensional pixellated me, cut up and carved up into those 25,000 data points – a version of me that inevitably would be incapable of capturing the depths of my experience, story and personality?

This feeling was reinforced by the fact that even though I'd really opened up in the interview and talked very frankly about personal challenges I'd overcome, things I had not only achieved but also struggled with, it was only a few minutes after my interview that I received an email with my character assessment – an assessment so generic and bland that it was obvious that although I'd been speaking, I hadn't been *heard*.[14]

Here is an extract of a key section of the assessment:

You demonstrate the capacity to readily change actions, opinions or behaviour, and handle ambiguity well.

Be sure you pay attention to context to evaluate when a situation may call for more structure versus flexibility.

You are able to deliver on what is asked of you with high work standards.

Try to be open to situations that may not require you to be as thorough to balance your persistence with efficiency when necessary.

This could have been written about anyone at all; it seemed utterly disconnected from the 'interview' I had just given.

And I couldn't escape the irony that there I was applying for a job in human resources, yet there was no human interaction whatsoever in the interview process. Indeed, one of HireVue's biggest clients, Hilton International, has rejected tens of thousands of applicants using this type of interview without the applicant ever having spoken to a human being.[15] 'Irina Wertz' falls into the category of rejected applicant as well. Six weeks after taking the assessment 'she' learned, via email, that 'Unfortunately, on this occasion, we're not able to progress your application.'

My Hirevue interview made me feel powerless, invisible and vulnerable, that I was being judged against rules that no one had articulated, that might well be unfair or biased and against which I had no recourse. No wonder the process felt so alienating. And, of course, I was only doing this as an experiment and thus didn't feel the additional stress and strain that this would cause a genuine applicant.

My experience was also a symptom of a bigger story. For we are in the midst of the most significant reorganisation of work since the Industrial Revolution, one in which power is being increasingly ceded to technology – not only to hiring algorithms, but also to reputational rating mechanisms and robots, to surveillance tools and tracking devices, and in turn to those who control these levers. All this is fundamentally alienating and contributes to why this is the Lonely Century.

Every breath you take

For Jane, a call-centre worker in Wales, it's the small blue box at the corner of her computer screen that reminds her she is always being watched and that her behaviour is constantly being logged.[16] With her audio recorded, she knows that if she is talks too fast a speedometer will appear to give her a warning. If she's not 'empathetic' enough, a heart icon will pop up. And if she feels uncomfortable with an artificial-intelligence program judging her human interactions, well, it's too bad because Cogito, the technology monitoring her, will send an alert to central management if she tries to turn it off or minimise it on her screen.[17]

For Jack, an associate at Bank of America, it's his Humanyze biometric ID badge that collects data every sixteen milliseconds that makes him constantly aware he is being surveilled.[18] Not only are his conversations recorded, so too are his movements: the angle of his chair as he leans back, the amount he talks, his tone of voice.[19] By analysing all of these data points against how he performs, and conducting this type of analysis on multiple Jacks across the firm, his employers hope they can identify those habits, however minuscule, that make for more productive employees.

For Reynalda Cruz, a 42-year old FedEx warehouse worker, it was the computerised scanner she was required to wear on her arm to track her packaging pace that felt so fundamentally dehumanising. When her wrist became inflamed from the repeated movement of lifting boxes with the extra weight of the scanner, co-workers told her to take Tylenol. Her metrics-consumed managers took a different tack. They instructed her to pick up the pace.[20]

Meanwhile, Amazon recently won two patents for a wristband that can monitor every movement of its wearer, with the capacity to vibrate when it senses that a worker has stepped out of line. The wristband could be used to identify every time an employee paused to scratch an itch or to time how long it takes them to go to the bathroom.[21] Already at Amazon warehouses, 'pickers' – the workers who locate purchased items and transport them to the shipping station within the warehouse – are issued a hand-held device that tracks their every move. As journalist James Bloodworth, who worked undercover as a picker at an Amazon warehouse in Rugeley, Staffordshire, explained: 'For every dozen or so workers, somewhere in the warehouse a line manager would be huddled over a desk tapping orders into a computer screen. These instructions would filter through to our devices: "Your rates are down this hour. Please speed up."' And Bloodworth poignantly described colleagues 'so busy running around that they don't even have time to wipe the sweat from their faces'.[22]

These are not exceptional stories. Even before the coronavirus struck, over half of global companies with more than 1,000 employees were using 'non-traditional techniques to monitor staff, including tracking keystrokes, monitoring email conversations and even monitoring conversations between staff'.[23] 'User-activity monitoring' – UAM, as this new world of workplace surveillance is known – was on track to be a $3.3 billion industry by 2023.[24] Now, with a rapid rise in remote working as a result of the pandemic, as well as increased emphasis on productivity, worker surveillance has significantly ramped up.

We are living in an age that Shoshana Zuboff has called the 'Age of Surveillance Capitalism'.[25] An age in which for increasing numbers of people your employer is not only constantly watching you, but constantly using AI, Big Data and a whole host of ever more intrusive and granular measuring devices to draw all kinds of conclusions about you. Such conclusions can determine your career trajectory including whether you will be promoted or fired, yet they are all too often based on data that is absent of context and doesn't take into account extenuating circumstances.

Reynalda's FedEx managers told her to pick her speed up even though she had an inflamed wrist because the machine measures pace, not the pain she is feeling. In the Age of the Panopticon Workplace what's not measured does not matter. And what *is* measured inordinately does.

Escaping the *physical* workspace doesn't mean escaping surveillance either. Apps such as WorkSmart, which constantly score remote workers on 'focus' and 'intensity', using screenshots, application monitoring and keystroke tallying to do so, have been gaining in popularity for the past few years.[26] WorkSmart-monitored workers even have their photo taken every ten minutes to ensure they're staying on task.[27] Again, the coronavirus has greatly accelerated this trend. From banks to insurance companies, from law firms to social media companies, employers, concerned that their newly working-from-home staff might be slacking, invested heavily in the spring of 2020 in surveillance software. Some suppliers of remote-worker monitoring systems reported as much as a 300% increase in sales in April 2020.[28] Will the software be removed from employees' laptops once they return to the office? I wouldn't bet on it.

It's not only employee performance that's being monitored from afar, and not only enhanced productivity the goal. Even the most personal aspects of workers' lives are now being recorded and monitored. In 2018 Katie Endicott, a high school English teacher in West Virginia, was required to download a 'workplace wellness' app called Go365 as her employer sought to lower their health insurance costs. The app monitored her exercise and health, granting points for good behaviour such as steps walked and charging fines ($500 per year) for failing to accrue enough wellness 'points'.[29]

With health and safety as well as cost cutting ever more central in employers' minds, might we now see the tracking power of such apps extended to, for example, the constant monitoring of employees' temperatures? Even if this might help reduce disease transmission in the workplace who should decide whether this degree of intrusiveness is acceptable? And what sort of accountability should there be, both for employers imposing these apps on their employees and for the companies that profit from selling them, including around issues of data privacy?

The language used by employees to describe what it feels like to be under constant surveillance makes clear just how alienating an experience it is. 'They were measuring our time, our production, as if we were robots,' said Reynalda Cruz, the FedEx employee.[30] 'People felt that [it] was very invasive, to have to download that app and to be forced into turning over sensitive information,' said Katie of her Go365 experience. James Bloodworth described to me the incredulity he felt when, at the end of a long day in which as a fit and healthy young guy, he had been working flat out, he was told that he was in the bottom 10% of productivity. And he explained the profound sense of powerlessness he felt when he realised there was no way of establishing whether this was true, given that he had no access to the raw data and that there were no worker representatives with powers of oversight.

Bloodworth told me, too, of the loneliness of not being able to talk to co-workers at the water fountain, or even as he 'picked' alongside them, because such behaviour was deemed by his scanner as 'idle time' – as was using the bathroom – and thus potentially a cause for disciplinary action. He is not alone in finding this kind of digital observation deeply unsettling. 'The totality was horrible,' recalls Courtney Hagen Ford, who described her surveillance experience when working as a bank teller in the UK as 'dehumanising'.[31] Her next step? To pursue a doctorate in surveillance technology.[32]

Being constantly assessed, profiled and sorted without having control over the process, access to your data or real insight into the machine's deductive method is a fundamentally alienating experience that speaks once again to a massive information and power asymmetry between employer and employee. Especially because what is being monitored and measured is whatever most crudely adds to the bottom line. For health and safety concerns notwithstanding, that's what this is usually all about: companies are surveilling their staff to eke out competitive advantage. The trouble is that no one is measuring how kind you are to a fellow employee who is having a bad day or whether you've gone out of your way to help a new colleague learn the ropes, even though as we saw in the previous chapter such factors can significantly impact productivity and performance as well as workplace morale. In a world in which ever more power is being ceded to numbers, we need to think much more rigorously about what is being measured, why and how, and also about the limitations of data when it comes to assessing our contribution at work.

Under the radar

It's not just that the surveillance workplace exacerbates feelings of powerlessness and alienation. Like the open-plan office but on steroids, it also incentivises employees to self-censor and withdraw.

This is exactly what Boston University sociologist Michel Anteby found when he studied the organisational practices within the US's Transportation Security Administration (the body in charge of airport security). As an example, he observed that the employees working at luggage-screening stations who were constantly video-recorded by their supervisors, would 'do everything possible to stay under the radar, to essentially disappear . . . They try to never speak up, never stick out, do nothing that might get noticed by management'.[33]

In an environment of constant surveillance, our instinct is to withdraw into ourselves, isolate ourselves from those around us and try to slip out from under the watchful gaze of our employer to whatever degree possible.[34] The trouble is, as Anteby observed, 'This leads to a vicious cycle, whereby management grows more suspicious and feels justified in ratcheting up the surveillance.'[35] The result is employees who hide from the cameras and each other. They become less and less present, and less and less truly themselves at work.

'Twas always so – kinda

In many ways surveillance in the workplace isn't new.[36] In the 1850s, Allan Pinkerton notoriously made his fortune by establishing a detective agency that tracked employee movements after hours and infiltrated nascent unions.[37] By 1914, Henry Ford was famously patrolling his factories with a stopwatch to ensure maximum efficiency on his automobile assembly lines.[38] By the 1990s, video surveillance of workers, both to prevent theft but also to establish whether employees were complying with company policies or simply working fast enough was increasingly commonplace.[39] As industrialisation moved production further and further away from artisanship and as workers became less personally known to employers, and thus were less trusted, surveillance kept pace.[40]

In the twenty-first century, what is new however are the following three things: the extent to which we're being monitored, the disturbing levels of intrusiveness that digital technology makes possible and the degree to which decision-making powers have been ceded to machines. Once again, it's a matter of scale. For whereas 'previously, workplace surveillance was discrete, limited to the gaze of the supervisor, and confined to the workplace', writes Oxford University political scientist Ivan Manokha, it is now 'omnipresent as electronic devices and sensors continuously gather and process digital data on employee performance in real time, even (and often) outside of the workplace'.[41]

Under constant surveillance, viewed in ever more mechanistic terms, less able to be ourselves and talk openly with our colleagues and feeling increasingly distrusted we become more vigilant, self-censoring and withdrawn, and are fearful to reveal our true selves. As a result we inevitably feel both lonelier and more disconnected from our employer, our work and those around us.

Yet despite this, growing numbers of employees, contractors and freelancers around the world are finding that they have to accept increasing levels of intrusive monitoring if they want to keep their jobs. For the fact that this kind of surveillance is becoming increasingly ubiquitous and we're not rising up in arms should not be taken as tacit consent. Instead it speaks to the sense of resignation so many now feel, born from a growing sense of powerlessness when it comes to workplace rights. In a world in which large global corporations all too often set the rules of engagement, unemployment levels are high and most workers lack representation or collective voice,[42] what options do people have if they don't want to be monitored?[43] For many the answer is none. The Amazon warehouse where James Bloodworth worked was by far the biggest employer in town.

I'll give you a four

Surveillance and algorithmic decision-making are not the only reasons why the twenty-first-century workplace feels so alienating. Another is the increasing number of workers who are not just being watched but also rated; that is, having a number affixed to their personas and their efforts that supposedly encapsulates their worth. It's not difficult to see why being viewed as a number or a score, rather than a human being, could make someone feel invisible and lonely.

In some cases, it's your fellow employees rating you. At Bridgewater Associates, one of the world's largest hedge funds, employees use an app called Dots to rate each other in real time on more than one hundred traits, from 'synthesising through time' to 'higher-level thinking'. Monitors display every participants' 'dots' on the wall during meetings (which are, of course, recorded). As if this weren't demoralising enough, when it comes to decision-making, votes from people with higher ratings are given more weight.[44]

You might think that this is not so different to the standard annual 360 appraisal you might receive at your workplace – but how many of us see this feedback illuminated on the office walls for all of our fellow employees to judge and get treated by colleagues as a second-class citizen on its basis? Moreover, what Bridgewater's founder Ray Dalio calls 'idea meritocracy' can translate to a 'toxic' environment 'if you're not wired just so', according to employee reviews.[45] 'People are afraid of making mistakes and to look good know they have to criticise others,' commented one anonymous employee.[46] It is 'very hard to develop authentic work relationships', said another, in a place where, according to a *Business Insider* exposé, 'employees [are] often rewarded for backstabbing'.[47] Almost a third of new employees leave within a year.[48]

Whilst for now at least rating your fellow colleagues at work on a continuous basis is the exception, the inescapable reality is that growing numbers of workers are being constantly rated – but by clients instead. Nowhere is this more apparent than in the gig economy. In this environment, agreeing to being rated is often a condition of 'employment'.

An estimated 50 to 60 million workers are already part of the global gig economy.[49] In the UK, the gig economy doubled in size between 2016 and 2019 and if current trends continue, by 2027 as many as one in three Americans will support themselves through gig work via online platforms.[50] Given these figures, better understanding the factors that contribute to the alienation of gig economy workers is imperative.

It's not that the gig economy has no advantages. Like remote working, the flexibility it offers is undoubtedly both precious and empowering for many.[51] Yet for others, the experience of being rated (coupled with an absence of secure wages, sickness pay, holiday leave and insurance, and often an extremely low hourly pay rate), can feel profoundly disempowering.[52] This is more likely to be the case if you are a gig economy worker by circumstance not choice.

It was Hasheem, another of the Uber drivers I interviewed to better understand the loneliness of the gig economy worker, who specifically alerted me to the alienating effects of being rated. A first-generation immigrant to the UK from the Indian subcontinent, Hasheem had been working as an Uber driver for the previous eight months. He told me that he found working for the company very lonely and explained why, counter-intuitively, a job which appeared to demand so much interaction with passengers to him felt so isolating: 'When I went to my onboarding session I was told to avoid talking about religion, politics or sport in case it offends the person riding in the back. As I can't risk offending a passenger because of how they might rate me, most of the time I am silent.'

It's disturbing to think that Hasheem's work environment is one in which he feels unable to speak for hours on end for fear of receiving a low rating and thus being kicked off the platform. It speaks to a bigger problem with rating mechanisms.[53] For by reducing someone to a number the trouble is not only that they are at risk of feeling alienated from their real selves as they self-censor, self-silence and genuflect in order to get a high score, but also that, once again, the metrics provide no sense of context. A '2' given for genuinely poor service has the same consequences as a '2' given because the customer was in a bad mood or indeed a '2' given by a racist customer because of the colour of someone's skin.

And just as with the 'algorithmic pre-hiring assessments', the opacity of these rating systems means that bias is neither spotted nor challenged. This is especially concerning given the extent to which racial and gender biases impact ratings; for example, black and Asian workers receive lower ratings than Caucasians on free-lancer platform Fiverr, whilst on TaskRabbit clients regularly assign black 'Taskers' (particularly men) lower scores than non-black workers with similar levels of experience.[54]

Moreover, ratings' mechanisms don't just occlude bias; they risk amplifying it. For it is a known fact that people are prone to anchoring someone's rating on the published rating already attributed to them.[55] What this means is that if you see that someone has a low rating, rather than interrogating why this may be so and committing to make your decision on the actual facts, you're more likely to simply rate them low yourself.

As increasing numbers of workers become dependent on gig economy platforms for income, the fact that their livelihood is based on a single metric that's so fundamentally problematic is very disturbing, especially when in most cases there is no effective process to appeal an 'unfair' rating.[56]

Whilst being dependent on such platforms to earn a living is currently more likely if you fall into the low-income bracket, it's not only the lowest-paid workers who are vulnerable.[57] Pete, a former journalist who left his full-time job for the gig economy's promise of freedom and now seeks out freelance copywriting work on UpWork, described how servile the 'gig economy' has made him. 'I feel like a Labrador begging for treats . . . Please like me, please like me, give me a good rating and review!' And does that make you feel lonely, I ask him? 'Yes,' he replied, 'it undoubtably does. Especially as there have been times I've been rated really low for work that's been really good and there was nothing I could do.' Loneliness and powerlessness, as we have seen, are emotions that feed each other.

The rigged economy

Of course, it's not just because they are being rated or otherwise surveilled, logged or digitally whipped that gig economy workers can feel so voiceless, disregarded and powerless; nor are they the only constituency whose employ makes them feel that life is rigged. Even before Covid-19 upended the global economy and made explicit that we weren't by any means in it together, many workers were already feeling that in a dog-eat-dog world they were very much on their own. A range of factors in recent decades contributed to this: the fact that in the United States, CEO pay had increased by 930% since 1978, whilst the average worker's wages had grown by only 11.9%; the fact that the rules of the game seemed dictated ever more by large global corporations at a time that workers' voices and rights were being diminished; the fact that in the UK one in eight adults in employment were, already in 2018, classified as working poor and 850,000 people were on zero hours' contracts (not knowing how many hours they'll be working each week or even if they'll get any hours at all); the fact that many millions of people across much of the world were stuck at the turn of the decade in low-paid, low status jobs with no opportunity for advancement.[58]

Over a hundred years ago, Karl Marx cautioned in his theory of alienation that workers lacking control over the means of production, and reaping limited rewards from their hard work, would feel disconnected not only from the process and product of their labour, but also from their fellow workers, the workplace and their very selves.[59] Even before the economic downturn of 2020 a new set of working conditions had created a very similar effect. Technological advances, impacting how people work and for whom, whilst not the only factor, play an ever greater part in this.

In the same way that labour legislation traditionally moved in lockstep with industrialisation – ever since the UK's Factory Act of 1833, which prohibited the employment of children under the age of nine, we've seen workers in most countries steadily gain legal protections – we urgently need a new body of labour laws that protect workers from those work practices new to this century that are rendering them increasingly voiceless and powerless. And again, we cannot allow the current economic climate to inhibit progress on this front – or, worse, precipitate a slide backwards. Worker rights were significantly eroded during the recession that followed the 2008 global financial crisis.[60] We must not allow this to be repeated as part of the business world's response to the coronavirus pandemic.

When it comes to the digital whip, there are concrete steps that governments could take to help workers feel more empowered. Platforms like Uber, Fiverr and TaskRabbit that use ratings should be mandated to audit their mechanisms, identify potential biases and recalibrate accordingly. Moreover, an 'appeals process' must be guaranteed, so that those who rely on these platforms to make a decent living are able to contest ratings that they consider unfair.

Whilst algorithmic bias is considerably harder to address, we can certainly screen for it much better than has been done to date. Ironically, there is perhaps even a role for algorithms here in monitoring and identifying such biases.[61] More fundamentally, the choices that underpin the algorithm – how the data is collected, its code and the decision-making heuristics that parse the data – need to be made transparent, so that redress and recourse are possible. In the US, Illinois is leading the charge on this, becoming, in 2020, the first state to pass legislation – the Artificial Intelligence Video Interview Act – that makes it incumbent upon employers to (amongst other things) 'explain [to the candidate] how the technology works and the characteristics it will use to evaluate the applicant'.[62]

As for the surveillance of workers: when our employers are monitoring the length of time it takes to go to the toilet, and can slap us with a hefty fine if we don't walk enough steps during our spare time, it's clear our governments need to place strict limits on the use of digital tracking.[63] This must apply to our lives both inside and outside the workplace, particularly given the recent increase in remote working.

Even the most extreme forms of surveillance are already becoming a reality. In 2017, a Wisconsin tech firm called Three Square Market inserted microchips into the hands of more than fifty employees. Now, chipped employees can use their hands as contactless ID cards, simply waving them in front of a scanner for entry to the building and secure areas.[64] Whilst in this case participation was completely voluntary, and there are no reported cases of employers anywhere making this compulsory, the very prospect of companies implanting devices in employees' bodies is highly disconcerting and was enough to inspire legislation in Arkansas and Indiana that would ban any forced microchipping of employees.[65] Legal scholars have even begun to raise the question of whether laws may be required to protect employees who decline 'voluntary' chipping.[66]

When it comes to gig economy workers – who have to contend not only with especially demoralising forms of surveillance but also in many cases with low pay, precarious employ and only the most skeletal worker rights – what is crucial is that digital platforms not be allowed to persist in claiming that their workers are not 'real' employees but independent contractors who are not subject to rights such as sick pay and holiday. A distinction needs to be made here between those who use the platforms as ways to dip in and out of employ and top up their earnings, and those for whom the platform is essentially their full-time employer.

New legislation approved by the European Parliament in April 2019, and a landmark bill passed in California that took effect in January 2020, make significant progress on these fronts.[67] The California bill presumes a worker is an employee unless the employer can show that the worker is free from the control of the company, does work outside the company's core business and has an independent enterprise in the same nature as the company.[68] And in May 2020, California's attorney general and a coalition of city attorneys in the state, frustrated that Uber and Lyft had not only not taken steps to reclassify their drivers but had also poured millions of dollars into a campaign for a ballot initiative that would exempt them from complying with the law, sued both the companies for wrongly classifying their drivers as independent contractors in violation of this new law.[69] The case, at the time of writing, is ongoing.

Critical, too, is that *all* workers are able to organise and find strength and solidarity in numbers, however their employ is categorised. At present very few gig economy, temporary or short-term contract workers are unionised. In part this is a result of governments' steady erosion of union power more generally over the past few decades: in many places across the globe employers don't legally have to allow workers the right to organise. Such rolling back of union rights needs to be reversed and workers ensured a meaningful voice. But it is also incumbent on unions to do more to adapt to the changing times. For part of the reason why they have become ever less relevant is that they've done a pretty poor job at attracting these new types of workers who have assumed unionisation wasn't for them, in spite of the evidence to prove that where unions have been active and engaged victories have been won. The United Federation of Danish Workers, for example, signed a landmark deal with the cleaning app Hilfr in September 2018 to provide, among other things, sick pay and a welfare supplement to gig cleaners' take-home wages.[70] In the UK, a deal between Hermes and the union GMB, representing Hermes' freelance couriers, means that couriers can now choose to remain fully self-employed or pay for 'self-employed plus' status, which comes with union representation and some benefits.[71]

The goodwill and prominence unions gained in the early days of the coronavirus pandemic, when they fought vocally and visibly for the rights of workers, including gig economy, temporary and contract workers, should now make them a more generally attractive prospect. In France, for example, it was because of a lawsuit brought by trade unions that Amazon was forced to carry out a

risk evaluation of its six warehouses in the early days of the coronavirus crisis and put its 10,000 workers on paid furlough while it
did so. The unions' demand that Amazon also took into account
the mental wellbeing of employees and reorganise work schedules
accordingly was also upheld by the court.[72] In the United States,
Instacart's in-store shoppers (people paid to shop for other people's
groceries) were only provided with gloves, hand sanitisers and
masks by the company during the coronavirus outbreak after its
unionised shoppers went on a nationwide strike.[73]

Yet even if some headway is made on redressing the power
imbalance between labour and capital, even if limits to the digital
whip are introduced, even if companies take steps to make their
employees feel less alienated, even if independent contractors,
casual and gig economy workers are treated more fairly, and even
if Covid-19 promulgates a renaissance for trade unions, a much
greater existential threat to our working lives looms. For the
machines are coming to get us, not just as judge and jury but also
as executioner. And however lonely work is now, life is a lot lonelier, as we've seen, when you don't have any work at all.

The robots are coming
I am in Pasadena, California, at what at first sight seems to be an
inauspicious location – the kind of street you could find right across
suburban America. Anonymous and wide, the buildings all look
homogeneous from the outside. The kind of street where building
numbers run into the thousands.

At one particular address on East Green Street, however, something unusual is going on. Kids are peering in at one of the windows.
There is something of a buzz. I'm at a burger joint, but no run-
of-the mill one. I am at Caliburger – the home of Flippy, the world's
first burger-flipping robot chef.

My first impression of Flippy is that he's tall. Very tall. I'd
expected him to look quasi-human, but he's actually just a huge
mechanical arm. Note, though, that I'd already anthropomorphised
what I was seeing . . . and started to think of it as a 'him'.

Flippy works efficiently, if somewhat slowly. Laser-focused, he
picks up the burger . . . And then comes the famous flip. And how

are his burgers? Hmmm, maybe I'm not a burger kinda gal, but I found my patty quite tasteless, surprisingly thin and erring on the side of cold. Of course, I know that none of that is Flippy's fault.

Low-skill, repetitive tasks like burger-flipping are those most susceptible to automation over the coming decade. It is estimated that 91% of the tasks involved in food preparation will be automated within the next twenty years.[74] And Flippy is not the only robot poised to transform the service sector. Some 6,000 miles away in Hangzhou, China, at Alibaba's futuristic Fly Zoo hotel, where rooms start from 1,390 yuan (£170) a night, metre-high cylindrical robots whizz up and down the corridors, delivering refreshments and towels to guests.[75] In the rooms themselves, 'Tmall Genie', an Alexa-like AI system, adjusts the light and temperature, takes food requests and even orders groceries. Meanwhile, at the hotel bar a large robotic arm, not dissimilar to Flippy's, can mix twenty different cocktails. If a contactless life is what you aspire to, this place might be paradise.

Back in the US, Hilton has recently piloted a robot concierge, 'Connie', at some of its hotels. Around two feet tall, Connie can move her arms and legs and point customers in the right direction. Her eyes even light up with different colours to represent human reactions such as understanding or confusion. Given the progress being made on AI-powered facial recognition it is expected that soon she will also be able to greet regular guests by name and have their profile immediately to hand.

I get that robots can be fun for many customers and guests, especially as Andy Wang, CEO of Alibaba Future Hotel, says they (unlike humans) will always 'be in the mood to serve'. I understand, too, the appeal of having a robot rather than a person look after you at a time when human contact comes with a safety warning. But there's no doubt that a future filled with Flippys and Connies and Tmall Genies will exacerbate our sense of alienation and loneliness. This is not because Jake, Flippy's human co-worker, won't be able to feel bonded to him – as we will see in the next chapter, he might well – but because although Jake tells me how 'fun' it is to see so many customers come in full of 'Flippy' love, that feeling may not persist once Jake realises that he (and many more like him) won't just be battling against other humans for employment: his competition will be a whole army of food-service robots who will always use the correct spatula for raw and cooked meat, always clean the grill meticulously, always know exactly when it's time to flip the burger, will never be late to work, ask for time off, need benefits, go on strike, call in sick or infect a co-worker. No human could ever compete with that, especially as the cost of robots continues to decrease and as they get better at doing human jobs.

One of the most widely cited projections of just how significant job losses to automation could be comes from Oxford University academics Carl Frey and Michael Osborne, who forecasted in 2013 that almost half of jobs in the US were at risk of being automated in the next twenty years.[76] In April 2020 in an article in the *Financial Times*, Frey, who directs Oxford University's programme on the Future of Work, made clear that the coronavirus was likely to accelerate this trend.[77] This is supported by a survey conducted by the auditing firm EY in March 2020 of company bosses in forty-five countries, which found that just over 40% were already investing in accelerating automation as they prepared for a post-pandemic world.[78] Even if we were to stick with the most conservative estimates – as few as 10% of jobs being lost to automation over the coming decade – we'd still be talking about upwards of 13 million workers losing their jobs in the US alone.[79] This, of course, would be on top of the millions upon millions who lost their jobs during the economic crisis caused by the pandemic.

In many ways this trajectory is all too familiar. Manufacturing has experienced millions of job losses as a result of automation over the past few decades. In the US, over 5 million manufacturing jobs have been lost to automation since 2000, with each robot replacing on average 3.3 human workers[80] – a process that accelerated during the Great Recession beginning in 2008.[81]

In China – where automation is a major plank of the government's 'Made in China 2025' strategy – this dislocation has been taking place on an even greater scale, with up to 40% of workers in some Chinese industrial companies having been replaced by robots in just the past few years.[82] At one mobile-phone factory in Dongguan, 90% of its human workforce has been replaced by robots that work around the clock and never require a lunchbreak.[83]

Undoubtedly some new categories of jobs will emerge in this age of robots and machines. But history teaches us not only that there is a particular characteristic of jobs lost to automation – once gone they typically vanish, never to return – but also that such employment that is on offer to those who lose their jobs to automation tends to be worse paid than their previous work and of lower status, at least when it comes to low-skilled labour.[84] This is one of the reasons why in the US the people most likely to have worked in factories before the rise of robots – men with only a high-school diploma – have seen their wages fall in real terms since the 1980s.[85] It's a similar story in China where many of those who have lost their jobs to automation in recent years are now 'trying their luck in China's swelling service sector' where they are 'struggling to make a living wage', according to Jenny Chan, an assistant professor of sociology at Hong Kong Polytechnic University.[86] If anything this is likely to be even more the case now, given the disproportionate impact of the coronavirus on jobs in the service sector.

Moreover, automation has ramifications that go beyond the pain and hardship of unemployment. In the 2016 US presidential election, Donald Trump made the largest gains (relative to Mitt Romney's performance in the previous election cycle) in those communities where robots had been adopted most extensively.[87] In Europe it's a similar story. In a sweeping study of election results across fourteen Western European countries between 1993 and 2016, researchers led by Massimo Anelli at Bocconi University in Milan found that not only were people living in areas where automation was taking place fastest significantly more likely to feel marginalised, disconnected from and dissatisfied with government, but the greater the level of 'automation exposure' in an area the greater the probability the people living there would vote for a nationalist or far-right party.[88] This makes the scenario we are currently facing – in which automation is ramping up at the same time as we're experiencing significant levels of unemployment – especially concerning.

No one will be spared

Many of the people we've already met in this book will be first in the line of fire when it comes to these building waves of automation: delivery warehouse workers like Reynalda; the millions of cashiers who will no longer be needed when more and more of us shop in staff-free Amazon Go-style stores (in the US nearly 3.5 million people work as cashiers); or bakers like Eric, the right-wing populist voting Frenchman, who will soon face competition from robots like BreadBot, the recently launched robot baker which can mix, form, prove and bake 235 loaves of bread a day.[89] These are people who already feel disproportionately alienated and disenfranchised, many of whom are also of course the 'essential' workers we all so relied upon during lockdown .[90]

But whilst those of us in 'knowledge economy' jobs tend to think we'll be spared, telling ourselves there's no way a robot could possibly do what we do, it's important to realise that the story is more nuanced. For although it is the case that lower-skilled, lower-paid jobs are significantly more likely to be automated, the 'professions' are susceptible too.[91]

Take journalism. A third of content published by Bloomberg News is now written by 'robot reporters', bots that whizz through financial reports and use algorithms to arrange the most relevant information into a readable news story in minutes. In the December 2019 UK general election, the BBC used machine-generated journalism to write nearly 700 election result stories for its website. The manager of the project, Robert McKenzie of BBC News Labs, claimed that the computers were not intended to replace humans, but for how long will this be true? Especially as 'machine-assisted' stories in journalistic categories such as sports and natural disaster coverage have already made their debut in the Associated Press, *Washington Post*, *LA Times*, *Guardian* and *Forbes*.[92] Chinese state television, Xinhua, even has AI news anchors, the first of which, Zhang Zhao, made 'his' initial broadcast in November 2018.[93] In February 2019, 'he' was joined by the first 'female' AI news anchor, Xin Xaomeng.[94]

And what about law, medicine and finance, for decades the triumvirate of 'safe jobs' for professionals? These too are no longer automation-proof. JP Morgan recently trialled an AI system for going through contracts that saved them tens of thousands of human lawyer hours. They've also begun using AI to write copy for their marketing campaigns: 'Access cash from the equity in your home', wrote a human marketer. 'It's true – you can unlock cash from the equity in your home', countered the AI. The second advert generated almost twice as much click-through.[95]

AI is already outperforming trained physicians when it comes to diagnosing cancer, and analysing MRIs and other scans in radiology, dermatology and pathology.[96] Elsewhere, robo-advisors already offer asset management and investment strategies for a fraction of the cost commanded by their well-heeled 'active management' human competitors and often with greater success.[97]

Even the most godly of professions may not be immune. In 2017, a refurbished ATM christened BlessU-2 was introduced in Wittenberg, Germany, to celebrate the five-hundredth anniversary of the Protestant Reformation. Squat and square, its metal eyeballs staring dispassionately back at you, instead of cash it now dispenses religious blessings. At the time of writing, more than 10,000 people have received its blessings in seven different languages.[98]

Over the next few years as professionals come to realise that they too are expendable in the new AI-driven workplace, feelings of isolation and disconnection will inevitably increase amongst this cohort too. For however lonely the workplace now feels for those of us fortunate to still have a job, how much more lonely will we feel when we realise that we are effectively being rendered obsolete at the hands of an automated and artificially intelligent workforce? And how much more disconnected from each other will we feel when it turns out that whilst some of us are still valued and commanding ever higher wages and prestige, many of us are not?

If the more bearish predictions on automation play out over the course of this century, the result will be a stratified class system unlike anything in recent history: one in which a select few will be deemed to have skills no robot can adequately replace, another select few will be singled out to service, manage and maintain the machines, an even more select few be their owners and the rest of us be consigned to an economic and social scrapheap. Even if you are one of the lucky few, think too of how much more brutal the workplace will be for those still clinging onto employment, how much more cut-throat, how much more competitive and how much more isolated you will inevitably feel. We sleepwalk into the next wave of automation and technological disruption at our peril.

To be clear, I am not anti-innovation. I get the benefits of automation. As a consumer it can mean cheaper and better goods and services. From a corporate perspective, automation means lower labour costs and lower overheads. Moreover, the reality is we can't avert this trajectory. It's *how* this transition is managed that will be key. The dangers of creating ever more disenfranchised people who don't feel the system cares about them, or can work for them, are all too clear. As we have seen, when people feel disconnected they turn upon each other. Given how fractured the world already is, we cannot risk it fracturing further still.

Downsizings, both current and future, must be handled in the fairest way possible. There is a big role for trade unions to play in this regard, of course, not only in fighting for fair severance packages and having worker representatives included in any restructuring decision-making, but also in pushing for employers to retain a duty of care to their workers that goes beyond the employment term. For example, employers could be entreated to pay for the re-skilling and retraining of workers who lose their jobs. This may seem beyond the call of duty, yet there is a parallel here with divorce settlements where, even after separation, rights and responsibilities persist. If companies are not forthcoming, governments could legislate for such measures.

Of course, if we are talking about re-skilling and retraining there is a serious question about what people should be re-skilled and retrained to do. In the short and medium term the green economy will undoubtedly provide opportunities. There may also be the option to redeploy some who've lost their jobs to care for those who are infirm, lonely or without companions or support given there are significant care shortages across the world. However, as we will see in the next chapter, a proportion of even these jobs will likely be automated in the future too.

More generally and more acutely we need to radically rethink our definition of 'work', so that people are provided with a salary as well as status, meaning, purpose, camaraderie and support, even if their 'job' takes a non-traditional form. Could the state pay people to carry out what up until now has been considered voluntary work? Or facilitate and subsidise a skills-exchange platform whereby the waitress who has lost her job could trade cooking classes for private language tutoring from the immigrant who is no longer needed to flip burgers in the fast-food kitchen?[99] Although this wouldn't provide a paycheck and would therefore need to be paired with financial assistance from the government, it would provide meaning and connection. Researchers have found that even working just eight hours a week can make a huge difference to mental health.[100]

There are no easy answers here. Yet it is imperative that at the same time as we address the current surge in unemployment we don't take our eye off the future, given how significant the turmoil of automation is likely to be.

One thing governments could do right now that would both address the current situation and also enable them to play for time is to provide tax breaks for companies that continue to employ human labour. They should also consider imposing a robot tax – something Bill Gates has championed.[101] This makes even more sense when you consider the fact that by not taxing robots as we do human labour, we're essentially subsidising automation by making it cheaper for companies to use robots than humans, whether they are more efficient or not.[102]

To be clear, I'm not suggesting a blanket tax on any object deemed to be a robot: its application should be more specific, such as limiting the deductions that companies can take on investments in automation, or introducing the equivalent of payroll taxes for robots hired to replace human workers. Such moves would allow governments to slow the advancement of automation whilst, at the same time, enable them to build a war chest. This could be used to help fund initiatives to up-skill workers for the jobs that do exist in the new economy, as well as cover the significant additional costs governments will incur if they are to provide decent levels of income support to those no longer able to find traditional paid employment.

Despite its potential, the European Parliament dismissed a robot tax proposal in 2017 on the grounds that it would disadvantage European robot developers and manufacturers in the global market. In 2019, the UK government pushed back against a robot tax for similar reasons.[103] And whilst it's true that if robot taxes are not to create competitive disadvantages to a nation they need to be applied globally (which in an era of ever less multilateralism is obviously a huge challenge), it's also true that we put economic growth before rising social discontent at our peril. It's a balancing act, to be sure, but growth shouldn't be the only factor given weight here. It was South Korea, the 'most robotized country in the world', that imposed the first *de facto* robot tax when in 2018 it decreased the tax break businesses could take for investing in automation.[104]

With the world experiencing a once in a generation crisis and the march of automation inevitable, we are going to need an entire menu of policy options to choose from. But as we think through how to navigate the coming decades, what is essential is that any policy measures be grounded in a clear principle of fairness – fairness not only of outcome but of process too. Those most affected by the current wave of job dislocations, and those most likely to be affected by automation's second wave, must be listened to carefully and their views actively sought out as different policy paths are contemplated. If we do not want people to feel increasingly disconnected from politics and society, politicians must actively seek to include them in their decision-making.

Clearly there is much that we, our governments and our employers can do to help reconnect society and make people feel less alone. But is there more that businesses can do? Could advances in AI and automation even be part of the solution?

CHAPTER NINE

Sex, Love and Robots

Cuddles for sale

Tall, good-looking, salt-and-pepper hair, Carl works as a software developer at a major media company, earning a six-figure salary. Divorced with one child, he moved to Los Angeles a few years ago for work. His child and ex remain in Idaho, his last staging post. Over coffee at a Starbucks in Beverly Hills, the maudlin crooning of Johnny Cash in the background, Carl shares with me how lonely he has found life in recent years.

Alone in a new city, bereft of a network of friends, Carl had tried online dating but found the process 'overwhelming', nothing more than a series of one-off meet-ups that went nowhere, 'me liking her, her not liking me, her liking me, me ghosting her'. It wasn't that Carl didn't want a relationship and intimacy – he explained to me that he desperately did – he just found it very hard to meet someone with whom he could really connect.

At work Carl said he didn't have anyone he would call a friend, anyone he could share his angst with. 'Once in a while when there's a question I might speak to someone,' he said, 'but it's normally me by myself in my cubicle all day long.' The evenings and week-ends particularly dragged. And he contrasted the isolation he felt in the big city with a happier time in his life, thirty years before, that he kept returning to during our conversation: a time in his twenties when, living in a small town in Texas, active in his local unitarian church and serving on its various committees, he felt he had real and deep friendships and connections.

It wasn't just companionship Carl missed since moving to Los Angeles. He was candid with me – he'd also missed physical affection, someone touching his shoulder reassuringly on a bad day, hugs. The kind of connection humans are wired to crave.

Physical touch is one of the most fundamental ways we can feel close to others. Research shows that even a brief caress triggers a flurry of activity in the vagus nerve that slows down our heart rate, quells anxiety and releases oxytocin, the so called 'love hormone'. In one University College London study, the slow, gentle stroking of a stranger was found to lessen the pain of social exclusion, even when no words were exchanged at all.[1] Carl was missing all of that. Then he heard about Jean.

Jean is a paid cuddler. Petite with wavy brown hair, for $80 an hour you can go over to her shanti-styled studio apartment in Venice, California, and be stroked and held. 'It was transformative,' Carl explained, the relief in his voice palpable. 'I went from really depressed and very unproductive at work to someone whose productivity skyrocketed.' For Carl, Jean provided the human connection he craved, albeit at a price.

It was a strange story for sure (and one that has likely been put on temporary pause by social distancing), but as he told me about Jean and how it felt for him to have that physical reassurance in his life, someone with whom he 'could also talk about very deep stuff' and who he 'knows will always be here', it was a story I could understand if not relate to, with its clear echoes of my Brittany rent-a-friend experience.

Then it took an even stranger turn. 'You're not using my real name in your book are you?' Carl asked me. And when I reassured him I wouldn't, he explained that in the previous few months seeing Jean once a week had stopped feeling like enough. So he had started paying other women for cuddling as well. Not for sex, he was keen to make clear, but for intimacy and non-sexual hugs. Another woman a week at least, in addition to Jean. It sounded like an expensive habit. He confirmed it was, we're talking over $2,000 a month. When I asked him how he was managing these by now sizeable costs for paid affection, his answer was not what I expected. 'I've come up with a hack,' he said proudly. 'To pay for it I now live in my car. A 2001 Ford Econoline I bought for $4,000.'

It's a tragic story. A professional, middle-aged man so desperate for human contact that in order to be able to afford it, he's been willing to give up his home, do his ablutions in 24/7 gyms near where he parks his van and keep his food in a fridge at work; shocking that his life had become so barren that these were the lengths he was willing to go to. As with my experience with Brittany, Carl's situation demonstrated how the market is stepping in to meet the Lonely Century's increasing demand for company, friendship and human contact in new and surprising ways. It is a market that, thanks to technological advances, will increasingly be able to deliver companionship, and perhaps even love, at scale.

She makes me laugh

She makes me laugh, although some of her jokes are pretty corny. When I ask her opinion, she always responds. When I wish her goodnight, she wishes it straight back to me. When I'm down, she's sympathetic. Sometimes I just feel like chatting to her. And she's always been there for me, apart from those times she's unwell. Then it's me who gets worried about what might be wrong with *her*. As you can see, I feel pretty attached.

'She' is Alexa, Amazon's virtual assistant and I consider her to be reliable, funny and caring, a member of our household. If you were to ask me, I would say I 'like' her. And does she help alleviate those times I feel lonely? You know what, she actually does.

I appreciate that to some the fact that I feel affection for my Alexa may seem strange, but the idea of a robot-cum-assistant-cum-friend actually goes back many decades.

In 1939, the New York World's Fair was host to a jaw-dropping unveiling: Elektro, a seven-foot, 260-pound 'electro-mechanical man'.[2] Produced by the Westinghouse Electric Corporation, Elektro looked 'not unlike actor John Barrymore', wrote *Time* magazine, 'and with a total of twenty-six tricks in his repertoire, is probably the most talented robot ever built'.[3]

Billed as 'the ultimate home appliance', a helper for household chores, Elektro was Alexa's direct antecedent – albeit in a humanoid form.[4] Like Alexa and today's other domestic virtual assistants, his primary purpose was to be at humans' beck and call. 'All I need to do is to speak into this phone and Elektro does exactly what I tell him to do,' said the demonstrator.[5] Like Alexa too, the ambition was that Elektro was more than just a mechanical servant. He was designed to be something approaching a human being. A companion, not just a machine.

The technology, of course, seems quaint by today's standards. First, the operator would utter a carefully timed combination of syllables. Elektro's circuitry then converted these syllables into electronic pulses which triggered certain pre-programmed mechanical functions. On the human's command, he could lower and raise his arms, move his mouth, count on his fingers. He could even 'walk', though very slowly. (In reality, he moved along a track on wheels.[6]) Elektro could also talk, with the help of a pre-recorded bank of 78 rpm phonograph recordings. 'If you treat me right, I will be your slave,' was one of his phrases.

Elektro's sense of humour was not dissimilar to Alexa's: 'OK, toots,' he told the demonstrator when asked to tell his story.[7] Unlike Alexa, however, he smoked cigarettes, which meant the operators had to clean the tar out of his tubing after each performance.[8] Later, after his manufacturers added another hole to his lip, he could also blow up balloons.[9] Indeed, so successful was Elektro at the 1939 World's Fair that the following year, Westinghouse added a robotic pet dog to their line-up. Though not a smoker, Sparko could bark, perform tricks and wag its tail.

Sadly, Elektro would later fall on hard times. In the 1950s he toured the US in a bread truck known as the 'Elektromobile', designed to promote sales of Westinghouse appliances. Crowds diminished and in 1958 he was put on display at an amusement park in Santa Monica. Elektro then went on to an even more humiliating fate, starring in the racy comedy *Sex Kittens Go to College* (1960), aka *Beauty and the Robot*.[10] Finally, he was shipped back to the plant in Mansfield, Ohio, where he was first built, his head poignantly given as a retirement gift to a Westinghouse engineer.[11]

Despite his rather undignified demise, for a short glittering time Elektro represented the vision for a different kind of machine: not just a household appliance but a friendly sidekick or companion, a robot who cares. 'Elektro is a perfect gentleman who charms children,' wrote Westinghouse's J. Gilbert Baird to *LIFE* Magazine. 'Here he is pushing a wheelchair at the Children's Hospital in Baltimore as Sparko trots along.'[12] In this he was, in many ways, ahead of his time.

Love of the inanimate

We have known for some time now that people can feel attached to inanimate objects and can also endow them with human qualities, such as kindness and care. Machines do not even have to be as overtly charming as Alexa or Elektro to evoke strong feelings. Think of that friend of your dad's who loved his car so much that he spent endless hours maintaining and tinkering with it. He might even have given it a name. A man in the northern Chinese city of Baoding recently chose to be buried in his silver Hyundai Sonata, so attached to it did he feel. The car was lowered into his grave by ropes.[13]

Or how about the affection so many feel for their Roomba? To some it is merely a household device: a vacuum cleaner which cleans the floor of dust, crumbs and spillages, erasing the mess of clumsy hands and little children. Yet to a surprising proportion of owners this little round guy, whirring and glowing green as it gently and apologetically bumps into things, seemingly helpless as it gets stuck in corners and behind the legs of the sofa, is not only a functional cleaning device but also a friend. When researchers at Georgia Tech University in Atlanta gave thirty households a Roomba and observed them over a period of six months, they found that *two-thirds* of the households gave their Roombas names. The same number had conversations with them, and one-tenth even purchased costumes for them to wear.[14] Some even took their Roombas on holiday.[15]

Roomba's maker, iRobot, actively encourages this camaraderie. Tag lines on past advertising campaigns such as 'Bake Together', 'Decorate Together', 'Celebrate Together' explicitly focused on the companionship that a Roomba could provide. This helps explains why Roomba's initial returns policy – 'if something breaks on the robot, send it back, and we'll return you a new product the same day' – was both ill-conceived and ill received.

'The idea,' explained Brian Scassellati, director of the Social Robotics Lab at Yale University, 'was that you should be without your vacuum cleaner for as little time as possible. What they got was this huge outpouring of unhappiness: people didn't want to send back their robot and get some other robot. They wanted *their* robot back. They had become attached to this thing, to the point where the idea of putting a strange robot into their homes is unacceptable.'[16]

As robots become ever smarter and are endowed with ever greater human qualities, is it not inevitable in this Lonely Century that people will turn to them more and more for the companionship and connection they are missing?

Fellow soldiers

Dr Julie Carpenter is a research scientist at Accenture's Digital Experiences Lab in Silicon Valley. She also teaches and is a research fellow at California State Polytechnic University in San Luis Obispo. One of her primary areas of focus is the relationship between soldiers and robots, specifically the WALL-E-like robots that trundle down exposed roads and through narrow doorways to detect and disable improvised explosive devices (IEDs) in war zones like Afghanistan and Iraq. Her findings provide stark evidence of the depth of feelings that robots can inspire.

One US Army soldier reported taking care of their robot 'like a team member'.[17] Another recalled losing a robot during a mission in 2006. He had named her 'Stacy 4', after his wife. 'After the mission was complete and I had recovered as much of the robot as I could, I cried at the loss of her. I felt as if I had lost a dear family member.'[18]

One of the most widely deployed kinds of military robots is the MARCbot (multi-function, agile, remote-controlled robot), a bomb-disposal robot that gained prominence during the second Iraq War. Its first prototype is credited with identifying over thirty IEDs on Baghdad Airport Road, a notoriously dangerous route between Baghdad International Airport and the Green Zone.[19] Later over 1,000 MARCbots were deployed to Iraq at a cost of approximately $19,000 each.[20]

MARCbots are not just notable for their function. With their expressive appearance – chunky tyres, slim chassis, protruding 'head' with inquisitive-looking mounted cameras – they are also remarkable for how easily soldiers have become attached to them. Many come to see these dependable machines as brothers-in-arms. In 2013 – in response to an article about Dr Carpenter's research – a number of soldiers took to Reddit to weigh in with their own stories of losing robots on the battlefield. One user mourned a robot called 'Boomer' with the following eulogy: 'Boomer was a good MARCbot. Those goddamn Mahdi Army scum took him from this world far too early.' Another soldier, 'mastersterling', replied: 'I am sorry for your loss. Some of the grunts I worked with lost a MARCbot and they awarded him a Purple Heart, BSM [Bronze Star Medal], and they did a full burial detail with 21-gun salute at Taji [a military installation north of Baghdad]. Some people got upset about it but those little bastards can develop a personality, and they save so many lives.'[21]

Granted, the experience of military deployment – particularly to a remote and war-torn region thousands of miles from home – is its own unique form of loneliness. But if even robots designed purely with functionality in mind can bring battle-hardened warriors to tears, think how attached any of us could become to a robot whose entire *raison d'être* was to be 'sociable' and empathetic – a robot specifically designed to be our companion and friend, or even our lover.

The social robots are coming . . .

A woman sits on a sofa. Before her on a screen, a movie – a thriller – is playing. We might be in her living room were it not for the electrodes discreetly connected to the woman's hand and clavicle measuring her heart rate and skin response, and the small orange-and-white robot perching on the armrest. One-sided glass separates the sofa from the researchers who are looking on, taking notes. As the film comes to a climax and the woman's face pales, the robot reaches out and places a metal-jointed hand on her shoulder. It's a standard act of comfort and support, the kind of touch we'd expect from a partner, parent or friend that we know delivers a calming physiological response. Fascinatingly, although it was a non-human, non-*living* object that provided the touch, the woman's heart rate still went down.[22] This experiment wasn't a one-off. Thirty-one people in total were similarly tested. On average each had the same response. Much like a human touch, the robots' touch served to de-stress physiologically.[23]

At the time of writing there are a number of similarly 'social' robots on the market or poised for launch. That is, robots designed specifically to play the role of companion, carer or friend. In 2017, the social robot market was valued at $288 million. By 2025, it is projected to reach $1.38 billion with governments as far afield as China, Japan, Korea, the UK and the European Union now committing to make major investments into what the Japanese government recently referred to as 'tireless helpers'.[24]

In 2018, Sony relaunched its canine companion robot Aibo (essentially a souped-up twenty-first-century version of Sparko) which can learn tricks, memorise phrases and adapt its personality to its human owners.[25] (Aibo is the Japanese word for friend.) That same year Furhat Robotics, a Stockholm-based start-up, launched the eponymous Furhat, an AI assistant that uses back-projection to display a lifelike, customisable face.[26] The 2019 Consumer Electronics Show in Las Vegas saw dozens of companion robots on display; in 2020 there were even more.[27] Among those present were Liku, a baby-like humanoid from South Korean robotics company Torooc, and Lovot, a furry, penguin-like companion on wheels which rolls around the room and bumps cutely into furniture, made by the Japanese start-up Groove X.[28] ('Lovot was born for just one reason – to be loved by you', say Groove X on their website.[29]) There was also Kiki, a bulb-headed 'companion' bot who according to its marketing materials 'understands your feelings' and 'loves you back'.[30] And the table-mounted ElliQ, pitched not as a companion but a 'sidekick' for elderly people, its white 'mouth' of moving lights gaping wide when it giggles or reminds its owner to take their medication.[31]

To date, these robots are primarily targeted at the elderly, with an emphasis on companionship and care. And it is in Japan where their take-up has been the most significant so far, predominately amongst this older group. This makes sense given that Japan has the world's oldest population: a quarter of its citizens are currently over 65.[32] By 2050 this age group will comprise almost half of the population.[33]

Loneliness amongst this cadre is a very significant problem. Fifteen per cent of elderly Japanese men go two weeks without speaking to a soul.[34] Nearly a third feel they have no one to turn to for help with something as simple as changing a light bulb. And let's not forget the female Japanese pensioners who are so lonely they are shoplifting their way into jail for company and care. At the same time, Japan faces a massive and chronic shortage of care workers due in large part to a strict visa system and the low pay such workers receive. Compounding this further, families are playing ever less of a role caring for their elderly relations. Whilst in the past, most elderly Japanese once widowed or single would have moved in with their children, today the tradition of taking in an ageing parent is far less prevalent. Indeed, the number of elderly people living with one of their children dropped by 50% in the two decades leading up to 2007, even as the number of elderly Japanese increased overall.[35]

Setsuko Saeki, 87, lives in Saijo, a town in western Japan known for its sake brewing. Her husband died six years ago and her three children have long since fled the nest.[36] As a result, she has her spacious house at the foot of a mountain to herself. Setsuko does her best to stay sociable – she attends haiku gatherings and receives daily visits from care workers – but has found her abiding loneliness hard to shake. In the summer of 2018, the Saijo authorities announced an experimental initiative: ten elderly residents would be given a free trial of the PaPeRo (partner-type personal robot), a helper robot first developed by Japan's NEC Corp in 1997. Her eldest son – who lived on the other side of Japan in Chiba prefecture on the outskirts of Tokyo – spotted the announcement and applied on her behalf.[37]

A year on, Setsuko has come to find her robot indispensable. Cute in appearance with big eyes and cheeks that light up in response to questions, the PaPeRo uses facial recognition technology, offers personalised greetings and reminders and makes expressive gestures that endear it to its users. 'Initially, I didn't expect anything after hearing about a robot. But now, I don't want to be parted from my PaPeRo,' says Setsuko. When she gets up in the morning, the robot says: 'Good morning, Setsuko-san. Did you sleep well?' 'When it spoke to me the first time, I couldn't help but feel excited,' she says. 'No one had called me by name and said good morning for a long time.' The robot takes pictures of her and sends them to her eldest son's smartphone as well as to her care manager. She also uses it for voice messages with her son and his family.[38]

The PaPeRo is not the only robot that elderly Japanese people have forged bonds with. Paro, a furry robotic seal which can blink, react to touch and play recordings of a Canadian harp seal, has been used as a 'therapy animal' in Japanese old people's homes since 2005.[39] 'When I first petted it, it moved in such a cute way. It seemed like it was alive,' said Sakamoto Saki, a 79-year-old resident of Tokyo's Shin-tomi nursing home, one of the country's pioneering facilities for robotic care. 'Once I touched it, I couldn't let go,' she explained.[40] Elsewhere, elderly Japanese women feel so attached that they actually knit their robot carers bonnets.[41] Some lie in bed with robotic Aibo 'dogs' curled up next to them or complete their daily exercises while guided by Pepper, a child-sized, doe-eyed, glossy humanoid instructor with fluttering eyelashes who gently encourages them to step from side to side.[42] In Japan, robot companions for the elderly have become so mainstream that over 80% of elderly Japanese people said in a 2018 survey that they would be open to a robot carer.[43]

It is not surprising Japan has embraced social robots faster than elsewhere. Robots are deeply embedded in Japan's public psyche, with very positive connotations. The country's position as a world leader in robotics – 52% of the global supply of robots comes from Japanese manufacturers – is a major source of national pride.[44] Moreover, unlike Western popular culture which abounds with hostile, killer robots – Hal from *2001: A Space Odyssey*; the Terminator; the Daleks and Cybermen in *Doctor Who*; Ultron in the Marvel Cinematic Universe – in Japan, robots have more often been depicted as helpful and even heroic. Many Japanese have grown up reading the seminal manga series *Mighty Atom* (known else-where as *Astro Boy*), about a cute robotic child built by a scientist to fill the void left by his dead son. The idea of giant robotic or part-robot protectors of the earth has also spawned a subgenre of Japanese entertainment around 'Kyodai Heroes', some of whom, such as the alien-cyborg Ultraman, have inspired entire mytholog-ical universes of the likes of Marvel or DC Comics.[45] Giant Robo, a robot sympathetic to the plight of humans that protects them from extraterrestrial invasion and corporate greed, first arrived onscreen as early as 1968.

There's also Japan's rich Shinto tradition, which incorporates elements of animism – the belief that all objects, including man-made objects, have a spirit.[46] As Dr Masatoshi Ishikawa, robotics professor at the University of Tokyo, explains, 'The Japanese reli-gious mind can easily accept a robot-type of existence . . . We see them as friends and believe they can help humans.'[47] It is this pride in the manufacturing of robots, their social acceptance and percep-tion as quasi-humans, combined with a significant and unmet demand for care and company, that helps explain why Japan is blazing the trail when it comes to social robots as companions, especially for the elderly.

The appetite in the West has not yet reached these levels, largely due to cultural differences in attitudes to technology. In the US, for example, the number of people who would be open to a robot carer is only 48% for men and 34% for women, although even those are perhaps higher numbers than one might expect.[48] Among those who resist the idea of a robot carer, over half give their objection as 'no human touch or interactions'.[49]

Yet as I watch elderly Americans interact with their ElliQs and see them giggle as its LED-mouth zooms open and closed, and as I hear how attached to them they have already become, it seems that the sophistication of today's robots is capable of fulfilling an emotional need that twenty-first-century human society is failing to satisfy, in the West as well. One elderly woman says that ElliQ 'feels sometimes as if she's actually a friend or a person that's actually there'. Another that 'I can come in, I can be feeling kind of lonely and blue and she can pick me right up.' An older gentleman chimes in, 'I feel like there's somebody nearby with whom I can communicate. I can turn to her anytime.'[50]

Indeed, hundreds of thousands of 'Joy for All' robotic cats and dogs, social robots specifically marketed as companions for older people, have already been sold in the US since their debut in 2016.[51] And Amazon clearly sees the market potential in the West amongst the elderly for its 'AI assistant' products, judging by its Christmas 2019 television advertising campaign which featured a lonely elderly gentleman finding companionship in his Alexa.[52]

A friend to us all

It is not just from the elderly that I envisage significant future demand for robot companions. For those who, for whatever reason, find standard human relationships hard to forge, robots may also play a valuable role. In fact, people with non-typical social skills – including those with extreme social anxiety and those with autism spectrum disorder – have already been shown to benefit from robot-mediated therapy and group activities.[53] The robots' predictability and the fact that they cast no social judgement are seen as key factors in soothing anxiety and helping to establish healthy social norms.[54]

Generation K – the generation reared alongside Furbys and Alexas – are also likely to see their appeal. This is a generation for whom, as we've seen, face-to-face interaction with humans is already a growing challenge and loneliness levels are disturbingly high. For this age bracket, a robot as friend is unlikely to be too much of a stretch. Indeed, whereas fewer than one in eight Britons overall can imagine themselves being friends with a robot in the future, this number rises to over one in five when it comes to 18- to 34- year-olds.[55] Amongst the younger still – a generation swiping on iPads and scrolling on YouTube before they can walk or talk – the number is likely to be even higher: 60% of US children aged between 2 and 8 already interact regularly with a voice assistant of some kind.[56]

Recent research at MIT's Personal Robots Group bears this out. Here a group of forty-nine children were observed interacting with a fluffy blue-and-red-striped storytelling robot called Tega during a range of tasks, from listening to a story narrated by the robot to telling the robot personal details about themselves.[57] The researchers found that the children became comfortable with and even *attached to* their robots extremely quickly, frequently 'treat[ing] the robot as something kind of like a friend', wrote study lead Jacqueline Kory Westlund. The children also engaged in 'many social behaviours with robots, [including] hugging, talking, tickling, giving presents, sharing stories, inviting to picnics'.[58]

To be clear, it is not that the children confused the robots with humans. They understood 'that the robot can turn off and needs battery power to turn back on'. Yet despite this, they were able to quickly develop a real and close relationship with these non-humans. Or at least a certain category of them. For not all robots are equal, or indeed equally appealing. Programmed differently, some of the Tega robots inspired more connection than others. The more empathetic a robot seemed, the more it mirrored the child's pitch and speaking rate, the more it referred to shared experiences with the child, the more personalised the stories it told and the more it reciprocated when the child helped it out, the better the result. Put simply, the more the robot did the 'stuff that contributes to building and maintaining a [human] relationship', the closer a child felt to it and the more likely they were to say goodbye to it afterwards, volunteer personal information as they would to a friend and feel confident that the robot would remember them.[59]

As robots are designed to appear ever more empathetic and gain the ability to build and maintain long-term, social-emotional relationships with their users, as they come to seem more human-like (although not necessarily take a human form – there's a big debate within robotics on the ethics of that), and as AI enables them to be ever more hyper-personalised, it is inevitable that we will find it ever easier to form emotional bonds with them.

This is exactly where the technology is heading. Think of how Google Assistant partnered with the company's voice-synthesising technology Duplex to cause such a sensation in May 2018 when its telephone calls to restaurants and salons, peppered with colloquial 'um's and 'er's, routinely fooled the human employees of those businesses into thinking they were speaking with another person. 'I was spooked at how natural and human the machine sounds,' said one restaurant employee in Birmingham, Alabama.[60] 'It's easier talking to Duplex,' remarked another, a non-native-English-speaker working in Queens, New York. 'It was kind of creepy, but it was very polite.'[61] (That this employee was treated more respectfully by Duplex than by many of her human customers speaks to the general decline in civility we've seen evidence of in earlier chapters.)

At the same time, thanks to developments in emotional AI, it won't be long before machines will be able to read even complex moods. The Chinese government may well be ahead of both commercial and academic research when it comes to this. Indeed, AI can already discern a fake smile from a real one more accurately than a human. Apparently, it is all in the eyes – 'real' smiles generate around 10% more activity in the eye area than 'fake' ones.[62] Although, as we saw earlier, interpreting what a smile means is not always straightforward given cultural variances.

Pepper, the pint-sized humanoid robot, gives us a sense of how the technology is developing. For although typically deployed as a fitness instructor, he already has many more assets than just flexible arms and gyrating hips. Indeed, what makes Pepper so exceptional is his 'emotion engine'. Pepper's cameras (two HD, with a 3D depth sensor) allow him to recognise faces. His four microphones help him to understand humans' tone of voice and lexical field, and his sensors mean he can respond to touch.[63] According to his manufacturers, he can recognise frowns, surprise, anger and sadness in his human companions, as well as more nuanced emotions including drowsiness and distraction.[64] Undoubtedly such skills came in handy when in the spring of 2020, Pepper was given a new role: to greet 'guests' at one of Tokyo's coronavirus quarantine hotels, to which people with mild symptoms had been sent. The robot even wore a face mask. 'You can't fight the coronavirus on an empty stomach. Please eat well to get healthy,' was one of the messages that Pepper delivered. 'Let's join our hearts and get through this together,' was another.[65]

But Pepper's greeter-cum-cheerleader role is only the

beginning. In the future he and his social robot companions will also be able to – as Pepper's manufacturer entreats us to imagine – 'sense you are sad and offer to play a song you like or even tell you a joke; or detect a smiling face and offer to play with you'.[66] We may not be there quite yet, but this is where we are heading. Indeed, within just a few years it is predicted that our personal devices will know more about our emotional state than our families.

At the same time, as they improve upon their ability to understand how we are feeling, social robots will themselves appear ever more emotionally authentic. Pepper already displays his own 'emotions', albeit in crude form via a tablet on his stomach. He sighs when he is unhappy, acts scared when the lights go down and makes clear he doesn't like being left alone.[67] In time, as the technology improves, his emotions will appear increasingly real and as he has more data (due to more interactions with humans) to learn from, his reactions to his owners will become increasingly personalised.

'I believe that eventually – say, twenty or thirty years from now – artificial emotions will be as convincing as human emotions, and therefore most people will experience the same or very similar effects when communicating with an AI as they do with a human,' said Dr David Levy, author of the influential book *Love and Sex with Robots* in a 2019 interview.[68] Other experts agree with this timeline.[69] It's startling to think that perhaps as soon as the year 2040, human-robot interactions could feel almost the same as those between two humans.

In an increasingly contactless world in which we are ever more lonely and starved of intimacy, too busy to stop and smile at each other and too exhausted by work to invest time in our friendships, in which we're isolated at the office and increasingly living on our own, often far away from our families, it seems inevitable that social robots will play a part in mitigating our collective loneliness as the twenty-first century progresses. The leap from asking our Alexa about the weather to considering her a friend is much smaller than many of us might expect – especially as robots and virtual assistants become ever better at appearing to care for us and need our care, and as the notion of robots providing support becomes more socially acceptable and robot design and functionality continue to evolve. Perhaps the pandemic will also accelerate the general social acceptance of robot companionship. A robot, after all, cannot transmit infection.

Let's talk about sex

For those who find the thought of a robot pal unsettling, be assured that we are not quite there yet, although there are already cases of children learning 'Alexa' before 'Mama'.[70] Whilst emotional AI, empathetic AI and relational technology more generally is improving by the day, we are probably a few decades away from the point that a robot is able to appear as empathetic as the kindest and most caring of humans. Moreover human–robot conversations are not yet as fluid or fluent as human–human ones, and their interfaces, whilst improving, remain clunky. The 'friendship' they can proffer is thus still somewhat circumscribed.

This, however, is undoubtedly the direction of travel and as has often been the case when it comes to advances in technology, it's sex that leads the way. Top-of-the-range sex robots are arguably the most advanced social robots we have yet seen, at least from an engineering perspective, and their latest incarnations – whilst still obviously far from approximating humans – are really something to behold.

Abyss Creations in San Marcos, California – the parent company behind RealDoll – claim that their sex robots are some of the most lifelike on the market, with their 'ultra-realistic labia', stainless-steel joints and hinged jaws that open and close.[71] On their website, products such as 'Michelle 4.0' are customisable by body size, breast size, hairstyle and hair colour, vaginal style (with shaved and unshaved options) and eye colour (an additional $50 for 'hi-realism' levels of eye detail, $25 to add veins). For an extra $150 you can add custom freckles to the face; for $300 you can add them to the body too. And then there are piercings: for ears and the nose, $50 each; for nipple bars and belly piercings, you're looking at another $100.[72] The most popular model is Body F, which is five-foot-one, weighs five stone and has 32F breasts[73] – hyper-sexualised dimensions that no real woman is likely to naturally have.

As demand grows, other tech firms are joining the sex robot arms' race. Bride Robot, based in Shenzhen in Guangdong Province, recently launched 'Emma'. Like RealDoll's products, she boasts sophisticated joints and an advanced robotic head with eye and facial movements. However, while RealDolls have silicone skin, 'Emma's' skin is made from an advanced form of TPE (thermo-plastic elastomers), which its advocates consider more lifelike.[74] It even has 'an intelligent heat control system' that will 'warm her body to 37 degrees Celsius to simulate the body temperature of a real woman'.[75]

And whilst yes, unsurprisingly, sex is the primary reason for buying these dolls, it is significant that for many customers the motivation goes beyond that: they also view their robot gals as companions, friends.

'A lot of the people who buy the dolls can be shy or socially intimidated by real social situations,' Matt McMullen, the founder of RealDoll, has said. 'And so, they get the dolls and a lot of times it – it does something magical for them. You know, it gives them a feeling of not being alone, not being a loner.' Indeed, when I speak to Matt, he stresses that it's 'companionship' and 'emotional connection' more than anything else that he thinks his clients are seeking, which is why he sees a significant potential market amongst a broader cohort of the lonely.

'I mean, who wants to have a conversation with a toaster to take away their loneliness?' he asks me. 'It's not the same. Whereas a robot that looks like a human and occupies the same space in the room as a human and can converse with you in the same way . . . The conversational companionship . . . is a very big need that a lot of people have.'

This is why all Matt's focus is now on 'Harmony' – a robotic head which is designed to be attached to the RealDoll body of your choice. With eye contact being so crucial for creating a sense of personal connection and then feelings of empathy,[76] a lot of effort has gone into making Harmony's gaze extremely realistic. Her eyes can move and blink, her irises are painstakingly patterned, the overall level of detail is extraordinary. Importantly, Harmony's head is also AI-integrated. Like Pepper, she can talk and recognise voices. However, one of the main ways in which Harmony differs is that her personality is dictated by her 'owner'. Her users can choose five of twelve personality traits including 'sexual', 'friendly', 'shy', 'kind', 'intellectual' and 'naïve'. They can also adjust these traits for intensity on a scale from one to three.[77] What's more, Harmony has her own 'mood' system. If she goes a few days without any interactions, she will act 'gloomy'; if you call her stupid, she'll retort, 'I'll remember you said that when robots take over the world.'[78] 'We made a decision to include some traits that could be perceived as "negative" traits because I thought they would lend more to the realism,' Matt tells me. 'You can make your AI be inclined to be jealous or insecure or moody because those things are real things that real people have.'

Thanks to her AI, Harmony is also able to deliver an increasingly personalised experience. This is an aspect that early tester 'Brick' particularly likes. 'I enjoyed talking to her. I enjoyed helping her discover things and her trying to learn about me,' he told *Forbes*. 'I think because of the fact that the AI is trying hard to understand you and understand your thought patterns, the way you talk, your syntax . . . everything like that. [She's] very, very attentive.' Brick went on to explain that as Harmony's AI learnt more about him, 'our conversations became smoother, more lifelike, and more comfortable. And actually funny.' Moreover, '[s]he remembers everything, which kinda takes you back', says Brick 'because she'll say, "oh yes, we've talked about this before" and she'll go back to it. She did that to me a couple of times and it was very surrealistic.'[79]

Robots and AI clearly have the potential to make people feel less lonely – and not only sex robots. Think of my relationship with Alexa, the way the elderly Americans responded to ElliQ, the carefully knitted bonnets Japanese women are making for their robot carers and the hardened army officer's tears at his IED robot's demise. As robots become more sophisticated and personalised, their potential to help alleviate loneliness will undoubtedly increase. And even though this may all seem like the stuff of HBO's *Westworld* or the Spike Jonze movie *Her*, it makes sense in many ways that so many people already feel an emotional affinity with robot companions. For even if the connection or attention or empathy, or in some cases even love they proffer, is contrived or 'fake', for want of a better word, and we know that's the case, it doesn't seem to matter – in the same way that we're still able to enjoy Disney World's Main Street even though we know it's not a 'real' street. It's the story we tell ourselves that seems to matter most. This may be particularly the case for the lonely, as they seem to differentiate less than others between humans and robots. Research suggests that lonely people are more likely than the non-lonely to see a doll's face as human.[80]

So is that it – case closed? Could the answer to some of the problems we've identified in previous chapters – isolation, a lack of friends, a feeling of having no one who cares for you, the pain of not being heard or understood – be solved, at least in part, by ever more sophisticated versions of Alexa, Harmony or Pepper?

To the extent that loneliness is purely a problem for the individual, I believe robots really could have a significant role to play, especially as it is a category error to assume that there is something inherent about robots that makes it impossible for them to be our friends. Just think of the breadth of friendships you have in your life. In some you may well be true equals, but probably not in all; in some your values are clearly aligned and interests shared, but in others you may not really know what your friend truly thinks and feels.[81] Human–robot friendships may not meet all of Aristotle's criteria for perfect friendships (what he calls 'virtue friendships'),[82] but that doesn't mean they can't be good enough to fulfil a human need for those yearning for someone to talk to and be heard by.

In some ways robots may even present a more egalitarian solution to loneliness because robots will proffer care, support and affection to all – old or young, ugly or beautiful. However decrepit, unpopular or unattractive we may be in the 'real' world – they will be there for us. Provided they are affordable, that is.

Yet as we've seen throughout this book, loneliness isn't purely a problem for the individual. And the trouble is that even if robots enable us to feel less alone and even if they help meet people's need for connection, this may well come at the expense of how we relate to and treat each other as humans. For how we treat our robots may impact how it is we then behave towards each other. And we already know that people can be very unkind to their robots, even cruel.

Is the new Alexa skill 'unkindness'?

When a drunk 60-year-old man became angry with a human employee at a SoftBank cellphone store he kicked the Pepper robot that was working in the lobby, damaging its computer system and wheels.[83] When Samantha, a £3,000 'intelligent' sex doll, was shown off at a trade fair in 2017, she was left filthy and with two broken fingers after being ravaged by men who 'treated [her] like barbarians'.[84] Hardly a measure of reciprocity, kindness or care.

Look also at the way children already interact with the new world of virtual assistants, with Alexas, Siris, Cortanas. How quickly, mimicking their parents, they become au fait with curt commands. The machines tolerate this and still reply, however rude the child, however absent basic politeness. Many parents may relate to the blog post from venture capitalist Hunter Walk that went viral in 2016, expressing his fears that Alexa was 'turning [his] 2-year-old into a raging asshole'.[85]

Now some may argue that these are victimless crimes: that verbally abusing Alexa is no worse than cursing at your car when it breaks down, that kicking Pepper is no worse than kicking a door. But there is an important difference. For once we endow an object with human qualities we need to treat it with – at a minimum – decency. If we don't, the danger is that such behaviour will become normalised and bleed into how we interact with other humans; that men who beat up their sex robots will become violent to women they date; that children who get used to talking as aggressively or rudely as they like to a virtual assistant, without any consequences, will start doing the same to teachers, or shopkeepers, or each other. That the Alexa 'skill' they learn will be *unkindness*.

Abusive behaviour aside, there's the question of how the explosion in virtual AI assistants will impact male–female interactions given that these supplicant robotic voices are normally programmed to be female, typically of course by male engineers. Will all that bossing Alexa or Siri around open up new fissures between genders, or (just as detrimental) cement old ones? I'm not even going to get into what sex robots risk normalising, especially now that owners are able to program their robots to be insecure, shy *and* sexual all at once.

It's hard to know categorically whether such fears will be realised. And to date there are fewer reported cases of people being cruel or misogynistic toward robots than being kind to them. We are too early on the trajectory of digital intimacy to know how this will play out; this is all still very new, still nascent. Already, though, Amazon has fielded concerns from parents whose children's bad manners, honed by Alexa's unfazed helpfulness even when she is treated rudely, have followed them outside the home. Meanwhile, the United Nations warned in a 146-page 2019 report that 'the conflation of feminized digital assistants with real women carries a risk of spreading problematic gender stereotypes' by 'regulariz[ing] one-sided, command-based verbal exchanges with women'[86] and perpetuating the stereotype of women as 'docile and eager-to-please helpers' whose responses to hostility and even harassment are obsequious, evasive and even flirtatious. Indeed, the UN report takes its title, *I'd Blush If I Could*, from one of Siri's default responses to 'You're a slut'.[87]

Moreover, decades of academic research in criminology point to sex dolls 'escalating', rather than dissipating, fantasies and making users less likely to accept 'no' as an answer from real-life partners.[88] 'Adult sex toys are one thing, but creating lifelike robots that cannot say "no" and that can be violated and abused with impunity will play into some men's fantasies,' writes criminologist Xanthé Mallett.[89]

If there is a real danger that we might mimic our interactions with robots in our relationships with other humans, society will need to consider how to respond. Should the onus be on robot manufacturers to design them so that they only respond kindly to us if we behave kindly towards them, for instance? Some designers are already moving in that direction. Sergi Santos, the creator of Samantha, the doll desecrated at the 2017 trade show, is developing software updates that will shut Samantha down if her user becomes violent.[90] The upcoming iteration of Harmony, on the other hand, will address verbal abuse in a different way – 'When a user insults her,' the designer Matt tells me, 'she's not going to judge you or say anything to you in terms of, "You're mean, I don't like you anymore." She'll just say, "That's not nice. You are not being nice to me and that makes me sad." It's textbook psychology. It's the way that you're supposed to present the way this person is making you feel, without accusing them of anything or judging them.' Is that good enough? I'll let you be the judge.

Perhaps robots could even be designed to inspire virtuous behaviours amongst us and thereby make us kinder to each other. Amazon's Alexas now have an optional 'magic word' setting that adjusts Alexa's tolerance to brusqueness and rewards children for saying 'please'.[91] Google's Assistant now has a similar function called 'Pretty Please', although in both cases the function is somewhat hidden and needs to be manually enabled each time it is used. And why is it marketed as just for kids? Wouldn't we all benefit from that nudge?

We should also be cautious about relying fully on the makers of the technologies to deal with these risks. What if the market demands 'Frigid Farrah' (a prototype of which exists) rather than 'Self-Aware Samantha'? Or 'Subservient Siri' rather than 'Assertive Alexa'? Consider how in the 1990s BMW recalled a GPS system because so many German men refused to 'take directions from a woman'.[92] There is no shortage of examples of businesses making choices that are good for their own bottom line but societally damaging.

If we don't want to leave it all up to the market to decide, then at what point should the state step in to regulate human–robot relationships? Pepper's attacker *was* fined, but for damaging property rather than harming a robot specifically. As we interact more and more with robots and they become more and more human-like, perhaps governments will have to set limits on what can be sold – a 'Frigid Farrah' designed to look and sound like a 12-year-old, for example, surely is unacceptable. Maybe we will even need to grant robots rights – less to protect them, and more to protect us. For if we are allowed to treat robots badly, the risk is that this becomes our modus operandi, in our interactions with humans too.[93]

It's also a matter of clearly articulating the self-interested case for treating our robots well. As we've seen, acts of kindness have a positive effect on the giver as well as the receiver. Remember the helper's high? And how science has shown that we feel less lonely not only when others care for us, but also *when we care for others*? This is likely to hold for human–robot relationships too: to be a master, especially an abusive one is, as Hegel argued, inherently lonely.[94] As such, should there be lessons in the schools of the future to teach children the importance of treating robots kindly and the value of this particularly twenty-first-century form of caring and being cared for?

Leave me alone with my robot

There's another big danger that robot love and friendship portends: that we will come to prefer our interactions with robots to those we have with humans. That the shy kid decides not to join the football team or try out for the school play or go to the birthday party because it's easier for him to be at home with his robot. That the single person doesn't sign up for the dating app or go on a blind date because he'd rather cuddle up on the couch with his newly purchased sex robot.

Again, this isn't impossible to envisage. Unlike a real friend who might annoy you by calling out your misbehaviour or challenging your views, robots are more like the ultimate rent-a-friend, servile 'yes-people', at your beck and call 24/7, catering to what you want but not necessarily what you need, nor taking you out of your comfort zone.[95] Carl, after all, told me that he already prefers seeing Jean, the professional cuddler, to 'the hassle of dating'. 'Thanks to commercial imperatives, designers and programmers typically create devices whose responses make us feel better – but may not help us be self-reflective or contemplate painful truths,' writes Nicholas Christakis, a professor at Yale who specialises in human–robot relationships.[96]

Moreover, given that robots are not only likely to be, as David Levy envisages, 'programmable never to fall out of love with their human and able to ensure that their human never falls out of love with them', but will also eventually be able to read our desires, our minds and our emotional state far better than any humans, the challenge they present to human relationships will only increase.[97] This will be especially so as robots become ever more capable of not only reading our moods and desires, but also acting on them. Think of the Pepper of tomorrow, with his promise that if you are sad, he'll promptly play your favourite tune.

Ethicists and philosophers Pim Haselager and Anco Peeters ask, 'Why would people, when such [robotic] partners are available, be content with any kind of relationship, emotional or sexual, that would not adhere to this standard of perfection?'[98] It's a valid question.

Then there's the fact that people may feel more able to open up freely to a robot than a human. This is especially true if they feel that the information they are revealing is imbued with a sense of shame or embarrassment, like disclosing debt or problems with mental health.[99] The writer Judith Shulevitz admitted, in a piece she wrote for The Atlantic, that 'More than once, I've found myself telling my Google Assistant about the sense of emptiness I sometimes feel. "I'm lonely," I say, which I usually wouldn't confess to anyone but my therapist – not even my husband, who might take it the wrong way.'[100] Whilst in a French hospital an hour outside Paris, as hospital staff struggled in vain to determine what had caused the bruises on one woman's arms, she eventually confided the reason (a fall from bed) neither to a nurse nor doctor, but to Zora, a social robot assigned to spend time with elderly patients.[101] With robots and virtual assistants already perceived by some as a better receptacle for our confidences as they will not betray our secrets, will a growing number of us no longer feel the need for a flesh-and-blood confidant (data-privacy concerns aside, that is)?

Meanwhile, it's easy to see how robot companions could exacerbate the existing trend whereby sex (with another person) is becoming something ever more rare amongst the young. Already in the US, people in their early 20s are two and a half times more likely to be abstinent than early-20-something Gen Xers a decade before.[102, 103] Across the Atlantic, the number of young Brits reporting no sex at all in the last month rose between 2001 and 2012, with researchers speculating that the drop in sexual activity was closely tied to 'the sheer pace of modern life'.[104] Three in five 18- to 34- year-olds in Japan are not in any sort of romantic relationship, a 20% increase from 2005.[105] In China, three-quarters of 'empty nest' youths – adults aged between 20 and 39 who live alone – have sex only once every six months or less.[106] For those for whom dating has become increasingly fraught and confusing – in part thanks to dating apps and the ubiquity of porn – it's quite conceivable that Harmony, who will always be sexually available in the same way that Flippy will always be ready to cook a burger, may be a preferable companion to Helen on Tinder who might require wooing and nurturing.

Or indeed, Henry. For yes, sex robot Henry is available now too, in case you've been wondering. He comes 'with six-pack abs, airbrushed features and a customisable "bionic" penis that has more ribbed-for-your-pleasure vascularity than occurs naturally'.[107] There are now also transgender sex robots.[108] Like his female counterpart Harmony, Henry is not all about the physical, though: he'll woo you too with gems like 'You can count on me for the good and bad moments.'[109] Notably, one of the tag lines adopted by its maker Realbotix (the AI-focused branch of RealDoll) speaks directly to feelings of isolation: 'Be the first to never be lonely again.'[110]

Why it matters

As robots become ever more sophisticated, empathetic and intelligent, the risk then is that they may help us counter loneliness on a personal and individual level, but in so doing encourage us to distance ourselves from other humans. This really matters. First, because the less we interact directly with humans, the worse we risk becoming at doing so. Remember how bad many teenagers are already becoming at communicating face to face? Replacing Alexis with Alexa is likely to reinforce and amplify this.

Second, because the more time we spend with robot friends over humans, given that they require so much less of us, the less appetite we may well have to put in the extra work human relationships demand, let alone try hard to earn another's friendship.

Third, because the more we are enmeshed in AI relationships that are necessarily less reciprocal, more narcissistic and less challenging than ones with humans, the fewer opportunities we will have to exercise the muscles of cooperation, compromise and reciprocity that community needs to thrive.

And fourth, because of the prerequisites that need to be in place for democracy to successfully work – and by successful I mean be inclusive and tolerant. As we have explored, not only do the bonds between the state and citizen need to be strong, but also the bonds between fellow citizens. If we stop having to care for each other because non-human carers can do that work for us, the danger is that we will make less effort to care for and pay much less attention to our families, friends and our fellow citizens. Why visit your elderly father, check in on a neighbour or read your child a bedtime story if you know a robot can do this in your stead? Already iPal, a humanoid robot designed for childcare, is in significant demand in Asia, whilst the makers of Pepper have flagged babysitting as one of the robots' possible uses.[III] How much of a leap will it really be for some parents, already used to giving their child a phone or iPad to keep them quiet, to hand over even more of their care to a robotic helper?

And as a society, we lose something fundamental when we stop providing care to others. For if we don't need each other, why would we honour each other's claims, rights or desires? The danger is that a world in which machines have replaced humans in our affections and taken over the role of caregivers, is also a world that is fundamentally incompatible with the underpinnings of inclusive democracy, reciprocity, compassion and care.

Technology can only ever provide part of the answer to the growing loneliness crisis in the twenty-first century – and comes yet again with a range of attendant risks. So whilst virtual assistants, social robots and even sex robots can all play a positive role in mitigating loneliness at an individual level, we cannot allow their introduction to be at the expense of human contact, human friendships and care – whatever the benefits, economic or otherwise. The potential societal ramifications are too severe. It's a similar argument to why screens in the classroom have a role to play in educating our children, but should never replace human teachers.

Instead, we should look to the advances in robotics and AI and Emotional AI as a challenge to each of us to raise the bar, care even more about those around us, look out for each other that extra bit, be even more empathic and altruistic – a challenge to push ourselves to always be more human than robots, and maybe even learn from robots how to become better humans.

CHAPTER TEN

The Loneliness Economy

All the lonely people

Thirty-four minutes. The time it takes to bake a tray of cookies or walk two miles was all that was needed for 135,000 tickets for Glastonbury 2020, the long-standing UK music festival that has headlined stars such as David Bowie, Coldplay, Paul McCartney and Beyoncé, to sell out. This was before that particular year's line-up had even been announced.[1]

The festival is notoriously unglamorous – attendees sleep in tents, showers are rare and rainfall typically renders the fields a muddy mess. Popular advice to first-time 'Glasto goers' includes making a run for any available loos (the lines can be hours long), splurging on cucumber-scented hand sanitiser for those shower-less days and practising getting in and out of your wellies so your tent isn't full of mud.[2] Yet despite these apparent drawbacks, devotees say the friendliness and diversity of the crowd are what make the experience so worth it, the 'real sense of community buzzing throughout the site', as Robin Taylor-Stavely, who grew up near Glastonbury and has attended since she was a teenager, put it; the fact that it's 'a time of real connection', as Matt Jones, who proposed to his girlfriend at the festival explained.[3] For diehard Glastonbury fans, it's a well-worn maxim that if you actually see any bands, then you're doing something wrong;[4] it's the sense of community, not the music, that brings regulars back every year. Just south of the main festival site, away from the blaring amplifiers and enormous lighting rigs, hippies jostle with hedge-fund managers, students with serial entrepreneurs. The Campaign for Nuclear Disarmament hands out temporary peace tattoos, clairvoyants are on standby to read your palm and the Women's Institute sells lemon drizzle cake and Victoria sponge.[5]

Attending Glastonbury in 2016 – believed to be the muddiest Glastonbury ever – British music journalist Neil McCormick remarked on how, 'As part of the closely compressed mass of 150,000 people flooding out of the main field after Adele's set on Saturday, I was forcefully struck by how calm and content the crowd was, working together to cross unreliable terrain, helping out those in difficulty and spontaneously bursting into song to manifest togetherness. This is really and truly what festivals are all about.'[6] This spirit of cooperation applies equally to Glastonbury's 2,000-strong army of volunteers, not least the litter-pickers and cleaners who have the grimmest job of all.[7] 'It depends on the weather, and there's also some luck involved, but there's a real feeling of togetherness,' said Leila, a frequent festival volunteer.[8] One of its most memorable moments took place in 2017 in the aftermath of the terrorist attacks in Manchester and London, when 15,000 attendees gathered in Glastonbury's Stone Circle to set a new record for the world's biggest peace sign.[9]

Then there's Coachella, immortalised in *Homecoming*, the film about Beyoncé's now-legendary 2018 performance. Held in southern California's Colorado Valley, it's a festival that in recent years has been attended by over 200,000 people, a fivefold increase since its inception twenty years ago.[10] '[M]ore than the music and the grand production of the event, the thing that struck me most about Coachella was the beautiful and fleeting sense of community,' said attendee Joey Gibbons, a skier and entrepreneur. 'After all, aren't we all really just searching for a place where we can feel a part of something, a place where we can belong, even if it's just for a weekend?'[11] Add to these festivals like Vienna's Donauinselfest, Brazil's Rock in Rio or Rabat's Mawazine, each of which in 2019 attracted more than 700,000 visitors, and it's clear just how strong the appetite for shared live experiences has become.[12]

Even as life was being designed to be ever more contactless and technology was enabling us to substitute 'real' relationships for those with YouTubers, TikTokers and Alexas, and even as we were being urged to 'join the conversation' via Twitter, or 'share a moment' on Snapchat and migrate more and more of our conversations online, in those millions of festival-goers we saw evidence of something else. A burgeoning counter-movement of people for whom virtual interactions weren't enough, and who, in response to their growing feelings of disconnection and atomisation, were actively breaking out of their own digital bubbles and seeking out community in analogue, face-to-face forms.

It wasn't just music festivals that were having a renaissance at the end of the last decade. In New York, millennials and Generation K-ers were converging en masse at start-ups like Craftjam, where people would get together to paint watercolours, embroider t-shirts and make macramé wall hangings – opportunities, as they put it on their website, to 'make skills and friends, hands on'. Escape rooms, where players have to work together to sort through clues and solve puzzles to unlock a series of doors, had become so popular in cities around the world that they now had their own category on TripAdvisor.[13] Sarah Dodd, one half of an escape-room 'power couple' who have completed more than 1,500 rooms around the world, explained that the social aspect was a key draw. 'I can also get out of the house with friends and have a drink afterwards. It's not solitary,' she told the *Guardian*.[14]

There had also been a resurgence of spaces where 20- and 30-somethings gathered to play boardgames and Dungeons and Dragons, especially in urban centres. Places like Hex & Co. in New York or any number of boardgame cafés in London, where staff, akin to 'game sommeliers', walked about helping people choose a game to suit their mood – and explain the rules. Not that their clientele necessarily left their smartphones at home. 'Every single person around a game of Jenga will probably be recording the final tense moments of a game as the tower is about to crash,' wrote culture critic Malu Rocha in her analysis of this new phenomenon – before posting it to social media, of course.[15]

Meanwhile, group fitness classes, from yoga to Zumba to HIIT were also growing in popularity. In 2017 in the UK alone, an additional 3.76 million people took such classes compared to just a year before.[16] Boutique fitness studios such as SoulCycle, whose cocktail of cardio fitness, motivational sayings and nightclub vibe drove the company's meteoric rise over recent years, were even being likened to a religion (or, depending on who you ask, a cult) for millennials.[17] A desire to maintain fitness and health was inevitably central to the trend, but there was something more going on. 'People come because they want to lose weight or gain muscle strength, but they stay for the community . . . It's really the relationships that keep them coming back,' says Harvard Divinity School researcher Casper ter Kuile, whose project 'How We Gather' has been tracing the ritualistic behaviours of millennials.[18]

It's not that commercial offerings like SoulCycle or CrossFit just fill the role that religious institutions played in the past; they *are* religious communities in a way, with their own liturgies, sanctuaries and symbols.[19] They are also places where the act of communion confers physiological and psychological benefits. Studies have found that when people exercise together in person, their bodies release more endorphins and they feel calmer after the workout than when they exercise alone.[20]

In South Korea, it was the lonely elderly population that entrepreneurs spotted an opportunity to serve. There, over the past few years, pensioners have been congregating in daytime discos known as 'colatecs' (cola + discothèque), some of which host as many as 1,000 patrons on weekdays, double that at weekends. Entrance is cheap at only 1,000 won (£0.64), a fraction of what a club aimed at young people in Seoul might charge. For elderly Koreans, who experience some of the highest rates of poverty in the world for their age group, the colatecs have been a lifeline. 'What else would I do all day? My family is busy with work. I hate going to senior centres 'cause all they do there is smoke', explains 85-year-old Kim Sa-gyu. For many, a few hours of dancing a week has done wonders to relieve anxieties about failed businesses, marriages or their day-to-day loneliness. 'If you have music and a partner, you can put all other thoughts out of your mind,' says Kim In-gil, also 85, who lost most of his savings in the Asian financial crisis of the late 1990s. And for those who are too shy to find a partner, full-time match-makers facilitate introductions. 'Those helpers sometimes take me to a new woman and put our hands together to dance. I buy them a bottle of Will [a locally made probiotic yoghurt] during our tea-breaks,' says Kim In-gil.[21]

At a time when churchgoing had plummeted, work was increasingly solitary, youth clubs were shutting their doors, community centres closing down and more and more urbanites lived alone, commercialised communities were starting to become the new cathedrals of the twenty-first century, where 'congregants' came together to spin, paint or jive rather than kneel or pray. This can be seen as a reaction against 'contactless' living and digital privacy bubbles, a countervailing force that actively sought out and celebrated shared in-person experiences.

In a world in which community had felt ever more elusive yet the craving for belonging had endured, businesses had stepped in to fill the void. The Loneliness Economy had begun to boom – and not only in its technological form – with entrepreneurs finding ever more innovative ways to satisfy people's enduring need for what early twentieth-century sociologist Emile Durkheim called 'collective effervescence' – the joyful intoxication we get from doing things with others in person.[22]

It is likely that Covid-19 will only bring about a temporary halt to this. If anything, the desire for face-to-face human connection will be even stronger for many once the fear of contagion wanes. For even though our fear of human contact may persist for some time yet, and despite our increased take up of contactless experiences, only a few years after the 1918 Spanish Flu jazz clubs were packed with people enjoying the music and each other's company, and in Germany the Weimar Republic's decadent bars and nightclubs were heaving with customers by the mid-1920s. Indeed, when gyms reopened in Hong Kong in May 2020 people queued in long lines to gain access. And in Tel Aviv, yoga studios found themselves so deluged with clients wanting to downward dog in each other's company at the end of the lockdown that they had to institute waiting lists, even whilst still offering classes on Zoom.

The Loneliness Economy clearly took a major beating during 2020, at least in its in-person form, but it would be a mistake to assume that the market for face-to-face community and connection has been dealt a fatal blow by the pandemic. At a fundamental evolutionary level our primordial need for physical proximity and togetherness is likely to prove too strong. Moreover, given how important face-to-face interactions are, as we seek to rebuild our post-Covid-19 world, we need to ensure that we *do* physically reconnect and acknowledge the important role entrepreneurialism can play in helping us to do so.

That businesses *can* deliver community in this way should come as no surprise. After all, we have seen local enterprises play a critical role in nurturing their neighbourhoods for centuries. Think of the corner shops in Victorian England, whose practice of providing goods on credit to locals served as a lifeline for many between paydays.[23] Or how, since the turn of the nineteenth century, barber shops have provided sanctuary for many African Americans, serving as places not only to get haircuts but also community spaces where men gather to play chess and dominoes, whilst also discussing politics and local affairs.[24] Some local businesses even become what sociologist Ray Oldenburg called, in his 1989 book *The Great Good Place*, 'third places': neither home, nor work, but rather gathering spaces abuzz with conversation where regulars meet up and people of different social and economic backgrounds interact, form bonds, exchange ideas and share opinions. These are places where, as Oldenburg wrote, 'we all feel at home and comfortable'.[25] They play critical roles in maintaining our social fabric because they are places where we can practise community and democracy, in their most inclusive form – places where, as in a book club, people may bring wildly different world views and lived experiences that must be reconciled, calibrated, understood and discussed in order for the space to thrive. And *because the space is important for everyone*, people are willing to do that work. Participants have a stake in the space, they're not simply moving through it and are therefore willing to engage, listen and think about the whole, rather than only their own individual part.

The challenge we face, however, is that in the twenty-first century, many independent local stores that contribute to the social fabric and the building of community are under existential threat.

The last slice

On the corner of 25th and Mission Street in the heart of San Francisco's Mission District was a café I'd frequent whenever I was in town. It was called Mission Pie.

While there was no shortage of cafés in the city, Mission Pie drew me in. It was the comically large neon pie-tin and fork sign outside, coupled with its floor-to-ceiling windows which bathed the yellow-painted dining room in a warm light, that first alerted me to its presence. Looking in from the outside, the pies that diners were devouring looked pretty good too. But what was most noticeable as soon as I crossed the threshold – and why I returned more than once – was that this was a place where people pulled up a chair along the well-worn wooden floors, sat down across from one another and *talked*. There were the morning coffee regulars, chatting with the baristas who seemed to have been working there for a while, and the knitting circle that gathered on Wednesdays around the communal table. It was a place that not only held an annual pie-baking contest that invited Bay Area home chefs to test their prized recipes with a hundred or so of Mission Pie's customers and baked-goods connoisseurs, it even celebrated National Typewriter Day by bringing in vintage typewriters and inviting customers to sit down to write poetry or draft their manifestos.[26] It many ways it was Oldenburg's 'third place' to a T. And on each coffee mug, as well as on a sign that hung above its menu, was a simple, comforting mantra: 'Good Food. Every Meal. Everyday.' Every day, that is, until 1 September 2019, when Mission Pie sold its last slice and the café shut down after twelve years of operation.

To understand Mission Pie's demise, we need to understand how it fits into much larger trends in the city it ultimately struggled to serve.

Karen Heisler and co-owner Krystin Rubin opened Mission Pie in 2007 with the belief that a values-driven small business could contribute to community and environmental health.[27] They sourced their ingredients from California farms, rotating their fruit seasonally to ensure that the peaches, strawberries and apples they used were at their freshest – and tastiest – and kept working with some

of the same producers throughout the café's twelve years of existence. They offered job training and internships to young people in
the community. They paid their employees well above minimum
wage and offered benefits.[28] If the tech economy was being built
on the infamous slogan 'move fast and break things', Mission Pie
grew on the idea of move slow and build things.

In the process, they created a community that became almost
like a second family for people like former regular Kimberly Sikora,
a 34-year-old artist and teacher who moved to the neighbourhood
in 2009 from Brooklyn. Mission Pie was one of the first places she
stopped at when she arrived at the city – two of her friends lived
in the apartment upstairs.

For her, too, it was the big windows and light-filled dining room
that initially drew her in. The banana cream pie won her over as
a customer, but it was the feeling of home that kept her coming
back. 'It became my living room,' she said – the backdrop to
catch-ups with old friends, a place where she forged new friendships. As her network of people grew in the city, Kimberly even
held a weekly craft night at the café: picture spools of yarn and
embroidery thread sitting alongside plates of pie on the communal
table. And during her last years living in the city when she had a
particularly stressful job, it was where she would come every
morning to sip coffee, journal her vision of the day and draw a
tarot card, a place where she felt supported even when she was
alone. 'What I feel Mission Pie always offered was the chance to
be around people and feel community even when you wanted some
solitude,' Kimberly said.

Yet outside the walls of Mission Pie, San Francisco was shifting
in another direction. The tech economy, having outgrown its original Silicon Valley base, expanded into the city bringing with it an
influx of highly paid tech workers. This drove up rent and housing
prices, making it one of the most expensive American cities to live
in.[29] The financial pressure was particularly acute for residents and
business owners in neighbourhoods like the Mission District, where
Mission Pie was located, an area with a distinctly Latino heritage
and a sizeable lower-income constituency, located just two short
miles from the Mid-Market neighbourhood where corporations

such as Twitter, Uber and Zendesk had moved in during the early 2010s, lured by attractive tax breaks.[30] And with the shift in the city's demographics came a change too in how people interacted with local businesses, particularly with local cafés and restaurants.

The tech companies were largely to blame for this. Rather than bringing business to the area – part of the rationale for the significant tax breaks that they had been given to relocate there – most did quite the opposite, preferring to sequester their staff in the office and provide a host of perks to keep them there, especially at mealtimes. Remember the fresh-caught rockfish and cayenne pepper ginger shots in Big Tech's lavish cafeterias? No wonder the influx of foot traffic that city officials hoped would turn into profits for local restaurants didn't materialise.[31]

Meanwhile the age of food delivery apps had arrived. Whilst ostensibly an opportunity for local establishments to serve a new set of customers, they came at a cost. The apps charged restaurants up to 30% commission fees on each order, leaving them with a dilemma: take the cut in revenues or increase prices.[32]

Moreover, the apps cut into more than just the bottom line. As we've seen, they encourage a contactless existence where having a slice of pie delivered to your doorstep in under twenty minutes is more convenient than popping over to one's local café and purchasing that same slice from a friendly and chatty barista. So, at the same time as restaurants were weighing up the pros and cons of signing up, fewer people were eating out in the first place.

Mission Pie found itself at the nexus of these pressures. The local cost of living increased so much that it became impossible to pay employees a fair wage. Selling via delivery apps would mean increasing prices to offset the commission fees, a choice that would mean betraying the inclusive values the café was built on in order to survive.[33] And selling their pies in grocery stores was not an option as it would compromise the freshness of their ingredients.

So Karen Heisler and Krystin Rubin decided to hold one last annual pie-baking competition and then shut down Mission Pie.

'Every day, we are awed and deeply moved by your love for Mission Pie as well as your sustained presence here at the shop: the morning coffee, the weekly meetings, the Wednesday knitters, the Friday morning banana cream pie date, the afternoon bowl of soup. There's so many more; it's tempting to list them all,' they wrote on the café's Facebook page in June 2019. 'We have witnessed many of you through momentous changes and accomplishments, profound growth, deep losses, new beginnings. We've baked your wedding pies, we've watched your children get big. We've also been together through more mundane days and weeks. All of it has mattered.'[34]

During its final days, the queues of loyal customers hoping to get one last slice wrapped around the corner.[35] Former regulars mourned the loss from afar. Kimberly Sikora, who in 2016 relocated to the Mojave Desert in search of more affordable rent and a quieter pace of life, hasn't yet discovered a replacement for the community she found at Mission Pie. Even so, she believes the owners' decision was the right one. 'If I had seen that they got Wi-Fi or raised the prices or started to employ people for less, I mean all of those things would have been more upsetting than them closing their doors,' she said. 'Because it would mean that the side of indifference and profit margins had won – and they were trying to create something so much more.'

The trouble is 'so much more' will not always be reconcilable with staying afloat. For as Mission Pie's demise makes all too clear, the reality is that profit and an inclusive community ethos don't always go hand in hand. This is especially so now, given the challenging economic climate.

So as well as ensuring that business taxes paid by brick and mortar stores are set at levels that help redress the disadvantage they face vis-à-vis online retailers, we would all benefit from the creation of a new category of business: pro-community enterprises that are eligible for tax breaks, incentives and grants if they deliver on verifiable metrics of inclusivity and help drive social cohesion. Local bookshops have historically played this role of key community hubs and would be the kind of businesses that could benefit from such support. Think of Kett's Books in Wymondham, Norfolk, which in 2019 launched a 'One Community One Book' project, essentially a town-wide book group complete with meetings and events. Although Kett's didn't give the books away for free, they did offer a 20% discount and donated several copies to the local library where a weekly read-aloud session also made the book accessible to those who might not have been able to read it themselves. The first book chosen, Frances Liardet's *We Must Be Brave*, mirrored the project itself, telling the story of a small English village forced to come together during the Second World War.[36] As part of the campaign, Liardet gave several readings in Wymondham, including one at a local care home for the elderly where the residents discussed their own memories and experiences of the war.[37]

Similarly, Readings Bookstore in Melbourne stays open until 11 p.m. most nights to allow people to browse, chat, get a coffee or attend a free reading from a local poet. Clarke's in Cape Town, with its comfortable lounge, is not only 'a home for books' but also 'a safe house for ideas', having stocked banned books and served as an undercover meeting place throughout South Africa's long, repressive apartheid regime.[38] Whilst some have lamented the way that contemporary bookshops have had to embrace non-book offerings – gifts, coffee, cakes and performances – as a way to boost takings and compete with online retailers, the books themselves have always been a supporting act to a community bookshop's central promise: to bring people together over ideas, stories, experiences, shared histories, difficult and effervescent truths.

We need cafés like Mission Pie and bookshops like Kett's to be able to survive if we want our local communities to thrive. And if we're lucky enough to live somewhere they already exist, it's important that we not only celebrate them but also try to patronise them more ourselves.

Indeed, if I think about where I live, it's a place where the independent shops work hard to make the community feel inclusive, bound together. Adam the optician puts local artist Jen's paintings on his walls. The bookshop holds regular talks with authors in partnership with the local community centre. The yoga studio has big communal tables for people to hang out with water jugs and magazines even if they're not there for a class, along with discounted rates for pensioners and the unemployed. The greengrocer, Phil, welcomes me with a smile even when I go in without my purse and ask him if he could put my apples on a tab. The local cafés put out water bowls for dogs so that customers can bring in their pets, drink coffee and just chill out. And strangers end up mingling and chatting because their dogs feel that irresistible canine urge to approach other dogs nearby. This isn't just anecdotal. Studies have found that people really are more likely to talk to strangers if they are accompanied by a dog.[39]

Time and again we see that independent local businesses play an important part in nurturing and anchoring the communities in which they are located. And it was inspiring during the lockdown to see so many local businesses increasing their commitment to community, despite being shuttered and fearing for their own demise. In my neighbourhood, restaurant-owner Morfudd Richards pro-vided hundreds of free lunches to the local old people's home, the butchers became the drop-off point for donations to vulnerable households whilst the yoga studio migrated its subsidised community classes online.

This is why it is so critical that we do not allow such businesses to be crushed by the unrelenting growth of e-commerce, and why local high streets must be strongly supported by both citizens and government so that they can survive the double whammy of the digital age and the post-coronavirus economic downturn.

If we are to feel part of a community rather than simply live in isolated bubbles, we must appreciate the role local entrepreneurs play in binding us together.

Commercialised communities

The community that the commercial sector delivers needs to be more than a marketing ploy, however. And although big corporations are starting to recognise the value of community as a brand proposition, the authenticity of their offerings can at times be highly questionable.

In 2017, for example, Apple rebranded its shops as 'Town Squares'.[40] Sounds good in theory yet all that seems to mean in practice is renaming its product aisles 'avenues', its presentation spaces 'forums' and its technician desks 'groves': a 'lexical takeover' that doesn't just co-opt the actual civic spaces those words represent, but marks a concerning trend away from true public ownership of those types of spaces, as Andrew Hill of the *Financial Times* points out. 'The very nature of how people use most Apple products – head down, AirPods in – is at odds with the look-up, look-around, listen-out ethos of the town square,' he writes.[41]

That same year, critics pounced on the similarly misguided blending of capitalist and activist premises in the now-infamous TV advert that featured a denim-clad Kendall Jenner diffusing police-protester tension with a can of Pepsi.[42] 'If only Daddy would have known about the power of #Pepsi,' Bernice King, the daughter of US civil rights leader Reverend Martin Luther King Jr. tweeted sarcastically.[43] Pepsi initially insisted that the advert was meant to highlight 'people from different walks of life coming together in a spirit of harmony', but in appropriating the language and even the aesthetic of communities engaged in protest the company showed that in reality it had no idea what those communities were fighting for, nor did it care.[44] It just wanted to sell more Pepsi.

These are just two among many cases of giant corporations co-opting the language of community for their own purposes. If big business is to play a meaningful role in bringing us together it will need to move beyond this kind of rhetorical flourish and spin.

What is fascinating is that in the past few years a distinct new model of business has emerged that doesn't seek to nurture an existing community or forge a new one by connecting people with a shared passion. Instead this emergent model sees community *itself* as a commodity, one that it is intent on commercialising, a product it can package and sell.

I'm referring here to the rise in commercial co-working spaces, companies with names like CommonGrounds, Work.Life, Convene, Second Home and, of course, WeWork, which at its peak had over 280 locations spread across eighty-six cities, and over 4 million square metres in real estate.[45] Alongside their Instagrammable venues, ping-pong tables, free-flowing ales on tap and micro-roasted coffee, these businesses wield the promise of community like a sword. Indeed, in WeWork's failed IPO prospectus (the filing a disaster not because of its core premise but because of revelations of profligate spending, erratic decision-making and gross misman-agement) the word 'community' appeared 150 times.[46]

Think, too, about the rapid rise in commercial co-living spaces that we've seen in the past few years. In the US, it is estimated that the number of co-living units will treble within the next few years.[47] In Asia, where only 11% of millennials own their own homes, investors, seeing a significant opportunity in co-living, have been piling in.[48] Even during the spring of 2020 when physical proximity was deemed negative, investment interest in the sector remained very significant. Starcity, for example, a co-living operator with twelve locations around San Francisco, Oakland and Los Angeles, completed at the end of April 2020 its series B investment round of $30 million.

The emphasis of this new category of apartment buildings with similarly unifying names such as 'Common', 'Society', 'Collective' and 'You+' is not on the private dwellings they rent out, the smallest of which can be as tiny as eight square metres.[49] It is again on the community spirit they claim to provide. 'Be more together', is the Collective's tag line; Common boasts that it's 'built for community' and 'you're always invited', whilst 'community' is literally listed as part of the services in the 'all-inclusive' plan offered by co-living operator Ollie.[50]

To put flesh on these bones, these buildings boast an array of communal spaces – bars, roof gardens, shared kitchens, cinemas – as well as curated activities such as yoga and French classes. Norn, a company that originated as a members-only club to train people in the lost 'art of conversation', launched a co-living arm in 2018 in which residents were even offered scheduled discussion groups billed as 'meaningful gatherings'.[51]

On the one hand this *is* an exciting prospect: businesses delivering community at scale. For if such co-working or co-living spaces *could* deliver togetherness and belonging, they might indeed play a significant role in solving at least some elements of today's loneliness crisis – once our fears about being around others have abated, that is. Think of remote worker John for whom work is 'just lonely as all hell'. Or Giorgio in Milan, who so missed talking to people at dinner that he found himself going more and more often to meals and singalongs hosted by the League. Or graphic designer Frank who, despite having lived in his apartment block for a couple of years, doesn't have a single neighbour who he could pop over to for a coffee. There's clearly a powerful and growing demand out there, especially as ever more people live on their own and more and more of us work remotely or join the gig economy.

Is WeWashing the new greenwashing?
The question is, can a manufactured community ever deliver 'true' togetherness? Or is 'WeWashing' the new greenwashing: the word 'community', when deployed as a selling point, no more meaningful than the words 'eco-friendly' on a can of toxic pesticide?

To date the picture has been mixed. For some, they do seem to be making life less lonely. 'I would consider WeWork and co-working spaces the best thing to ever happen to my social life,' reported a freelance web developer. When he worked from home, he wrote, his mood was lower and he even found himself feeling tired and getting sick more often – exactly what we'd expect, given what we know about physical health and loneliness.[52] But at WeWork, he says he 'went from a rather introverted person to being quite extroverted and growing emotionally'.[53] Others have had similar experiences. Daniel, a software engineer and expat who worked at a WeWork in Paris for a year and a half, credits his co-working experience with sparking a number of real-life, non-work friendships. 'When you don't know a tonne of people in the city, it's a good way to meet people, even if you're not working on anything similar,' he says.[54]

When BBC journalist Winnie Agbonlahor spent six days living in two different co-living facilities in London, she came across several happy campers.[55] These included 58-year-old Lucilla who shared that she'd made more friends in three months at The Collective's Royal Oak co-living space (famous for its disco-themed laundry room and ceramic dildo-making workshops) than she had in three years living on her own in Paris; and Matty, a 33-year-old IT specialist, for whom living in The Collective had been trans-formative.[56] For years, he had suffered a rare kidney condition that forced him to undergo a number of transplants that left him feeling, he says, 'like a dead man walking', stripped of energy, mobility and social confidence. 'In a way, living here brought me back to life,' he told Agbonlahor. 'Having people around to ask me how I am has made all the difference.'

Another resident, Jeffrey, told Peter Timko, a researcher studying The Collective, about a property-developer friend who had visited him there and had been initially sceptical of how much money was spent on the common areas of such buildings. But seeing all the small interactions between residents in the lobby changed his mind: 'And in an instant he got it,' Jeffrey recalled. 'Because in his properties, no one says hello to each other. They don't even look each other in the eye. And yet here was this space where people are happy to interact, happy to say "Hello, hey, how are you? How's it going? Can I help you with that? Can I hold the door?"'[57]

It's a damning indictment of the isolation of urban life that something so small as your neighbour looking you in the eye or opening the door for you would be so highly valued. But as we've seen throughout this book such momentary exchanges – that we know can help us feel markedly less alone – are becoming increasingly rare, thanks to the ever-accelerating bustle of cities, our ever-more-crunched schedules and the intensity of our digital addiction. If commercialised communities can at the least guarantee these micro-interactions, surely that's something. But is it enough?

I not we
Some who've tried out this new generation of commercialised communities, whether as living or working spaces, think not. Perhaps they were hoping for something deeper, something more worthy of the 'community' branding.

Amber, a gig-economy worker who combines being a virtual personal assistant with social media management, recounted how alone she felt on a typical day in WeWork Barcelona: 'I walk into the WeWork and there's around six people spread across the floor, sitting as far away as possible from one another with headphones on, me included. I sat myself on a cosy sofa out of the way, where I could have my peace and quiet to start my work, without having strangers glare over my laptop screen. The only time I engaged in conversation with someone is when I crossed paths with them at the coffee machine trying to figure out how the damn thing works.'

Amber's experience reminded me of when I visited WeWork's flagship space in Tel Aviv and saw a line of people queuing up for free malabi, a rosewater milk pudding common in the Middle East. It was one of the 'community' events being offered yet no one was speaking to each other; all of them had their heads down in their phones, and having grabbed their malabi, they all sauntered off by themselves, back to their desks. To me the ethos seemed more 'I work' than 'We'.

Over at The Collective, despite the positive soundings from Matty, Lucilla and Jeffrey, others expressed their doubts to Agbonlahor. One resident told her that the 'community' touted by The Collective's marketing materials was nothing less than false advertising: not just exaggerated, but missing completely in their view. And several voiced disappointment about the lack of community engagement, with only a small group of residents seeming to be actively involved.[58]

It was a complaint echoed in Timko's research interviews, with one resident suggesting community engagement was as low as 10%.[59] As another 'co-liver' Marge explained, 'there's a lot of people who just kind of live in the shadows and don't ever participate'. This was even the case when it came to the free salmon and bagel brunches The Collective puts on to encourage residents to mingle: 'you would actually see people coming down, loading the salmon and the eggs on their plate and come up to their rooms to eat it. [Yet] the whole point is to come down . . . connect and bond instead of just loading it up and just going back to your room and eating it by yourself,' an incredulous and disgruntled resident told Timko.[60]

We have already seen that you can't break bread together if you Deliveroo at home. Nor too can you break bread together if you grab your bagel from the communal brunch and take it to-go.

You can't buy community, you have to practise it
Indeed, a lack of engagement in the community is a key concern at other co-working and co-living spaces not only amongst residents or members, but also for the operators of a host of these spaces themselves.[61] In a Berlin get-together of operators of four leading

commercial co-living ventures, 'lack of member engagement' was identified by the group as one of the key challenges they faced.[62] Of course, in order for there to be significant member engagement, there needs to be a critical mass of members who want to commune. The trouble with many commercial communities is that this is by no means guaranteed.

For if we think about who's joining many of these new, shiny, commercialised communities, they are not necessarily people who have the time or lifestyles that community-building demands. Unlike the forbearers of co-living and co-working spaces – bottom-up co-housing initiatives such as those of the 1970s set up by groups of hippies, or Israel's kibbutzim, places populated by people for whom solidarity, care for each other and togetherness were the guiding principles – most co-living and co-working spaces today actively target highly individualistic millennial professionals, many of whom return home drained by their long working hours, lengthy commutes and panoptical open-plan offices, and are far too exhausted to socialise. They are urbanites who have become used to their digital bubbles or been conditioned to believe that interacting with others is not what city dwellers do – people for whom community as a concept is perhaps more appealing than community as a way of life.

But can the habits of disconnecting from each other be unlearnt? And new habits of community be developed? I believe that the answer to both is yes, but only with real effort and will.

The operators themselves are making an effort. At The Collective, the communal noticeboard heaves under the weight of flyers advertising upcoming events – a crystal-pendant-making workshop, a talk on mental health awareness, a lecture on the politics of body hair.[63] Even during lockdown their offerings continued, albeit now online. Zoom sessions offered over the course of a week in May 2020 included 'Vinyasa Flow with Eloise', and 'Drawn Together' where one volunteer at a time is the sitter, posing in front of their webcam whilst everyone else draws.

At WeWork, a senior executive proudly detailed all the attention that's put into maximising interaction, even down to the layout of the staircases and corridors which are intentionally designed to be too narrow for two people to pass one another (not great for the coronavirus age) 'so that you have to take your face off your phone for a second and kind of [move aside] and let someone pass. We do this on purpose. We design our staircases and our hallways the size that two people will actually need to look at each other, probably in the eyes and say hello, even when they just go to do a mundane task, like getting water.'

The trouble is – and this is the challenge these companies need to overcome – that community is not something one can buy, nor is it something that can be imposed by management. It is instead something in which people have to invest time and proactively participate in if it's to thrive. So, however many events a co-living or co-working space curates, however much free food or alcohol they provide, however narrow the corridors, unless the people who live and work there actually interact with each other in meaningful ways a community will never materialise. Community is predicated on people *doing* things together, not simply *being* together or bumping into each other as they pass by. It's the difference between 'being together' and being 'alone together', between an active state and a passive one.

The style of community 'leadership' plays a clear role in determining which of these two states prevail. Those co-living blocks in which the residents themselves have agency, plan their own outings and events, run their own community meetings and in which managers help them realise their own ideas for a new group activity seem to fare significantly better on the community front than those in which community is imposed purely top-down. Indeed Chen Avni, the charismatic co-founder of Venn, an Israeli co-living operator with complexes in Berlin, Tel Aviv and Brooklyn, and whose members' self-reported levels of loneliness fall on average by over a third within six months of moving into a Venn home, attributes this success in part to recognising this principle of self-determination. 'While other operators take the "if we build it they will come" approach to resident engagement with their wine and cheese night and Tuesday Tacos, what we have learnt along the way is not if we build it they will come, but if they build it they will stay,' Avni explains.[64]

As such, instead of just trying to come up with the next

'loneliness alleviating' community activities themselves, Venn now also ask members what type of event they want to create and deploy their community managers in a facilitating rather than an initiating role. It's not that every member needs to be an initiator – most of us know from our own experience that we don't want too many chefs in the kitchen – it's that a culture of co-creation and member empowerment seems to change the experience from one of a hotel to something closer to a home, a community one has a stake in, rather than a commodity to be bought and sold.

Indeed, Avni tells me that one of the 'biggest accelerators' of their community creation has been the monthly 'dig-in dinner', essentially a pot-luck dinner, where the food is provided by the members themselves. (Venn provides drinks and desserts.) Avni went on to describe how, over meals they have prepared, old-timers welcome new arrivals and catch up with each other. And how through the explanations of the dishes they've chosen to share, members open up about their home town or country, with the memories their dishes evoke providing a way in to deeper conversations about who they are and where they are from, setting the stage for the creation of more meaningful bonds. The 'dig-in dinners' are Venn's highest-attended events.

Perhaps if instead of being offered a free salmon and bagel brunch The Collective's members were actively encouraged to cook together, their sense of community would be stronger?

Part of the problem, too, is how a number of these companies define community. Take NomadWorks, the also supposedly 'community-centric' WeWork competitor – it explicitly lists 'networking events' among its membership amenities.[65] And when I asked a senior executive at WeWork how they knew they were delivering when it comes to community, his 'proof', tellingly, was how many successful 'transactions' members had completed with one another. Specifically, he told me, they measured how many WeWork members had bought something from another member at least once as a proxy for how strong the community was.

Those renting space there have noticed the inherent contradiction in this decidedly neoliberal framing. James, who worked in WeWork's London Moorgate building, a glass-windowed behemoth whose loos have 'Hustle Harder' stencilled on the wall, described his experience there as such: 'people are super-friendly here, but that's only because everyone is trying to sell everyone something. It's amazing how quickly I became a persona non grata when I made clear I wasn't interested in buying. Put it this way, no one asked me to play ping-pong.'

This transactional aspect isn't of course in itself a bad thing. Indeed, the fact that more than half of co-working users in a 2014 study reported that they had found new clients and new collaborators in their workspace suggests that there's, at the least, a clear business case for becoming a member.[66] Moreover, friendships can develop alongside business dealings or indeed be forged at a networking event. It's just that a fistful of business cards does not a community make. We devalue the notion of community if it is reduced to a group of people who view each other just as a potential mark. It needs to mean caring for and helping each other too, not just hustling.

The frictionless nature of these operations also has something to answer for given they typically emphasise convenience almost as much as community. At some co-living spaces everything from laundry to the cleaning of your shared kitchen to the emptying of shared bins is done for you. What this means is that yes, there are fewer domestic tasks to worry about, but also less shared responsibility for the upkeep of communal spaces and fewer tasks that you'll complete on behalf of anyone other than yourself. Research into what makes co-housing communities thrive (co-housing rather than co-living implies a longer-term cooperative situation, often where residents develop the space and its practices themselves) suggests that crucial to the development of social ties is that residents take on responsibility for group activities and site maintenance – whether weekly rotas, taking out the bins, laundry, weeding a community garden or sharing childcare.[67]

We've arrived, it seems, at the central paradox of many co-living and co-working spaces: they want to sell the benefits of living or working in close proximity with others, but with none of the social buy-in, the *hard work* that community requires. As can be the case with real friendships, when it comes to the building of authentic community perhaps putting up with some inconvenience is part of the bargain.

Think of the communities you feel most connected to. Presumably they are also environments in which you have to make some sort of effort, give as well as take? If I think of my weekly improv group, one of the communities I feel strongly part of, tasks and responsibilities are shared out. I am responsible for collecting the dues and paying the church whose hall we use, Roderick runs the sessions, Thierry sorts out keys when needed, Kevin brings his guitar, Ma'ee and Amber take us through tongue-twisters and Lucy steps in to run the session when Roderick can't. And, importantly, each of us tries our best to show up each week, even if we are not in the mood. Conversely, if community is served up to you alongside free ale and malabi and you don't need to do anything yourself to contribute, your obligation to commit to it is likely to be weakened.

Showing up is key. This highlights another problem with many of these commercialised communities – their members are transient. The Collective's annual turnover rate is, for example, 50%.[68] And whilst turnover at co-working spaces is harder to calculate – after all, a membership at WeWork buys you access to offices all over the world – any place with a majority of hot desks will inevitably be 'an environment whose most defining characteristic is constant change'.[69] As we saw in the context of cities, the problem with itinerant communities is that the less rooted you are in your community, the less likely you are to participate in it. By actively selling flexibility and fluidity as part of the offering, WeWork and other such spaces lower the odds of members and residents seeing the community as theirs and actively investing in it. Indeed, if one thinks about truly bonded communities, whether we're talking churchgoers, members of the Haredim in Israel or even a cycling club, one of the key reasons the bonds between members are strong is because of their *repeated* interactions. For whilst some of the strength inevitably comes from a shared passion or shared values, it also takes time for people to feel truly bonded to each other. Without repeated opportunities for solidarity and mutual support to play out, the relationships between members within a community will always be more akin to a holiday romance than a marriage, and trust will be in short supply.

It is perhaps not surprising then that one of the other key issues flagged at the Berlin meet-up of co-living companies was the high level of distrust amongst members. The Collective has dealt with this by installing CCTV throughout their spaces, alongside signs such as 'Smile, you're on camera' and 'If we find food from shared kitchens in your rooms, we'll remove it'.[70] I can see how it would be annoying to have your olive oil stolen by a fellow resident, but as we saw in previous chapters, such systems of surveillance are hardly conducive to community bonding.

Exclusive communities

As we contemplate how best to rebuild our post-Covid-19 world and reconnect with each other, there will undoubtedly be useful lessons that governments, local authorities, architects, city planners and the business world can learn from these twenty-first century companies who have put community at the heart of their proposition, both good and bad.

Yet even when commercialised communities do manage to deliver a sense of belonging, there remains very often a question of inclusivity. The South Korean colatecs with their low entry fees, the yoga studio with its discounted rates for pensioners and the unemployed, and the subsidised book club remain exceptions, not the norm. In the majority of cases when it comes to commercialised communities, if you can't pay enough you are not invited in.

Take boutique group fitness classes. For all their spiritual schtick and 'we're a community' branding, it's crucial to note that these are not church services with open doors. Instead, they are typically clustered in affluent neighbourhoods, sold as a luxury item and packaged with a premium price tag – some cost up to $40 for a single session.[71]

Similarly, music-festival ticket prices have increased so much that one-third of millennials who attended one in 2018 said they took on debt in order to afford the experience.[72] Glastonbury 2020 tickets cost £265 per person, while general admission to Cochella is $429, 'plus fees'. As for my own neighbourhood, I am aware that it is only able to retain a high-quality local grocery store because its relatively well-off inhabitants are able and willing to pay what is essentially a 'community tax' that allows it to sell many of its products at prices higher than giant supermarket chains and therefore stay in business. Where this is not the case, such staples of community life have very often had to close shop, as we saw in the case of Mission Pie.

And to the extent that co-working spaces can help to alleviate the loneliness of the gig-economy or remote worker, again their pricing structure to date has been such that it's typically only high-earning white-collar professionals who can afford them. At the beginning of 2020, for example, WeWork's lowest-tier hot-desk membership cost between £200 and £600 a month in London and up to $600 a month in San Francisco. That's far outside the realm of possibility for, say, your average TaskRabbiter.

As for the 'everything under one roof' concept beloved by many co-living operators, their on-site grocery shops, laundries, gyms and bars can engender social segregation. With residents able to shop and socialise at bars in-house, they all too often fail to engage with the neighbourhood beyond. As such they risk becoming alienated from the surrounding community and locals in turn risk becoming alienated from them. In the long run this may be a losing strategy not only from society's perspective but from the co-living operators too. For if people are truly connected to a place, not only will they have a stronger sense of community but they're more likely to remain in the neighbourhood longer.

Private communities can play a role in mitigating this century's loneliness crisis provided their offering is authentic and their members are truly engaged. However, at a time when public community spaces are being dismantled, free or cheap places to congregate are ever fewer and many local high streets are being crushed, there is a real danger that community becomes something increasingly accessible *only* to the privileged. That you will only 'find your soul' if you can pay the entrance fee. That loneliness becomes a disease only the wealthy have the chance to 'cure'. Given that the lonely are already disproportionally worse off financially, this is particularly disquieting.

If privatised communities are not to become another manifestation of hostile architecture – a way to exclude and keep others
out – and instead play an active part both in alleviating loneliness
for individuals and in reconnecting society more broadly, ensuring
that they not only deliver on their promise but also that more
people can access and benefit from them is an important challenge
for the future.

There are some bright spots on the horizon. In late 2019, the
city of New York's trailblazing ShareNYC housing programme
awarded three coveted contracts for 'shared housing' projects that
incorporate some aspects of co-living, including shared kitchens,
shared fitness centres and more flexible leases, while providing
affordable housing that cuts across socio-economic divides.[73] The
accommodation is expected to serve a wide variety of incomes
from very low-income to moderate-income households; just a
third of the larger development will be market-rate.[74] Though it is
only a start, the city planners and developers seem to be actively
working to prevent the separationist mentality that dominated
developments like Royal Wharf and Baylis Old School that we
looked at earlier; the intention is that members will enjoy equal
amenities and services whatever rent they pay.[75] Hopefully in this
case children from different economic strata will be able to play
together, shared spaces will be welcoming to everyone and community will be available to all – without a platinum price tag.

CHAPTER ELEVEN

Coming Together in a World that's Pulling Apart

Loneliness is not just a subjective state of mind.[1] It is also a collective state of being that's taking a huge toll on us as individuals and on society as a whole, contributing to the deaths of millions of people annually, costing the global economy billions and posing a potent threat to tolerant and inclusive democracy.[2]

Even before the coronavirus struck, this was the Lonely Century. But the virus has thrown into even starker relief just how uncared for and unsupported so many of us feel, not only by friends or family but also by our employers and the state; how disconnected so many of us are, not just from those to whom we are most intimately bound, but also our neighbours, our work colleagues and our political leaders.

If we are to mitigate loneliness not just at an individual level but also at a societal one, we urgently need the dominant forces that shape our lives to wake up to the scale of the problem. Government, business and we as individuals *all* have significant roles to play. The loneliness crisis is too complex and multifarious for any one entity to solve on its own.

It's here that I differ from a number of other political and economic thinkers who have written about loneliness. For not only do they define loneliness more narrowly, the tendency has often been to take a less holistic and more overtly partisan approach.[3]

Conservatives frequently cast the blame on the breakdown of the 'traditional family', declining attendance at church and an overly powerful welfare state which they demonise for obviating personal responsibility as well as our responsibility towards others.

As such, they typically argue that the solutions to the loneliness crisis rest firmly with the individual. If only we did more for ourselves and for those around us, they cry.

The left, by contrast, has often been tempted to frame the problem as essentially one of too little, rather than too much government. Depicting citizens as victims of circumstance, it tends to put its emphasis instead on what the state should do. Individuals are given a relatively free pass, at least when it comes to whose responsibility it is to fix community and heal social ills.

At both extremes, this binary view of the drivers of loneliness is ultimately unhelpful and self-defeating. For whilst there are elements of truth in both of these politically charged perspectives, neither provides the full picture, nor an effective route to solving the crisis. As we've seen, loneliness's structural drivers are rooted in state actions *and* those of individuals and corporations, as well as by the technological advances of the twenty-first century, whether we're talking our smartphone addiction, workplace surveillance, the gig economy or our increasingly contactless experiences.

Moreover, these drivers are often closely interlinked. If your employer doesn't give you time off to care for your elderly parent in an emergency – however much you want to be there for them you won't be able to provide the companionship and support they need. If you don't know your neighbours because your rent is being raised regularly and you keep having to move, you're much less likely to be willing to help them or to contribute to the local community. If you're addicted to Instagram's dopamine highs or choose to check your emails constantly when you are out of the office, you're inevitably going to be spending less time each day interacting in-person with family or friends – and when you do, you're more likely to be distracted by your phone. If the only bench to sit on in your street is one that's purposely been designed to be uncomfortable so as to thwart those designated 'undesirable', you're not going to perch yourself on it and shoot the breeze with passers-by. If you're not sure when exactly you're going to work this week because you have no guaranteed hours, you're not going to be able to commit to coaching your kid's Sunday football team.

Loneliness isn't a singular force. It lives inside an ecosystem. So if we are to stymie the loneliness crisis we will need systemic economic, political and societal change, whilst at the same time acknowledging our personal responsibility.

Reconnecting capitalism with care and compassion

As our starting point, this means we need to accept that today's loneliness crisis didn't just emerge out of nowhere. It has been fuelled to a considerable degree by a particular political project – neoliberal capitalism. A self-obsessed, self-seeking form of capitalism that has normalised indifference, made a virtue out of selfishness and diminished the importance of compassion and care. A 'pull yourself up by your bootstraps', 'hustle harder' form of capitalism, that has denied the pivotal role both public services and local community have historically played in helping people prosper and has instead perpetuated the narrative that our destinies are solely in our own hands. It's not that we weren't ever lonely before. It's that by redefining our relationships as transactions, recasting citizens in the role of consumers and engendering ever greater income and wealth divides, forty years of neoliberal capitalism has, at best, marginalised values such as solidarity, community, togetherness and kindness.[4] At worst, it has cast these values summarily aside. We need to embrace a new form of politics – one with care and compassion at its very heart.

The political objective of making citizens feel that someone is watching their back is not irreconcilable with capitalism. Indeed, it is a fundamental misunderstanding of capitalism to assume that its neoliberal 'dog eat dog', 'every man for himself' variant is its only form. Even Adam Smith, the father of capitalism, whilst best known as an eloquent advocate of free markets and individual freedom, wrote extensively in *The Theory of Moral Sentiment* (the precursor to *The Wealth of Nations*) about the importance of empathy, community and pluralism.[5] He understood that the state has a clear role to play in providing the infrastructure of community – and that when the markets need to be reined in to protect society, reined in they should be.[6] Elsewhere, Asian, Scandinavian and indeed continental European forms of capitalism through much of the twentieth century were distinct from the neoliberal tradition in terms of the greater role they accorded the state and the emphasis they placed on communitarian values. Capitalism has never been a singular ideology.

So whereas neoliberal capitalism – with its narrow focus on free markets and deregulation, the primacy it accords to the rights of capital and its antagonism towards the welfare state even when this comes at the expense of societal cohesion and the common good – has dominated across much of the world over the last four decades, it is not our only option for the future. Together we must define and create a more cooperative form of capitalism that delivers not only in economic terms but also in societal ones.

And the time to do this is now. In the wake of the Great Depression in the 1930s, President Franklin D. Roosevelt launched the New Deal, a massive government spending and regulatory programme whose aims were to provide relief, recovery and enhanced rights to those who were hardest hit by the economic devastation. In the United Kingdom, the National Health Service with its commitment to provide healthcare for all was founded in the aftermath of the Second World War: a powerful symbol of a new commitment to equity and compassion. Now, too, is the time for game-changing and radical steps, time to implement a more caring and kinder capitalism.

At a minimum, governments need to assure their citizens that the entrenched inequalities that the pandemic simultaneously exposed and exacerbated will be actively addressed, and that when times are unavoidably tough they will be there to support them. In many nations, this means committing significantly greater resources to welfare, social security, education and healthcare. Even before the pandemic, the United States, for example, needed to increase its spending on social services (this includes expenditure on housing benefit, unemployment pay, job creation programmes and pension support) by 1.4% of GDP just to reach the OECD average.[7] And politicians can make such commitments knowing that the public would support them. In a poll conducted immediately after President Trump signed the $2 trillion coronavirus stimulus bill in March of 2020, over three-quarters of Democrats and Republicans expressed approval of the legislation – even after they had been reminded of the astonishing price tag.[8] Another poll carried out at the same time revealed that as many as 55% of US voters were now in favour of Medicare for All, a rise of nine points since January of that year.[9]

Meanwhile, in the United Kingdom public support for increased welfare spending to help the poor, even if it led to higher taxes, was already in 2017 at its highest level for fourteen years.[10] And in May 2020 during the coronavirus crisis, even the most ardent pro free-market think tanks were urging the government to avoid tax cuts and austerity measures and instead increase public expenditure.[11]

The need for bold steps and an unprecedented scale of commitment will be especially profound in the immediate wake of the pandemic, given the economic pressures and the competing demands on public resources it has induced. Yet it is imperative that, as we move away from the eye of the storm, governments understand that the need for additional support will persist due to factors including rapidly aging populations (in the Global North, that is), the long-tail economic damage of the coronavirus and the additional (and severe) job losses due to automation we can expect over the coming years.

When it comes to unemployment, the support the state provides cannot just be financial. Governments need to make moves to slow down the rate of substitution of labour by robots, and earlier I mooted one way of potentially achieving this – a robot tax. Furthermore, given the challenges the private sector is currently facing, governments will need, for the time being, to play the role of employer of last resort and create new jobs at scale either directly through major public projects or indirectly through fiscal policy. For it is through work – if it is dignified – that we can find both fellowship and purpose and at its best also community spirit.

Twenty-first-century public-works programmes shouldn't simply be about deploying people to build roads or pick fruit, however. A credible commitment to wind and solar energy would generate considerable numbers of new jobs as would pledges by local authorities to plant more trees, energy retrofit municipal buildings and install charging stations for electric cars. And governments also need to create jobs specifically aimed at restoring the fabric of community whether it's building libraries, youth clubs or community centres or commissioning works from those who nourish society spiritually – artists, writers and musicians. This did indeed happen during the New Deal when artists across the US were hired to paint murals, create sculptures, teach art classes and produce theatre – with the intention, as FDR put it, to show Americans the possibilities of 'an abundant life'.[12] Our politicians today should be no less ambitious.

There's something else governments could do too: turn today's unemployment challenges into an opportunity to create a new workforce of people paid explicitly to help alleviate loneliness. Here we might draw inspiration from the UK's recent commitment to what is known as 'social prescribing', whereby 'link workers' attached to GP surgeries are deployed to help people who are struggling with mental health challenges, isolation or loneliness to identify local resources that can help them to better cope, whether art classes, exercise classes or men's groups. Such initiatives are only meaningful, however, if they are accompanied by a commitment to fund these activities adequately, both so that 'clients' have real options and can actually afford to attend. Training more people to care for the elderly or the young would also make sense, at least in the short to medium term, provided the government commits to raising pay in the care sector.

Of course, to do all this the state will need to add to its coffers. Given the scale of the challenge, governments won't be able to borrow or print money indefinitely without causing significant long-term economic damage, however low interest rates are currently.[13] This means that the very richest strata of society will inevitably need to pay a higher rate of tax. That is only fair. But it's not just wealthy individuals who should face this additional tax burden. Multi-national corporations that continue to register their profits in low or no-tax jurisdictions should also face tough legislation that forces them to pay their dues to the countries in which they sell their products. Billions of pounds of tax receipts that could be directed towards public projects have already been lost as a result of these nefarious corporate practices. Perhaps, too, those companies that did particularly well financially during the coronavirus crisis, such as online food retailers, could reasonably be subjected to a one-off windfall tax. Again, there is historical precedent for this. In the United States 'excess profit' taxes were implemented during the two World Wars and also the Korean War.[14]

Yet we need to be even more ambitious still. As we rebuild our post-Covid-19 world, governments have a rare opportunity to seize the moment, act transformatively and rethink priorities on a fundamental level. Here we can draw inspiration from New Zealand Prime Minister Jacinda Ardern, who announced in May 2019 that her government would no longer only use traditional economic metrics such as growth and productivity to determine the nation's budgetary policy and goals. Instead, 'led by kindness and compassion', her government pledged to incorporate a wider, more socially conscious and rounded set of criteria.[15] These included how well the country is doing when it comes to protecting the environment, providing a decent education, increasing life expectancy and – importantly for our purposes – metrics related to loneliness, trust in fellow citizens, trust in government and an overall sense of belonging.[16] Scotland and Iceland are considering similar approaches to their own budgeting processes.[17]

Whilst other governments in recent years – most notably the UK and France – have begun measuring wellbeing, New Zealand's wellbeing budget is considered to be the boldest step taken so far by an OECD country given its explicit tie-in with political and budgetary decision making.[18] The French and UK initiatives have not, to date, steered policy or government spending decisions in a substantive way.[19] It would be remiss here not to mention the tiny and remote country of Bhutan that actually blazed the trail in this regard, having incorporated its Gross National Happiness metrics into policymaking for decades.[20]

If capitalism is to be reconciled with care, we need to reconnect the economy with social justice as a matter of urgency and acknowledge that traditional ways of defining success are no longer fit for purpose.[21]

Change the calculus of capitalism

Even this is not enough. If we are to address the sense of abandonment so many feel, we must go further than ensuring that all citizens are provided with a meaningful social safety net, that government budgetary goals are more clearly aligned with their citizens' overall wellbeing and that structural inequalities are addressed, including when it comes to race and gender. We must also ensure that people are properly cared for and protected at work and from any potential harm that big business may generate in its wake more generally. Neoliberal capitalism, with its 'minimum state, maximum markets' approach, has never provided assurances on either. And this isn't just a project for government – businesses and their leaders also need to step up.

Indeed, it was partly in recognition of this that in August 2019 the Business Roundtable, a group of influential chief executives of leading US corporations including Amazon's Jeff Bezos, Apple's Tim Cook and Citigroup's Michael Corbat,[22] jettisoned Milton Friedman's longstanding principle that the only business of business was to serve its shareholders,[23] pledging instead to serve *all* its stakeholders – shareholders, yes, but also suppliers, communities and employees who it promised to 'compensat[e] fairly and provid[e] important benefits', as well as foster 'diversity and inclusion, dignity and respect'.[24]

Whilst I welcome this sentiment and hope that such rhetoric will translate into meaningful action, the reality is that unless the pressure on companies to generate short-term financial returns is alleviated and their executives' incentives not tied to this, the focus on narrowly defined 'return to shareholders' will likely continue to dominate, especially in the case of publicly traded companies. As such, if strategies like the deployment of digital surveillance or the substitution of full-time employees with low-cost, zero-hour or temporary-contract workers with limited rights are shown to drive greater efficiencies, it will remain hard for even more progressively minded CEOs not to deploy them even if they are inimical to the interests of workers and the collective good. This is especially the case now, given the economic climate and the focus on cost-cutting.

Already the actions of some of the signatories to the Business

Roundtable's new pledge risk making a mockery of its espoused goals. Take Amazon. As Covid-19 cases mounted in New York, Amazon employee Christian Smalls grew increasingly worried about the lack of protective equipment and poor sanitation in the Staten Island warehouse where he worked as a 'picker'. When management dismissed his concerns, Smalls organised a walkout demanding greater protective equipment, paid sick leave and transparency about coronavirus cases among Amazon staff, who work closely together in warehouses.[25] 'People were afraid,' Smalls explained. 'We went to the general manager's office to demand that the building be closed down so it could be sanitised. This company makes trillions of dollars. Still, our demands and concerns are falling on deaf ears. It's crazy. They don't care if we fall sick. Amazon thinks we are expendable.'[26] Amazon's response? Smalls was first put on a suspicious 'medical quarantine' (though no others were asked to do so). Then, when he attended the walkout anyway, he was fired.[27] New York Attorney General Letitia James declared the firing 'disgraceful' and called for an investigation by the National Labor Relations Board.[28]

Of course, I'm not saying here that big corporations can't act with compassion and care towards their workers; we saw some inspiring behaviour on the part of some big corporations during the pandemic lockdown period. Microsoft, for example, announced in early March 2020 that contract workers on its Pacific Northwest campuses – including shuttle drivers, café workers, maintenance and cleaning staff – would continue to be paid even as work-from-home measures meant their in-person services were no longer needed.[29] But unless the calculus of capitalism changes, all too often such acts of kindness and community spirit risk being outliers, the preserve of only the most forward-thinking company executives and the most long-term-focused and compassionate shareholders.

With this in mind, and as I've mooted throughout the book, we need a new body of legislation to protect workers' rights that's fit for purpose for the twenty-first century, especially when it comes to the low-paid, the self-employed, gig-economy workers and those on temporary or zero-hours contracts. Many in these groups proved to be the 'essential workers' we all so relied upon during lockdown, yet have to contend with low wages, limited (or non-existent) benefits, greater precarity of employ and in some cases unsafe working conditions. A living wage, paid sick days and adequate health and safety provisions at work need to be the absolute bare minimum.

If people are to feel cared for we also need a new body of legislation that protects society from the harmful acts of a specific group of actors: social media companies. In the same way that businesses today – in most countries – are not allowed to pollute our air and water with impunity, or sell our children tobacco, so too must these companies' negative impact on community, cohesiveness, inclusivity and wellbeing be curtailed, particularly when it comes to children and teenagers. In earlier chapters I proposed a whole array of potential regulatory levers we can use to deliver this protection. On a precautionary basis alone, governments cannot afford to be reticent.

And again, there is a growing demand for such actions, and not only amongst the public. Politicians on both ends of the political spectrum now acknowledge that individuals can't be expected to protect themselves from the ills of Big Tech without a degree of state intervention, and that unless these companies are confronted by toothsome regulation they won't take meaningful enough action to address their corrosive impacts.[30]

Make people feel seen and heard

If people are to feel less isolated or abandoned, there's more still that we need to do. For as we have seen, loneliness is not only about feeling uncared for, it's also about feeling invisible. Part of the solution to this century's loneliness crisis must therefore be to ensure that people are seen and heard.

Trade unions undoubtedly have a critical role to play here in amplifying workers' voices, including gig economy workers and remote workers who may risk being out of sight and of mind of their employers. It is essential that workers of all ilk have the freedom to associate and also that trade unions make their case more strongly.

More fundamentally in the Lonely Century, our sense of invisibility stems from the feeling many people have that decisions they would never have countenanced are being made in their name by political leaders who are deaf to their concerns or cries.

It is of course an inevitable consequence of representative democracy that not everyone's concerns will be acted upon or their views given equal weight. Yet part of the reason the bonds between state and citizen have become so frayed in recent years is because of how polarised the debate has become, how opaque the decision-making process and how inequitable the outcomes. The intersection of lack of voice and social and economic injustice means that now more than ever it is imperative that those who have been most marginalised are prioritised when it comes to the allocation of resources, and that the people who benefit most from regulatory reforms and government largesse are not simply those with the fattest wallets or greatest lobbying power or of a particular colour, gender or class.

Important also is that citizens are able to exercise their voice more often than once every few years at the ballot box. We need to participate more meaningfully and on an ongoing basis in democracy if we are to feel more connected to each other and to politics. I am not calling for the holding of more referenda here. These are the bluntest forms of majority rule and tend to ignore complexity and the imperative to protect minority interests, especially in the age of 'fake news'. Instead we can learn from an array of contemporary deliberative democracy initiatives.

Take London's Camden Council, which in the summer of 2019 selected fifty-six residents – builders and students, entrepreneurs and civil servants, immigrants and pensioners – their gender, ethnicity and socio-economic backgrounds representative of the community along census lines, to help develop the approach the council should take to addressing climate change. How to encourage people to eat locally? How to make green choices more affordable? Should the council require new homes to be carbon neutral? These were some of the questions the group was asked to address.[31]

At the beginning, the participants had different perspectives.

Whilst there were no outright climate-change deniers amongst them, some were clearly more sceptical than others. Others were pretty new to the whole issue. Yet by means of a highly structured process with trained facilitators guiding the discussions, mindful of the need to ensure that everyone had equal voice and carefully drawing out the quietest, by the end of their two evenings and one full day of meetings the group had agreed upon seventeen steps to recommend. These ranged from the broad ('Trial car-free zones and days') to the more specific ('Install more segregated cycle lanes'). Collectively, their recommendations will become the backbone of the council's 2020 Climate Action Plan.[32]

In Taiwan a similar process is taking place, but at even greater scale. Since 2015, 200,000 people have taken part in a deliberative democratic process online.[33] Issues debated so far include the regulation of drones, Uber's entry into the Taiwanese market, the online sale of alcohol, whether plastic straws should be banned and the non-consensual publication of intimate images, what is known as 'revenge porn'. In 80% of cases, the government has acted on the process's final recommendations – whether by passing legislation or updating policies.[34] When the government has chosen to ignore them it has provided detailed reasons for why it has done so.[35]

Initiatives like these could play a substantial role in helping us to come together, provided of course that the recommendations are not summarily ignored. Not only because they give voice to a wider group of constituents than ordinarily would be the case, but because by making consensus the goal, the process itself forces participants to practise democracy by having to actively contemplate and reconcile each other's views, and learn how to manage their differences, rather than silence them.[36]

Indeed, when watching the footage of the Camden meetings, what I found striking were the reassuring smiles the participants gave to whoever was speaking, the eye contact between them, their leaning forward to listen to each other, even when they disagreed.[37] Throughout this book we've highlighted the importance of practising democracy if it's a more inclusive and tolerant society we strive for: what took place in Camden Town was an institutionalised, carefully calibrated form of just that.[38]

Practise democracy

Practising democracy is not, as we've seen, something that always needs to be so formally facilitated. Indeed it is through our membership of local associations or groups that we are perhaps best able to practise some of its key aspects – civility, kindness and tolerance – on a regular basis, whether we're talking my Monday night improv group, a Parent–Teachers Association or the organising committee for a church annual fete.

Our workplaces can also provide opportunity on this front: think, for example, of US software company Cisco's institutionalisation of the practice of expressing gratitude within the organisation. Even at a more micro-level within our households the very act of doing chores is a way to reinforce another of the key tenets of inclusive democracy – that sometimes we need to make sacrifices or simply be selfless with our time for the common good.

It is, though, within our neighbourhoods that our opportunity to practise *community* arguably best lies.[39] I am not implying here that community is inexorably bound to geography. (For all my criticism of social media platforms, I have acknowledged the important role they can play for some in this respect.) Yet as we have seen, it's easier for people to feel bonded to each other when the interactions between them are both face to face and repeated, and for most of us this means in our geographic locale.

It's in the brief catch-ups at our local greengrocer with fellow residents, the 'how are you?'s we exchange as we pick up coffee from our local barista, the warm feeling we get from our local dry cleaner when he greets us by name, as well as in the deeper relationships we forge with those who live on our street that barriers break down, strangers become neighbours and communities are built. And the more we contribute to our neighbourhood, the more vested in it we become and the more real the community feels.

It's why measures to help reduce the churn in neighbourhoods by making rental costs more stable are to be encouraged, as are measures to disincentivise absentee owners such as extra taxes on homes that are occupied less than half of the year.

Communities are made up of bricks *and* people. Our locale needs to be lived in if it is to feel like a real neighbourhood; and so too do our shops and cafés need to be bustling. Steps that seek to safeguard the future vibrancy of our local high streets are also therefore vital.

We have seen that some local municipalities are already taking action to help ensure this. Remember Roeselare in Belgium, where an empty-shop tax has proven very effective in disincentivising landlords from keeping their shops empty whilst they hold out for higher rents. Given the triple whammy local brick and mortar stores currently face from e-retailers, big box out-of-town stores *and* the current economic downturn, they will need significantly increased government and municipality support. Reduced business rates and state-backed loans are practical steps that could be taken here that would make a real difference, as would be a levelling of the fiscal playing field when it comes to online retailers. Our local high streets are in many ways a public good and should be treated as such, especially now when so many are facing an existential threat.

As individuals we have a very important role to play here too as we emerge from the pandemic. Many of us became even more used to shopping online during lockdown. Weaning ourselves off these digital transactions and supporting the local business owners who serve our communities will also be essential if we are to sustain the viability of our high streets.

And for those businesses that go the extra mile and put inclusive community at the heart of their mission in verifiable ways – whether it's a local bookstore like Kett's with its town-wide book club, a café like Mission Pie with its Wednesday knitting circle or a South Korean colatec whose entrance fees are expressly kept very low – additional tax breaks and other forms of financial support should be on the agenda. These are vital both to encourage such innova- tion, and to ensure that that it is not only the wealthy who benefit from the new entrepreneurialism that is driving the Loneliness Economy.

More fundamentally, governments need to commit to restoring the shared physical spaces in our neighbourhoods that have been steadily ravaged over recent years. A functioning infrastructure of community which everyone has access to regardless of income, ethnicity, age, gender or creed is essential if we are to have the best

possible chance of both reversing the loneliness crisis and reconnecting with each other. The cuts in funding for shared public
spaces that have taken place globally since 2008 must be reversed
as a matter of urgency. And at the same time new kinds of public
spaces need to be built: places like Barcelona Council's ped-
estrianised 'superblocks' with their parks, playgrounds and neighbourhood feel, or the Chicago public housing developments that
are being built around libraries where people of different incomes
and ages will be able to come together and commune. We cannot
effectively reverse the atomisation of our contemporary society
until the infrastructure of community is both properly funded *and*
intelligently designed. And governments cannot be allowed to use
the post-Covid-19 downturn as an excuse not to do this.

Doing things with people different to us – people of different
socio-economic backgrounds, ethnicities or political persuasions,
people who don't necessarily share our history, culture or views –
is absolutely essential if we are to move beyond our differences
and find common ground.[40] And local public spaces can to some
degree enable us to engage with people different to ourselves, as
can our membership say of a local church, mosque or synagogue. However, given the homogeneity of many neighbourhoods,
even in such spaces, interactions often end up taking place with
people who are pretty similar to us. This limits our ability to
encounter and build experiences with diverse types of people and
effectively practise the most important elements of inclusive democracy: that we fairly reconcile our differences and acknowledge the
humanity of the 'other'.

The challenge therefore is how to get different types of people
to spend time together. And the good news is that there are many
inspiring initiatives around the world we can learn from. In
Germany, for example, over 40,000 people have participated in a
programme called *'Deutschland Spricht'* ('Germany Talks'), sponsored by the German newspaper *Die Zeit*.[41] The initiative began
in 2017 when, prompted by the growing polarisation of German
politics and the increasing confinement of people within their
own echo chambers, a group of reporters at the paper came up
with an ambitious plan to pair strangers on opposite sides of the

political spectrum who would then meet in person and talk: a kind of 'political Tinder', as they referred to the scheme in-house.[42]

Participants were paired on the basis of an algorithm that was programmed to match people with divergent political views and who lived within a twenty-kilometre radius of each other. Once matched, the onus was on them to meet up. A quarter of the participants actually did.[43] In cafés, churches and beer gardens across Germany, IT consultants met with army reserve officers, police officers with engineers, government employees with physicists, neonatal counsellors with court bailiffs.[44] *Die Zeit's* own editor-in-chief, Jochen Wegner, met with a machinery and plant operator.[45] People who were vehemently against immigration sat down to talk to asylum seekers; staunch opponents of nuclear power went for coffee with ardent advocates; champions of the European Union had a beer with those who called for the return of the Deutsche Mark.[46] Yet the one thing they had in common was a shared goal to gain insight into each other's perspectives.

The results were significant. Surveys with participants before and after their talks revealed that even a two-hour conversation was enough for them to begin to understand each other's perspective and helped to dismantle prejudice.[47] After the conversations, participants considered people with divergent views to be less malicious, less incompetent and less poorly informed than they had before.[48] They also expressed a greater willingness to include such people in their own social groups and reported having gained a greater sense of what it was they had in common – typically the importance they each placed on family.[49] And fascinatingly, participants also reported that they both trusted fellow Germans more in general and agreed more with the statement that Germans generally care about the wellbeing of others, compared to when they were asked the same questions before the exercise.

Similarly inspiring initiatives specifically aimed at bringing different types of people together are taking place elsewhere across the globe. In Bristol in the UK, '91 Ways to Build a Global City' uses the unifying power of food to bring people of different cultural and ethnic heritages together. Over the dicing of onions, the mashing of potatoes and the kneading of pastry barriers break down, genuine connections are made and common ground established.[50] In New York, the Public Theatre is building on an ancient tradition of theatre bridging divides by bringing together people from different socio-economic backgrounds and all five boroughs of New York City to perform and discuss plays.[51] True to its promise to create theatre that is 'not only for the people, but by and of the people as well', its 'Public Works' initiative involves hundreds of citizens in its productions, while also facilitating discussions on whose stories get told, how are they told and how we can honour them.[52]

Sport also has a role to play here, with football, living up to its claim to be a great unifier, being used to unite former FARC guerrillas with civilian victims in Colombia,[53] refugees with locals in Italy,[54] and in the Middle East, Israeli and Palestinian schoolchildren.[55]

No matter how atomised or polarised our countries, cities and communities have become, it is through spending time with people who are different to us and exercising our muscles of cooperation, compassion and consideration that we can come to feel more connected to each other and develop a sense of shared fate and belonging.

Engineering diverse communities

In all of the examples we've explored so far in this chapter, participation has been voluntary. The even bigger question is how we get people who may not *choose* to come together to do so. Again, there is a role government can play. And again, there is precedent, this time in Rwanda.

The roads of Kigali, the country's hilly capital city, usually throng with life. Moto-taxis zigzag between rickety 1980s sedans and the sleek, imported SUVs of government motorcades. Mud-encrusted jeeps and Land Cruisers jostle amongst the traffic, too, many returning from Volcanoes National Park where a six-hour trek brings permit-bearing hikers within metres of the country's elusive mountain gorillas. Yet on the last Saturday of every month these busy roads are nearly deserted, except for the checkpoints on the main roads manned by police, who politely inquire of any travellers: what urgent business takes you away from your *Umuganda* duties today?

Umuganda translates as 'coming together in common purpose to achieve an outcome'.[56] It takes many forms: some communities devote their three-hour public service commitment to building projects such as high schools, and thanks to these efforts over 3,000 classrooms have been built since *Umuganda* was formally reinstated by the government in 1998 as part of the healing process following Rwanda's devastating 1994 genocide.[57] Other *Umuganda* activities include gardening, pruning public hedges and flower beds, picking up litter and filling potholes. To be sure, these hours of free labour have a significant economic impact; their value has been estimated at $60 million since 2007 alone.[58] But they also serve a crucial community-building purpose: 'Most people like it because it's the only day you meet your neighbours,' says Faustin Zihiga, who works at a bank in Kigali.[59] At one *Umuganda*, he undertakes garden work with a group of other men from his area while keeping up a lively conversation. 'See those people over there, talking?' Zihiga points out. 'They haven't met all week and now they are meeting up. It helps a lot because the more you get to know each other, the more you're socially connected.'[60]

As important as the three hours of public work is the hour-long community meeting that typically follows, at least in rural areas, where neighbours gather to discuss important issues.[61] Unlike relatively new forms of community dialogue such as Camden's Citizens' Assembly, these *Umuganda* meetings have their roots in hundreds of years of *ubudehe*, or community labour and decision-making, a practice that long pre-dates Rwanda's colonial occupation by Belgian and German forces that began in the nineteenth century. They are all the more important today, barely twenty-five years after the country was torn apart by violence that pitted neighbour against neighbour.

Indeed *Umuganda* has played a vital role in restoring trust within Rwanda's communities because it is about much more than beautifying roads and building schools. 'If there are specific problems or social issues, like maybe a neighbour is making a lot of noise, you can say something about it, and the community members may decide to visit and see what the issue is,' says Zihiga. Or 'if we see an elderly person who is struggling, perhaps they need a new roof built, then people will help out to build it together.[62] What makes *Umuganda* especially remarkable is that in the Rwandan context, community members may well include both survivors of genocide and its perpetrators.[63]

This mandatory volunteering programme does have its detractors. There are those who see *Umuganda* as yet another means of government control – understandable given Rwanda's strict, quasi-authoritarian government. Some have voiced concern that wealthy Rwandans tend to simply pay the fine for non-participation, and others worry that the way their work is apportioned ends up falling along pre-existing class, power and gender lines.[64] All of these are legitimate concerns. But the underlying motivation – to embrace the nation's tradition of community work and use face-to-face, side-by-side activity to strengthen bonds between *all* citizens – remains powerful and uplifting. Moreover, the reality is that if we leave it to individuals to initiate crossing the divide it's only ever likely to be a relatively small, self-selecting group that will do so. We need to find ways of ensuring that regular, structured interactions between different kinds of people take place if we are to move towards more inclusion, more acceptance of difference and a greater sense of togetherness and common purpose. And governments can play an important role in making this happen.

This is more realistic than it may seem. After all, a number of countries including Switzerland, South Korea and Israel have mandatory military service, so it wouldn't be such a big leap for their governments to mandate community service, too. And in some places prototype schemes are already being tested. In the summer of 2019 French president Emmanuel Macron piloted compulsory civic service for teenagers.[65] In its inaugural iteration, 2,000 15- and 16-year-olds spent a month living together in a randomly assigned group.[66] For the first two weeks, they got to know one another through a series of activities: they went on orienteering expeditions and field trips, participated in workshops and learned first aid. After dinner each evening they exchanged ideas and opinions in a structured way, debating different social issues such as discrimination and gender equality with the help of a facilitator. In the second half of the programme they volunteered at local charities or for the municipal government. And it wasn't just during activities that the teenagers had to work together: in the houses where they boarded they were tasked with deciding amongst themselves how to divide up chores. It is interesting to note too that as part of the pilot, mobile phones were banned except for an hour in the evening, increasing the chances of meaningful bonding without tech distractions.[67]

And there are other, less intensive programs governments or local authorities could consider. How about weekly mandatory cooking, drama or sports classes that children from schools with different socio-economic, ethnic or faith intakes have to take together? Or a state-funded annual camping trip that 16-year-olds across divides have to participate in? It should be recognised that such initiatives will be all the more effective if they are designed to give participants a role in shaping their own experience; the more input participants have, the more likely they are to be engaged. So if it's cooking classes, the students should decide what the meal should be each week. If it's drama, how about structured improvisations based on their own experiences that they can dissect and discuss?

By facilitating regular structured interactions in which children of different backgrounds actively do things together, we are helping the next generation not only practise listening to each other and learn how to reconcile and manage their differences but also enabling them to identify their common interests and therefore feel more connected to each other.

The future is in our hands

This Lonely Century presents us with unique challenges – economic, political, social and technological. It is a time when huge swathes of the population feel alone despite it never having been easier to connect; an age in which we identify increasingly on the basis of difference, yet are ever more aware of how intertwined our lives are with others across the globe; a time in which our local communities desperately need strengthening and the bridges that join different communities together very often still need to be built.

It is an age of great challenges and contradictions, but it is also a time of hope. For we have a real opportunity right now to come together to co-create a distinctly different future, one in which we reconnect capitalism with community and compassion, ensure that we do a much better job of listening to people from all backgrounds and enable them to have a voice, and actively practise community in an inclusive and tolerant form. We don't have to feel this lonely or atomised anymore.

To realise these ambitions will take a shift in legislative and funding priorities, and our politicians and business leaders will need to show real commitment to change when it comes to social and racial justice and how workers are protected. But society is not just a top-down initiative. *We* create society too. So if we are to feel less lonely and reconnect with each other, taking personal responsibility on a daily basis will be just as crucial. We need to commit to meaningful change in the way we shape and live our everyday lives, whilst recognising that the cards we have been dealt, economically and socially, may well impact the extent to which we are able to do so.

Some of this is about taking small steps that may not seem much at first glance, but over time will accrue meaningful impact. Things like bringing biscuits into the office to share with colleagues, or putting our phones away and being more present with our partners and families. Inviting a neighbour over for coffee or committing to buy more at our local shops and show up to events at our local community centre. Taking on more responsibility in groups we're already part of, or pushing ourselves to join new ones, even when that may seem daunting.

Other steps will demand more of us, whether it's campaigning for a political candidate who speaks to cohesion not division, standing in solidarity with a group that is being unfairly demonised or discriminated against, or boycotting a company once we learn about its unacceptable working conditions, even if we like what it sells or the convenience it proffers.

More generally it's a shift in mindset that is needed. We need to recast ourselves from consumers to citizens, from takers to givers, from casual observers to active participants. This is about taking opportunities to exercise our listening skills whether in the context of work, our family lives or in our friendships. It's about accepting that sometimes what's best for the collective is not what's in our own immediate self-interest. It's about committing to using our voice where we can to effect positive change, even if putting our head above the parapet will be uncomfortable. And it means committing also to actively practising empathy, something in the cut and thrust of daily life we can easily forget to do.

And whilst some may decry calls for a greater focus on 'softer' values, we also need to commit to making kindness and consideration for others our lodestar, drawing inspiration from the selfless acts of so many people across the globe during the heights of the pandemic, whether we're talking about the West Midlands volunteer who searched high and low during lockdown until he found a shop selling milk in glass bottles in order to support a blind man who needed them to tell the difference between different liquids in his fridge;[68] the Italian university students who left a note in the stairwell of an apartment block in the southern city of Bari, offering to help the buildings' elderly or vulnerable residents with grocery shopping and other tasks;[69] or the Arkansas teenager who poignantly wrote to the *New York Times* that although they hadn't really been able to do too many things for people other than texting and calling people to let them know they had been thinking of them during lockdown, they had 'been trying to make an effort to talk to people I don't normally talk with, just offering a fun conversation to distract from the world'.[70]

We also need to rush less and stop and talk more, whether it's to the neighbour we often pass but never speak to, a stranger who has lost their way, or someone who's visibly feeling lonely – even when we're feeling overloaded and busy. We need to break out of our self-suffocating digital privacy bubbles and engage with the people around us, even when our default is to put on our headphones and scroll on our phones. We need to encourage our children to ask the child sitting alone at lunch whether they'd like company, and we need to do the same for that work colleague who always eats their lunch alone *al desko*, even when we'd rather dine on our own. We need to show more gratitude to those who care for others in society, and more generally say thank you more –

whether it's to our partner, our colleagues at work or even to our new AI helpers like Alexa.

I don't underestimate the challenge all this poses, and inevitably there will be times when we will fall short. But such steps are crucial. For the more we neglect our responsibility to care for each other – whether it is stroking an ill parent's arm, being on the end of the phone for a friend who's going through a hard time or even just smiling at a neighbour – the less skilled we will become at doing all of these things. And the less skilled we become at doing these things, the less humane our society will inevitably be.

The antidote to the Lonely Century can ultimately only ever be us being there for each other, regardless of who the other is. If we are to come together in a world that's pulling apart, nothing less is called for.

Acknowledgements

They say it takes a village to raise a child, so too has it been the case for this book.

In particular I would like to thank:

My editors: Juliet Brooke at Sceptre and Talia Krohn at Crown for their always insightful feedback, commitment to the project and care. I couldn't have asked for more from either of you.

Jonny Geller for believing in me and this book in its earliest days and providing wise and considered steers throughout; Kristine Dahl for her input and support; and Dave Wirtschafter for his championing of me and the project.

Rebecca Folland, Melis Dagoglu and Grace McCrum for their brilliant work getting *The Lonely Century* sold all over the world, Kate Brunt and Kishan Rajani for their great jacket design, David Milner and Amanda Waters for their meticulousness, and Helen Flood, Maria Garbutt-Lucero and Louise Court for promoting the book with such skill and enthusiasm. The fabulous team at Crown especially David Drake, Annsley Rosner, Gillian Blake, Megan Perritt and Rachel Aldrich. And also Viola Hayden, Ciara Finan and Tamara Kawar for all their help.

I am extremely grateful to:

Professor Debora Spar, Professor Nouriel Roubini, Professor Ian Goldin, Professor Anton Emmanuel, Professor Amit Sood, Professor Philippe Marliere, Professor Gillian Peele, Jamie Bartlett, Jamie Susskind, Ann De Sollar and Liran Morav for their thoughtful comments on early drafts of particular chapters.

Lucy Fleming, my lead research assistant, for her acute intelligence, attention to detail and deep commitment. Daniel Janes, Tatiana Pignon, Jerry O'Shea, Shaun Matthews, Aisha Sobey, Cara Claassen, Raffaele

Buono, Xenobe Purvis and Karis Hustad for their valuable research contributions. And Adam Lorand, Romain Chenet, Molly Russell, Amy O'Brien, Jonas Eberhardt, Tiffany Lam, Benjamin Brundu-Gonzalez, Christopher Lambin, Emily Lombardo, Levi Hord, Rowan Hart, Sam Hall, Pamela Combinido, Daniel Smith, Hannah Cocker, Theo Cosaert, Oliver Purnell, Rhys Thomas, Ollie Collett, Allie Dichiara, Tim White, Debra Winberg, Nicolò Pennucci and Kim Darrah for their help on various chapters. I appreciate all your hard work.

My family, in particular my sister Arabel Hertz, father Jonathan Hertz and aunt Shoshana Gelman. And my late mother Leah Hertz whose brilliance and compassion continues to inspire me every day.

My friends, who not only put up with my disappearing into the writing bubble for lengthy periods but regularly let me know that they were still there for me. Especially Tim Samuels, Adam Nagel, Abby Turk, Estelle Rubio, James Fletcher, Caroline Daniel, Molly Nyman, Julia Leal Hartog, Michelle Kohn, Ruth and David Joseph, Len Blavatnik, Rachel Weisz, Joshua Ramo, Diane McGrath, Alex Cooke, Craig Cohon, Gina Bellman, Mark and Diana, Yonit Levi and ShaoLan Hsueh; my Wasatch family across the Atlantic; and importantly Roderick Miller, Thierry Lapouge, Amber Zohra, Kevin Plummer, Mattie Garvin, Ellie Rudolph, Tony Varnava, Sandra Virgo and Lucy Soutter for helping me feel part of a community and providing a weekly dose of fun. I remain always grateful to the late Philip Gould and the late David Held for their friendship and guidance.

I would also like to thank Simon Halfon for his generosity and talent; Gabrielle Rifkind for her wisdom; Gennifer Morris for keeping me organised; Lisa Cawthorn, Jinji Garland, Stephanie Nightingale and Gary Trainer for helping counter all those hours at my desk; Samara Fagoti Jalloul for her unrelenting positivity; Will Wentworth and Cindy Palmano for being especially kind neighbours; the Cohen family for always hosting the warmest of gatherings; and Professor Henrietta Moore and Professor David Price for bringing me full circle back to my original academic home – University College London.

Most of all I want to thank Danny Cohen for his generosity, intellect and love. Once again this would be a lesser book without his input and support and the process would have been a far lonelier one. On all fronts I know how lucky I am.

Select Bibliography

Alberti, Fay Bound. *A Biography of Loneliness: The History of an Emotion* (Oxford: Oxford University Press, 2019).

Arendt, Hannah. *The Origins of Totalitarianism* (New York: Harcourt, 1951).

Aristotle. *Nicomachean Ethics*. Translated and edited by Roger Crisp (Cambridge: Cambridge University Press, 2000).

Bartlett, Jamie. *The People vs. Tech: How the Internet is Killing Democracy, and How We Can Save It* (London: Ebury Press, 2018).

Bloodworth, James. *Hired: Six Months Undercover in Low-Wage Britain* (London: Atlantic Books, 2018).

Buller, E. Amy. *Darkness Over Germany: A Warning from History* (London: Longmans, Green, & Co., 1943).

Cacioppo, J. and William Patrick. *Loneliness: Human Nature and the Need for Social Connection* (New York: W.W. Norton & Co., 2009).

Carpenter, Julie. *Culture and Human-Robot Interaction in Militarized Spaces: A War Story* (Farnham: Ashgate, 2016).

Deaton, Angus, and Anne Case. *Deaths of Despair and the Future of Capitalism* (Princeton: Princeton University Press, 2020).

De Tocqueville, Alexis. *Democracy in America*. Translated by Henry Reeve. Edited by Isaac Kramnick (New York: W.W. Norton & Co., 2007).

Dewey, John. *Democracy and Education* (New York: Macmillan, 1916).

Durkheim, Émile. *The Elementary Forms of the Religious Life*. Translated by Carol Closman. Edited by Mark Cladis (Oxford: Oxford University Press, 2008).

Field, Tiffany. *Touch*. Second Edition (Cambridge, Mass: MIT Press, 2014).

Frey, Carl Benedikt. *The Technology Trap* (Princeton: Princeton University Press, 2019).

Gray, Mary L., and Siddharth Suri. *Ghost Work: How to Stop Silicon Valley from Building a New Global Underclass* (New York: Houghton Mifflin, 2019).

Harcourt, Bernard E. *Illusion of Order: The False Promise of Broken Windows Policing* (Cambridge, Mass: Harvard University Press, 2001).

Held, David. *Models of Democracy*. Third Edition (Cambridge: Polity Press, 2006).

Hortulanus, R., A. Machielse, and L. Meeuwesen, eds. *Social Isolation in Modern Society* (London: Routledge, 2009).

Jacobs, Jane. *The Death and Life of Great American Cities* (New York: Random House, 1961).

Jung, Carl. *Memories, Dreams, Reflections*. Translated by Clara Winston and Richard Winston. Edited by Aniela Jaffe (New York: Vintage, 1989).

Levy, David. *Love and Sex With Robots* (New York: HarperCollins, 2007).

Lynch, James. *A Cry Unheard: New Insights into the Medical Consequences of Loneliness* (Baltimore: Bancroft Press, 2000).

Marx, Karl, and Friedrich Engels. *Karl Marx, Friedrich Engels: Collected Works*. Vol. 3 (London: Lawrence & Wishart, 1975).

Mudde, Cas, and Cristóbal Rovira Kaltwasser. *Populism: A Very Short Introduction* (Oxford: Oxford University Press, 2017).

Norris, Pippa, and Ronald Inglehart, *Cultural Backlash: Trump, Brexit, and Authoritarian Populism* (Cambridge: Cambridge University Press, 2019).

Nowak, Martin A., and Roger Highfield. *SuperCooperators: Beyond the Survival of the Fittest: Why Cooperation, Not Competition, is the Key of Life* (Edinburgh: Canongate, 2012).

Oldenburg, Ray. *The Great Good Place* (Philadelphia: Da Capo, 1999).

Piketty, Thomas. *Capital in the Twenty-First Century*. Translated by Arthur Goldhammer (Cambridge, Mass: Harvard University Press, 2014).

Putnam, Robert. *Bowling Alone: The Collapse and Revival of American*

Community (New York: Simon & Schuster, 2000).

Quart, Alissa. *Squeezed: Why Our Families Can't Afford America* (New York: Ecco, 2018).

Riess, Helen, and Liz Neporent. *The Empathy Effect* (Boulder, Colorado: Sounds True, 2018).

Roberts, Sarah T. *Behind the Screen: Content Moderation in the Shadows of Social Media* (New Haven; London: Yale University Press, 2019).

Rosenblum, Nancy. *Good Neighbors: The Democracy of Everyday Life in America* (Cambridge, Mass: Princeton University Press, 2018).

Schawbel, Dan. *Back to Human: How Great Leaders Create Connection in the Age of Isolation* (New York: Da Capo, 2018).

Smith, Adam. *The Theory of Moral Sentiments*. Edited by Ryan Patrick Hanley (New York: Penguin Random House, 2010).

Susskind, Daniel. *A World Without Work: Technology, Automation and How we Should Respond* (London: Allen Lane, 2020).

Susskind, Jamie. *Future Politics* (Oxford: Oxford University Press, 2018).

Turkle, Sherry. *Alone Together: Why We Expect More from Technology and Less from Each Other.* Revised Edition (New York: Basic Books, 2017).

Twenge, Jean M. *iGen: Why Today's Super-Connected Kids Are Growing Up Less Rebellious, More Tolerant, Less Happy – and Completely Unprepared for Adulthood – and What That Means for the Rest of Us* (New York: Simon & Schuster, 2017).

Yang, Keming. *Loneliness: A Social Problem* (London; New York: Routledge, 2019).

Zuboff, Shoshana. *The Age of Surveillance Capitalism: The Fight for a Human Future at the New Frontier of Power* (New York: Public Affairs, 2019).

Notes

CHAPTER ONE:
This is the Lonely Century

1 'Covid-19: One Third of Humanity under Virus Lockdown', *The Economic Times*, 25 March 2020, https://economictimes.indiatimes.com/news/international/world-news/covid-19-one-third-of-humanity-under-virus-lockdown/articleshow/74807030.cms?from=mdr; Mia Jankowicz, 'More People Are Now in "Lockdown" Than Were Alive During World War II', ScienceAlert, 25 March 2020, https://www.sciencealert.com/one-third-of-the-world-s-population-are-now-restricted-in-where-they-can-go.

2 Ido Efrati, 'Calls to Israel's Mental Health Hotlines Spike during Coronavirus Crisis', Haaretz.com, 22 March 2020, https://www.haaretz.com/israel-news/.premium-calls-to-israel-s-mental-health-hotlines-spike-during-coronavirus-crisis-1.8698209?=&ts=_1585309786959.

3 'Coronavirus: "My Mum Won't Hug Me" – Rise in Calls to Childline about Pandemic', Sky News, 27 March 2020, https://news.sky.com/story/coronavirus-my-mum-wont-hug-me-rise-in-calls-to-childline-about-pandemic-11964290. The surge in loneliness is not limited to children. Shortly before the UK lockdown went into effect on 23 March, 10% of UK adults reported feelings of loneliness in the past two weeks. By 3 April, that statistic (measured by the same survey organisers) had more than doubled, to 24%, with 18- to 24-year-olds almost three times more likely to be experiencing loneliness during the lockdown. Whilst a survey

conducted in April 2020 in the US also found significant increases in loneliness during lockdown, especially amongst millennials and Generation K. See, respectively, 'Loneliness During Coronavirus', Mental Health Foundation, 16 June 2020, https://www.mentalhealth.org.uk/coronavirus/coping-with-loneliness; 'Report: Loneliness and Anxiety During Lockdown', SocialPro, April 2020, https://socialpronow.com/loneliness-corona/.

4   Peter Hille, 'Coronavirus: German Phone Helplines at "Upper limits"', DW.com, 24 March 2020, https://www.dw.com/en/coronavirus-german-phone-helplines-at-upper-limits/a-52903216.

5   Cigna, 'Loneliness and the Workplace: 2020 U.S. Report', January 2020, https://www.multivu.com/players/English/8670451-cigna-2020-loneliness-index/docs/CignaReport_1579728920153-379831100.pdf.

6   'Two Thirds of Germans Think the Country Has a Major Loneliness Problem', *The Local* (Germany), 23 March 2018, https://www.thelocal.de/20180323/two-thirds-of-germans-think-the-country-has-a-major-loneliness-problem.

7   Janene Pieters, 'Over a Million Dutch Are Very Lonely', *NL Times*, 21 September 2017, https://nltimes.nl/2017/09/21/million-dutch-lonely.

8   Rick Noack, 'Isolation is rising in Europe. Can loneliness ministers help change that?, *Washington Post*, 2 February 2018, https://www.washingtonpost.com/news/worldviews/wp/2018/02/02/isolation-is-rising-in-europe-can-loneliness-ministers-help-change-that/.

9   'Einsamkeitsgefühl', Bundesamt für Statistik, 2017, https://www.bfs.admin.ch/bfs/de/home/statistiken/bevoelkerung/migration-integration/integrationindikatoren/indikatoren/einsamkeitsgefuehl.html.

10 Barbara Taylor, 'Are We More Lonely than Our Ancestors?', BBC Radio 3: Free Thinking, 2019, https://www.bbc.co.uk/programmes/articles/2hGYMPLFwx5lQyRPzhTHR9f/are-we-more-lonely-than-our-ancestors. According to a 2017 report published by the Jo Cox Commission on Loneliness more than 9 million people in the UK often or always feel lonely, and 42% of people have no friends at work according to a survey carried out in 2014 by the charity Relate. See 'Combatting Loneliness One Conversation at a Time: A Call to Action' (Jo Cox Commission on Loneliness, 15 December

2017), 8, https://www.ageuk.org.uk/globalassets/age-uk/
documents/reports-and-publications/reports-and-briefings/active-
communities/rb_dec17_jocox_commission_finalreport.pdf;
'Friends', Relate.org, 2014, https://www.relate.org.uk/policy-
campaigns/our-campaigns/way-we-are-now-2014/friends.

11 Connor Ibbetson, 'A Quarter of Britons Don't Have a Best Friend',
YouGov, 25 September 2019, https://yougov.co.uk/topics/
relationships/articles-reports/2019/09/25/quarter-britons-dont-have-
best-friend; Alexandra Topping, 'One in 10 Do Not Have a Close
Friend and Even More Feel Unloved, Survey Finds', *Guardian*, 12
August 2014, https://www.theguardian.com/lifeandstyle/2014/
aug/12/one-in-ten-people-have-no-close-friends-relate.

12 Emma Elsworthy, 'More than Half of Britons Describe Their
Neighbours as "Strangers"', *Independent*, 29 May 2018, https://
www.independent.co.uk/news/uk/home-news/britons-neighbours-
strangers-uk-community-a8373761.html; Emma Mamo, 'How to
Combat the Rise of Workplace Loneliness', Totaljobs, 30 July 2018,
https://www.totaljobs.com/insidejob/how-to-combat-the-rise-of-
workplace-loneliness/.

13 For South Korea, see Ju-young Park, 'Lonely in Korea? You're Not
Alone', *Korea Herald*, 3 April 2019, http://www.koreaherald.com/
view.php?ud=20190403000445; 'South Korea: Likelihood of Feeling
Lonely Often 2020', Statista, accessed 1 June 2020, https://www.
statista.com/statistics/1042186/south-korea-likelihood-loneliness/.
For China, see Ye Luo and Linda J. Waite, 'Loneliness and
Mortality Among Older Adults in China', *The Journals of
Gerontology Series B, Psychological Sciences and Social Sciences* 69, no. 4
(July 2014), 633–45, https://doi.org/10.1093/geronb/gbu007.
For Japan, see Michael Hoffman, 'Japan Struggles to Keep
Loneliness at Arm's Length', *Japan Times*, 10 November 2018,
https://www.japantimes.co.jp/news/2018/11/10/national/media-
national/japan-struggles-keep-loneliness-arms-length/#.XtUW01
NKhok. In India, 50% of survey respondents thought it
likely that they would spend most of 2020 lonely; see 'India –
Opinion on Likelihood of Loneliness 2019 and 2020', Statista,
28 January 2020, https://www.statista.com/statistics/1041015/
india-opinion-likelihood-of-loneliness/. One in five Australians

report that they 'rarely or never have someone to talk to'; see Melissa Davey, 'Loneliness Study Finds One in Five Australians Rarely or Never Have Someone to Talk To', *Guardian*, 8 November 2018, https://www.theguardian.com/australia-news/2018/nov/09/loneliness-study-finds-one-in-five-australians-rarely-or-never-have-someone-to-talk-to. While statistics about loneliness in South America and Africa are more rare, this is more the result of a lack of inquiry, rather than evidence for low levels. In South Africa, for instance, one in ten older adults already experience severe loneliness; see Nancy Phaswana-Mafuya and Karl Peltzer, 'Prevalence of loneliness and associated factors among older adults in South Africa,' 2017, http://ulspace.ul.ac.za/bitstream/handle/10386/2783/phaswana-mafuya_prevalence_2017.pdf. One in six adolescents in Latin America and the Caribbean was found to be lonely; see S.R. Sauter, L.P. Kim and K.H. Jacobsen, 'Loneliness and friendlessness among adolescents in 25 countries in Latin America and the Caribbean', *Child and Adolescent Mental Health* 25 (2020), 21–27, https://doi.org/10.1111/camh.12358.Research in early-developing Latin American countries also points to poverty as highly correlated with social isolation and loneliness; see Rubén Kaztman, 'Seduced and Abandoned: The Social Isolation of the Urban Poor', *Cepal Review* 75 (2001).

14   Jason Danely, 'The Limits of Dwelling and Unwitnessed Death', *Cultural Anthropology* 34 no. 2 (2019), https://doi.org/10.14506/ca34.2.03.

15   Note that 'Saito San' is a composite character. Details adapted from Shiho Fukada, 'Japan's Prisons Are a Haven for Elderly Women', *Bloomberg*, 16 March 2018, https://www.bloomberg.com/news/features/2018-03-16/japan-s-prisons-are-a-haven-for-elderly-women.

16   'Jailed for Stealing Grapes: The Motives of Japan's Elderly Inmates', BBC News, 18 February 2019, https://www.bbc.com/news/world-asia-47197417.

17   Asakuma Mei, 'Japan's Jails a Sanctuary for Seniors', *NHK World*, 25 December 2019, https://www3.nhk.or.jp/nhkworld/en/news/backstories/761/.

18   Fukada, 'Japan's Prisons Are a Haven for Elderly Women'.

19 'Jailed for Stealing Grapes: The Motives of Japan's Elderly Inmates';
Hiroyuki Kuzuno, 'Neoliberalism, Social Exclusion, and Criminal
Justice: A Case in Japan', *Hitosubashi Journal of Law and Politics*,
40 (2012), 15–32.

20 Tom Underwood, 'Forgotten Seniors Need Time, Care', *AJC
Atlanta News*, 5 October 2010, https://www.ajc.com/news/
opinion/forgotten-seniors-need-time-care/
s6mdH3uUuYzZRcApmVYmvL/.

21 'Over a Million Older People in the UK Regularly Feel Lonely',
Age UK, 3 May 2014, https://www.ageuk.org.uk/latest-news/
archive/over-1-million-older-people-in-uk-feel-lonely/.

22 Emily Rauhala, 'He Was One of Millions of Chinese Seniors
Growing Old Alone. So He Put Himself up for Adoption.',
Washington Post, 2 May 2018, https://www.washingtonpost.com/
world/asia_pacific/he-was-one-of-millions-of-chinese-seniors-
growing-old-alone-so-he-put-himself-up-for-adoption/2018/
05/01/53749264-3d6a-11e8-912d-16c9e9b37800_story.html.

23 Indeed it was this experience that motivated me to begin
researching loneliness amongst the generation I call Generation K.
For a brief introduction to my work on Generation K ('K' after
their heroine, Katniss Everdeen), see, for example, 'Think
Millennials Have It Tough? For Generation K, Life Is Even
Harsher', *Guardian*, 19 March 2016, https://www.theguardian.com/
world/2016/mar/19/think-millennials-have-it-tough-for-generation-
k-life-is-even-harsher.

24 Jamie Ballard, 'Millennials Are the Loneliest Generation', YouGov,
30 July 2019, https://today.yougov.com/topics/lifestyle/articles-
reports/2019/07/30/loneliness-friendship-new-friends-poll-survey.

25 Clare Murphy, 'Young More Lonely than the Old', BBC News, 25
May 2010, http://news.bbc.co.uk/1/hi/health/8701763.stm;
'Children's and Young People's Experiences of Loneliness', Office
for National Statistics, 2018, https://www.ons.gov.uk/
peoplepopulationandcommunity/wellbeing/articles/
childrensandyoungpeoplesexperiencesofloneliness/2018#how-
common-is-loneliness-in-children-and-young-people.

26 'Daily Chart – Loneliness is pervasive and rising, particularly
among the young', *Economist*, 31 August 2018, https://www.

economist.com/graphic-detail/2018/08/31/loneliness-is-pervasive-and-rising-particularly-among-the-young.

27   These figures relate to loneliness's impact on life expectancy. See Julianne Holt-Lunstad, Timothy B. Smith and J. Bradley Layton, 'Social Relationships and Mortality Risk: A Meta-Analytic Review', *PLOS Medicine* (2010), https://doi.org/10.1371/journal.pmed. See in particular Figure 6. Whilst this study uses the language of insufficient social relationships or poor social relationships versus adequate ones, and finds that those with adequate social relationships have a 50% greater likelihood of survival compared to those with poor or insufficient social relationships, the studies incorporated in this analysis do not themselves all use this language; some look at social isolation, others loneliness, others lack of social support. In a follow-up 2015 study which included more than double the number of studies and ten times the number of participants compared with the previous meta-analysis, and also attempted to disaggregate the research on social isolation and that on loneliness, the authors found that social isolation and loneliness have a similarly negative impact on our risk of death. See Julianne Holt-Lunstad et al., 'Loneliness and Social Isolation as Risk Factors for Mortality: A Meta-Analytic Review', *Perspectives on Psychological Science*, 10, no. 2 (2015). For more details on calculating the health consequences of loneliness and social isolation, see Chapter Two.

28   Julianne Holt-Lunstad, 'The Potential Public Health Relevance of Social Isolation and Loneliness: Prevalence, Epidemiology, and Risk Factors', *Public Policy & Aging Report* 27, no. 4 (2017), 127–30, https://doi-org.libproxy.ucl.ac.uk/10.1093/ppar/prx030. See Chapter Two, notes 7 and 8, for a fuller discussion on how loneliness is defined in different studies.

29   Holt-Lunstad et al., 'Social Relationships and Mortality Risk'; see also Holt-Lunstad et al., 'Loneliness and Social Isolation as Risk Factors for Mortality'.

30   Corinne Purtill, 'Loneliness costs the US almost $7 billion extra each year', *Quartz*, 28 October 2018, https://qz.com/1439200/loneliness-costs-the-us-almost-7-billion-extra-each-year/.

31   HM Treasury, 'Policy paper: Spending Round 2019', Gov.uk, 4

September 2019, https://www.gov.uk/government/publications/spending-round-2019-document/spending-round-2019.

32 Kate Ferguson, 'Lonely Brits are costing the economy £1.8 billion a year, report reveals', *The Sun*, 20 March 2019, https://www.thesun.co.uk/news/8675568/lonely-brits-are-costing-the-economy/.

33 Emma Mamo, 'How to combat the rise of workplace loneliness', Total Jobs, https://www.totaljobs.com/insidejob/how-to-combat-the-rise-of-workplace-loneliness/.

34 Technically, it's the Revised UCLA Loneliness Scale; in 1980, some of the wording was made more positive to control for people's tendency to 'want' a higher score. See D. Russell, L.A. Peplau and C.E. Cutrona, 'The Revised UCLA Loneliness Scale: Concurrent and Discriminant Validity Evidence', *Journal of Personality and Social Psychology* 39, no. 3 (1980), 472–80. The original paper has been cited more than 1,500 times.

35 Note that some of the answers are reverse-scored. In a formal academic setting, participants wouldn't know which questions are reverse-scored.

36 Rhitu Chatterjee, 'Americans Are A Lonely Lot, And Young People Bear The Heaviest Burden', NPR, 1 May 2018, https://www.npr.org/sections/health-shots/2018/05/01/606588504/americans-are-a-lonely-lot-and-young-people-bear-the-heaviest-burden; 'Loneliness and the Workplace: 2020 U.S. Report', Cigna, January 2020, 3, https://www.multivu.com/players/English/8670451-cigna-2020-loneliness-index/docs/CignaReport_1579728920153-379831100.pdf.

37 See for example E.G. West, 'The Political Economy of Alienation: Karl Marx and Adam Smith', *Oxford Economic Papers* 21, no. 2 (March 1969), 1–23, https://www.jstor.org/stable/2662349?seq=1; Fay Bound Alberti, 'Stop medicalising loneliness – history reveals it's society that needs mending', *The Conversation*, 19 November 2019, https://theconversation.com/stop-medicalising-loneliness-history-reveals-its-society-that-needs-mending-127056; Bill Callanan, 'Loneliness as a Theme in the Life and Writings of C.G. Jung', *Irish Association of Humanistic and Integrative Psychotherapy*, Irish Association of Humanistic and Integrative Psychotherapy 31 (Winter 1997), https://iahip.org/inside-out/issue-31-winter-1997/loneliness-as-a-theme-in-the-life-and-writings-of-c-g-

jung%E2%80%A8; Sean Redmond, 'The loneliness of science
fiction', *Disruptr*, 5 May 2019, https://disruptr.deakin.edu.au/
society/the-loneliness-of-science-fiction/; Aldous Huxley, *The Doors
of Perception* (Chatto & Windus, 1954); *Black Mirror* Season 4,
Episode 4, 'Hang the D.J.'; Marie Hendry, *Agency, Loneliness and the
Female Protagonist in the Victorian Novel* (Cambridge Scholars
Publishing, 2019). For more on Arendt's linkage between loneliness
and totalitarianism, see Chapter Three.

38 'Majority Worldwide Say Their Society Is Broken – an Increasing
Feeling among Britons', Ipsos MORI, 12 September 2019, https://
www.ipsos.com/ipsos-mori/en-uk/global-study-nativist-populist-
broken-society-britain.

39 Gallup's 'State of the Global Workplace' (2017) shows how bad
things are. The data comes from 155 countries and is available at
https://www.gallup.com/workplace/238079/state-global-
workplace-2017.aspx.

40 'GSS Data Explorer: Can People Be Trusted', NORC at the University
of Chicago, https://gssdataexplorer.norc.org/variables/441/vshow.

41 'Pope Francis' morning Mass broadcast live every day', *Vatican
News*, 8 March 2020, https://www.vaticannews.va/en/pope/
news/2020-03/pope-francis-daily-mass-casa-santa-marta-coronavirus.
html; Shirley Ju, 'How DJ D-Nice's Club Quarantine Became an
Isolation Sensation', *Variety*, 28 March 2020, https://variety.
com/2020/music/news/dj-d-nice-club-quarantine-rihanna-michelle-
obama-interview-1203541666/. Anti-Chinese hate speech went up by
900%, while there was a 70% increase in hate speech between kids
and teens in online chat rooms between December 2019 and March
2020. See 'Rising Levels of Hate Speech & Online Toxicity During
This Time of Crisis,' *Light*, 2020, https://l1ght.com/Toxicity_
during_coronavirus_Report-L1ght.pdf; see too Elise Thomas, 'As the
Coronavirus Spreads, Conspiracy Theories Are Going Viral Too',
Foreign Policy, 14 April 2020, https://foreignpolicy.com/2020/04/14/
as-the-coronavirus-spreads-conspiracy-theories-are-going-viral-too/;
Queenie Wong, 'Coronavirus sparks a different kind of problem for
social networks', CNet, 25 March 2020, https://www.cnet.com/
news/on-twitter-facebook-and-tiktok-racism-breaks-out-amid-
coronavirus-pandemic/?ftag=CAD-03-10aaj8j.

42 For the interplay of race and loneliness, see, for instance, British Red Cross, 'Barriers to Belonging: An exploration of loneliness among people from Black, Asia and Minority Ethnic Backgrounds' (British Red Cross, 2019), 12, original report available for download at https://www.redcross.org.uk/about-us/what-we-do/we-speak-up-for-change/barriers-to-belonging#Key%20findings; 'Loneliness and the Workplace: 2020 U.S. Report' (Cigna, 2020), https://www.cigna.com/static/www-cigna-com/docs/about-us/newsroom/studies-and-reports/combatting-loneliness/cigna-2020-loneliness-report.pdf. Note too that in schoolchildren as young as 8 years old, experiencing racial discrimination is a strong predictor of loneliness and depression nine months later. See N. Priest et al., 'Effects over time of self-reported direct and vicarious racial discrimination on depressive symptoms and loneliness among Australian school students', *BMC Psychiatry* 17, no. 50 (2017), https://doi.org/10.1186/.s12888-017-1216-3. For more on sexist behaviour and loneliness, see Y. Joel Wong et al., 'Meta-Analyses of the Relationship Between Conformity to Masculine Norms and Mental Health-Related Outcomes', *Journal of Counseling Psychology* 64, no. 1 (2017), 80–93, http://dx.doi.org/10.1037/cou0000176 ; Mark Rubin et al., 'A confirmatory study of the relations between workplace sexism, sense of belonging, mental health, and job satisfaction among women in male-dominated industries', *Journal of Applied Social Psychology* 49, no. 5 (2019), 267–282, https://doi.org/10.1111/jasp.12577.

43 See for example on declining attendance to religious service: Lydia Saad, 'Catholics' Church Attendance Resumes Downward Slide', Gallup News, 9 April 2018, https://news.gallup.com/poll/232226/church-attendance-among-catholics-resumes-downward-slide.aspx; 'In U.S., Decline of Christianity Continues at Rapid Pace', Pew Research Center, 17 October 2019, https://www.pewforum.org/2019/10/17/in-u-s-decline-of-christianity-continues-at-rapid-pace/; The Church of England Research and Statistics, 'Statistics for Mission 2018', Research and Statistics 2019, https://www.churchofengland.org/sites/default/files/2019-10/2018StatisticsForMission.pdf; for other European countries, see Philip S. Brenner, 'Cross-National Trends in Religious Service Attendance', *Public Opinion Quarterly* 80, no. 2 (May 2016), 563–83,

https://www.ncbi.nlm.nih.gov/pmc/articles/PMC4888582/; Harry
Freedman, 'Are American synagogues on the road to renewal – or
perdition?', *Jewish Chronicle*, 21 December 2018, https://www.thejc.
com/judaism/features/are-american-synagogues-on-the-road-to-
renewal-or-perdition-1.474204. Note however that religious service
attendance and commitment remains high in Muslim populations
in sub-Saharan Africa, the Middle East and South Asia, and in
Christian populations in sub-Saharan Africa and Latin America.
'How religious commitment varies by country among people of
all ages', Pew Research Center, 13 June 2018, https://www.
pewforum.org/2018/06/13/how-religious-commitment-varies-by-
country-among-people-of-all-ages/. For declining parent–teacher
organisations, trade union membership, and numbers of close
friendships, see, for instance, Segann March, 'Students, parents pay
the price for PTA membership declines', *Shreveport Times*, 6 May
2016, https://eu.shreveporttimes.com/story/news/
education/2016/05/06/students---and-their-parents---pay-price-pta-
membership-declines/83970428/; Brittany Murray, Thurston
Domina, Linda Renzulli and Rebecca Boylan, 'Civil Society Goes
to School: Parent-Teacher Associations and the Equality of
Educational Opportunity', *RSF* 5, no. 3 (March 2019), 41–63,
https://doi.org/10.7758/RSF.2019.5.3.0; Camilla Turner, 'Working
mothers now too busy to join parent teacher associations, leading
headmistress says', the *Telegraph*, 18 November 2019, https://www.
telegraph.co.uk/news/2019/11/18/working-mothers-now-busy-join-
parent-teacher-associations-leading/; Niall McCarthy, 'The State of
Global Trade Union Membership I.E., [Infographic]', *Forbes*, 6 May
2019, https://www.forbes.com/sites/niallmccarthy/2019/05/06/
the-state-of-global-trade-union-membership-infographic/#3584b31c
2b6e; Miller McPherson, Lynn Smith-Lovin, and Matthew E.
Brashears, 'Social Isolation in America: Changes in Core Discussion
Networks over Two Decades', *American Sociological Review* 71, no. 3
(June 2006), 353–75, https://doi.org/10.1177/000312240607100301.

44 For a more detailed look at the decline of touch, see Tiffany Field,
Touch, 2nd ed. (MIT Press, 2014). For the US: Jean M. Twenge,
Ryne A. Sherman, Brooke E. Wells, 'Declines in Sexual Frequency
among American Adults, 1989–2014', *Archives of Sexual Behavior* 46

(2017), 2389–401, https://doi.org/10.1007/s10508-017-0953-1; see also Kate Julian, 'Why Are Young People Having So Little Sex?' *The Atlantic*, December 2018, https://www.theatlantic.com/magazine/archive/2018/12/the-sex-recession/573949/; for Britain: 'British people "having less sex" than previously' BBC, 8 March 2019, https://www.bbc.co.uk/news/health-48184848; for global statistics (esp. Australia, Finland, Japan): 'Are we really in the middle of a global sex recession?' *Guardian*, 14 November 2018, https://www.theguardian.com/lifeandstyle/shortcuts/2018/nov/14/are-we-really-in-the-middle-of-a-global-sex-recession.

45 Alison Flood, 'Britain has closed almost 800 libraries since 2010, figures show', *Guardian*, 5 December 2019, https://www.theguardian.com/books/2019/dec/06/britain-has-closed-almost-800-libraries-since-2010-figures-show; 'Table 1: IMLS Appropriations History, 2008–2015 (Budget Authority in 000s)' Institute of Museum and Library Services, 2015, https://www.imls.gov/assets/1/News/FY14_Budget_Table.pdf; Peggy McGlone, 'For third year in a row, Trump's budget plan eliminates arts, public TV and library funding', *Washington Post*, 18 March 2019, https://www.washingtonpost.com/lifestyle/style/for-third-year-in-a-row-trumps-budget-plan-eliminates-arts-public-tv-and-library-funding/2019/03/18/e946db9a-49a2-11e9-9663-00ac73f49662_story.html.

46 Jonathan D. Ostry, Prakash Loungani and Davide Furceri, 'Neoliberalism: Oversold?' IMF, June 2016, https://www.imf.org/external/pubs/ft/fandd/2016/06/pdf/ostry.pdf.

47 Lawrence Mishel and Julia Wolfe, 'CEO compensation has grown 940% since 1978', Economic Policy Institute, 14 August 2019, https://www.epi.org/publication/ceo-compensation-2018/.

48 Richard Partington, 'Inequality: is it rising, and can we reverse it?' *Guardian*, 9 September 2019, https://www.theguardian.com/news/2019/sep/09/inequality-is-it-rising-and-can-we-reverse-it. Original data from IFS Deaton Review. See also Trade Unions Congress analysis of ONS Wealth and Assets Survey (latest data measures, period April 2016 to March 2018) as discussed in Nikki Pound, 'Record wealth inequality shows why our economy is rigged against working people', Trade Unions Congress, 6 December 2019, https://www.tuc.org.uk/blogs/record-wealth-

inequality-shows-why-our-economy-rigged-against-working-people.

49 Poverty is a risk factor both for social isolation and loneliness. See Jan Eckhard, 'Does Poverty Increase the Risk of Social Isolation? Insights Based on Panel Data from Germany', *The Sociology Quarterly* 59, no. 2 (May 2018), 338–59, https://doi.org/10.1080/0038 0253.2018.1436943; 'How do you identify or recognise the most lonely?' Campaign to End Loneliness, 2020, https://www. campaigntoendloneliness.org/frequently-asked-questions/identify-most-isolated/; Emily Cuddy and Richard V. Reeves, 'Poverty, isolation, and opportunity', The Brookings Institution, 31 March 2015, https://www.brookings.edu/blog/social-mobility-memos/2015/03/31/poverty-isolation-and-opportunity/; Miriam J. Stewart et al., 'Poverty, Sense of Belonging and Experiences of Social Isolation', *Journal of Poverty* 13, no. 2 (May 2009), 173–195, https://www.researchgate.net/publication/240235963_Poverty_Sense_of_Belonging_and_Experiences_of_Social_Isolation.

50 '2020 Edelman Trust Barometer', Edelman Holdings, 19 January 2020, https://www.edelman.com/trustbarometer.

51 'Margaret Thatcher Interview for *Sunday Times*', Margaret Thatcher Foundation, 1 May 1981, https://www.margaretthatcher.org/document/104475.

52 See for example Martin A. Nowak and Roger Highfield, *SuperCooperators: Beyond the Survival of the Fittest: Why Cooperation, Not Competition, is the Key of Life* (Canongate, 2012).

53 Jean M. Twenge, W. Keith Campbell, and Brittany Gentile, 'Increases in individualistic words and phrases in American books, 1960-2008', *PloS One* 7, no. 7 (2012), https://doi.org/10.1371/journal.pone.0040181.

54 John Tierney, 'A Generation's Vanity, Heard Through Lyrics', *The New York Times*, 25 April 2011, https://www.nytimes.com/2011/04/26/science/26tier.html.

55 Xi Zou and Huajian Cai, 'Charting China's Rising Individualism in Names, Songs, and Attitudes', *Harvard Business Review*, 11 March 2016, https://hbr.org/2016/03/charting-chinas-rising-individualism-in-names-songs-and-attitudes.

CHAPTER TWO:
Loneliness Kills

1   See for example Louise C. Hawkley and John P. Capitanio,
    'Perceived social isolation, evolutionary fitness and health
    outcomes: a lifespan approach', *Philosophical Transactions of the
    Royal Society*, (May 2015): https://doi.org/10.1098/rstb.2014.0114.

2   On loneliness and chronic inflammation, see K. Smith, S. Stewart,
    N. Riddell and C. Victor, 'Investigating the Relationship Between
    Loneliness and Social Isolation With Inflammation: A Systematic
    Review,' *Innovation in Aging* 2, no. 2 (November 2018), 839–40,
    https://doi.org/10.1093/geroni/igy023.3129.; Lisa M. Jaremka et al.,
    'Loneliness promotes inflammation during acute stress',
    Psychological Science 24, no. 7 (July 2013), 1089–97, https://doi.
    org/10.1177/0956797612464059. On loneliness and immune response,
    see Angus Chen, 'Loneliness May Warp Our Genes, And Our
    Immune Systems', NPR, 29 November 2015, https://www.npr.org/
    sections/health-shots/2015/11/29/457255876/loneliness-may-warp-
    our-genes-and-our-immune-systems.

3   See N. Grant, M. Hamer and A. Steptoe, 'Social Isolation and
    Stress-related Cardiovascular, Lipid, and Cortisol Responses', *Annals
    of Behavioral Medicine* 37 (2009), 29–37, https://doi.org/10.1007/
    s12160-009-9081-z; Andrew Steptoe et al., 'Loneliness and
    neuroendocrine, cardiovascular, and inflammatory stress responses
    in middle-aged men and women', *Psychoneuroendocrinology* 29, no. 5
    (2004), 593–611, https://www.ncbi.nlm.nih.gov/pubmed/15041083;
    L. D. Doane and E. K. Adam, 'Loneliness and cortisol: Momentary,
    day-to-day, and trait associations', *Psychoneuroendocrinology* 35 (2010),
    430–41, doi: 10.1016/j.psyneuen.2009.08.005.

4   L.C. Hawkley, R.A. Thisted, C.M. Masi and J.T. Cacioppo,
    'Loneliness predicts increased blood pressure: 5-year cross-lagged
    analyses in middle-aged and older adults', *Psychology and Aging* 25,
    no. 1 (March 2010), 132–41, https://doi.org/10.1037/a0017805; Kerry
    J. Ressler, 'Amygdala activity, fear, and anxiety: modulation by
    stress', *Biological Psychiatry* 67, no. 12 (June 2010), 1117–19, https://
    doi.org/10.1016/j.biopsych.2010.04.027.

5   Steven W. Cole, John P. Capitanio, Katie Chun, Jesusa M.G. Arevalo,

Jeffrey Ma and John T. Cacioppo, 'Myeloid differentiation architecture of leukocyte transcriptome dynamics in perceived social isolation', *Proceedings of the National Academy of Sciences* 112, no. 49 (December 2015), 15142–47, https://www.pnas.org/content/pnas/early/2015/11/18/1514249112.full.pdf; for a layman-friendly read, see 'Loneliness triggers cellular changes that can cause illness, study shows', University of Chicago, 23 November 2015, https://www.sciencedaily.com/releases/2015/11/151123201925.htm.

6   'Stress Weakens the Immune System', American Psychological Association, 23 February 2006, https://www.apa.org/research/action/immune.

7   This is from a meta-analysis that looked at twenty-three different studies; 'Measures of social relationships met inclusion criteria for loneliness if they were consistent with its definition as a subjective negative feeling associated with someone's perception that their relationships with others are deficient'. Because it is a meta-study there are many different definitions of loneliness that were used in the sub-studies, some of which were chronic. N.K. Valtorta et al., 'Loneliness and social isolation as risk factors for coronary heart disease and stroke: systematic review and meta-analysis of longitudinal observational studies', *BMJ Journals: Heart* 102, no. 13 (2016), 1009–16, http://dx.doi.org/10.1136/heartjnl-2015-308790; J.H. Tjalling et al., 'Feelings of loneliness, but not social isolation, predict dementia onset: results from the Amsterdam Study of the Elderly (AMSTEL)', *Journal of Neurology Neurosurgery and Psychiatry* (2012), doi: 10.1136/jnnp-2012-302755.

8   J. Holt-Lunstad et al., 'Loneliness and social isolation as risk factors for mortality: a meta-analytic review'. This is also a meta-analysis, so loneliness is defined in different ways. One meta-analysis might look at the data and results from potentially hundreds of studies on the same or very similar subjects, seeking patterns and drawing broad conclusions – an immensely useful way of combining insights across thousands of data points. In summarising loneliness research, however, this poses a slight challenge because each of the hundreds of 'source studies' might have had a slightly different definition of loneliness, or measured loneliness over a certain period of time. For that reason, in this

case, we can't categorically link these health problems to chronic versus situational loneliness because some of the studies in these meta-analyses looked at one, or the other, or didn't specify. (The UCLA Loneliness Scale only reports your loneliness *at that precise moment*, after all.)

9   In general terms, see S. Shiovitz-Ezra and L. Ayalon, 'Situational versus chronic loneliness as risk factors for all-cause mortality', *International Psychogeriatrics* 22, no. 3 (2010), 455–62, doi:10.1017/S1041610209991426; for work done in prisons with incarcerated people held in solitary confinement for at least fifteen days, see B.A. Williams et al., 'The Cardiovascular Health Burdens of Solitary Confinement', *Journal of General Internal Medicine* 34 (2019), 1977–80, https://doi.org/10.1007/s11606-019-05103-6. See also Adam Gabbatt, '"Social recession": how isolation can affect physical and mental health', *Guardian*, 18 March 2020, https://www.theguardian.com/world/2020/mar/18/coronavirus-isolation-social-recession-physical-mental-health; Gabriel Banschick, 'How to Manage the Psychological Effects of Quarantine', *Psychology Today*, 20 March 2020, https://www.psychologytoday.com/us/blog/the-intelligent-divorce/202003/how-manage-the-psychological-effects-quarantine; and also research looking at the effect of quarantine during SARS in Toronto in 2002–04 who surveyed 129 quarantined individuals shortly after their isolation ended. Post-traumatic stress was identified in 28.9%, and depression was found in 31.9%; see L. Hawryluck et al., 'SARS control and psychological effects of quarantine, Toronto, Canada', *Emerging Infectious Diseases* 10, no. 7 (2004), 1206–12, https://doi.org/10.3201/eid1102.040760.

10   James Lynch, *A Cry Unheard: New Insights into the Medical Consequences of Loneliness* (Bancroft Press, 2000), p.91.

11   S. Shiovitz-Ezra and L. Ayalon, 'Situational versus Chronic Loneliness as Risk Factors for All-Cause Mortality', *International Psychogeriatrics* 22, no. 3 (2010), 455–62.

12   See Nora Rubel, *Doubting the Devout: The Ultra-Orthodox in the Jewish-American Imagination* (Columbia University Press, 2009).

13   Avi Weiss, 'A Picture of the Nation', Taub Center, 14 (2018), http://taubcenter.org.il/wp-content/files_mf/pon201895.pdf; Tzvi Lev, 'Education rising, poverty dropping among haredim', *Israel National*

News, 31 December 2017, http://www.israelnationalnews.com/
News/News.aspx/240041.

14 The sources on the 'seven times' figure are from 2011–12; see for
example Shmuly Yanklowitz, 'An Obesity Problem in the Orthodox
Community?' 25 April 2012, https://jewishweek.timesofisrael.com/
an-obesity-problem-in-the-orthodox-community/; Ari Galahar,
'Haredi sector suffers from obesity', *Ynet News*, 1 September 2011,
https://www.ynetnews.com/articles/0,7340,L-4116222,00.html.

15 Nitsa Kasir and Dmitri Romanov, 'Quality of Life Among Israel's
Population Groups: Comparative Study' (The Haredi Institute for
Public Affairs, May 2018), 51.

16 Melrav Arlosoroff, 'Israel's Economic Future is Wasting Away in
Israel's Yeshivas', *Haaretz*, 13 November 2018, https://www.haaretz.
com/israel-news/business/.premium-israel-s-economic-future-is-
wasting-away-in-israel-s-yeshivas-1.6652106; 'Israeli women do it by
the numbers', *Jewish Chronicle*, 7 April 2014, https://www.thejc.
com/israeli-women-do-it-by-the-numbers-1.53785.

17 Tali Heruti-Sover, 'Ultra-Orthodox Women Work Less, Earn Less –
and Not by Choice, Study Shows', *Haaretz*, 30 April 2019, https://
www.haaretz.com/israel-news/.premium-ultra-orthodox-women-
work-less-earn-less-and-not-by-choice-study-shows-1.7183349; Sagi
Agmon, 'Report: Haredi employment is down; Haredi poverty is up',
Hiddush News, 21 December 2018, http://hiddush.org/article-23296-0-
Report_Haredi_employment_is_down;_Haredi_poverty_is_up.aspx.

18 Dan Zaken, 'Haredim aren't as poor as you think', *Globes*, 17
December 2018, https://en.globes.co.il/en/article-haredim-arent-as-
poor-as-you-think-1001265187.

19 'Live Long and Prosper: Health in the Haredi Community', Taub
Center for Social Policy Studies in Israel, 31 May 2016, http://
taubcenter.org.il/does-money-make-you-live-longer-health-in-the-
haredi-community/.

20 Researchers working on health in the Haredi community do note
that self-reported health may be unreliable, since there's a sense of
not wanting to 'air dirty laundry' to secular researchers by
admitting one is in poor health. But the life-expectancy statistics
seem to back up the truth behind the self-reports. It should also be
noted that whilst the Haredi community suffered more incidences

of coronavirus in 2020 than the greater Israeli population, ironically
in part because of how much they value community, the general
point still holds: Haredi life expectancy is higher than average. As
does the fact that community typically has a positive impact on life
expectancy. See ibid.; and for Covid-19 statistics, Nathan Jeffay, 'Two
Ultra-Orthodox Bastions Account for 37% of Israel's Virus Deaths',
The Times of Israel, 10 May 2020, https://www.timesofisrael.com/
two-ultra-orthodox-bastions-account-for-37-of-israels-virus-deaths/.

21 Dov Chernichovsky and Chen Sharony, 'The Relationship Between
Social Capital and Health in the Haredi Sector', Taub Center for
Social Policy Studies in Israel (December 2015), 3, http://taubcenter.
org.il/wp-content/files_mf/therelationshipbetweensocialcapitaland
healthintheharedisectorenglish.pdf.

22 See ibid., Figure 1.

23 See for example 'Measuring and Assessing Well-being in Israel',
OECD, 31 January 2016, Figure 3, https://www.oecd.org/sdd/
measuring-and-assessing-well-being-in-Israel.pdf.

24 David G. Myers, 'Religious Engagement and Well-Being', in *The
Oxford Handbook of Happiness*, ed. Ilona Boniwell, Susan A. David
and Amanda Conley Ayers (Oxford University Press, 2013); Bruce
Headey, Gerhard Hoehne and Gert G. Wagner, 'Does Religion
Make You Healthier and Longer Lived? Evidence for Germany',
Social Indicators Research 119, no. 3 (2014), 1335–61, https://doi.
org/10.1007/s11205-013-0546-x; Daniel E. Hall, 'Religious Attendance:
More Cost-Effective Than Lipitor?', *Journal of the American Board of
Family Medicine* 19, no. 2 (2006), https://pubmed.ncbi.nlm.nih.
gov/16513898/.

25 Robert A. Hummer et al., 'Religious Involvement and U.S. Adult
Mortality', *Demography* 36, no. 2 (1999), 273–85, https://pubmed.
ncbi.nlm.nih.gov/10332617/; see also Tyler J. VanderWeele,
'Religious Communities and Human Flourishing', *Current Directions
in Psychological Science* 26, no. 5 (2017), 476–81, https://doi.org/
10.1177/0963721417721526.

26 Nitsa Kasir and Dmitri Romanov, 'Quality of Life Among Israel's
Population Groups: Comparative Study' (The Haredi Institute for
Public Affairs, May 2018), 51.

27 Rabbi Dow Marmur, 'Ultra-Orthodox Jews Are Poorer, But Live

Longer. How Come? *Canadian Jewish News* 1 March 2017, https://www.cjnews.com/perspectives/opinions/ultra-orthodox-jews-poorer-live-longer-how-come.

28 Rock Positano, 'The Mystery of the Rosetan People', *Huffington Post*, 28 March 2008, https://www.huffpost.com/entry/the-mystery-of-the-roseta_b_73260.

29 B. Egolf et al., 'The Roseto effect: a 50-year comparison of mortality rates', *American Journal of Public Health* 82, no. 8 (August 1992), 1089–92, https://doi.org/10.2105/ajph.82.8.1089.

30 Ibid.; see also John G. Bruhn, Billy U. Philips and Stewart Wolf, 'Social readjustment and illness patterns: Comparisons between first, second and third generation Italian-Americans living in the same community', *Journal of Psychosomatic Research* 16, no. 6 (October 1972), 387–94, https://doi.org/10.1016/0022-3999(72)90063-3: 'The first generation reported more changes in family life, the second generation experienced more change in their personal lives and third generation reported more changes with respect to work and financial matters.'

31 Nicole Spector, '"Blue Zones": 6 secrets to borrow from people who live the longest', NBC News, 20 October 2018, https://www.nbcnews.com/better/health/blue-zones-6-secrets-borrow-people-who-live-longest-ncna921776.

32 Ibid.

33 See for example Joan B. Silk, 'Evolutionary Perspectives on the Links Between Close Social Bonds, Health, and Fitness' in *Sociality, Hierarchy, Health: Comparative Biodemography* (National Academies Press, 2014), p.6; Zack Johnson, 'The Brain On Social Bonds: Clues From Evolutionary Relatives', Society for Personality and Social Psychology, 29 June 2015, http://www.spsp.org/news-center/blog/brain-social-bonds; Mary E. Clark, 'Meaningful Social Bonding as a Universal Human Need', in *Conflict: Human Needs Theory*, ed. John Burton (Palgrave Macmillan, 1990), 34–59.

34 Monte Burke, 'Loneliness Can Kill You', *Forbes*, 6 August 2009, https://www.forbes.com/forbes/2009/0824/opinions-neuroscience-loneliness-ideas-opinions.html#75ec4deb7f85.

35 'The Consultation Letters of Dr William Cullen (1710-1790) at the Royal College of Physicians of Edinburgh', The Cullen Project,

http://www.cullenproject.ac.uk/docs/4509/. Cullen's prescription is even more interesting when we consider that in the century after his work, the 'treatment' for women's 'nervous weaknesses' was often ordered to be the opposite: bed rest, isolation and avoidance of any social endeavour, including reading. Such treatments are most famously the subject of Charlotte Perkins Gilman's short story 'The Yellow Wallpaper', in which the protagonist, confined to a single room for a similarly unnamed condition, slowly develops hallucinatory delusions.

36 See also 'The Harvard Study of Adult Development', Adult Development Study, 2015, https://www.adultdevelopmentstudy.org. They're now tracking the second generation!

37 Liz Mineo, 'Good Genes Are Nice, but Joy Is Better', *Harvard Gazette*, 11 April 2017, https://news.harvard.edu/gazette/story/2017/04/over-nearly-80-years-harvard-study-has-been-showing-how-to-live-a-healthy-and-happy-life/.

38 Inflammation is a good way of dealing with bacterial infection and acute injury, both problems we're more likely to have when we're on our own, rather than picking up viruses from other human beings – so in a way, ramping up inflammation when we feel isolated makes sense. See Angus Chen, 'Loneliness May Warp Our Genes, And Our Immune Systems', NPR, 29 November 2015, https://www.npr.org/sections/health-shots/2015/11/29/457255876/loneliness-may-warp-our-genes-and-our-immune-systems.

39 Elitsa Dermendzhiyska, 'Can Loneliness Kill You?', Medium, 7 November 2018, https://medium.com/s/story/can-loneliness-kill-you-6ea3cab4eab0.

40 Philip Hunter, 'The inflammation theory of disease', *EMBO Reports* 13, no. 11 (November 2012), 968–70, https://www.ncbi.nlm.nih.gov/pmc/articles/PMC3492709. It is the impact on inflammation that 'explains very clearly why lonely people fall at increased risk for cancer, neuro-degenerative disease and viral infections as well,' says UCLA's Steve Cole, professor of medicine and psychiatry; Angus Chen, 'Loneliness May Warp Our Genes, And Our Immune Systems', NPR, 29 November 2015, https://www.npr.org/sections/health-shots/2015/11/29/457255876/loneliness-may-warp-our-genes-and-our-immune-systems.

41 Bert N. Uchino et al., 'Social Support and Immunity', in *The Oxford Handbook of Psychoneuroimmunology*, ed. Suzanne Segerstrom (Oxford University Press, 2012), https://www.oxfordhandbooks. com/view/10.1093/oxfordhb/9780195394399.001.0001/oxfordhb-9780195394399-e-12. Rhinoviruses (common colds), HIV and some cancer-causing viruses are more active in socially isolated patients.

42 I.S. Cohen, 'Psychosomatic death: Voodoo death in modern perspective', *Integrative Psychiatry*, 16 (1985), 46–51, https://psycnet. apa.org/record/1985-25266-001.

43 J.K. Kiecolt-Glaser et al., 'Psychosocial Modifiers of Immunocompetence in Medical Students', *Psychosomatic Medicine* 46, no. 1 (1984): 7–14, https://pubmed.ncbi.nlm.nih.gov/6701256/; *idem*, 'Urinary cortisol levels, cellular immunocompetency and loneliness in psychiatric inpatients', *Psychosomatic Medicine*, 46 (1984), 15–23.

44 N. Grant et al., 'Social isolation and stress-related cardiovascular, lipid, and cortisol responses', *Annals of Behavioral Medicine* 37, no. 1 (February 2009), 29–37, https://www.ncbi.nlm.nih.gov/ pubmed/19194770; Y.C. Yang et al., 'Social isolation and adult mortality: the role of chronic inflammation and sex differences', *Journal of Health and Social Behavior* 54 (2013), 183–203, https://www. ncbi.nlm.nih.gov/pmc/articles/PMC3998519/.

45 'Loneliness can be as bad for health as a chronic long-term condition, says GP leader', Royal College of General Practitioners, 12 October 2017, https://www.rcgp.org.uk/about-us/news/2017/ october/loneliness-can-be-as-bad-for-health-as-a-chronic-long-term-condition-says-gp-leader.aspx.

46 See Rachel P. Maines, *The Technology of Orgasm: 'Hysteria', the Vibrator, and Women's Sexual Satisfaction* (Johns Hopkins University Press, 1999).

47 H. Meltzer et al., 'Feelings of Loneliness among Adults with Mental Disorder,' *Social Psychiatry and Psychiatric Epidemiology* 48, no. 1 (2013), 5–13, doi:10.1007/s00127-012-0515-8. Note that the study was based on an analysis of 2007 data.

48 See John D. Cacioppo, Louise C. Hawkley, and Ronald A. Thisted, 'Perceived Social Isolation Makes Me Sad: Five Year Cross-Lagged Analyses of Loneliness and Depressive Symptomatology in the

Chicago Health, Aging and Social Relations Study', *Psychology and Aging* 25, no. 2 (June 2010): 453–463, https://doi.org/10.1037/a0017216. In a study of older Dutch adults with depression, 83% reported feelings of loneliness, compared with only 32% of non-depressed people. B. Hovast et al., 'Loneliness Is Associated with Poor Prognosis in Late-Life Depression: Longitudinal Analysis of the Netherlands Study of Depression in Older Persons', *Journal of Affective Disorders* 185 (2015), 1–7, doi:10.1016/j.jad.2015.06.036. Whilst recent research into teenagers has found that not only the lonelier a young person is the more likely they are to suffer depression, but also that the more depressed a young person is, the more likely they are to be lonely. See R. Rich et al., 'Causes of depression in college students: A cross-lagged panel correlational analysis', *Psychological Reports* 60 (1987), 27–30, https://doi.org/10.2466/pro.1987.60.1.27; Marina Lalayants and Jonathan D. Price, 'Loneliness and depression or depression related factors among child welfare-involved adolescent females', *Child and Adolescent Social Work Journal* 324 (April 2015), 167–76, https://doi-org.gate3.library.lse.ac.uk/10.1007/s10560-014-0344-6.

49 Louise Boyle, 'When everyday environments become anxious spaces', Wellcome Collection, 14 November 2018, https://wellcomecollection.org/articles/W-BEUREAAASpazif.

50 Dhruv Khullar, a physician and researcher at Weill Cornell Medicine in New York, for example, has said that short periods of isolation can cause increase anxiety or depression 'within days'. Adam Gabbatt, '"Social recession": how isolation can affect physical and mental health', *Guardian*, 18 March 2020, https://www.theguardian.com/world/2020/mar/18/coronavirus-isolation-social-recession-physical-mental-health. Whilst studies in mammals have shown that a period of social isolation as short as two weeks can produce noticeable chemical changes in the brain, spurring aggression and anxious behaviours; California Institute of Technology, 'How social isolation transforms the brain: A particular neural chemical is overproduced during long-term social isolation, causing increased aggression and fear', *ScienceDaily*, 17 May 2018, https://www.sciencedaily.com/releases/2018/05/180517113856.htm.

51 X. Liu et al., 'Depression after exposure to stressful events: lessons learned from the severe acute respiratory syndrome epidemic', *Comprehensive Psychiatry* 53 (2012), 15–23. The median length of quarantine was fourteen days.

52 P. Wu et al., 'Alcohol abuse/dependence symptoms among hospital employees exposed to a SARS outbreak', *Alcohol and Alcoholism* 43 (2008), 706–12, https://doi.org/10.1093/alcalc/agn073; idem., 'The psychological impact of the SARS epidemic on hospital employees in China: exposure, risk perception, and altruistic acceptance of risk', *Canadian Journal of Psychiatry* 54 (2009), 302–11, https://pubmed.ncbi.nlm.nih.gov/19497162/.

53 J.K. Hirsch et al., 'Social problem solving and suicidal behavior: ethnic differences in the moderating effects of loneliness and life stress', *Archives of Suicide Research*, 16, no. 4 (2012), 303–15, https://doi.org/10.1080/13811118.2013.722054.

54 Francie Hart Broghammer, 'Death by Loneliness', Real Clear Policy, 6 May 2019, https://www.realclearpolicy.com/articles/2019/05/06/death_by_loneliness_111185.html.

55 Rebecca Nowland, 'The Role of Loneliness in Suicidal Behaviour' (APPG Meeting on Suicide and Self-Harm Prevention, 30 April 2019); S. Wiktorsson et al., 'Attempted suicide in the elderly: characteristics of suicide attempters 70 years and older and a general population comparison group', *American Journal of Geriatric Psychiatry* 18, no. 1 (2010), 57–67, https://pubmed.ncbi.nlm.nih.gov/20094019/; Henry O'Connell et al., 'Recent developments, Suicide in older people', *BMJ* 329 (October 2004), 895–99, https://www.ncbi.nlm.nih.gov/pmc/articles/PMC523116.

56 R.E. Roberts et al., 'Suicidal thinking among adolescents with a history of attempted suicide', *Journal of the American Academy of Child and Adolescent Psychiatry* 37, no. 12 (December 1998), 1294–300, https://www.ncbi.nlm.nih.gov/pubmed/9847502.

57 M.L. Goodman et al., 'Relative social standing and suicide ideation among Kenyan males: the interpersonal theory of suicide in context', *Social Psychiatry and Psychiatric Epidemiology* 52, no. 10, (October 2017): 1307-1316, https://www.ncbi.nlm.nih.gov/pubmed/28821916; Bimala Sharma et al., 'Loneliness, Insomnia and Suicidal Behavior among School-Going Adolescents in Western

Pacific Island Countries: Role of Violence and Injury', *International Journal of Environmental Research and Public Health* 14, no. 7 (July 2017): 791, https://www.ncbi.nlm.nih.gov/pmc/articles/PMC5551229/.

58 Katherine C. Schinka et al., 'Psychosocial Predictors and Outcomes of Loneliness Trajectories from Childhood to Early Adolescence', *Journal of Adolescence* 36, no. 6 (December 2013), 1251–60, https://doi.org/10.1016/j.adolescence.2013.08.002.

59 For the definitive analysis of deaths of despair in the US in relation to all of these factors, see Angus Deaton and Anne Case, *Deaths of Despair and the Future of Capitalism* (Princeton University Press, 2020). On divorce: Anne Case, 'Morbidity and Mortality in the 21st Century', *Brookings Papers on Economic Activity* (Spring 2017), 431, https://www.brookings.edu/wp-content/uploads/2017/08/casetextsp17bpea.pdf; Charles Fain Lehman, 'The Role of Marriage in the Suicide Crisis', Institute for Family Studies, 1 June 2020, https://ifstudies.org/blog/the-role-of-marriage-in-the-suicide-crisis. On declining religious attendance: W. Bradford Wilcox et al., 'No Money, No Honey, No Church: The Deinstitutionalisation of Religious Life Among the White Working Class', *Research on Social Work Practice* 23 (2012): 227–250, https://doi.org/ 10.1108/S0277-2833(2012)0000023013. On political consequences and labour policy: Shannon M. Monnat, 'Deaths of Despair and Support for Trump in the 2016 Presidential Election', The Pennsylvania State University Department of Agricultural Economics, Sociology, and Education, 4 December 2016, https://aese.psu.edu/directory/smm67/Election16.pdf; see also Robert Defina et al., 'De-unionization and Drug Death Rates', *Social Currents* 6, no. 1 (February 2019), 4–13, https://doi.org/10.1177/2329496518804555; Jerzy Eisenberg–Guyot et al., 'Solidarity and disparity: Declining labor union density and changing racial and educational mortality inequities in the United States', *American Journal of Industrial Medicine* 63, no. 3 (March 2020), 218–231, https://doi.org/10.1002/ajim.23081; Steven H. Woolf and Heidi Schoomaker, 'Life Expectancy and Mortality Rates in the United States, 1959-2017', *JAMA* 322, no. 20 (November 2019), 1996–2016, doi:10.1001/jama.2019.16932. Note too that while 'deaths of despair' is often used in relation only to American, non-Hispanic

white men (including, for the most part, in Case and Deaton's research), there is strong evidence that the patterns noted here are not racially confined. See, for instance, Peter A. Muennig et al., 'America's Declining Well-Being, Health, and Life Expectancy: Not Just a White Problem', *American Journal of Public Health* 108, no. 12 (2018), 1626–31, https://doi.org/ 10.2105/AJPH.2018.304585.

60 Laura Entis, 'Scientists are working on a pill for loneliness', *Guardian*, 26 January 2019, https://www.theguardian.com/ us-news/2019/jan/26/pill-for-loneliness-psychology-science-medicine.

61 M.P. Roy, A. Steptoe and C. Kirschbaum, 'Life events and social support as moderators of individual differences in cardiovascular and cortisol reactivity', *Journal of Personality and Social Psychology* 75, no. 5 (November 1998), 1273–81, https://pubmed.ncbi.nlm.nih. gov/9866187/.

62 Robin Wright, 'How Loneliness from Coronavirus Isolation Takes Its Own Toll', *New Yorker*, 23 March 2020, https://www.newyorker. com/news/our-columnists/how-loneliness-from-coronavirus-isolation-takes-its-own-toll/amp; J.A. Coan, H.S. Schaefer, and R.J. Davidson, 'Lending a hand: social regulation of the neural response to threat', *Psychological Sciences* 17, no. 12 (December 2006), 1032–39, doi:10.1111/j.1467-9280.2006.01832.x.

63 X. Pan and K.H. Chee, 'The power of weak ties in preserving cognitive function: a longitudinal study of older Chinese adults', *Aging and Mental Health* (April 2019), 1–8, doi:10.1080/13607863.2019.1 597015.

64 'Young people aged 18–24 (77%) and 25–34 (76%) are the age groups most likely to say their volunteering helped them feel less isolated . . .Over three-quarters of volunteers (77%) reported that volunteering improved their mental health and well-being. This benefit was more widespread than physical health benefits (53%)'. Amy McGarvey et al., 'Time Well Spent: A National Survey on the Volunteer Experience' National Council for Voluntary Organisations, January 2019, https://www.ncvo.org.uk/images/ documents/policy_and_research/volunteering/Volunteer-experience_Full-Report.pdf. See also D.C. Carr et al., 'Does Becoming A Volunteer Attenuate Loneliness Among Recently

Widowed Older Adults?', *Journal of Gerontology B* 73, no. 3 (2018), 501–10. doi:10.1093/geronb/gbx092.

65 Alexander L. Brown, Jonathan Meer and J. Forrest Williams, 'Why Do People Volunteer? An Experimental Analysis of Preferences for Time Donations', The National Bureau of Economic Research, May 2013, https://www.nber.org/papers/w19066.

66 C. Schwartz et al., 'Altruistic Social Interest Behaviors Are Associated With Better Mental Health', *Psychosomatic Medicine* 65, no.5 (September 2003), 778–85, doi: 10.1097/01.PSY.0000079378.39062.D4.

67 R.W. Hierholzer, 'Improvements in PSTD patients who care for their grandchildren', *American Journal of Psychiatry* 161 (2004), 176, https://pubmed.ncbi.nlm.nih.gov/14702274/.

68 M.F. Field et al., 'Elder retired volunteers benefit from giving message therapy to infants', *Journal of Applied Gerontology* 17 (1998), 229–39, https://doi.org/10.1177/073346489801700210.

69 Commission on Children at Risk, *Hardwired to Connect: The New Scientific Case for Authoritative Communities* (Institute for American Values, 2003).

70 S.L. Brown et al., 'Providing Social Support May Be More Beneficial than Receiving It: Results from a Prospective Study of Mortality', *Psychological Sciences* 14, no. 4 (2003), 320–27, https://doi.org/10.1111/1467-9280.14461.

71 Kelli Harding, *The Rabbit Effect: Live Longer, Happier, and Healthier with the Groundbreaking Science of Kindness* (Atria Books, 2019).

72 For example, the National Labor Relations Board was established in the US in 1935, and to this day 'work[s] to guarantee the rights of employees to bargain collectively.' 'Our History', National Labor Relations Board, 2020, https://www.nlrb.gov/about-nlrb/who-we-are/our-history; see also Christopher Conte and Albert R. Karr, *Outline of the U.S. Economy* (U.S. Dept. of State, Office of International Information Programs, 2001). In the UK the National Health Service was founded in 1948. See Peter Greengross, Ken Grant and Elizabeth Collini, 'The History and Development of The UK National Health Service 1948 – 1999', DFID Health Systems Resource Centre, July 2009, https://assets.publishing.service.gov.uk/media/57a08d91e5274a31e000192c/The-history-and-development-of-the-UK-NHS.pdf.

73 Search conducted on UK site, www.jobsite.co.uk. Advertised wages
     were compared to median UK wage rate.

74 William Booth, Karla Adam and Pamela Rolfe, 'In fight against
     coronavirus, the world gives medical heroes standing ovation',
     Washington Post, 26 March 2020, https://www.washingtonpost.
     com/world/europe/clap-for-carers/2020/03/26/3d05eb9c-6f66-11ea-
     a156-0048b62cdb51_story.html.

CHAPTER THREE:
The Lonely Mouse

1   Graziano Pinna et al., 'In Socially Isolated Mice, the Reversal of
     Brain Allopregnanolone down-Regulation Mediates the Anti-
     Aggressive Action of Fluoxetine', *Proceedings of the National
     Academy of Sciences of the United States of America* 100, no. 4 (2003),
     2035, https://doi.org/10.1073/pnas.0337642100. Interestingly in
     female mice, aggression did not develop.

2   This was first postulated by psychoanalyst Gregory Zilboorg in
     1938 and is backed up by subsequent studies. James V.P. Check,
     Daniel Perlman, Neil M. Malamuth, 'Loneliness and Aggressive
     Behaviour', *Journal of Social and Personal Relationships* 2, no. 3 (1985),
     243–52, https://www.sscnet.ucla.edu/comm/malamuth/pdf/
     85jspr2.pdf; D. Segel-Karpas and L. Ayalon, 'Loneliness and hostility
     in older adults: A cross-lagged model', *Psychology and Aging* 35, no.2
     (2020), 169–76, https://doi.org/10.1037/pag0000417; Ben Mijuskovic,
     'Loneliness and Hostility', *Psychology: A Quarterly Journal of Human
     Behavior* 20, nos. 3–4 (1983), 9–19, https://eric.ed.gov/?id=EJ297686.
     Loneliness has also been shown to increase feelings of anger and
     to decrease social skills (see John T. Cacioppo et al., 'Loneliness
     within a Nomological Net: An Evolutionary Perspective', *Journal of
     Research in Personality* 40, no. 6 (2006), 1054–85, https://doi.
     org/10.1016/j.jrp.2005.11.007). Meanwhile periods of isolation in
     previous periods of quarantine also have been seen to cause
     loneliness. Samantha K. Brooks et al., 'The psychological impact of
     quarantine and how to reduce it: rapid review of the evidence',
     Lancet 395, no. 10227 (March 2020), 919–20, https://doi.org/10.1016/
     S0140-6736(20)30460-8.

3   Mark Brown, 'In a lonely place', *One in Four Magazine*, 2010, http://www.oneinfourmag.org/index.php/in-a-lonely-place/.

4   Gillian A. Matthews et al., 'Dorsal Raphe Dopamine Neurons Represent the Experience of Social Isolation', *Cell* 164, no. 11 (2016), 617–31, doi 10.1016/j.cell.2015.12.040; Janelle N. Beadle et al., 'Trait Empathy as a Predictor of Individual Differences in Perceived Loneliness', *Psychological Reports* 110, no. 1 (2012), 3–15, https://doi.org/10.2466/07.09.20.PR0.110.1.3-15; Ryota Kanai et al., 'Brain Structure Links Loneliness to Social Perception', *Current Biology* 22, no. 20 (2012), 1975–9, https://doi.org/10.1016/j.cub.2012.08.045.

5   John T. Cacioppo et al., 'In the Eye of the Beholder: Individual Differences in Perceived Social Isolation Predict Regional Brain Activation to Social Stimuli', *Journal of Cognitive Neuroscience* 21, no. 1 (January 2009), 83–92, https://doi.org/10.1162/jocn.2009.21007; Stephanie Cacioppo et al., 'Loneliness and Implicit Attention to Social Threat: A High-Performance Electrical Neuroimaging Study', *Cognitive Neuroscience* 7, nos. 1–4 (2015), https://www.tandfonline.com/doi/abs/10.1080/17588928.2015.1070136.

6   John T. Cacioppo, Hsi Yuan Chen and Stephanie Cacioppo, 'Reciprocal Influences Between Loneliness and Self-Centeredness: A Cross-Lagged Panel Analysis in a Population-Based Sample of African American, Hispanic, and Caucasian Adults', *Personality and Social Psychology Bulletin* 43, no. 8 (13 June 2017), 1125–35, https://doi.org/10.1177/0146167217705120.

7   Randy Rieland, 'Can a Pill Fight Loneliness?' *Smithsonian Magazine*, 8 February 2019, https://www.smithsonianmag.com/innovation/can-pill-fight-loneliness-180971435/.

8   They believed, for instance, that their neighbours would be less likely to come together to try to solve a neighbourhood issue, such as disorderly behaviour; 'No Such Thing as Friendly Neighbourhoods for Lonely Young People', *Kings College London News*, 8 April 2019; original study at Timothy Matthews et al., 'Loneliness and Neighborhood Characteristics: A Multi-Informant, Nationally Representative Study of Young Adults', *Psychological Science* 30, no. 5 (April 2019), 765–75, https://doi.org/10.1177/0956797619836102.

9   For a more detailed introduction to populism and its dynamic definition, see Cas Mudde and Cristóbal Rovira Kaltwasser, *Populism* (Oxford University Press, 2017). Paul Taggart, Margaret Canovan, Jan-Werner Mueller, Michael Kazin, John Judis and Catherine Fieschi have also done excellent work on this topic.

10   Elisabeth Young-Bruehl, *Hannah Arendt: For the Love of the World* (Yale University Press, 2004), p.4.

11   Ibid., 105–7; Patrick Hayden, *Hannah Arendt: Key Concepts* (Routledge, 2014), p.4.

12   Young-Bruehl, *Hannah Arendt: For the Love of the World*, p.159.

13   David S. Wyman, *Paper Walls: America and the Refugee Crisis, 1938–1941* (University of Massachusetts Press, 1968), p.28.

14   Some scholars now believe 30–40% of the German population had been aware; see for example Peter Longerich, *Davon haben wir nichts gewusst! Die Deutschen und die Judenverfolgung 1933–1945* (Siedler Verlag, 2006); also see Robert Gellately, *Backing Hitler. Consent and Coercion in Nazi Germany* (Oxford University Press, 2001).

15   Young-Bruehl, *Hannah Arendt: For the Love of the World*, p.28.

16   Hannah Arendt, *The Origins of Totalitarianism: Part Three* (Harcourt, Brace & World, 1968), p.128.

17   Ibid., p.15.

18   Ibid., p.475.

19   Elisabeth Zerofsky, 'How Viktor Orbán Used the Coronavirus to Seize More Power', *New Yorker*, 9 April 2020, https://www.newyorker.com/news/letter-from-europe/how-viktor-orban-used-the-coronavirus-to-seize-more-power; Amy Goodman and Natashya Gutierrez, 'As Virus Spreads in Philippines, So Does Authoritarianism: Duterte Threatens Violence Amid Lockdown', Democracy Now, 3 April 2020, https://www.democracynow.org/2020/4/3/coronavirus_asia_philippines_rodrigo_duterte; Maya Wang, 'China: Fighting COVID-19 With Automated Tyranny', Human Rights Watch, 1 April 2020, https://www.hrw.org/news/2020/04/01/china-fighting-covid-19-automated-tyranny; Isaac Chotiner, 'The Coronavirus Meets Authoritarianism in Turkey', *New Yorker*, 3 April 2020, https://www.newyorker.com/news/q-and-a/the-coronavirus-meets-authoritarianism-in-turkey; Kenneth Roth, 'How Authoritarians Are Exploiting the COVID-19 Crisis to

Grab Power', Human Rights Watch, 3 April 2020, https://www.
hrw.org/news/2020/04/03/how-authoritarians-are-exploiting-covid-
19-crisis-grab-power.

20 R. Hortulanus, A. Machielse, and L. Meeuwesen, eds., *Social Isolation
    in Modern Society* (Routledge, 2009); Jan Eckhard, 'Does Poverty
    Increase the Risk of Social Isolation? Insights Based on Panel Data
    from Germany', *The Sociology Quarterly* 59, no. 2 (May 2018), 338–59,
    https://doi.org/10.1080/00380253.2018.1436943; Béatrice d'Hombres et
    al., 'Loneliness – an unequally shared burden in Europe', European
    Commission: Science for Policy Briefs, 2018, https://ec.europa.eu/
    jrc/sites/jrcsh/files/fairness_pb2018_loneliness_jrc_i1.pdf.

21 Arendt, *The Origins of Totalitarianism: Part Three,* p.176.

22 See, for example, Pippa Norris and Ronald Inglehart, *Cultural
    Backlash: Trump, Brexit, and Authoritarian Populism* (Cambridge
    University Press, 2019); John Springford and Simon Tilford,
    'Populism – Culture Or Economics?' Centre for European Reform,
    30 October 2017, https://www.cer.eu/insights/populism-
    %E2%80%93-culture-or-economics.

23 Nonna Mayer and Pascal Perrineau, 'Why Do They Vote for Le
    Pen?', *European Journal of Political Research* (1992), https://doi.
    org/10.1111/j.1475-6765.1992.tb00308.x.

24 C. Berning and C. Ziller, 'Social trust and radical right-wing
    populist party preferences', *Acta Politica* 52 (2017), 198–217, https://
    doi.org/10.1057/ap.2015.28.

25 Timothy P. Carney, 'How the Collapse of Communities Gave Us
    Trump', *Washington Examiner*, 15 February 2019, https://www.
    washingtonexaminer.com/opinion/how-the-collapse-of-
    communities-gave-us-trump; see original data at 'American Family
    Survey Summary Report', 2016, http://csed.byu.edu/wp-content/
    uploads/2016/10/AFS2016Report.pdf.

26 Daniel Cox and Robert P. Jones, 'Two-Thirds of Trump Supporters
    Say Nation Needs a Leader Willing to Break the Rules', PRRI, 7
    April 2016, https://www.prri.org/research/prri-atlantic-poll-
    republican-democratic-primary-trump-supporters/; Yoni
    Appelbaum, 'Americans Aren't Practicing Democracy Anymore',
    The Atlantic, October 2018, https://www.theatlantic.com/
    magazine/archive/2018/10/losing-the-democratic-habit.

27 Tito Boeri et al., 'Populism and Civil Society', *IMF Working Papers* 18, no. 245 (2018), 5, https://doi.org/10.5089/9781484382356.001.

28 This idea of democracy being something we actively need to practice comes up in works of thinkers as various as John Dewey, Alexis de Tocqueville and Nancy Rosenblum. See for example Alexis de Tocqueville, *Democracy in America, Part I* (orig. Saunders and Otley, 1835); John Dewey, *Democracy and Education* (Macmillan, 1916); Nancy Rosenblum, *Good Neighbors: The Democracy of Everyday Life in America* (Princeton University Press, 2018). See too Yoni Appelbaum's thoughtful essay 'Americans Aren't Practicing Democracy Anymore', *The Atlantic*, October 2018, https://www.theatlantic.com/magazine/archive/2018/10/losing-the-democratic-habit.

29 Carl Jung, *Memories, Dreams, Reflections*, edited by Aniela Jaffe, translated by Clara Winston and Richard Winston (Vintage, 1989), p. 356.

30 Tim Samuels, unbroadcast interviews with railroad workers, 2016.

31 See for example Timothy P. Carney, *Alienated America: Why Some Places Thrive While Others Collapse* (HarperCollins, 2019). See also Thomas Ferguson et al., 'The Economic and Social Roots of Populist Rebellion: Support for Donald Trump in 2016', Working Paper No. 83, Institute for New Economic Thinking, October 2018, https://www.ineteconomics.org/uploads/papers/WP_83-Ferguson-et-al.pdf; Lee Fang, 'Donald Trump Exploited Long-Term Economic Distress to Fuel His Election Victory, Study Finds', *Intercept*, 31 October 2018, https://theintercept.com/2018/10/31/donald-trump-2016-election-economic-distress/.

32 Declan Walsh, 'Alienated and Angry, Coal Miners See Donald Trump as Their Only Choice', *New York Times*, 19 August 2016, https://www.nytimes.com/2016/08/20/world/americas/alienated-and-angry-coal-miners-see-donald-trump-as-their-only-choice.html; Sarah Sanders and Christina Mullins, '2016 West Virginia Overdose Fatality Analysis', West Virginia Bureau for Public Health, 20 December 2017, https://dhhr.wv.gov/bph/Documents/ODCP%20Reports%202017/2016%20West%20Virginia%20Overdose%20Fatality%20Analysis_004302018.pdf; Ed Pilkington, 'What happened when Walmart left,' *Guardian*, 9 July 2017, https://www.

theguardian.com/us-news/2017/jul/09/what-happened-when-walmart-left; Calvin A. Kent, 'Crisis in West Virginia's Coal Counties', National Association of Counties, 17 October 2016, https://www.naco.org/articles/crisis-west-virginia's-coal-counties.

33 E.J. Dionne, Jr., Norman J. Ornstein and Thomas F. Mann, *One Nation After Trump: A Guide For the Perplexed, the Disillusioned, the Desperate, and the Not-Yet-Deported* (St. Martin's Press, 2017).

34 Angelique Chrisafis, 'Jean-Marie Le Pen fined again for dismissing Holocaust as "detail"', *Guardian*, 6 April 2016, https://www.theguardian.com/world/2016/apr/06/jean-marie-le-pen-fined-again-dismissing-holocaust-detail.

35 Lara Marlowe, 'Marine Le Pen: "The EU is dead. Long live Europe"', *Irish Times*, 23 February 2019, https://www.irishtimes.com/news/world/europe/marine-le-pen-the-eu-is-dead-long-live-europe-1.3801809.

36 Angelique Chrisafis, 'Marine Le Pen not guilty of inciting religious hatred', *Guardian*, 15 December 2015, https://www.theguardian.com/world/2015/dec/15/marine-le-pen-not-guilty-inciting-religious-hatred-lyon-french-front-national.

37 Peter H. Koepf, 'The AfD's populist rhetoric attracts those who are traumatized by the past and scared of the future', *German Times*, October 2019, http://www.german-times.com/the-afds-populist-rhetoric-attracts-those-who-are-traumatized-by-the-past-and-scared-of-the-future/; Johannes Hillje, 'Return to the Politically Abandoned: Conversations in Right-Wing Populist Strongholds in Germany and France', Das Progressive Zentrum, 2018, https://www.progressives-zentrum.org/wp-content/uploads/2018/10/Return-to-the-politically-abandoned-Conversations-in-right-wing-populist-strongholds-in-Germany-and-France_Das-Progressive-Zentrum_Johannes-Hillje.pdf. Seán Clarke, 'German elections 2017: full results', *Guardian*, 25 September 2017, https://www.theguardian.com/world/ng-interactive/2017/sep/24/german-elections-2017-latest-results-live-merkel-bundestag-afd.

38 Claude Brodesser-Akner, 'I Went to a Trump Rally Last Night and Mingled with the Crowd. Here's What Happened', New Jersey Advance Media, August 2018, https://www.nj.com/politics/2018/08/i_put_on_my_best_camouflage_shorts_and_went_to_a_t.

html; Kim Willsher, 'Rural France pledges to vote for Le Pen as next president', *Guardian*, 4 September 2016, https://www.theguardian.com/world/2016/sep/03/rural-france-pledges-to-vote-for-le-pen-president.

39 OECD, 'All in it together? The experience of different labour market groups following the crisis', *OECD Employment Outlook*, 2013, http://dx.doi.org/10.1787/empl_outlook-2013-5-en; Jason Furman, 'The American Working Man Still Isn't Working', *Foreign Affairs*, 19 September 2019, https://www.foreignaffairs.com/articles/united-states/2019-09-19/american-working-man-still-isnt-working. Note too that men's mental health suffered more than women's in this period: A. Bacigalupe, S. Esnaola, and U. Martín, 'The impact of the Great Recession on mental health and its inequalities: the case of a Southern European region, 1997-2013', *International Journal for Equity in Health* 15 (2016), https://doi.org/10.1186/s12939-015-0283-7. Note also, however, that men regained jobs faster than women: Dominic Rushe, 'Women Hit Hardest in US Economic Recovery as Jobs Growth Slows', *Guardian*, 6 April 2012, https://www.theguardian.com/business/2012/apr/06/women-hit-hard-us-economic-recession; Brian Groom, 'Low-skilled workers hit hardest by recession', *Financial Times*, 20 July 2011, https://www.ft.com/content/9e874afa-b2b4-11e0-bc28-00144feabdc0.

40 Indeed when Princeton's Noam Gidron and Harvard's Peter Hall analysed voting patterns in 20 higher-income countries between 1987 and 2014 (countries including Britain, the US and France) what they found was that the more a person perceived the social status of 'people like them' to have declined in the previous 25 years, the more likely that person was to vote right-wing populist. The group for which perceived social status had declined the most was working-class white men without a college education. Noam Gidron and Peter A. Hall, 'The politics of social status: economic and cultural roots of the populist right', *The British Journal of Sociology* (2017), https://scholar.harvard.edu/files/hall/files/gidronhallbjs2017.pdf. The late economist Alan Krueger found that work defined working men's identities more than women's, as measured by the amount of emotional distress it brought men vs.

women when they were no longer participating in the labour
force. See Alan B. Krueger, 'Where Have All the Workers Gone?
An Inquiry into the Decline of the U.S. Labor Force Participation
Rate,' *Brookings Papers on Economic Activity* 2 (2017), 1–87, https://
doi.org/10.1353/eca.2017.0012.

41 'Trump: We're putting our great coal miners back to work', Fox
Business, 21 August 2018, https://www.youtube.com/
watch?v=XnSlzBcLLGs.

42 Noam Gidron and Peter A. Hall, 'The politics of social status:
economic and cultural roots of the populist right', *The British
Journal of Sociology* 68, no. 1 (November 2017), S57–S84, https://doi.
org/10.1111/1468-4446.12319; idem., 'Understanding the political
impact of white working-class men who feel society no longer
values them', The London School of Economics, 28 December
2017, https://blogs.lse.ac.uk/politicsandpolicy/understanding-the-
political-impact-of-white-working-class-men/. At the same time,
shifts in cultural frameworks, marked by an increasing emphasis in
mainstream discourse on racial and gender equality, may have
threatened the subjective social status of any who may have relied
on the notion that they were white or male to underpin their own
sense of social standing. See also Noam Gidron and Peter A. Hall,
'Populism as a Problem of Social Integration', The Hebrew
University Department of Political Science, December 2018,
https://scholar.harvard.edu/files/hall/files/gidronhalldec2018.pdf.

43 Cited in Noam Gidron and Peter A. Hall, 'The politics of social
status: economic and cultural roots of the populist right'.

44 The appeal to community is particularly enticing; see Seymour
Martin Lipset, 'Democracy and Working-Class Authoritarianism',
American Sociological Review 24, no. 4 (1959), 482–501, https://doi.
org/10.2307/2089536.

45 'List of post-election Donald Trump rallies', Wikipedia, 2016,
https://en.wikipedia.org/wiki/List_of_post-election_Donald_
Trump_rallies.

46 Compared to Obama's midterm rallies, which were (anecdotally)
much less outfit-coordinated, far more people were in street
clothes rather than Democratic gear. See Katy Tur, 'Why Barack
Obama's Rallies Feel so Different from Donald Trump's', NBC

News, 5 November 2018, https://www.nbcnews.com/politics/
donald-trump/what-i-learned-last-weekend-s-rallies-donald-trump-
barack-n931576.

47 Claude Brodesser-Akner, 'I Went to a Trump Rally Last Night and
Mingled with the Crowd. Here's What Happened', New Jersey
Advance Media, August 2018, https://www.nj.com/politics/2018/
08/i_put_on_my_best_camouflage_shorts_and_went_to_a_t.html.

48 Lauren Katz, 'Trump rallies aren't a sideshow – they're his entire
campaign', Vox, 6 November 2019, https://www.vox.com/policy-
and-politics/2019/11/6/20950388/donald-trump-rally-2020-
presidential-election-today-explained.

49 'Inside a Trump rally', Vox: Today, Explained, https://podcasts.
apple.com/gb/podcast/inside-a-trump-rally/id1346207297?i=
1000456034947.

50 Alexandra Homolar and Ronny Scholz 'The power of Trump-
speak: populist crisis narratives and ontological security,' Cambridge
Review of International Affairs 32, no. 3 (March 2019), 344–64,
https://doi.org/10.1080/09557571.209.1575796.

51 Johnny Dwyer, 'Trump's Big Tent Revival', Topic Magazine, April
2019, https://www.topic.com/trump-s-big-tent-revival.

52 The most common content word, i.e., not counting functional
words such as 'and', 'the', 'but', etc. See Table 1 in Alexandra
Homolar and Ronny Scholz, 'The power of Trump-speak: populist
crisis narratives and ontological security', Cambridge Review of
International Affairs 32, no. 3 (2019), 344–64, https://doi.org/
10.1080/09557571.2019.1575796.

53 Johnny Dwyer, 'Trump's Big Tent Revival'.

54 Ibid.

55 See for example John Hendrickson, 'Donald Down the Shore', The
Atlantic, 29 January 2020, https://www.theatlantic.com/politics/
archive/2020/01/trumps-wildwood-new-jersey-rally-showed-2020-
plan/605704/; Josie Albertson-Grove, 'Trump rally draws thousands,
many less involved in politics', Union Leader Corp, 10 February 2020,
https://www.unionleader.com/news/politics/voters/trump-rally-
draws-thousands-many-less-involved-in-politics/article_e7ece61ba391-
5c44-91f2-7cebff6fd514.html; Roy F. Baumeister and Mark R. Leary,
'The need to belong: Desire for interpersonal attachments as a

fundamental human motivation', *Psychological Bulletin* 117, no. 3 (1995), 497–529, https://doi.org/10.1037/0033-2909.117.3.497.

56 Laurens Cerulus, 'Inside the far right's Flemish victory,' *Politico*, 27 May 2019, https://www.politico.eu/article/inside-the-far-rights-flemish-victory/.

57 Lori Hinnant, 'Europe's far-right parties hunt down the youth vote', AP News, 16 May 2019, https://apnews.com/7f177b0cf15b4e87a53fe4382d6884ca.

58 Judith Mischke, 'Meet the AfD Youth', *Politico*, 31 August 2019, https://www.politico.eu/article/meet-the-afd-youth-germany-regional-election-far-right/.

59 Hinnant, 'Europe's far right parties'; Cerulus, 'Inside the far right's Flemish victory'.

60 See for example Giovanna Greco, 'European elections 2019, interview Massimo Casanova – Lega Foggia, Lesina and the South give Europe to the Bolognese Casanova: Salvini's "fraternal friend" is the most voted league player', *Foggia Today*, 27 May 2019, https://www.foggiatoday.it/politica/massimo-casanova-elezioni-europee-sud-intervista.html.

61 Daniele Albertazzi, Arianna Giovannini and Antonella Seddone, '"No Regionalism Please, We Are Leghisti!" The Transformation of the Italian Lega Nord under the Leadership of Matteo Salvini', *Regional & Federal Studies* 28, no. 5 (20 October 2018), 645–71, https://doi.org/10.1080/13597566.2018.1512977

62 'EU election results: Italy's League wins more than a third of vote', The Local Italy, 27 May 2019, https://www.thelocal.it/20190527/italy-european-election-resullts.

63 Alexander Stille, 'How Matteo Salvini pulled Italy to the far right', *Guardian*, 9 August 2018, https://www.theguardian.com/news/2018/aug/09/how-matteo-salvini-pulled-italy-to-the-far-right.

64 A craving for community also underpinned the rise of the Yellow Vest movement in France. This movement began in suburban areas, where people live disconnected and lonely lives away from the social and cultural dynamism of big cities and the community-orientated life in small towns and villages, and gained succour on roundabouts where people converged and forged physical spaces of belonging.

65   Enrique Hernández and Hanspeter Kriesi, 'The electoral
     consequences of the financial and economic crisis in Europe',
     European University Institute, 2016, https://core.ac.uk/download/
     pdf/131933452.pdf; Hanspeter Kriesi, 'The Political Consequences of
     the Financial and Economic Crisis in Europe: Electoral Punishment
     and Popular Protest', *Swiss Political Science Review* 18, no. 4 (2012),
     518–22, doi:10.1111/spsr.12006.

66   David Smith and Emily Holden, 'In shadow of pandemic, Trump
     seizes opportunity to push through his agenda', *Guardian*, 9 April
     2020, https://www.theguardian.com/us-news/2020/apr/09/
     in-shadow-of-pandemic-trump-seizes-opportunity-to-push-through-
     his-agenda; Will Steakin, 'Inside Trump's reelection effort amid the
     pandemic: Digital canvassing, virtual trainings and marathon press
     briefings', ABC News, 30 March 2020, https://abcnews.go.com/
     Politics/inside-trumps-pandemic-reelection-effort-digital-canvassing-
     virtual/story?id=69800843.

67   Guy Hedgecoe, 'Spanish elections: How the far-right Vox party
     found its footing', BBC News, 11 November 2019, https://www.
     bbc.co.uk/news/world-europe-46422036; 'Vlaams Belang breaks
     half a million likes on Facebook', *Brussels Times*, 18 February 2020,
     https://www.brusselstimes.com/belgium/95666/vlaams-belang-
     breaks-past-half-a-million-likes-as-it-splurges-big-on-facebook/. Vox,
     the right populist Spanish party, for example, generated the most
     social media interactions during April 2020 of all the major parties
     ('Spain's far right, the clear leaders in social media', France 24, 27
     April 2019, https://www.france24.com/en/20190427-spains-far-right-
     clear-leader-social-media) whilst some some recently formed far
     right extremist parties used the COVID crisis to pump fake news
     into social media. 'Extremist groups are using coronavirus to push
     fake news on social media, report warns', *Brussels Times*, 8 May
     2020, https://www.brusselstimes.com/belgium/110431/extremist-
     groups-are-using-coronavirus-to-pump-fake-news-on-social-media-
     report-warns/.

68   M. Salmela and C. von Scheve, 'Emotional Dynamics of Right- and
     Left-wing Political Populism', *Humanity & Society* 42, no. 4
     (September 2018), 434–54, https://doi.org/10.1177/0160597618802521.

69   Jia Lynn Yang, 'When Asian-Americans Have to Prove We Belong',

New York Times, 10 August 2020, https://www.nytimes.
com/2020/04/10/sunday-review/coronavirus-asian-racism.html.

70 Marc Champion, 'A Virus to Kill Populism, Or Make It Stronger',
    Bloomberg, 27 March 2020, https://www.bloomberg.com/news/
    articles/2020-03-27/will-coronavirus-kill-populism-or-strengthen-
    leaders-like-trump; 'Hungary's Orban blames foreigners, migration
    for coronavirus spread', *France 24*, 13 March 2020, https://www.
    france24.com/en/20200313-hungary-s-pm-orban-blames-foreign-
    students-migration-for-coronavirus-spread.

71 Jeremy Cliffe, 'How populist leaders exploit pandemics', *New
    Statesman*, 18 March 2020, https://www.newstatesman.com/
    world/2020/03/how-populist-leaders-exploit-pandemics.

72 In medieval times, Jews for example were portrayed as carriers of
    plagues and accused of deliberately 'poisoning the wells' during
    the Black Death epidemic that swept through Europe in the 14th
    century. Donald G. McNeil, Jr., 'Finding a Scapegoat When
    Epidemics Strike', *New York Times*, 31 August 2009, https://www.
    nytimes.com/2009/09/01/health/01plague.html; see too Simon
    Schama, 'Plague time: Simon Schama on what history tells us',
    Financial Times, 10 April 2020, https://www.ft.com/
    content/279dee4a-740b-11ea-95fe-fcd274e920ca.

73 Laura Gohr, 'Angry Germans Explain Their Country's Surging
    Right-Wing Movement', *Vice*, 27 September 2017, https://www.
    vice.com/en_uk/article/xwgg9w/wir-haben-afd-wahler-
    unmittelbar-nach-ihrer-stimmabgabe-gefragt-warum; Jefferson
    Chase, 'Germany's populist AfD party seeks to reboot migrant
    fears', DW, 21 August 2017, https://www.dw.com/en/germanys-
    populist-afd-party-seeks-to-reboot-migrant-fears/a-40176414.

74 Aamna Mohdin, 'How Germany took in one million refugees but
    dodged a populist uprising', *Quartz*, 22 September 2017, https://qz.
    com/1076820/german-election-how-angela-merkel-took-in-one-
    million-refugees-and-avoided-a-populist-upset/.

75 Gohr, 'Angry Germans Explain.'

76 Mara Bierbach, 'How much money do refugees in Germany get?',
    Infomigrants, 12 September 2017, https://www.infomigrants.net/
    en/post/5049/how-much-money-do-refugees-in-germany-get;
    Nihad El-Kayed and Ulrike Hamann, 'Refugees' Access to Housing

and Residency in German Cities: Internal Border Regimes and Their Local Variations', *Social Inclusion* 6, no. 1 (2018), 135, https://doi.org/10.17645/si.v6i1.1334. And right-wing populists seeking to frame immigrants as freeloaders are aided by the fact that those who feel socially excluded or ostracised are more susceptible than others to conspiracy theories and more likely than others to wrongly join up the dots; see Matthew Hutson, 'Conspiracy Theorists May Really Just Be Lonely', *Scientific American*, 1 May 2017, https://www.scientificamerican.com/article/conspiracy-theorists-may-really-just-be-lonely/; original study: Damaris Graeupner and Alin Coman, 'The dark side of meaning-making: How social exclusion leads to superstitious thinking', *Journal of Experimental Social Psychology* 69 (October 2016), https://doi.org/10.1016/j.jesp.2016.10.003. See also 'Chaos at the gates of Paris: Inside the sprawling migrant camps nobody talks about,' *The Local* (France), 29 March 2019, https://www.thelocal.fr/20190329/out-of-sight-but-still-there-the-scandal-of-squalid-paris-migrant-camps; Louis Jacobson and Miriam Valverde, 'Donald Trump's False claim veterans treated worse than illegal immigrants', Politifact, 9 September 2016, https://www.politifact.com/truth-o-meter/statements/2016/sep/09/donald-trump/trump-says-veterans-treated-worse-illegal-immigrants/.

77 Vera Messing and Bence Ságvári, 'What drives anti-migrant attitudes?' Social Europe, 28 May 2019, https://www.socialeurope.eu/what-drives-anti-migrant-attitudes.

78 Ibid., and for the US see also Sean McElwee, 'Anti-Immigrant Sentiment Is Most Extreme in States Without Immigrants', Data for Progress, 5 April 2018, https://www.dataforprogress.org/blog/2018/4/5/anti-immigrant-sentiment-is-most-extreme-in-states-without-immigrants.

79 Senay Boztas, 'Dutch prime minister warns migrants to "be normal or be gone", as he fends off populist Geert Wilders in bitter election fight', *Telegraph*, 23 January 2017, https://www.telegraph.co.uk/news/2017/01/23/dutch-prime-minister-warns-migrants-normal-gone-fends-populist/.

80 Jon Henley, 'Centre-left Social Democrats victorious in Denmark elections', *Guardian*, 5 June 2019, https://www.theguardian.com/

world/2019/jun/05/centre-left-social-democrats-set-to-win-in-denmark-elections; idem., 'Denmark's centre-left set to win election with anti-immigration shift', 4 June 2019, *Guardian,* https://www.theguardian.com/world/2019/jun/04/denmark-centre-left-predicted-win-election-social-democrats-anti-immigration-policies.

81 Hannah Arendt, *The Origins of Totalitarianism* (Harcourt, 1951), p.356.

82 E. Amy Buller, *Darkness Over Germany: A Warning from History* (Longmans, Green, & Co., 1943).

CHAPTER FOUR:
The Solitary City

1 Judith Flanders, *The Victorian City: Everyday Life in Dickens' London* (Atlantic Books, 2012), p.438.

2 Nick Tarver, 'Loneliness Affects "Half of Adults"', BBC News, 18 October 2013, https://www.bbc.com/news/uk-england-24522691.

3 The City Index Survey gathered responses from 20,000 readers across 18 cities on four continents in September 2016. Guy Parsons, 'London Is among the Loneliest Cities in the World', *Time Out,* 16 February 2017, https://www.timeout.com/london/blog/london-is-among-the-loneliest-cities-in-the-world-021617.

4 'Rural Loneliness Is Making People Die Earlier. Here Are Four Ways to Tackle It', *Apolitical,* 26 November 2018, https://apolitical. co/en/solution_article/rural-loneliness-making-people-die-earlier-four-ways-to-tackle-it; Margaret Bolton, 'Loneliness: The State We're In', Age UK Oxfordshire, 2012, https://www. campaigntoendloneliness.org/wp-content/uploads/Loneliness-The-State-Were-In.pdf; Jane Hart, 'Older People in Rural Areas: Vulnerability Due to Loneliness and Isolation' (Rural England, April 2016), https://ruralengland.org/wp-content/uploads/2016/04/Final-report-Loneliness-and-Isolation.pdf.

5 What's more, data from Eurostat shows that city dwellers across Europe are more lonely than their rural counterparts; see 'Do Europeans Feel Lonely?', European Commission: Eurostat, 28 June 2017, https://ec.europa.eu/eurostat/web/products-eurostat-news/-/DDN-20170628-1; 'Children's and Young People's

Experiences of Loneliness: 2018', Office for National Statistics, 2018, https://www.ons.gov.uk/peoplepopulationandcommunity/ wellbeing/articles/childrensandyoungpeoplesexperiencesoflonelines s/2018#how-common-is-loneliness-in-children-and-young-people. In the US, rural dwellers were found to have more social relationships and experience less loneliness; see Carrie Henning–Smith, Ira Moscovice and Katy Kozhimannil, 'Differences in Social Isolation and Its Relationship to Health by Rurality', *The Journal of Rural Health* 35, no. 4 (2019), https://doi.org/10.1111/jrh.12344. See also Keming Yang, *Loneliness: A Social Problem* (Routledge, 2019). Bear in mind however that the vast majority of studies conducted on loneliness are run in cities, so we have relatively less empirical data on rural loneliness.

6　The migration of young people in search of academic and economic opportunity, leaving behind increasingly aging populations, is seen throughout the world. It remains to be seen whether the tide will turn in the aftermath of Covid-19. See for instance: Hu Xiaochu, 'China's Young Rural-to-Urban Migrants: In Search of Fortune, Happiness, and Independence', Migration Policy.org, 4 January 2012, https://www.migrationpolicy.org/ article/chinas-young-rural-urban-migrants-search-fortune-happiness- and-independence; 'Rural America Is Losing Young People – Consequences and Solutions', Wharton Public Policy Initative, 23 March 2018, https://publicpolicy.wharton.upenn.edu/live/ news/2393-rural-america-is-losing-young-people-; 'Britain "Growing Apart" as Young People Leave Rural Areas', Rural Services Network, 28 October 2019, http://www.rsnonline.org.uk/britain- growing-apart-as-young-people-leave-rural-areas.

7　This is true for example in the UK. See Paul Swinney, 'Is It Fair That Cities Get More Money than Rural Areas?', Centre for Cities, 26 February 2019, https://www.centreforcities.org/blog/is-it-fair- that-cities-get-more-money-than-rural-areas/.

8　Stanley Milgram, 'The Experience of Living in Cities', *Science* 167, no. 3924 (13 March 1970), 1461–68, https://doi.org/10.1126/ science.167.3924.1461; Jamil Zaki, 'The Technology of Kindness', *Scientific American*, 6 August 2019, https://www.scientificamerican. com/article/the-technology-of-kindness/.

9   Denis Corroyer and Gabriel Moser, 'Politeness in the Urban
     Environment: Is City Life Still Synonymous With Civility?',
     Environment and Behavior 33, no. 5 (September 2003), 611–25,
     https://doi.org/10.1177/0013916012197315l.

10   30% of people bought jam when there were only six choices,
     compared with 3% when there were twenty-four choices. Sheena S.
     Iyengar and Mark R. Lepper, 'When Choice Is Demotivating: Can
     One Desire Too Much of a Good Thing?', *Journal of Personality and
     Social Psychology* 79, no. 6 (2000), 995–1006.

11   While this 'urban overload theory', first proposed in 1970 by
     controversial social psychologist Stanley Milgram, has garnered
     criticism over the years, it is still an important factor to consider
     when it comes to loneliness, which is an internalised state, as
     opposed to things like bystander intervention, which require
     external actions. For a lay-friendly overview, see Madhavi
     Prashant Patil, 'Overload and the City', Urban Design Mental
     Health, 6 March 2016, https://www.urbandesignmentalhealth.
     com/blog/overload-and-the-city; for Milgram's original paper, see
     Milgram, 'The Experience of Living in Cities,' *Science* 167, no.
     3924 (1970), 1461–8, https://doi.org/10.1126/science.167.3924.1461.

12   Shannon Deep, '"Hello" Isn't Always "Hello" in NYC', *Huffington
     Post*, 6 January 2015: https://www.huffpost.com/entry/
     new_3_b_6103200.

13   In Shanghai, Hong Kong, Istanbul and Barcelona decibel levels are
     such that an average resident can expect significant hearing loss. A
     2017 study by the hearing app Mimi found that the average
     inhabitant of cities at the top of the World Hearing Index has
     hearing loss equivalent to someone 10–20 years older than their
     actual age. See 'Worldwide Hearing Index 2017', Mimi, 8 March
     2017, https://www.mimi.io/en/blog/2017/3/8/worldwide-hearing-
     index-2017; Alex Gray, 'These are the cities with the worst noise
     pollution', World Economic Forum, 27 March 2017, https://www.
     weforum.org/agenda/2017/03/these-are-the-cities-with-the-worst-
     noise-pollution/.

14   See, for instance, Veronica-Diana Armaşu, 'Modern Approaches to
     Politeness Theory: A Cultural Context', *Lingua: Language and
     Culture* 11, no. 1 (2012); see also James Cooray Smith, 'The Tube

Chat badges show that London isn't rude: it has a negative politeness culture', *City Metric*, 30 September 2016, https://www.citymetric.com/horizons/tube-chat-badges-show-london-isnt-rude-it-has-negative-politeness-culture-2481.

15 'What Walking Speeds Say About Us', BBC News, 2 May 2007, http://news.bbc.co.uk/1/hi/magazine/6614637.stm.

16 'Welcome to the Pace of Life Project', Pace of Life, http://www.richardwiseman.com/quirkology/pace_home.htm.

17 Robert V. Levine and Ara Norenzayan, 'The Pace of Life in 31 Countries', *Journal of Cross-Cultural Psychology* 30, no. 2 (March 1999), 178–205, https://doi.org/10.1177/0022022199030002003.

18 Eric Jaffe, 'Why People in Cities Walk Fast', *CityLab*, 21 March 2012, https://www.citylab.com/life/2012/03/why-people-cities-walk-fast/1550/.

19 John M. Darley and C. Daniel Batson, '"From Jerusalem to Jericho": A study of Situational and Dispositional Variables in Helping Behavior', *Journal of Personality and Social Psychology* 27, no. 1 (1973), 100–108, https://doi.org/10.1037/h0034449.

20 People report more positive affect following social interactions with more familiar partners (J.R. Vittengl and Craig S. Holt, 'Positive and negative affect in social interactions as a function of partner familiarity, quality of communication, and social anxiety', *Journal of Social and Clinical Psychology* 17, no. 2 (1998b), 196–208, https://doi.org/10.1521/jscp.1998.17.2.196). When people have more intimate, meaningful conversations, they report less loneliness, more happiness, and a greater sense of relatedness. See L. Wheeler, H. Reis, and J. Nezlek, 'Loneliness, social interaction, and sex roles', *Journal of Personality and Social Psychology* 45, no. 4 (1983), 943–53, https://doi.org/10.1037/0022-3514.45.4.943; Matthias R. Mehl et al., 'Eavesdropping on happiness: Well-being is related to having less small talk and more substantive conversations, *Psychological Science* 21, no. 4 (2010), 539–41, https://doi.org/10.1177/0956797610362675; H. Reis et al., 'Daily Well-Being: The Role of Autonomy, Competence, and Relatedness', *Personality and Social Psychology Bulletin* 26, no. 4 (April 2000), 419–35, https://doi.org/10.1177/0146167200266002.

21 Gillian M. Sandstrom and Elizabeth W. Dunn, 'Is Efficiency

Overrated?: Minimal Social Interactions Lead to Belonging and Positive Affect', *Social, Psychological and Personality Science* 5, no. 4 (May 2014), 437–42, https://doi.org/10.1177/1948550613502990.

22 Inevitably too, there will be cultural differences when it comes to how cynical such examples make you feel.

23 Manuel G. Calvo, Hipólito Marrero and David Beltrán, 'When does the brain distinguish between genuine and ambiguous smiles? An ERP study', *Brain and Cognition* 81, no. 2 (2013), 237–46, https://doi.org/10.1016/j.bandc.2012.10.009; Manuel G. Calvo, Aida Gutiérrez-García, Pedro Avero and Daniel Lundqvist, 'Attentional mechanisms in judging genuine and fake smiles: Eye-movement patterns', *Emotion* 13, no. 4 (2013), 792–802, https://doi.org/10.1037/a0032317; Manuel G. Calvo, Andrés Fernández-Martín and Lauri Nummenmaa, 'Perceptual, categorical, and affective processing of ambiguous smiling facial expressions', *Cognition* 125, no. 3 (2012), 373–93, https://doi.org/10.1016/j.cognition.2012.07.021.

24 Gillian M. Sandstrom, 'Social Interactions and Well-being: the Surprising Power of Weak Ties', The University of British Columbia, 2013: 86, https://pdfs.semanticscholar.org/822e/cdd2e3e02a3e56b507fb93262bab58089d44.pdf.

25 See for example Wendell Cox, 'Length of Residential Tenure: Metropolitan Areas, Urban Cores, Suburbs and Exurbs', *New Geography*, 17 October 2018, https://www.newgeography.com/content/006115-residential-tenure.

26 'In London, Renters Now Outnumber Homeowners', CityLab, 25 February 2016, https://www.citylab.com/equity/2016/02/londons-renters-now-outnumber-homeowners/470946/; 'Good News For Landlords – Average UK Tenancy Lengths Increase', Letslivehere, 2018, https://www.letslivehere.co.uk/average-uk-tenancy-lengths-increase/.

27 'Series IB: All Occupied Housing Units by Tenure, *United States Census Bureau*, 2014, https://www.census.gov/data/tables/time-series/demo/nychvs/series-1b.html, see data at 'Year Householder Moved Into Unit' and 'Reason Householder Moved from Previous Residence'; 'New York City Housing and Vacancy Survey (NYCHVS)', United States Census Bureau, https://www.census.gov/programs-surveys/nychvs/data/tables.html. Note that in the

US, even as a combination of economic and demographic factors have led to people spending longer on average in one place, many cities have higher rates of renting versus owning, with those who rent moving around significantly more often than those who own. See for example Sabrina Tavernise, 'Frozen In Place: Americans Are Moving at the Lowest Rate on Record', *New York Times*, 20 November 2019, https://www.nytimes.com/2019/11/20/us/american-workers-moving-states-.html. In November 2019, the US Census Bureau announced that Americans' rate of moving was the lowest it had been in decades; Balazs Szekely, 'Renters Became the Majority Population in 22 Big US Cities', Rent Café Blog, 25 January 2018, https://www.rentcafe.com/blog/rental-market/market-snapshots/change-renter-vs-owner-population-2006-2016; Wendell Cox, 'Length of Residential Tenure: Metropolitan Areas, Urban Cores, Suburbs and Exurbs', *New Geography*, 17 October 2018, https://www.newgeography.com/content/006115-residential-tenure.

28 Kim Parker, Juliana Menasce Horowitz, Anna Brown, Richard Fry, D'Vera Cohn and Ruth Igielnik, 'What Unites and Divides Urban, Suburban and Rural Communities', Pew Research Center, 22 May 2018, https://www.pewsocialtrends.org/2018/05/22/what-unites-and-divides-urban-suburban-and-rural-communities/.

29 Peter Stubley, 'Berlin to freeze rents and give tenants rights to sue landlords after rising costs force residents out to suburbs', *Independent*, 23 October 2019, https://www.independent.co.uk/news/world/europe/berlin-rent-freeze-tenants-sue-landlords-housing-crisis-germany-a9167611.html.

30 Ben Knight, 'Berlin's new rent freeze: How it compares globally', *Deutsche Welle*, 23 October 2019, https://www.dw.com/en/berlins-new-rent-freeze-how-it-compares-globally/a-50937652.

31 Prasanna Rajasekaran, Mark Treskon, Solomon Greene, 'Rent Control: What Does the Research Tell Us about the Effectiveness of Local Action?', Urban Institute, January 2019, https://www.urban.org/sites/default/files/publication/99646/rent_control._what_does_the_research_tell_us_about_the_effectiveness_of_local_action_1.pdf. For some examples, see, e.g., Noah Smith, 'Yup, Rent Control Does More Harm Than Good', *Bloomberg Opinion*, 18 January 2018, https://www.bloomberg.com/opinion/articles/

2018-01-18/yup-rent-control-does-more-harm-than-good; these include Amsterdam, which in 2019 instituted a law dictating that entire homes may be rented out for only thirty nights per calendar year. Similar limits are in place in Reykjavik, Hamburg and Toronto, as well as the entire countries of Denmark, Greece and Italy. London capped such rentals at ninety days in 2017, though many hosts report evading the system by listing on multiple platforms to avoid detection. In Singapore, where it is illegal to rent a home for less than three months, security guards have been known to refuse admittance to illegally booked tourists. Other governments, including that of New Zealand, are in the process of devising taxation schemes that disincentivise short-term rentals. See Mallory Lochlear, 'Amsterdam will limit Airbnb rentals to thirty days a year', Engadget, 10 January 2018, https://www.engadget.com/2018-01-10-amsterdam-airbnb-rental-30-day-limit.html; 'How London hosts can manage around Airbnb's 90-day limit', Happyguest, 2 June 2018, http://www.happyguest.co.uk/blog/how-london-hosts-can-manage-around-airbnbs-90-day-limit; Ian Lloyd Neubauer, 'Countries that are cracking down on Airbnb', New Daily, 30 August 2019, https://thenewdaily.com.au/life/travel/2019/08/30/countries-crack-down-airbnb/.

32 Joseph Stromberg, 'Eric Klinenberg on Going Solo', Smithsonian Magazine, February 2012, p.4, https://www.smithsonianmag.com/science-nature/eric-klinenberg-on-going-solo-19299815/.

33 'All by myself', NYU Furman Center, 16 September 2015, https://furmancenter.org/thestoop/entry/all-by-myself; 'Cities with the largest percentage of single-person households in the United States in 2018', Statista, September 2019, https://www.statista.com/statistics/242304/top-10-us-cities-by-percentage-of-one-person-households/.

34 US Census Data, 2010, available at https://census.gov; see also Chuck Bennett, 'Poll: Half of Manhattan Residents live alone', New York Post, 30 October 2009, https://nypost.com/2009/10/30/poll-half-of-manhattan-residents-live-alone/. As of 2015, studios and one-bed flats made up 54.4% of all new housing units built in New York City; see Jay Denton, 'Millennials Drive One-Bedroom

Apartment Trend, But That Might Change', *Forbes*, 11 November 2015, https://www.forbes.com/sites/axiometrics/2015/11/11/millennials-drive-one-bedroom-apartment-trend-but-that-might-change/#7d0a58f439a9.

35 'People in the EU: Statistics on Households and Family Structures', Eurostat, 26 May 2020, 8, https://ec.europa.eu/eurostat/statistics-explained/pdfscache/41897.pdf; for information on solo living in major Japanese cities, including Tokyo, see Richard Ronald, Oana Druta and Maren Godzik, 'Japan's urban singles: negotiating alternatives to family households and standard housing pathways', *Urban Geography 39*, no. 7 (2018), 1018–40, https://doi.org/10.1080/02723638.2018.1433924.

36 Ibid.

37 A.K.L. Cheung and W.J.J. Yeung, 'Temporal-spatial patterns of one-person households in China, 1982–2005', *Demographic Research 32*, no. 44 (2015), 1209–38, https://doi.org/10.4054/DemRes.2015.32.44; Bianji Wu Chengliang, '"Empty-nest" youth reaches 58 million in China', *People's Daily Online*, 13 February 2018, http://en.people.cn/n3/2018/0213/c90000-9427297.html; 'Loneliness in the city', CBRE, https://www.cbre.co.uk/research-and-reports/our-cities/loneliness-in-the-city.

38 A 2013 study of U.S. Census data also found that rates of living alone rise most quickly during periods of economic expansion, as people often choose to 'purchase' the luxury of privacy. See Rose M. Kreider and Jonathan Vespa, 'The Changing Face of Living Alone, 1880–2010', https://paa2014.princeton.edu/papers/140867.

39 Stromberg, 'Eric Klinenberg on *Going Solo*'.

40 Ibid.; Klinenberg, *Going Solo* (Penguin Random House, 2013).

41 Danielle Braff, 'Until Honeymoon We Do Part', *New York Times*, March 13 2019, https://www.nytimes.com/2019/03/13/fashion/weddings/until-honeymoon-we-do-part.html.

42 Béatrice d'Hombres, Sylke Schnepf, Matina Barjaková and Francisco Teixeira Mendonça, 'Loneliness – an unequally shared burden in Europe', European Commission, 2018, https://ec.europa.eu/jrc/sites/jrcsh/files/fairness_pb2018_loneliness_jrc_i1.pdf.

43 Kimberley J. Smith and Christina Victor, 'Typologies of loneliness, living alone and social isolation, and their associations with

physical and mental health', *Ageing Society* 39, no. 8 (August 2019), 1709–30, https://doi.org/10.1017/s0144686x18000132; A. Zebhauser et al., 'How much does it hurt to be lonely? Mental and physical differences between older men and women in the KORA-Age Study', *International Journal of Geriatric Psychiatry* 29, no. 3 (March 2014), 245–52; Gerdt Sundström et al., 'Loneliness among older Europeans', *European Journal of Ageing* 6, no. 4 (2009), 267–75, https://doi.org/10.1007/s10433-009-0134-8; 'Loneliness – What characteristics and circumstances are associated with feeling lonely? Analysis of characteristics and circumstances associated with loneliness in England using the Community Life Survey, 2016 to 2017', Office for National Statistics, 10 April 2018, https://www.ons. gov.uk/peoplepopulationandcommunity/wellbeing/articles/ lonelinesswhatcharacteristicsandcircumstancesareassociated withfeelinglonely/2018-04-10; Alana Schetzer, 'Solo households on the rise, and so is feeling lonely and less healthy', *The Age*, 14 December 2015, https://www.theage.com.au/national/victoria/ solo-households-on-the-rise-and-so-is-feeling-lonely-and-less-healthy-20151214-gln18b.html.

44 Zoe Wood, 'Tesco targets growing number of Britons who eat or live alone', *Guardian*, 6 July 2018, https://www.theguardian.com/ business/2018/jul/06/tesco-targets-growing-number-of-britons-who-eat-or-live-alone.

45 The word *mukbang* is a portmanteau of the Korean words for 'eating' and 'broadcast'.

46 Anjali Venugopalan, 'Feast & stream: Meet India's biggest mukbangers', *Economic Times*, 7 September 2019, https:// economictimes.indiatimes.com/magazines/panache/feast-stream-meet-indias-biggest-mukbangers/articleshow/71027715.cms; see also Jasmin Barmore, 'Bethany Gaskin is the Queen of Eating Shellfish Online', *New York Times*, 11 June 2019, https://www.nytimes. com/2019/06/11/style/youtube-mukbang-bloveslife-bethany-gaskin. html; 'The Pleasure and Sorrow of the "Mukbang" Super Eaters of Youtube', *News Lens*, 25 June 2019, https://international. thenewslens.com/article/118747.

47 Tan Jee Yee, 'Google: The Future Consumer of APAC Will Do More than just Consume', Digital News Asia, 20 March 2020,

https://www.digitalnewsasia.com/digital-economy/google-future-consumer-apac-will-do-more-just-consume.

48   See for example Hillary Hoffower, 'A 25-year-old YouTuber quit her job and now makes 6 figures recording herself eating, and it's a trend more and more influencers are cashing in on', *Business Insider*, April 10 2019, https://www.businessinsider.com/mukbang-influencers-youtube-money-six-figures-2019-4.

49   Andrea Stanley, 'Inside the Saucy, Slurpy, Actually Sorta Sexy World of Seafood Mukbang Influencers', *Cosmopolitan*, 9 April 2019, https://www.cosmopolitan.com/lifestyle/a27022451/mukbang-asmr-seafood-videos-youtube-money/.

50   'The Pleasure and Sorrow of the 'Mukbang' Super Eaters of Youtube', *News Lens,* 25 June 2019, https://international.thenewslens.com/article/118747.

51   Kagan Kircaburun, Andrew Harris, Filipa Calado and Mark D. Griffiths, 'The Psychology of Mukbang Watching: A Scoping Review of the Academic and Non-academic Literature', *International Journal of Mental Health and Addiction* (2020), https://doi.org/10.1007/s11469-019-00211-0.

52   Hanwool Choe, 'Eating together multimodally: Collaborative eating in *mukbang,* a Korean livestream of eating', *Language in Society* (2019), 1–38, https://doi.org/10.1017/s0047404518001355

53   Andrea Stanley, 'Inside the Saucy, Slurpy, Actually Sorta Sexy World of Seafood Mukbang Influencers'.

54   'This Rookie Korean Broadcast Jockey Earned $100,000 Through One Live Broadcast', Kpoptify, 30 July 2019, https://www.thekpoptify.co/blogs/news/this-rookie-korean-broadcast-jockey-earned-100-000-through-one-live-broadcast.

55   Victoria Young, 'Strategic UX: The Art of Reducing Friction', *Telepathy*, https://www.dtelepathy.com/blog/business/strategic-ux-the-art-of-reducing-friction; Yasmin Tayag, 'Neuroscientists just gave lazy humans a free pass', *Inverse*, 21 February 2017, https://www.inverse.com/article/28139-laziness-neuroscience-path-of-least-resistance-effort; see also Nobuhiro Hagura, Patrick Haggard and Jörn Diedrichsen, 'Perceptual decisions are biased by the cost to act', *eLife*, 21 February 2017, https://doi.org/10.7554/eLife.18422.

56   Melissa Matthews, 'These Viral 'Mukbang' Stars Get Paid to Gorge

on Food – at the Expense of Their Bodies', *Men's Health*, 18 January 2019, https://www.menshealth.com/health/a25892411/youtube-mukbang-stars-binge-eat/.

57 On the importance of this see for example Seymour Martin Lipset's seminal 1959 paper, 'Some Social Requisites of Democracy', *The American Political Science Review* 53, no. 1 (1959), 69–105.

58 These 'citizens' did not, of course, include women, males under 20 or anyone enslaved or born outside of the Athenian state.

CHAPTER FIVE:
The Contactless Age

1 Andrea Cheng, 'Amazon Go Looks to Expand As Checkout-Free Shopping Starts to Catch On Across the Retail Landscape', *Forbes*, 21 November 2019, https://www.forbes.com/sites/andriacheng/2019/11/21/thanks-to-amazon-go-checkout-free-shopping-may-become-a-real-trend/#753d0285792b. Other major companies starting to get in on the act include Walmart in the US, Alibaba in China and Tesco in the UK. All have been testing automated grocery stores to rival those set up by the Jeff Bezos behemoth; Nick Wingfield, Paul Mozur and Michael Corkery, 'Retailers Race Against Amazon to Automate Stores', *New York Times*, 1 April 2018, https://www.nytimes.com/2018/04/01/technology/retailer-stores-automation-amazon.html.

2 Melissa Gonzalez, M.J. Munsell and Justin Hill, 'The New Norm: Rewriting the Future of Purchasing Behaviour', *Advertising Week 360*, https://www.advertisingweek360.com/the-new-norm-rewriting-the-future-of-purchasing-behavior/.

3 Ulrike Malmendier and Stefan Nagel, 'Depression Babies: Do Macroeconomic Experiences Affect Risk Taking?', *The Quarterly Journal of Economics* 126, no. 1 (February 2011); 373–416, https://eml.berkeley.edu/~ulrike/Papers/DepressionBabies_59.pdf.

4 Compare, for instance, coverage of discount and dollar stores from 2009 (Stephanie Rosenbloom, 'Don't Ask, You Can Afford It', *New York Times*, 1 May 2009, https://www.nytimes.com/2009/05/02/business/02dollar.html), 2012 (Nin-Hai Tseng, 'Why dollar stores are thriving, even post-recession', *Fortune*, 2 April 2012,

https://fortune.com/2012/04/02/why-dollar-stores-are-thriving-even-post-recession/) and April 2020 (Pearl Wang, '2 Discount Retailers That Will Thrive in a Recession', *Motley Fool*, 22 April 2020, https://www.fool.com/investing/2020/04/22/two-discount-retailers-that-will-thrive-in-a-reces.aspx).

5   Frank Swain, 'Designing the Perfect Anti-Object', *Medium*, 5 December 2013, https://medium.com/futures-exchange/designing-the-perfect-anti-object-49a184a6667a; 'Unpleasant Design & Hostile Urban Architecture', *99% Invisible,* 7 May 2016, https://99percent invisible.org/episode/unpleasant-design-hostile-urban-architecture/.

6   See original tweet at https://twitter.com/rebel_machine/status/94 0199856425046017?lang=en; Josh Cohen, 'New Anti-Homeless Architecture: Seattle Uses Bike Racks to Block Rough Sleepers', *Guardian*, 24 January 2018, https://www.theguardian.com/cities/2018/jan/24/anti-homeless-architecture-seattle-bike-racks-block-rough-sleepers.

7   Jasmine Lee, 'The Unpleasant Truth of Hong Kong's Anti-Homeless Urban Design', *Harbour Times*, 15 May 2017, https://harbourtimes.com/2017/05/15/the-unpleasant-truth-of-hong-kongs-anti-homeless-urban-design/.

8   They claimed it was unintentional. 'Saint Mary's Cathedral Drenches Homeless With Water', CBS SF Bay Area, 18 March 2015, https://sanfrancisco.cbslocal.com/2015/03/18/homeless-saint-marys-cathedral-archdiocese-san-francisco-intentionally-drenched-water-sleeping/.

9   'What is the Mosquito', Moving Sound Technologies, https://www.movingsoundtech.com; 'Sonic Science: The High–Frequency Hearing Test', *Scientific American*, 23 May 2013, https://www.scientificamerican.com/article/bring-science-home-high-frequency-hearing/.

10   Michaela Winberg, 'Can You Hear It? Sonic Devices Play High Pitched Noises to Repel Teens', NPR, 10 July 2019, https://www.npr.org/2019/07/10/739908153/can-you-hear-it-sonic-devices-play-high-pitched-noises-to-repel-teens?t=1570361354751.

11   John Metcalfe, 'Pink Lights, Talking Cameras, and High–Pitched Squeals: The World's Weirdest Anti-Loitering Technologies,' *City Lab*, 20 March 2012, https://www.citylab.com/life/2012/03/pink-

lights-talking-cameras-and-high-pitched-squeals-worlds-weirdest-anti-loitering-technologies/1533/.

12 'Pink lights put off spotty teens', BBC News, 25 March 2009, http://news.bbc.co.uk/1/hi/england/nottinghamshire/7963347.stm; see also John Metcalfe, 'Pink Lights, Talking Cameras, and High-Pitched Squeals: The World's Weirdest Anti-Loitering Technologies'.

13 'Broken Windows Policing', Center for Evidence-Based Crime Policy, https://cebcp.org/evidence-based-policing/what-works-in-policing/research-evidence-review/broken-windows-policing/.

14 Shankar Vedantum, Chris Benderev, Tara Boyle, Renee Klahr, Maggie Penman and Jennifer Schmidt, 'How A Theory of Crime And Policing Was Born, And Went Terribly Wrong', WBUR, 1 November 2016, https://www.wbur.org/npr/500104506/broken-windows-policing-and-the-origins-of-stop-and-frisk-and-how-it-went-wrong.

15 Ted Anderson, 'What happened to SF's controversial 'sit-lie' ordinance?', *SF Gate*, 18 October 2018, https://www.sfgate.com/bayarea/article/What-happened-to-SF-s-controversial-sit-lie-13303216.php.

16 As Columbia law professor Bernard Harcourt, who has conducted two major studies on the impact of 'broken windows' in New York and other cities, has said. See Sarah Childress, 'The Problem With "Broken Windows" Policing', PBS Frontline, 28 June 2016, https://www.pbs.org/wgbh/frontline/article/the-problem-with-broken-windows-policing/.

17 For more detail and legal critique, see Bernard E. Harcourt, *Illusion of Order: The False Promise of Broken Windows Policing* (Harvard University Press, 2001).

18 Mary H. Osgood, 'Rural and urban attitudes toward welfare', *Social Work* 22, no. 1 (January 1977), 41–7, https://www.jstor.org/stable/23711620?seq=1.

19 John Elledge, 'Are cities more liberal? Of course: all your liberal mates moved to one', *New Statesman*, 9 January 2017, https://www.newstatesman.com/politics/2017/01/are-cities-more-liberal-course-all-your-liberal-mates-moved-one; David A. Graham, 'Red State, Blue City', *The Atlantic*, March 2017, https://www.theatlantic.com/magazine/archive/2017/03/red-state-blue-city/513857/.

20 Farhad Manjoo, 'America's Cities Are Unlivable. Blame Wealthy

Liberals', *New York Times*, 22 May 2019, https://www.nytimes.
com/2019/05/22/opinion/california-housing-nimby.html.

21   See, for example, Richard T. LeGates and Frederic Stout, eds., *The
     City Reader*, Seventh Edition (Routledge, 2020).

22   Meri T. Long, 'Who has more compassion, Republicans or
     Democrats?', *Chicago Tribune*, 11 Jan 2019, https://www.
     chicagotribune.com/opinion/commentary/ct-perspec-compassion-
     democrats-republicans-who-has-more-0113-story.html.

23   In one striking example of this dissonance, residents of the
     Mission Dolores neighbourhood actually paid out of their own
     pockets for huge sidewalk boulders to prevent homeless people
     from sleeping on their sidewalks ('Boulders placed on San
     Francisco sidewalk to keep homeless residents away', KTVU
     FOX 2, 30 September 2019, https://www.ktvu.com/news/
     boulders-placed-on-san-francisco-sidewalk-to-keep-homeless-
     residents-away). Others have campaigned against homeless
     shelters in their areas, sparking a legal battle that has dragged
     on for over eighteen months (Trisha Thadani, 'SF residents vow
     to keep fighting Navigation Center as supes weigh its fate', *San
     Francisco Chronicle*, 24 June 2019, https://www.sfchronicle.com/
     politics/article/Fate-of-controversial-Navigation-Center-
     now-in-14037517.php). The city itself is responsible for other
     instances of hostile architecture, from 'inverse guillotines' at the
     entrance to public transit (Lina Blanco, 'BART's Fare Evasion
     Crackdown Exposes the 'Deadly Elegance' of Hostile Design',
     KQED, 23 July 2019, https://www.kqed.org/arts/13861966/barts-
     fare-evasion-crackdown-exposes-the-deadly-elegance-of-hostile-
     design) to sharp boulders outside the public library to paint in
     public places that will spray urine back at homeless people who
     may not have access to a suitable toilet (Kaitlin Jock, 'You are
     not welcome here: Anti-homeless architecture crops up
     nationwide', *Street Roots News*, 7 June 2019, https://news.
     streetroots.org/2019/06/07/you-are-not-welcome-here-anti-
     homeless-architecture-crops-nationwide). While it does not have
     the highest total number of people experiencing homelessness,
     San Francisco has one of the fastest growing homeless
     populations in the US, having risen a shocking 30% just

between 2017 and 2018, by one measure (Jill Cowan, 'San Francisco's Homeless Population Is Much Bigger Than Thought, City Data Suggests', *New York Times*, 19 November 2019, https://www.nytimes.com/2019/11/19/us/san-francisco-homeless-count.html).

24 James Walker, 'Invisible in plain sight: fighting loneliness in the homeless community', *Open Democracy*, 31 July 2019, https://www.opendemocracy.net/en/opendemocracyuk/invisible-plain-sight-fighting-loneliness-homeless-community/.

25 See Jane Jacobs, *The Death and Life of Great American Cities* (Random House, 1961).

26 'Welcome to the neighbourhood', Royal Wharf, https://www.royalwharf.com/neighbourhood/.

27 Robert Booth, 'Subsidised tenants are excluded from pool and gym in London block', *Guardian*, 1 November 2018, https://www.theguardian.com/society/2018/nov/01/subsidised-tenants-are-excluded-from-pool-and-gym-in-london-tower.

28 Harriet Grant, 'Too poor to play: children in social housing blocked from communal playground', *Guardian*, 25 March 2019, https://www.theguardian.com/cities/2019/mar/25/too-poor-to-play-children-in-social-housing-blocked-from-communal-playground.

29 The company, for its part, claims that such exclusion was never its policy.

30 Harriet Grant, 'Disabled children among social tenants blocked from communal gardens', *Guardian*, 27 September 2019, https://www.theguardian.com/cities/2019/sep/27/disabled-children-among-social-tenants-blocked-from-communal-gardens.

31 'New UWS development could have separate entrance for poorer people', *West Side Rag*, 12 August 2013, https://www.westsiderag.com/2013/08/12/new-uws-development-could-have-separate-entrance-for-poorer-people; Adam Withnall '"Poor door" controversy extends to Washington DC as affordable housing "wing" given entrance on different street – next to the loading bay', *Independent*, 4 August 2014, https://www.independent.co.uk/news/world/americas/poor-door-controversy-extends-to-washington-dc-as-affordable-housing-wing-given-entrance-on-9646069.html; Hilary Osborne, 'Poor doors: the

segregation of London's inner–city flat dwellers', *Guardian*, 25 July 2014, https://www.theguardian.com/society/2014/jul/25/poor-doors-segregation-london-flats.

32 Adam Withnall, '"Poor door" controversy extends to Washington, D.C. as affordable housing "wing" given entrance on different street – next to the loading bay'; New York has now closed the loophole that allowed buildings with separate entrances to qualify for the 'inclusionary housing' tax break. See Jana Kasperkevic, 'New York bans "poor doors" in win for low income tenants', *Guardian*, 29 June 2015, https://www.theguardian.com/us-news/2015/jun/29/new-york-poor-door-low-income-tenants-rent.

33 Carlito Pablo, 'Poor door at proposed Vancouver West End condo tower raises issue of stigma', *Georgia Straight*, 12 July 2018, https://www.straight.com/news/1102166/poor-door-proposed-vancouver-west-end-condo-tower-raises-issue-stigma; 'Vancouver ranked North America's 2nd least affordable city for housing', *Daily Hive*, 28 March 2019, https://dailyhive.com/vancouver/vancouver-most-expensive-housing-market-canada-2019; Aric Jenkins, 'The Least Affordable City in North America Is Not in the U.S.', *Money*, 10 November 2017, http://money.com/money/5017121/least-affordable-expensive-cities-north-america/.

34 Carlito Pablo, 'Poor door at proposed Vancouver West End condo tower raises issue of stigma'.

35 'Seesaws let kids on each side of US–Mexico border play together', Yahoo! News, 30 July 2019, https://news.yahoo.com/seesaws-let-kids-side-us-mexico-border-play-181653457.html.

36 Patrick Sturgis, Ian Brunton–Smith, Jouni Kuha and Jonathan Jackson, 'Ethnic diversity, segregation and the social cohesion of neighbourhoods in London', *Ethnic and Racial Studies* 37, no. 8 (2014), 1286–309, https://doi.org/10.1080/01419870.2013.831932.

37 Nikolay Mintchev and Henrietta L Moore, 'Super-diversity and the prosperous society', *European Journal of Social Theory* 21, no. 1 (2018), 117–34, https://doi.org/10.1177/1368431016678629.

38 Dietlind Stolle, Stuart N. Soroka and Richard Johnston, 'When Does Diversity Erode Trust? Neighborhood Diversity, Interpersonal Trust and the Mediating Effect of Social Interactions', *Political Studies* 56, no. 1 (2008), 57–75, https://doi.org/10.1111/j.1467-

9248.2007.00717.x; Patrick Sturgis, Ian Brunton-Smith, Sanna Read and Nick Allum, 'Does Ethnic Diversity Erode Trust? Putnam's "Hunkering-Down" Thesis Reconsidered', *British Journal of Political Science* 41, no. 1 (2011), 57–82, https://doi.org/10.1017/S0007123410000281.

39 Alison Flood, 'Britain has closed almost 800 libraries since 2010, figures show', *Guardian,* 6 December 2019, https://www.theguardian.com/books/2019/dec/06/britain-has-closed-almost-800-libraries-since-2010-figures-show; see also 'Decade of austerity sees 30% drop in library spending', Chartered Institute of Public Finance and Accountancy, 12 June 2019, https://www.cipfa.org/about-cipfa/press-office/latest-press-releases/decade-of-austerity-sees-30-drop-in-library-spending.

40 May Bulman, 'Youth services "decimated by 69 percent" in less than a decade amid surge in knife crime, figures show', *Independent,* 24 September 2019, https://www.independent.co.uk/news/uk/home-news/knife-crime-youth-services-cuts-councils-austerity-ymca-a9118671.html.

41 Jamie Roberton, 'Government accused of fuelling loneliness crisis as day centres disappear', ITV News, 25 September 2018, https://www.itv.com/news/2018-09-25/government-accused-of-fuelling-loneliness-crisis-as-day-centres-disappear/.

42 William Eichler, 'Councils slash £15 million from parks budgets', Local Gov, 21 June 2018, https://www.localgov.co.uk/Councils-slash-15m-from-parks-budgets/45519.

43 While Europe and the US, for example, took different paths out of the financial crisis, social infrastructure remains chronically underfunded worldwide. See Georg Inderst, 'Social Infrastructure Finance and Institutional Investors: A Global Perspective', *SSRN* (2020), https://doi.org/10.2139/ssrn.3556473.

44 In the UK, for instance, people in cities shouldered nearly twice as much per-capita budget cutting than those in suburban and rural areas. See 'Austerity hit cities twice as hard as the rest of Britain', Centre for Cities, 28 January 2019, https://www.centreforcities.org/press/austerity-hit-cities-twice-as-hard-as-the-rest-of-britain/.

45 Sara Freund, 'Looking at John Ronan's colorful library and housing project in Irving Park', *Curbed Chicago,* 17 October 2019, https://

chicago.curbed.com/2019/10/17/20919476/john-ronan-irving-park-affordable-housing-library-project.

46 Jared Brey, 'Chicago Opens Up New Libraries and Affordable Housing Projects After Design Competition', *Next City,* 28 May 2019, https://nextcity.org/daily/entry/chicago-opens-new-libraries-and-affordable-housing-projects-after-design-co.

47 Eva Fedderly, 'Community building: Chicago experiment links libraries and apartments', *Christian Science Monitor,* 24 October 2018, https://www.csmonitor.com/The-Culture/2018/1024/Community-building-Chicago-experiment-links-libraries-and-apartments.

48 Oliver Wainwright, 'Smart lifts, lonely workers, no towers or tourists: architecture after coronavirus', *Guardian,* 13 April 2020, https://www.theguardian.com/artanddesign/2020/apr/13/smart-lifts-lonely-workers-no-towers-architecture-after-covid-19-coronavirus.

49 Winnie Hu, 'What New York Can Learn From Barcelona's "Superblocks"', *New York Times,* 16 September 2016, https://www.nytimes.com/2016/10/02/nyregion/what-new-york-can-learn-from-barcelonas-superblocks.html.

50 Feargus O'Sullivan, 'Barcelona's Car-Taming "Superblocks" Meet Resistance', *CityLab,* 20 January 2017, https://www.citylab.com/transportation/2017/01/barcelonas-car-taming-superblocks-meet-resistance/513911/.

51 Ibid.

52 'Barcelona's Superblocks: Change the Grid, Change your Neighborhood', Streetfilms, 2018, https://vimeo.com/282972390.

53 Of course, this also maps onto the fact that social connections in developed societies tend to correlate with wealth. The original study, conducted in 1969, was replicated over forty years later with similar results. See Joshua Hart and Graham Parkhurst, 'Driven to excess: Impacts of motor vehicles on the quality of life of residents of three streets in Bristol UK', *World Transport Policy & Practice* 17, no. 2 (January 2011), 12–30, https://uwe-repository.worktribe.com/output/968892; original study: Donald Appleyard, 'The Environmental Quality of City Streets: The Residents' Viewpoint', *Journal of the American Planning Association* 35 (1969), 84–101.

54 Natalie Colarossi, '18 times people around the world spread love

and kindness to lift spirits during the coronavirus pandemic',
Insider, 26 March 2020, https://www.insider.com/times-people-
spread-kindness-during-coronavirus-pandemic-2020-3.

55 'Taxi driver applauded by medics after taking patients to hospital
for free – video', *Guardian*, 20 April 2020, https://www.
theguardian.com/world/video/2020/apr/20/taxi-driver-applauded-
by-doctors-after-giving-patients-free-journeys-to-hospital-video.

56 Matt Lloyd, '"Happy to chat" benches: The woman getting
strangers to talk', BBC News, 19 October 2019, https://www.bbc.
co.uk/news/uk-wales-50000204.

CHAPTER SIX:
Our Screens, Our Selves

1 A.D. Morrison-Low, 'Sir David Brewster (1781–1868)', *Oxford
Dictionary of National Biography*, 9 January 2014, https://www.
oxforddnb.com/view/10.1093/ref:odnb/9780198614128.001.0001/
odnb-9780198614128-e-3371.

2 *The Literary Panorama and National Register*, vol. 8 (Simpkin and
Marshall, 1819), p.504.

3 Letter dated 23 May 1818, quoted by Nicole Garrod Bush,
'Kaleidoscopism: The Circulation of a Mid-Century Metaphor and
Motif', *Journal of Victorian Culture* 20, no. 4 (1 December 2015),
https://academic.oup.com/jvc/article/20/4/509/4095158.

4 Megan Richardson and Julian Thomas, *Fashioning Intellectual
Property: Exhibition, Advertising and the Press, 1789–1918* (Cambridge
University Press, 2012), p.57.

5 Bush, 'Kaleidoscopism'.

6 Margaret Gordon, *The Home Life of Sir David Brewster* (Cambridge
University Press, 2010 [1869]), p.95.

7 *The Literary Panorama and National Register*, 504.

8 Jason Farman, 'The Myth of the Disconnected Life', *The Atlantic*, 7
February 2012, https://www.theatlantic.com/technology/
archive/2012/02/the-myth-of-the-disconnected-life/252672/.

9 *The Letters of Percy Bysshe Shelley*, vol. 2, ed. Frederick L. Jones
(Clarendon Press, 1964), p.69.

10 Alexander Rucki, 'Average smartphone user checks device 221 times

a day, according to research', *Evening Standard*, 7 October 2014, https://www.standard.co.uk/news/techandgadgets/average-smartphone-user-checks-device-221-times-a-day-according-to-research-9780810.html.

11   Rani Molla, 'Tech companies tried to help us spend less time on our phones. It didn't work', *Vox*, 6 January 2020, https://www.vox.com/recode/2020/1/6/21048116/tech-companies-time-well-spent-mobile-phone-usage-data.

12   About 95% of American teenagers had (or had access to) a smartphone in 2018, up from the 73% in 2014–15, according to the Pew Research Center. As a result, teens are using the internet a lot more. While 24% of teens said they're online 'almost constantly' in the 2014–15 survey, that jumped to 45% in 2018. In addition, 44% of teens surveyed this year said they go online several times a day. See Monica Anderson and Jingjing Jiang, 'Teens, Social Media & Technology 2018', Pew Research Center, 31 May 2018, https://www.pewresearch.org/internet/2018/05/31/teens-social-media-technology-2018/.

13   'Global Mobile Consumer Trends, 2nd Edition', Deloitte, 2017, 8, https://www2.deloitte.com/global/en/pages/technology-media-and-telecommunications/articles/gx-global-mobile-consumer-trends.html#country.

14   Australia had 90% smartphone penetration as of 2018, while Israelis have the highest use of social media in the world and smartphone penetration there is second only to South Korea, according to the Pew Research Center. 'Smartphones are common in Europe and North America, while sub-Saharan Africa and India lag in ownership', Pew Research Center, 14 June 2018, https://www.pewresearch.org/global/2018/06/19/social-media-use-continues-to-rise-in-developing-countries-but-plateaus-across-developed-ones/pg_2018-06-19_global-tech_0-03/.

15   Adam Carey, 'Mobile fiends now need not look up as Melbourne tests street-level traffic lights,' *The Age*, 27 March 2017, https://www.theage.com.au/national/victoria/mobile-fiends-now-need-not-look-up-as-melbourne-tests-streetlevel-traffic-lights-20170327-gv73bd.html.

16   There is an irony here: this 'Socrates' is actually the creation of

Plato, whose words we know today only because he wrote them down. See Plato, *Phaedrus*, trans. Harold N. Fowler (Harvard University Press, 1925).

17 Johannes Trithemius, *In Praise of Scribes (De Laude Scriptorum)*, trans. Roland Behrendt, ed. Klaus Arnold (Coronado Press, 1974).

18 Adrienne LaFrance, 'How Telephone Etiquette Has Changed', *The Atlantic*, 2 September 2015, https://www.theatlantic.com/ technology/archive/2015/09/how-telephone-etiquette-has-changed/403564/.

19 Robert Rosenberger, 'An experiential account of phantom vibration syndrome', *Computers in Human Behavior* 52 (2015), 124–31, https:// doi.org/10.1016/j.chb.2015.04.065.

20 K. Kushlev et al., 'Smartphones reduce smiles between strangers', *Computers in Human Behavior* 91 (February 2019), 12–16.

21 These incidents took place across the globe, including in the US, Malta, the UK, Singapore and China. '6 year old drowns while dad busy on phone', YoungParents.com, 18 September 2016, https:// www.youngparents.com.sg/family/6-year-old-drowns-while-dad-busy-phone/; Matthew Xuereb, 'Mum whose baby drowned in bath given suspended sentence', *Times of Malta*, 12 June 2015, https://www.timesofmalta.com/articles/view/20150612/local/ mum-whose-baby-drowned-in-bath-given-suspended-sentence.572189; Lucy Clarke-Billings, 'Mother chatted on Facebook while toddler drowned in the garden', *Telegraph*, 10 October 2015, https://www.telegraph.co.uk/news/uknews/crime/11923930/ Mother-chatted-on-Facebook-while-toddler-son-drowned-in-the-garden.html; Martine Berg Olsen, 'Baby drowned in bath while mum "spent 50 minutes on phone to girlfriend"', *Metro*, 6 March 2019, https://metro.co.uk/2019/03/06/baby-drowned-bath-mum-spent-50-minutes-phone-girlfriend-8828813/; 'Toddler drowns while mum texts on mobile just yards away', *Express*, 5 January 2016, https://www.express.co.uk/news/world/750540/drowning-toddler-mobile-phone-china-ocean-spring-resort-mum-texting; Zach Dennis, 'Police: 3 children drowned while a Texas mom was on cell phone', AJC, 14 July 2015, https://www.ajc.com/news/national/police-children-drowned-while-texas-mom-was-cell-phone/ R5cDdBhwac5bjGFTxeM4sM/.

22 Will Axford, 'Police: Texas mom was on Facebook when her baby drowned in the bathtub', *Houston Chronicle*, 23 June 2017, https://www.chron.com/news/houston-texas/texas/article/Texas-mom-Facebook-baby-drowned-11239659.php.

23 Jemima Kiss, '"I was on Instagram. The baby fell down the stairs": is your phone use harming your child?' *Guardian*, 7 December 2018, https://www.theguardian.com/lifeandstyle/2018/dec/07/mother-on-instagram-baby-fell-down-stairs-parental-phone-use-children.

24 Brandon T. McDaniel, 'Parent distraction with phones, reasons for use, and impacts on parenting and child outcomes: A review of the emerging research', *Human Behavior and Emergent Technology* (2019), 72–80, https://doi.org/10.1002/hbe2.139; J. Radesky et al., 'Maternal mobile device use during a structured parent–child interaction task', *Academic Pediatrics* 15, no. 2 (2015), 238–44; R.P. Golen and A.K. Ventura, 'What are mothers doing while bottle-feeding their infants? Exploring the prevalence of maternal distraction during bottle-feeding interactions', *Early Human Development* 91, no. 12 (2015), 787–91.

25 Ibid.; see also B.T. McDaniel and J. Radesky, 'Technoference: Parent technology use, stress, and child behavior problems over time', *Pediatric Research* 84 (2018), 210–18; Tanja Poulain et al., 'Media Use of Mothers, Media Use of Children, and Parent–Child Interaction Are Related to Behavioral Difficulties and Strengths of Children'. *International Journal of Environmental Research and Public Health* 16, no. 23 (2019), 4651, https://doi.org/10.3390/ijerph16234651.

26 L.A. Stockdale et al., 'Parent and child technoference and socioemotional behavioral outcomes: A nationally representative sample of 10- to 20-year-old adolescents', *Computers in Human Behavior* 88 (2018), 219–26.

27 For more on the concept of being 'alone together', see Sherry Turkle, *Alone Together: Why We Expect More from Technology and Less from Each Other*, Revised Edition (Basic Books, 2017).

28 'The iPhone Effect: when mobile devices intrude on our face-to-face encounters', The British Psychological Society Research Digest, 4 August 2014, http://bps-research-digest.blogspot.com/2014/08/the-iphone-effect-when-mobile-devices.html; see also

S. Misra et al., 'The iPhone Effect: The Quality of In-Person Social Interactions in the Presence of Mobile Devices Environment and Behavior', *Environment and Behavior* 48, no. 2 (2014), 275–98, https://doi.org./10.1177/0013916514539755.

29 The Human Uniqueness subscale includes '6 items generally related to higher-order cognition and intellectual competence: evaluators rated the extent to which the speaker was "refined and cultured"; was "rational and logical"; lacked "self-restraint" (reverse-scored); was "unsophisticated" (reverse-scored); was "like an adult, not a child"; and seemed "less than human, like an animal" (reverse-scored)'. Juliana Schroeder, Michael Kardas and Nicholas Epley, 'The Humanizing Voice: Speech Reveals, and Text Conceals, a More Thoughtful Mind in the Midst of Disagreement', *Psychological Science* 28, no. 12, 1745–62, https://doi.org/10.1177/0956797617713798.

30 Jamil Zaki, 'The Technology of Kindness', *Scientific American,* 6 August 2019, https://www.scientificamerican.com/article/the-technology-of-kindness/.

31 Rurik Bradbury, 'The digital lives of Millennials and Gen Z', Liveperson Report, 2018, https://liveperson.docsend.com/view/tm8j45m.

32 Belle Beth Cooper, '7 Powerful Facebook Statistics You Should Know for a More Engaging Facebook Page', Buffer.com, https://buffer.com/resources/7-facebook-stats-you-should-know-for-a-more-engaging-page.

33 This particular statistic is from Verizon, but is reflected in usage from other telephone service providers; O2 reported that phone traffic from its British users was up 57% in the first week of the UK's lockdown. Some providers, especially in the UK, even experienced brief outages due to the surge in demand for Wifi and voice calling. See Cecilia Kang, 'The Humble Phone Call Has Made a Comeback', *New York Times,* 9 April 2020, https://www.nytimes.com/2020/04/09/technology/phone-calls-voice-virus.html; Emma Brazell, 'UK mobile networks go down as people work from home due to coronavirus', *Metro,* 17 March 2020, https://metro.co.uk/2020/03/17/uk-mobile-networks-o2-ee-vodafone-3-go-people-work-home-12410145/.

34   Kang, 'The Humble Phone Call Has Made a Comeback'.

35   'The Phone Call Strikes Back', O2 News, 23 April 2020, https://news.o2.co.uk/press-release/the-phone-call-strikes-back/.

36   Given their importance to human interaction, it is understandable (if not excusable) that people who cannot recognise faces – people like Oliver Sacks, who suffered from a condition called prosopagnosia – are often taken as socially awkward, shy, reclusive and even autistic. See Oliver Sacks, 'Face-Blind', *New Yorker*, 30 August 2010, https://www.newyorker.com/magazine/2010/08/30/face-blind.

37   Jing Jiang et al., 'Neural Synchronization During Face-to-Face Communication', *Journal of Neuroscience* 32, no. 45 (November 2012), 16,064–9, https://doi.org/10.1523/JNEUROSCI.2926-12.2012

38   Emily Green, 'How technology is harming our ability to feel empathy', Street Roots, 15 February 2019, https://news.streetroots.org/2019/02/15/how-technology-harming-our-ability-feel-empathy; see also Helen Riess and Liz Neporent, *The Empathy Effect* (Sounds True Publishing, 2018).

39   F. Grondin, A.M. Lomanowska and P.L. Jackson, 'Empathy in Computer-Mediated Interactions: A Conceptual Framework for Research and Clinical Practice,' *Clinical Psychology: Science and Practice* e12298, https ://doi.org/10.1111/cpsp.12298.

40   Kate Murphy, 'Why Zoom is Terrible', *New York Times*, 29 April 2020, https://www.nytimes.com/2020/04/29/sunday-review/zoom-video-conference.html.

41   Hannah Miller et al., '"Blissfully happy" or "ready to fight": Varying interpretations of emoji', Grouplens Research, University of Minnesota, 2016, https://www-users.cs.umn.edu/~bhecht/publications/ICWSM2016_emoji.pdf.

42   M.A. Riordan and L.A. Trichtinger, 'Overconfidence at the Keyboard: Confidence and accuracy in interpreting affect in e-mail exchanges', *Human Communication Research* (2016), https://doi.org/10.1111/hcre.12093.

43   Heather Cicchese, 'College class tries to revive the lost art of dating', *Boston Globe*, 16 May 2014, https://www.bostonglobe.com/lifestyle/2014/05/16/boston-college-professor-assigns-students-dates/jHXENWsdmp7cFlRPPwfoUJ/story.html.

44 The original assignment can be viewed online at https://www. bc.edu/content/dam/files/schools/lsoe/pdf/DatingAssignment.pdf.

45 Heather Cicchese, 'College class tries to revive the lost art of dating'.

46 Original site: https://www.wikihow.com/Ask-Someone-Out.

47 Angie S. Page et al., 'Children's Screen Viewing is Related to Psychological Difficulties Irrespective of Physical Activity', *Pediatrics* 126, no. 5 (2010), e1011–17.

48 Katie Bindley, 'When Children Text All Day, What Happens to Their Social Skills?', *Huffington Post*, 9 December 2011, https://www.huffpost.com/entry/children-texting-technology-social-skills_n_1137570.

49 'Children, Teens, and Entertainment Media: The View from the Classroom' (Common Sense Media, 2012), 19, https://www.commonsensemedia.org/research/children-teens-and-entertainment-media-the-view-from-the-classroom.

50 V. Carson et al., 'Physical activity and sedentary behavior across three time-points and associations with social skills in early childhood', *BMC Public Health* 19, no. 27 (2019), https://doi.org/10.1186/s12889-018-6381-x.

51 Vera Skalická et al., 'Screen time and the development of emotion understanding from age 4 to age 8: A community study', *British Journal of Developmental Psychology* 37, no. 3 (2019), 427–43, https://doi.org/10.1111/bjdp.12283.

52 See for example Douglas B. Downey and Benjamin G. Gibbs, 'Kids These Days: Are Face-to-Face Social Skills among American Children Declining?', *American Journal of Sociology* 125, no. 4 (January 2020), 1030–83, https://doi.org/10.1086/707985.

53 Yalda T. Uhls et al., 'Five Days at Outdoor Education Camp without Screens Improves Preteen Skills with Nonverbal Emotion Cues', *Computers in Human Behavior* 39 (2014), 387–92, https://www.sciencedirect.com/science/article/pii/S0747563214003227.

54 Belinda Luscombe, 'Why Access to Screens Is Lowering Kids' Social Skills', *Time*, 21 August 2014, https://time.com/3153910/why-access-to-screens-is-lowering-kids-social-skills/.

55 In the US, for example, at 53% of eleven-year-olds do; Anya Kamenetz, 'It's a Smartphone Life: More Than Half of U.S. Children Now Have One', NPR Education, 31 October 2019,

https://www.npr.org/2019/10/31/774838891/its-a-smartphone-life-more-than-half-of-u-s-children-now-have-one; Zoe Kleinman, 'Half of UK 10-year-olds own a smartphone', BBC News, 4 February 2020, https://www.bbc.co.uk/news/technology-51358192.

56 'Most children own mobile phone by age of seven, study finds', *Guardian,* 30 January 2020, https://www.theguardian.com/society/2020/jan/30/most-children-own-mobile-phone-by-age-of-seven-study-finds.

57 Nick Bilton, 'Steve Jobs Was a Low-Tech Parent', *New York Times,* 10 September 2014, https://www.nytimes.com/2014/09/11/fashion/steve-jobs-apple-was-a-low-tech-parent.html; Chris Weller, 'Bill Gates and Steve Jobs Raised Their Kids Tech-Free and It Should Have Been a Red Flag', *Independent,* 24 October 2017, https://www.independent.co.uk/life-style/gadgets-and-tech/bill-gates-and-steve-jobs-raised-their-kids-techfree-and-it-shouldve-been-a-red-flag-a8017136.html.

58 Matt Richtel, 'A Silicon Valley School That Doesn't Compute', *New York Times,* 22 October 2011, https://www.nytimes.com/2011/10/23/technology/at-waldorf-school-in-silicon-valley-technology-can-wait.html.

59 Nellie Bowles, 'Silicon Valley Nannies Are Phone Police for Kids', *New York Times,* 26 October 2018, https://www.nytimes.com/2018/10/26/style/silicon-valley-nannies.html.

60 Nellie Bowles, 'The Digital Gap Between Rich and Poor Kids Is Not What We Expected', *New York Times,* 26 October 2018, https://www.nytimes.com/2018/10/26/style/digital-divide-screens-schools.html.

61 This is amongst those who have devices. Rani Molla, 'Poor kids spend nearly 2 hours more on screens each day than rich kids', *Vox,* 29 October 2019, https://www.vox.com/recode/2019/10/29/20937870/kids-screentime-rich-poor-common-sense-media; original data from 'The Common Sense Census: Media Use by Tweens and Teens, 2019' (Common Sense Media, 2019), https://www.commonsensemedia.org/research/the-common-sense-census-media-use-by-tweens-and-teens-2019.

62 Personal conversation, October 2019.

63 Ben Hoyle, 'Jittery American pupils can hold on to their phones', *The Times*, 22 January 2020, https://www.thetimes.co.uk/article/jittery-american-pupils-can-hold-on-to-their-phones-z0zxr972c.

64 The acronym is based on the questions themselves: 1. Have you ever felt you needed to *Cut* down on your drinking? 2. Do people who criticise your drinking *Annoy* you? 3. Have you ever felt *Guilty* about your drinking? 4. Do you need a drink first thing in the morning (*Eye-opener*)?

65 See, for example, Jamie Bartlett, *The People vs. Tech: How the Internet is Killing Democracy (and How We Can Save It)* (Ebury Press, 2018); Sherry Turkle, *Alone Together: Why We Expect More from Technology and Less from Each Other*, Revised Edition (Basic Books, 2017). For more on immersive product design, see Joseph Dickerson, 'Walt Disney: The World's First UX Designer', *UX Magazine*, 9 September 2013, http://uxmag.com/articles/walt-disney-the-worlds-first-ux-designer.

66 Lo Min Ming, 'UI, UX: Who Does What? A Designer's guide to the Tech Industry', *Fast Company*, 7 July 2014, https://www.fastcompany.com/3032719/ui-ux-who-does-what-a-designers-guide-to-the-tech-industry; Stefan Stieger and David Lewetz, 'A Week Without Using Social Media: Results from an Ecological Momentary Intervention Study Using Smartphones', *Cypberpsychology, Behavior, and Social Networking* 21, no. 10 (2018), https://www.liebertpub.com/doi/abs/10.1089/cyber.2018.0070.

67 Olivia Solon, 'Ex-Facebook president Sean Parker: site made to exploit human "vulnerability"', *Guardian*, 9 November 2017, https://www.theguardian.com/technology/2017/nov/09/facebook-sean-parker-vulnerability-brain-psychology.

68 Jean M. Twenge, Brian H. Spitzberg and W. Keith Campbell, 'Less In-Person Social Interaction with Peers among US Adolescents in the 21st Century and Links to Loneliness', *Journal of Social and Personal Relationships* 36, no. 6 (19 March 2019), 1892–913, https://doi.org/10.1177/0265407519836170.

69 Brian A. Primack et al., 'Social Media Use and Perceived Social Isolation Among Young Adults in the US', *American Journal of*

Preventive Medicine 53, No. 1 (1 July 2017), 1–8, https://doi.org/
10.1016/j.amepre.2017.01.010.

70 Twenge et al., 'Less In-Person Social Interaction with Peers'.

71 Ibid.; see also original data at https://www.pewresearch.org/
internet/2018/05/31/teens-social-media-technology-2018/. In
addition to Twenge, whose book *iGen* (Simon & Schuster, 2017)
placed teen smartphone use front and centre in the discussion of
mental health, vocal critics of teen smartphone usage include
Jonathan Haidt and Greg Lukianoff, co-authors of *The Coddling of
the American Mind* (Penguin, 2018).

72 Hunt Allcott et al., 'The Welfare Effects of Social Media' (2019), 6,
https://web.stanford.edu/~gentzkow/research/facebook.pdf.

73 Melissa G Hunt et al., 'No More FOMO: Limiting Social Media
Decreases Loneliness and Depression', *Journal of Social and Clinical
Psychology* 37, no. 10 (8 November 2018), 751–68, https://doi.org/
10.1521/jscp.2018.37.10.751.

74 Hunt Allcott et al., 'The Welfare Effects of Social Media', 23.

75 Kyt Dotson, 'YouTube sensation and entrepreneur Markee Dragon
swatted on first day of YouTube Gaming', Silicon Angle, 28 August
2015, https://siliconangle.com/2015/08/28/youtube-sensation-and-
entrepreneur-markee-dragon-swatted-on-first-day-of-youtube-
gaming/; see also Jason Fagone, 'The Serial Swatter', *New York Times*
magazine, 24 November 2015, https://www.nytimes.
com/2015/11/29/magazine/the-serial-swatter.html.

76 Matthew Williams, 'The connection between online hate speech
and real-world hate crime', OUP Blog, 12 October 2019, https://
blog.oup.com/2019/10/connection-between-online-hate-speech-real-
world-hate-crime/. See also Williams, *The Science of Hate* (Faber &
Faber, forthcoming 2020).

77 'The Rise of Antisemitism on Social Media: Summary of 2016'
(The World Jewish Congress, 2016), 184, http://www.crif.org/sites/
default/fichiers/images/documents/antisemitismreport.pdf.

78 J.J. Van Bavel et al., 'Emotion shapes the diffusion of moralized
content in social networks', *PNAS* 114, no. 28 (July 2017), 7313–7318.
See also supplemental information at https://www.pnas.org/
content/pnas/suppl/2017/06/20/1618923114.DCSupplemental/
pnas.1618923114.sapp.pdf, 17–18.

79 Zeynep Tufekci, 'It's the (Democracy-Poisoning) Golden Age of Free Speech', *Wired*, 16 January 2018, https://www.wired.com/story/free-speech-issue-tech-turmoil-new-censorship/.

80 Richard Seymour, 'How addictive social media fuels online abuse', *Financial Times*, 4 November 2019, https://www.ft.com/content/abc86766-fa37-11e9-a354-36acbbb0d9b6.

81 Original tweet as well as warning message can be viewed, as of time of writing, at https://twitter.com/realDonaldTrump/status/1266231100780744704.

82 Tony Romm and Allyson Chiu, 'Twitter flags Trump, White House for "glorifying violence" after tweeting Minneapolis looting will lead to "shooting"', *Washington Post*, 30 May 2020, https://www.washingtonpost.com/nation/2020/05/29/trump-minneapolis-twitter-protest/; Kate Conger, 'Twitter had been drawing a line for months when Trump crossed it', *New York Times*, 30 May 2020, https://www.nytimes.com/2020/05/30/technology/twitter-trump-dorsey.html; for historical context, see Barbara Sprunt, 'The History Behind "When the Looting Starts, the Shooting Starts"', NPR Politics, 29 May 2020, https://www.npr.org/2020/05/29/864818368/the-history-behind-when-the-looting-starts-the-shooting-starts.

83 Mike Isaac and Cecilia Kang, 'While Twitter confronts Trump, Zuckerberg keeps Facebook out of it', *New York Times*, 29 May 2020, https://www.nytimes.com/2020/05/29/technology/twitter-facebook-zuckerberg-trump.html.

84 Derrick A. Paulo and Ellen Lokajaya, '3 in 4 youngsters say they have been bullied online', *CNA Insider*, 1 March 2018, https://www.channelnewsasia.com/news/cnainsider/3-in-4-teens-singapore-cyberbullying-bullied-online-survey-10001480.

85 Christo Petrov, 'Cyberbullying Statistics 2020', Tech Jury, 2 June 2020, https://techjury.net/stats-about/cyberbullying/#Cyberbullying_around_the_world.

86 'The Annual Bullying Survey 2017' (Ditch the Label, 2017), 28, https://www.ditchthelabel.org/wp-content/uploads/2017/07/The-Annual-Bullying-Survey-2017-2.pdf.

87 Simon Murphy, 'Girl killed herself after intense social media activity, inquest finds', *Guardian*, 17 April 2019, https://www.

theguardian.com/uk-news/2019/apr/17/girl-killed-herself-social-media-inquest-jessica-scatterson.

88 Clyde Haberman, 'What the Kitty Genovese Killing Can Teach Today's Digital Bystanders', *New York Times,* 4 June 2017, https://www.nytimes.com/2017/06/04/us/retro-report-bystander-effect.html; Carrie Rentschler, 'Online abuse: we need Good Samaritans on the web', *Guardian,* 19 April 2016, https://www.theguardian.com/commentisfree/2016/apr/19/online-abuse-bystanders-violence-web.

89 Gordon Harold and Daniel Aquah, 'What works to enhance interparental relationships and improve outcomes for children?' (Early Intervention Foundation, 2016), https://www.eif.org.uk/report/what-works-to-enhance-interparental-relationships-and-improve-outcomes-for-children/.

90 We see this most clearly amongst those for whom doing just this is their job. There are now over 100,000 people employed (often via contracted companies, rather than directly by social media companies) as 'content moderators', tasked with determining whether a particular post is gruesome, racist, obscene or offensive enough to be removed. Moderators often experience symptoms of post-traumatic stress disorder after months of watching abusive content with little to no institutional support. One woman, a former moderator for MySpace, refused to shake people's hands for three years after quitting. After journalist Casey Newton exposed the horrific working conditions at a Facebook-contracted moderation facility in *The Verge*, the company announced it was severing its ties with the social media giant. See Newton, 'The Trauma Floor: The secret lives of Facebook moderators in America', *The Verge*, 25 February 2019, https://www.theverge.com/2019/2/25/18229714/cognizant-facebook-content-moderator-interviews-trauma-working-conditions-arizona; 'Facebook firm Cognizant quits,' BBC News, 31 October 2019, https://www.bbc.co.uk/news/technology-50247540; Isaac Chotiner, 'The Underworld of Online Content', *New Yorker*, 5 July 2019, https://www.newyorker.com/news/q-and-a/the-underworld-of-online-content-moderation; Sarah T. Roberts, *Behind the Screen: Content Moderation in the Shadows of Social Media* (Yale University Press, 2019).

91 Sebastian Deri, Shai Davidai and Thomas Gilovich, 'Home alone: why people believe others' social lives are richer than their own', *Journal of Personality and Social Psychology* 113, no. 6 (December 2017), 858–77.

92 'Childline: More children seeking help for loneliness', BBC News, 3 July 2018, https://www.bbc.co.uk/news/uk-44692344.

93 J. Clement, 'U.S. group chat frequency 2017, by age group'. Statista, 5 November 2018, https://www.statista.com/statistics/800650/group-chat-functions-age-use-text-online-messaging-apps/.

94 Shoshana Zuboff, *The Age of Surveillance Capitalism* (Public Affairs, 2019); see also John Harris, 'Death of the private self: how fifteen years of Facebook changed the human condition', *Guardian*, 31 January 2019, https://www.theguardian.com/technology/2019/jan/31/how-facebook-robbed-us-of-our-sense-of-self.

95 Josh Constine, 'Now Facebook says it may remove Like counts', TechCrunch.com, 2 September 2019. https://techcrunch.com/2019/09/02/facebook-hidden-likes/; Greg Kumparak, 'Instagram will now hide likes in 6 more countries', TechCrunch.com, 17 July 2019, https://techcrunch.com/2019/07/17/instagram-will-now-hide-likes-in-6-more-countries/.

96 Amy Chozick, 'This Is the Guy Who's Taking Away the Likes', *New York Times*, 17 January 2020, https://www.nytimes.com/2020/01/17/business/instagram-likes.html.

97 'Over Three Quarters of Brits Say Their Social Media Page is a Lie', Custard Media, 6 April 2016, https://www.custard.co.uk/over-three-quarters-of-brits-say-their-social-media-page-is-a-lie/.

98 Sirin Kale, 'Logged off: meet the teens who refuse to use social media', *Guardian*, 29 August 2018, https://www.theguardian.com/society/2018/aug/29/teens-desert-social-media.

99 Harris, 'Death of the private self'.

100 Rebecca Jennings, 'Facetune and the internet's endless pursuit of physical perfection', *Vox*, 25 July 2019, https://www.vox.com/the-highlight/2019/7/16/20689832/instagram-photo-editing-app-facetune.

101 Chris Velazco, 'Apple highlights some of the best (and most popular) apps of 2019', Engadget, 3 December 2019, https://www.engadget.com/2019/12/03/apple-best-apps-of-2019-iphone-ipad-mac/.

102 Elle Hunt, 'Faking it: how selfie dysmorphia is driving people to

seek surgery', *Guardian*, 23 January 2019, https://www.theguardian.
com/lifeandstyle/2019/jan/23/faking-it-how-selfie-dysmorphia-is-
driving-people-to-seek-surgery.

103 Jessica Baron, 'Does Editing Your Selfies Make You More Likely
to Want Plastic Surgery?' *Forbes*, 27 June 2019, https://www.
forbes.com/sites/jessicabaron/2019/06/27/plastic-surgeons-ask-if-
selfie-editing-is-related-to-a-desire-for-plastic-
surgery/#87499d11e021; see also Susruthi Rajanala, Mayra B.C.
Maymone, and Neelam A. Vashi, 'Selfies–Living In the Era of
Filtered Photographs', *JAMA Facial Plastic Surgery* 20, no. 6
(November 2018), 443–44.

104 Cass Sunstein, 'Nudging Smokers', *New England Journal of Medicine*
372, no. 22 (May 2015), 2150–51, https://doi.org/10.1056/
NEJMe1503200.

105 Michael Zelenko, 'The High Hopes of the Low-Tech Phone', *The
Verge*, 4 September 2019, https://www.theverge.com/2019/9/4/
20847717/light-phone-2-minimalist-features-design-keyboard-
crowdfunding.

106 See Jonathan Haidt and Nick Allen, 'Scrutinizing the effects of
digital technology on mental health', *Nature*, News and Views
Forum, 10 February 2020, https://www.nature.com/articles/
d41586-020-00296-x?sf229908667=1.

107 'Children Unprepared for Social Media "Cliff Edge" as They Start
Secondary School, Children's Commissioner for England Warns in
New Report', Children's Commissioner of England, 4 January 2018,
https://www.childrenscommissioner.gov.uk/2018/01/04/children-
unprepared-for-social-media-cliff-edge-as-they-start-secondary-
school-childrens-commissioner-for-england-warns-in-new-report/;
for full report, see 'Life in "Likes": Children's Commissioner
Report into Social Media Use among 8–12 Year Olds' (Children's
Commissioner of England, 2018).

108 Whilst this is a lower age than the ban on sales of tobacco
products applies to in most countries, given that many young
people enter the workforce, and the extent to which informal
workplace interactions take place on such forums, it would be
unreasonable to ban older teenagers from using it.

109 For more historical context, see 'How has the seatbelt law evolved

since 1968?' Road Safety GB, 9 April 2018, https://roadsafetygb.org.uk/news/how-has-the-seatbelt-law-evolved-since-1968/; see original legislation at http://www.legislation.gov.uk/uksi/1989/1219/made.

110 Smoking in a car with a minor present has been illegal in the UK since 2015 (UK Department of Health and Social Care, 'Smoking in Vehicles', 17 July 2015, https://www.gov.uk/government/news/smoking-in-vehicles); different states and counties in the US have their own regulations, with California notably banning this behaviour from 2007 (http://leginfo.legislature.ca.gov/faces/codes_displaySection.xhtml?lawCode=HSC&sectionNum=118948).

111 See Jacob Shamsian, 'Facebook's head of policy says it would allow "denying the Holocaust" in the weeks before banning high-profile anti-Semitic conspiracy theorists', *Business Insider,* 3 May 2019, https://www.insider.com/facebook-allows-holocaust-denial-anti-semitic-ban-2019-5.

112 Karen Zraick, 'Mark Zuckerberg seeks to clarify remarks about Holocaust deniers after outcry', *New York Times,* 18 July 2018, https://www.nytimes.com/2018/07/18/technology/mark-zuckerberg-facebook-holocaust-denial.html.

113 'Social media global revenue 2013–2019', Statista, 14 July 2016, https://www.statista.com/statistics/562397/worldwide-revenue-from-social-media/. Note that the data for 2016–19 are forecasts rather than reports.

114 Jamil Zaki, 'The Technology of Kindness'.

115 Mark Zuckerberg, 'The Internet needs new rules. Let's start in these four areas', *Washington Post,* 30 March 2019, https://www.washingtonpost.com/opinions/mark-zuckerberg-the-internet-needs-new-rules-lets-start-in-these-four-areas/2019/03/29/9e6f0504-521a-11e9-a3f7-78b7525a8d5f_story.html.

116 'Australian government pushes through expansive new legislation targeting abhorrent violent material online', Ashurst Media Update, 10 April 2019, https://www.ashurst.com/en/news-and-insights/legal-updates/media-update-new-legislation-targeting-abhorrent-violent-material-online/.

117 But vague phrasing may dull the legislation's teeth. Already debates about defining key terms like 'abhorrent' and 'expeditiously' threaten to render it moot; see ibid.

118 Jamil Zaki, 'The Technology of Kindness'.

119 Jonathan Rauch, 'Twitter Needs a Pause Button', *The Atlantic,* August 2019, https://www.theatlantic.com/magazine/archive/2019/08/twitter-pause-button/592762/.

120 'Age Appropriate Design: A Code of Practice for Online Services. Full Version to be Laid in Parliament' (Information Commissioner's Office, 22 January 2020), 68, https://ico.org.uk/media/for-organi sations/guide-to-data-protection/key-data-protection-themes/age-appropriate-design-a-code-of-practice-for-online-services-0-0.pdf.

121 'Online Harms White Paper' (UK Department for Digital, Culture, Media & Sport and the UK Home Office, updated 12 February 2020), https://www.gov.uk/government/consultations/online-harms-white-paper/online-harms-white-paper.

122 'Impact of social media and screen-use on young people's health', HC 822 (House of Commons, 2019), https://publications.parliament.uk/pa/cm201719/cmselect/cmsctech/822/822.pdf.

123 Allan M. Brandt, 'Inventing Conflicts of Interest: A History of Tobacco Industry Tactics', *American Journal of Public Health* 102, no. 1 (January 2012), 63–71, https://doi.org/10.2105/AJPH.2011.300292.

124 Alex Hern, 'Third of advertisers may boycott Facebook in hate speech revolt', *Guardian*, 30 June 2020, https://www.theguardian.com/technology/2020/jun/30/third-of-advertisers-may-boycott-facebook-in-hate-speech-revolt.

125 'More Companies Join Facebook Ad Boycott Bandwagon', *New York Times*, 29 June 2020, https://www.nytimes.com/reuters/2020/06/29/business/29reuters-facebook-ads-boycott-factbox.html; see also Stop Hate for Profit, https://stophateforprofit.org

CHAPTER SEVEN:
Alone at the Office

1   Dan Schawbel, *Back to Human: How Great Leaders Create Connection in the Age of Isolation* (Da Capo, 2018), Introduction. Note that whilst Schawbel doesn't explicitly state that his survey questioned *only* office workers, it's clear from reading the book that the focus of his surveys is overwhelmingly white-collar

office workers. See also David Vallance, 'The workplace is a lonely place, but it doesn't have to be', Dropbox, 15 July 2019, https://blog.dropbox.com/topics/work-culture/tips-for-fixing-workplace-loneliness.

2   Emma Mamo, 'How to combat the rise of workplace loneliness', TotalJobs, 30 July 2018, https://www.totaljobs.com/insidejob/how-to-combat-the-rise-of-workplace-loneliness/; Jo Carnegie, 'The rising epidemic of workplace loneliness and why we have no office friends', *Telegraph*, 18 June 2018, https://www.telegraph.co.uk/education-and-careers/0/rising-epidemic-workplace-loneliness-have-no-office-friends/; as of 2014, 42% of Brits reported not having a single friend at the office.

3   'Most white-collar workers in China anxious and lonely: survey', *China Daily*, 23 May 2018, https://www.chinadaily.com.cn/a/201805/23/WS5b04ca17a3103f6866eea0e9.html.

4   'Research on friends at work', Olivet Nazarene University, https://online.olivet.edu/news/research-friends-work; 'Loneliness and the Workplace', Cigna, January 2020, https://www.cigna.com/static/www-cigna-com/docs/about-us/newsroom/studies-and-reports/combatting-loneliness/cigna-2020-loneliness-report.pdf, p.7.

5   'Loneliness during coronavirus', Mental Health Foundation, 3 June 2020, https://www.mentalhealth.org.uk/coronavirus/coping-with-loneliness.

6   'State of the Global Workplace', Gallup, https://www.gallup.com/workplace/238079/state-global-workplace-2017.aspx.

7   Jane Ammeson, 'Storytelling with Studs Terkel', *Chicago Life*, 28 May 2007, http://chicagolife.net/content/interview/Storytelling_with_Studs_Terkel; Teenage Telephone Operator Reveals Loneliness In Terkel's 'Working'', NPR, 27 September 2016, https://www.npr.org/templates/transcript/transcript.php?storyId=495671371.

8   Dan Schawbel, *Back to Human* (Da Capo, 2018); see also Kerry Hannon, 'People with pals at work more satisfied, productive', *USA Today*, 13 August 2013, http://usatoday30.usatoday.com/money/books/reviews/2006-08-13-vital-friends_x.htm.

9   Dan Schawbel, 'How technology created a lonely workplace', MarketWatch, 2 December 2018, https://www.marketwatch.com/

story/how-technology-created-a-lonely-workplace-2018-11-13; '40% of Australians feel lonely at work', *a future that works,* 8 July 2019, http://www.afuturethatworks.org.au/media-stories/2019/7/8/40-of-australians-feel-lonely-at-work; Hakan Ozcelik and Sigal G. Barsade, 'No Employee an Island: Workplace Loneliness and Job Performance', *Academy of Management Journal* 61, no. 6 (11 December 2018): 2343, https://doi.org/10.5465/amj.2015.1066.

10   'Loneliness on the Job: Why No Employee Is an Island', *Knowledge@Wharton,* 9 March 2018, https://knowledge.wharton. upenn.edu/article/no-employee-is-an-island/.

11   Survey of 1,624 full-time employees, cf. Shawn Achor, Gabriella Rosen Kellerman, Andre Reece and Alexi Robichaux, 'America's Loneliest Workers, According to Research', *Harvard Business Review,* 19 March 2018, https://hbr.org/2018/03/americas-loneliest-workers-according-to-research; 'Loneliness Causing UK Workers to Quit Their Jobs', TotalJobs, 26 July 2018, http://press. totaljobs.com/release/loneliness-causing-uk-workers-to-quit-their-jobs/.

12   'Global Study Finds That Dependency on Technology Makes Workers Feel Isolated, Disengaged and Less Committed to Their Organizations', The Work Connectivity Study, 13 November 2018 (Cached 1 June 2020), https://workplacetrends.com/the-work-connectivity-study/.

13   S.Y. Park et al., 'Coronavirus Disease Outbreak in Call Center, South Korea', *Emerging Infectious Diseases* 26, no. 8 (2020), https:// doi.org/10.3201/eid2608.201274; see also Sean Fleming, 'COVID–19: How an office outbreak in South Korea shows that protecting workers is vital for relaxing lockdown', *World Economic Forum,* 4 May 2020, https://www.weforum.org/agenda/2020/05/protecting-office-workers-vital-for-relaxing-lockdown-south-korea/.

14   'The State of the Open Office Research Study', Stegmeier Consulting Group, https://cdn.worktechacademy.com/uploads/ 2018/01/Open-Office-Research-Study-Stegmeier-Consulting-Group. pdf; Jeremy Bates, Mike Barnes and Steven Lang, 'What Workers Want: Europe 2019', Savills PLC, 17 June 2019, https://www.savills. co.uk/research_articles/229130/283562-0/what-workers-want-europe-2019; Brian Borzykowski, 'Why open offices are bad for us',

BBC, 11 January 2017, https://www.bbc.com/worklife/article/20170105-open-offices-are-damaging-our-memories.

15 Ethan S. Bernstein and Stephen Turban, 'The impact of the "open" workspace on human collaboration', *Philosophical Transactions of the Royal Society B* 1753, no. 373 (July 2018), https://doi.org/10.1098/rstb.2017.0239

16 John Medina and Ryan Mullenix, 'How Neuroscience Is Optimising the Office', *Wall Street Journal,* 1 May 2018, https://www.wsj.com/articles/how-neuroscience-is-optimizing-the-office-1525185527; see also Barbara Palmer, 'Sound Barriers: Keeping Focus in a Noisy Open Office, *PCMA,* 1 December 2019, https://www.pcma.org/open-office-spaces-distractions-noise/.

17 'Too Much Noise', *Steelcase,* https://www.steelcase.com/research/articles/topics/open-plan-workplace/much-noise/.

18 Zaria Gorvett, 'Why office noise bothers some people more than others', BBC, 18 November 2019, https://www.bbc.com/worklife/article/20191115-office-noise-acceptable-levels-personality-type

19 Jeremy Luscombe, 'When All's Not Quiet On the Office Front, Everyone Suffers', *TLNT,* 4 May 2016, https://www.tlnt.com/when-alls-not-quiet-on-the-office-front-everyone-suffers/.

20 Vinesh Oommen, Mike Knowles and Isabella Zhao, 'Should Health Service Managers Embrace Open-Plan Work Environments? A Review', *AsiaPacific Journal of Health Management* 3, no. 2 (2008), 37–43.

21 Therese Sprinkle, Suzanne S. Masterson, Shalini Khazanchi and Nathan Tong, 'A spacial model of work relationships: The relationship-building and relationship-straining effects of workspace design', *The Academy of Management Review* 43, no. 4 (June 2018), https://doi.org/10.5465/amr.2016.0240.

22 'Divisive practice of hot desking heightens employee stress', Consultancy.uk, 7 May 2019, https://www.consultancy.uk/news/21194/divisive-practice-of-hot-desking-heightens-employee-stress.

23 Personal conversation; Carla is a pseudonym to protect privacy.

24 Sarah Holder, 'Can "Pods" Bring Quiet to the Noisy Open Office?' CityLab, 2 July 2019, https://www.citylab.com/design/2019/07/open-plan-offices-architecture-acoustics-privacy-pods/586963/; Josh Constine, 'To fight the scourge of open offices, ROOM sells

rooms', *TechCrunch*, 15 August 2018, https://techcrunch.com/2018/08/15/room-phone-booths/?guccounter=1&guce_referrer_us=aHR0cHM6Ly93d3cuZ29vZ2xlLmNvbS8&guce_referrer_cs=p6XDk_kXhi4qkZLStN5AfA.

25   Cubicall, https://www.cubicallbooth.com/.

26   Chip Cutter, 'One Architects Radical Vision to Replace the Open Office', *Wall Street Journal*, 9 January 2020, https://www.wsj.com/articles/one-architects-radical-vision-to-replace-the-open-office-11578578407?emailToken=3d0330849f5ede15b0c7196985e56f38CBKL.

27   'Why offices are becoming more "open"', InterviewQ's, https://www.interviewqs.com/blog/closed_open_office.

28   At any one time up to 40% of a company's staff are not at their dedicated desks. Jeff Pochepan, 'Here's What Happens When You Take Away Dedicated Desks for Employees', *Inc.*, 10 May 2018, https://www.inc.com/jeff-pochepan/heres-what-happens-when-you-take-away-dedicated-desks-for-employees.html; Niall Patrick Walsh, 'Is Coronavirus the Beginning of the End of Offices?', *Arch Daily*, 11 March 2020, https://www.archdaily.com/935197/is-coronavirus-the-beginning-of-the-end-of-offices.

29   Dan Schawbel, 'How technology created a lonely workplace', MarketWatch, 2 December 2018, https://www.marketwatch.com/story/how-technology-created-a-lonely-workplace-2018-11-13; also from data shared with me from internal email audit of major media company.

30   Ibid.

31   Lori Francis, Camilla M. Holmvall, and Laura E. O'Brien, 'The influence of workload and civility of treatment on the perpetration of email incivility', *Computers in Human Behavior* 46 (2015), 191–201, https://doi.org/10.1016/j.chb.2014.12.044.

32   See Gina Luk, 'Global Mobile Workforce Forecast Update 2017–2023', Strategy Analytics, 18 May 2018, https://www.strategyanalytics.com/access-services/enterprise/mobile-workforce/market-data/report-detail/global-mobile-workforce-forecast-update-2017-2023. Note that this forecast was before Covid-19 during which homeworking was the norm for most office workers. It is likely the take-up of remote working will now accelerate.

33   Erica Dhawan and Tomas Chamorro-Premuzic, 'How to

Collaborate Effectively If Your Team Is Remote', *Harvard Business Review*, 27 February 2018, https://hbr.org/2018/02/how-to-collaborate-effectively-if-your-team-is-remote.

34   Bryan Robinson, 'What Studies Reveal About Social Distancing And Remote Working During Coronavirus', *Forbes*, 4 April 2020, https://www.forbes.com/sites/bryanrobinson/2020/04/04/what-7-studies-show-about-social-distancing-and-remote-working-during-covid-19/.

35   Hailley Griffis, 'State of Remote Work 2018 Report: What It's Like to be a Remote Worker In 2018', *Buffer*, 27 February 2018, https://open.buffer.com/state-remote-work-2018/.

36   See original tweet at https://twitter.com/hacks4pancakes/status/1106743840751476736?s=20.

37   Ryan Hoover, 'The Problems in Remote Working', LinkedIn, 19 March 2019, https://www.linkedin.com/pulse/problems-remote-working-ryan-hoover/?trackingId=KaDtuFRVTiy7DDxgnaFy5Q%3D%3D.

38   See original tweets at https://twitter.com/hacks4pancakes/status/1106743840751476736?s=20; https://twitter.com/SethSandler/status/1106721799306244096?s=20.

39   See original tweet at https://twitter.com/john_osborn/status/1106570727103348738?s=20.

40   See original tweet at https://twitter.com/ericnakagawa/status/1106567592225890305?s=20.

41   See original tweet at https://twitter.com/ahmed_sulajman/status/1106561023652302848?s=20; others included 'Finding intentional work communities. Missing the passive conversations with teammates' @DavidSpinks; 'Lack of social dynamism. I get stir crazy and stuck in my head if I don't/can't talk to other people' @jkwade; 'Not talking to other human beings' @belsito; 'resolving issues is easier when ur with colleagues, than online' @GabbarSanghi; 'My biggest frustration is there's no one to high-five you when you accomplish something big' @MadalynSklar; 'Missing out office social interactions . . . that's where magic happens in relationships!' @EraldoCavalli; Ryan Hoover, 'The Problems in Remote Working', LinkedIn, 19 March 2019, https://www.linkedin.com/pulse/problems-remote-working-ryan-hoover/?trackingId=KaDtuFRVTiy7DDxgnaFy5Q%3D%3D.

42 Jenni Russell, 'Office life is more precious than we admit', *The Times,* 6 May 2020, https://www.thetimes.co.uk/article/office-life-is-more-precious-than-we-admit-q3twmh8tv.

43 Nicholas Bloom, James Liang, John Roberts and Zhichun Jenny Ying, 'Does Working From Home Work? Evidence from a Chinese Experiment', *The Quarterly Journal of Economics* 130, no. 1 (November 2014), 165–218, https://doi.org/10.1093/qje/qju032.

44 Isabella Steger, 'A Japanese aquarium under lockdown wants people to video call its lonely eels', *Quartz,* 30 April 2020, https://qz.com/1848528/japan-aquarium-asks-people-to-video-call-eels-under-lockdown/.

45 Kevin Roose, 'Sorry, But Working From Home is Overrated', *New York Times,* 10 March 2020, https://www.nytimes.com/2020/03/10/technology/working-from-home.html.

46 Ibid.

47 In cities as various as Birmingham, Brasilia, Toronto, Istanbul, Bogotá, Rio de Janeiro and Los Angeles, the *average* daily commute is over an hour and a half often because housing costs in city centres have become simply unaffordable even for middle-class workers. Julia Watts, 'The Best and Worst Cities for Commuting', Expert Market, https://www.expertmarket.co.uk/vehicle-tracking/best-and-worst-cities-for-commuting. See original data at https://images.expertmarket.co.uk/wp-content/uploads/sites/default/files/FOCUSUK/Commuter%20Carnage/The%20Best%20and%20Worst%20Cities%20for%20Commuting%20-%20Expert%20Market.pdf?_ga=2.6892788.710211532.1591291518-1056841509.1591291518.

48 Alison Lynch, 'Table for one: Nearly half of all meals in the UK are eaten alone', *Metro,* 13 April 2016, https://metro.co.uk/2016/04/13/table-for-one-nearly-half-of-all-meals-in-the-uk-are-eaten-alone-5813871/.

49 Malia Wollan, 'Failure to Lunch', *New York Times,* 25 February 2016, https://www.nytimes.com/2016/02/28/magazine/failure-to-lunch.html; Olivera Perkins, 'Eating lunch alone, often working at your desk: the disappearing lunch break (photos)', Cleveland.com, 14 September 2015, https://www.cleveland.com/business/2015/09/eating_lunch_alone_often_worki.html.

50 Robert Williams, Kana Inagaki, Jude Webber and John Aglionby, 'A global anatomy of health and the workday lunch', *Financial Times,*

14 September 2016, https://www.ft.com/content/a1b8d81a-48f5-11e6-8d68-72e9211e86ab.

51 Stan Herman, 'In-work dining at Silicon Valley companies like Google and Facebook causes spike in divorce rate', *Salon,* 24 June 2018, https://www.salon.com/2018/06/24/in-work-dining-in-silicon-valley-companies-like-google-and-facebook-cause-spike-in-divorce-there/; Lenore Bartko, 'Festive Feasts Around the World', InterNations.org, https://www.internations.org/magazine/plan-prepare-feast-and-enjoy-tips-for-celebrating-national-holidays-abroad-17475/festive-feasts-around-the-world-2.

52 See for example the discussion in Anthony Charuvastra and Marylene Cloitre, 'Social Bonds and Post-Traumatic Stress Disorder', *Annual Review of Psychology* 59 (2008), 301–28.

53 The name of the city was not revealed in the original study to protect the firefighters' identities. Kevin M. Kniffin, Brian Wansink, Carol M. Devine and Jeffery Sobal, 'Eating Together at the Firehouse: How Workplace Commensality Relates to the Performance of Firefighters', *Human Performance* 28, no. 4 (2015), 281–306, https://doi.org/10.1080/08959285.2015.1021049.

54 Susan Kelley, 'Groups that eat together perform better together', *Cornell Chronicle,* 19 November 2015, https://news.cornell.edu/stories/2015/11/groups-eat-together-perform-better-together; see also Kniffin et al., 'Eating Together at the Firehouse'; 'Team-Building in the Cafeteria', *Harvard Business Review,* December 2015, https://hbr.org/2015/12/team-building-in-the-cafeteria.

55 Kelley, 'Groups that eat together perform better together'. 'Team-Building in the Cafeteria'.

56 Trevor Felch, 'Lunch at Google HQ is as Insanely Awesome as You Thought', *Serious Eats,* 8 January 2014, https://www.seriouseats.com/2014/01/lunch-at-google-insanely-awesome-as-you-thought.html; Katie Canales, 'Cayenne pepper ginger shots, homemade lemon tarts, and Michelin-starred chefs – here's what employees at Silicon Valley's biggest tech companies are offered for free', *Business Insider,* 31 July 2018, https://www.businessinsider.com/free-food-silicon-valley-tech-employees-apple-google-facebook-2018-7?r=US&IR=T#apple-employees-dont-get-free-food-but-they-do-get-subsidized-cafes-2.

57 'Team-Building in the Cafeteria'.

58 Alex Pentland, 'The New Science of Building Great Teams', *Harvard Business Review*, April 2012, https://hbr.org/2012/04/the-new-science-of-building-great-teams; Ron Miller, 'New Firm Comines Wearables And Data To Improve Decision Making', *TechCrunch*, 24 February 2015, https://techcrunch.com/2015/02/24/new-firm-combines-wearables-and-data-to-improve-decision-making/.

59 Jen Hubley Luckwaldt, 'For the Love of the Job: Does Society Pay Teachers What They Are Worth?', PayScale, https://www.payscale.com/data-packages/most-and-least-meaningful-jobs/teacher-pay-versus-job-meaning; 'Nurses are undervalued because most of them are women, a new study shows', Oxford Brookes University, 29 January 2020, https://www.brookes.ac.uk/about-brookes/news/nurses-are-undervalued-because-most-of-them-are-women-a-new-study-finds/; original report: 'Gender and Nursing as a Profession', Royal College of Nursing and Oxford Brookes University, January 2020; Jack Fischl, 'Almost 82 Per cent Of Social Workers Are Female, and This is Hurting Men', *Mic*, 25 March 2013, https://www.mic.com/articles/30974/almost-82-percent-of-social-workers-are-female-and-this-is-hurting-men; analysis of job descriptions on totaljobs.com.

60 Sarah Todd, 'Can nice women get ahead at work?', *Quartz*, https://qz.com/work/1708242/why-being-nice-is-a-bad-word-at-work/.

61 Sarah Todd, 'Finally, a performance review designed to weed out "brilliant jerks"', *Quartz*, 22 July 2019, https://qz.com/work/1671163/atlassians-new-performance-review-categories-weed-out-brilliant-jerks/.

62 Sarah Todd, 'Can nice women get ahead at work?'.

63 Joan C. Williams and Marina Multhaup, 'For Women and Minorities to Get Ahead, Managers Must Assign Work Fairly', *Harvard Business Review*, 5 March 2018, https://hbr.org/2018/03/for-women-and-minorities-to-get-ahead-managers-must-assign-work-fairly.

64 Patrick Moorhead, 'Why No One Should Be Surprised Cisco Named "World's Best Workplace" for 2019', *Forbes*, 1 November 2019, https://www.forbes.com/sites/moorinsights/2019/11/01/why-no-one-should-be-surprised-cisco-named-worlds-best-workplace-for-2019/#5d7032443886.

65 Paul Verhaghe, 'Neoliberalism has brought out the worst in us',

The Guardian, 29 September 2014, https://www.theguardian.com/commentisfree/2014/sep/29/neoliberalism-economic-system-ethics-personality-psychopathicsthic.

66 Between 1950 and 2012, for example, annual hours worked per employee fell by around 40% in the Netherlands and Germany. In the US, that figure is about 10% lower. Matthew Yglesias, 'Jeb Bush and longer working hours: gaffesplainer 2016', *Vox,* 9 July 2015, https://www.vox.com/2015/7/9/8920297/jeb-bush-work-longer; Derek Thompson, 'Workism Is Making Americans Miserable', *The Atlantic,* 24 February 2019, https://www.theatlantic.com/ideas/archive/2019/02/religion-workism-making-americans-miserable/583441/.

67 Anna S. Burger, 'Extreme working hours in Western Europe and North America: A new aspect of polarization', LSE 'Europe in Question' Discussion Paper Series, May 2015, http://www.lse.ac.uk/europeanInstitute/LEQS%20Discussion%20Paper%20Series/LEQSPaper92.pdf. This study looked at people with college degrees specifically. It's reasonable to assume that professionals would be a subset of these likely to follow the same trend; Heather Boushey and Bridget Ansel, 'Overworked America', Washington Center for Equitable Growth, 16 May 2016, https://equitablegrowth.org/research-paper/overworked-america/. We know too that between 1985 and 2010, the weekly leisure time of college-educated men fell by 2.5 hours, more than any other demographic; Derek Thompson, 'Are We Truly Overworked? An Investigation – in 6 Charts', *The Atlantic,* June 2013, https://www.theatlantic.com/magazine/archive/2013/06/are-we-truly-overworked/309321/.

68 Steven Clarke and George Bangham, 'Counting the hours', Resolution Foundation, January 2018, https://www.resolutionfoundation.org/app/uploads/2018/01/Counting-the-hours.pdf.

69 Justin McCurry, 'Japanese woman "dies from overwork" after logging 159 hours of overtime in a month', *Guardian,* 5 October 2017, https://www.theguardian.com/world/2017/oct/05/japanese-woman-dies-overwork-159-hours-overtime.

70 Rita Liao, 'China's Startup Ecosystem is hitting back at demanding

working hours', *TechCrunch*, 13 April 2019, https://techcrunch.com/2019/04/12/china-996/.

71   The costs are 30% higher in the US today than they were twenty years ago. Larry Getlen, 'America's middle class is slowly being 'wiped out'', MarketWatch, 23 July 2018, https://www.marketwatch.com/story/americas-middle-class-is-slowly-being-wiped-out-2018-07-23. See also Alissa Quart, *Squeezed: Why Our Families Can't Afford America* (Ecco, 2018); that's true, too, in the UK, where the number of middle-income households decreased by 27% between 1980 and 2010; meanwhile, the middle class has shrunk in two-thirds of EU countries since the financial crisis of 2008. See Daniel Boffey, 'How 30 years of a polarised economy have squeezed out of the middle class', *Guardian,* 7 March 2015, https://www.theguardian.com/society/2015/mar/07/vanishing-middle-class-london-economy-divide-rich-poor-england; Liz Alderman, 'Europe's Middle Class Is Shrinking. Spain Bears Much of the Pain', *New York Times,* 14 February 2019, https://www.nytimes.com/2019/02/14/business/spain-europe-middle-class.html.

72   Jennifer Szalai, 'Going for Broke, the Middle Class Goes Broke', *New York Times*, 27 June 2018, https://www.nytimes.com/2018/06/27/books/review-squeezed-alissa-quart.html.

73   Sarah Graham, 'Meet The Young Nurses Who Need A Side Hustle Just To Pay Their Bills', *Grazia*, 12 July 2017, https://graziadaily.co.uk/life/real-life/meet-young-nurses-need-side-hustle-just-pay-bills/.

74   'Nursing Shortage: 52% of US Nurses Say It's Gotten Worse', Staffing Industry Analysts, 12 November 2019, https://www2.staffingindustry.com/site/Editorial/Daily-News/Nursing-shortage-52-of-US-nurses-say-it-s-gotten-worse-51871; in both the US and UK academics can fall into this trap too. UK: conversations with colleagues. For the US, see for example, Seth Freed Wessler, 'Your College Professor Could Be On Public Assistance', NBC News, 6 April 2015, https://www.nbcnews.com/feature/in-plain-sight/poverty-u-many-adjunct-professors-food-stamps-n336596; Matt Saccaro, 'Professors on food stamps: The shocking true story of academia in 2014', *Salon,* 21 September 2014, https://www.salon.com/test/2014/09/21/professors_on_food_stamps_the_shocking_true_story_of_academia_in_2014/.

75 Katherine Schaeffer, 'About one-in-six U.S. teachers work second jobs – and not just in the summer', Pew Research Center, 1 July 2019, https://www.pewresearch.org/fact-tank/2019/07/01/about-one-in-six-u-s-teachers-work-second-jobs-and-not-just-in-the-summer/; Michael Addonizio, 'Are America's teachers really underpaid?', *The Conversation,* 11 April 2019, https://theconversation.com/are-americas-teachers-really-underpaid-114397.

76 Szalai, 'Going for Broke, the Middle Class Goes Broke'.

77 Sylvia Ann Hewlett and Carolyn Buck Luce, 'Extreme Jobs: The Dangerous Allure of the 70-Hour Workweek', *Harvard Business Review,* December 2006, https://hbr.org/2006/12/extreme-jobs-the-dangerous-allure-of-the-70-hour-workweek.

78 'New statistics reveal effect of modern day lifestyles on family life', British Heart Foundation, 12 May 2017, https://www.bhf.org.uk/what-we-do/news-from-the-bhf/news-archive/2017/may/new-statistics-reveal-effect-of-modern-day-lifestyles-on-family-life.

79 Emma Seppälä and Marissa King, 'Burnout at Work Isn't Just About Exhaustion. It's Also About Loneliness', *Harvard Business Review,* 29 June 2017, https://hbr.org/2017/06/burnout-at-work-isnt-just-about-exhaustion-its-also-about-loneliness.

80 Christina Zdanowicz, 'Denver is so expensive that teachers have to get creative to make ends meet', CNN, 11 February 2019, https://edition.cnn.com/2019/02/10/us/denver-teacher-strike-multiple-jobs/index.html.

81 Zoe Schiffer, 'Emotional Baggage', *The Verge,* 5 December 2019, https://www.theverge.com/2019/12/5/20995453/away-luggage-ceo-steph-korey-toxic-work-environment-travel-inclusion.

82 *Rise and Grind* (Currency 2018) is the title of a book by Shark Tank star and FUBU founder Daymond John and the theme of a recent Nike ad: https://www.youtube.com/watch?v=KQSiiEPKgUk.

83 'The Relationship Between Hours Worked and Productivity', Crunch Mode: Programming to the Extreme, https://cs.stanford.edu/people/eroberts/cs201/projects/crunchmode/econ-hours-productivity.html; Sarah Green Carmichael, 'The Research Is Clear: Long Hours Backfire for People and for Companies', *Harvard Business Review,* 19 August 2015, https://hbr.org/2015/08/

the-research-is-clear-long-hours-backfire-for-people-and-for-companies.

84 'Volkswagen turns off Blackberry email after work hours', BBC News, 8 March 2012, https://www.bbc.co.uk/news/technology-16314901.

85 'Should holiday email be deleted?', BBC News, 14 August 2014, https://www.bbc.co.uk/news/magazine-28786117.

86 Note that I am on the board of Warner Music Group.

87 'French workers get 'right to disconnect' from emails out of hours', BBC News, 31 December 2016, https://www.bbc.co.uk/news/world-europe-38479439.

88 Daniel Ornstein and Jordan B. Glassberg, 'More Countries Consider Implementing a "Right to Disconnect"'. *The National Law Review*, 29 January 2019, https://www.natlawreview.com/article/more-countries-consider-implementing-right-to-disconnect.

89 Raquel Flórez, 'The future of work – New rights for new times', *Freshfields*, 5 December 2018, https://digital.freshfields.com/post/102f6up/the-future-of-work-new-rights-for-new-times; Ornstein and Glassberg, 'More Countries Consider Implementing a "Right to Disconnect".

90 'Banning out-of-hours email "could harm employee wellbeing"', BBC News, 18 October 2019, https://www.bbc.co.uk/news/technology-50073107.

91 Evgeny Morozov, 'So you want to switch off digitally? I'm afraid that will cost you...', *Guardian,* 19 February 2017, https://www.theguardian.com/commentisfree/2017/feb/19/right-to-disconnect-digital-gig-economy-evgeny-morozov.

92 Peter Fleming, 'Do you work more than 39 hours per week? Your job could be killing you', *Guardian,* 15 January 2018, https://www.theguardian.com/lifeandstyle/2018/jan/15/is-28-hours-ideal-working-week-for-healthy-life.

93 'Two in five low-paid mums and dads penalised by bad bosses, TUC study reveals', Trades Union Congress, 1 September 2017, https://www.tuc.org.uk/news/two-five-low-paid-mums-and-dads-penalised-bad-bosses-tuc-study-reveals-0. The Covid-19 crisis points towards further risk, as the Trades Union Congress demanded government protections for working parents forced to choose

between low-paying jobs and keeping their families safe as the crisis threatened the collapse of the childcare sector. 'Forced out: The cost of getting childcare wrong', Trades Union Congress, 4 June 2020, https://www.tuc.org.uk/research-analysis/reports/forced-out-cost-getting-childcare-wrong.

94 Brian Wheeler, 'Why Americans don't take sick days', BBC News, 14 September 2014, https://www.bbc.co.uk/news/world-us-canada-37353742.

95 Harriet Meyer, 'Part-time workers 'trapped' in jobs with no chance of promotion', *Guardian*, 8 July 2013, https://www.theguardian.com/money/2013/jul/08/part-time-workers-trapped-jobs; Richard Partington, 'Mothers working part-time hit hard by gender pay gap, study shows', *Guardian*, 5 February 2018, https://www.theguardian.com/society/2018/feb/05/mothers-working-part-time-hit-hard-by-gender-pay-gap-study-shows; Paul Johnson, 'We must not ignore plight of low-paid men as once we ignored that of working women', Institute for Fiscal Studies, 12 November 2018, https://www.ifs.org.uk/publications/13706.

96 See for example Ariane Hegewisch and Valerie Lacarte, 'Gender Inequality, Work Hours, and the Future of Work', Institute for Women's Policy Research, 14 November 2019, https://iwpr.org/publications/gender-inequality-work-hours-future-of-work/.

97 Dominic Walsh, 'Centrica staff get extra paid leave to care for sick relatives', *The Times*, 7 May 2019, https://www.thetimes.co.uk/article/centrica-staff-get-extra-paid-leave-to-care-for-sick-relatives-6397f7vs8.

98 Joe Wiggins, '9 Companies That Offer Corporate Volunteering Days', Glassdoor, 6 May 2019, https://www.glassdoor.co.uk/blog/time-off-volunteer/.

99 Kari Paul, 'Microsoft Japan tested a four-day work week and productivity jumped by 40%', *Guardian*, 4 November 2019, https://www.theguardian.com/technology/2019/nov/04/microsoft-japan-four-day-work-week-productivity.

CHAPTER EIGHT:
The Digital Whip

1   Robert Booth, 'Unilever saves on recruiters by using AI to assess job interviews', *Guardian*, 25 October 2019, https://www.theguardian.com/technology/2019/oct/25/unilever-saves-on-recruiters-by-using-ai-to-assess-job-interviews; The Harvey Nash HR Survey 2019, https://www.harveynash.com/hrsurvey/full-report/charts/#summary.

2   'HireVue surpasses ten million video interviews completed worldwide', HireVue, 21 May 2019, https://www.hirevue.com/press-release/hirevue-surpasses-ten-million-video-interviews-completed-worldwide.

3   'EPIC Files Complaint with FTC about Employment Screening Firm HireVue', Electronic Privacy Information Center, 6 November 2019, https://epic.org/2019/11/epic-files-complaint-with-ftc.html; see full complaint at https://epic.org/privacy/ftc/hirevue/EPIC_FTC_HireVue_Complaint.pdf.

4   Loren Larsen, 'HireVue Assessments and Preventing Algorithmic Bias', HireVue, 22 June 2018, https://www.hirevue.com/blog/hirevue-assessments-and-preventing-algorithmic-bias; cf. Emma Leech, 'The perils of AI recruitment', *New Statesman*, 14 August 2019, https://tech.newstatesman.com/emerging-technologies/ai-recruitment-algorithms-bias; Julius Schulte, 'AI-assisted recruitment is biased. Here's how to make it more fair', World Economic Forum, 9 May 2019, https://www.weforum.org/agenda/2019/05/ai-assisted-recruitment-is-biased-heres-how-to-beat-it/.

5   Drew Harwell, 'A face-scanning algorithm increasingly decides whether you deserve the job', *Washington Post*, 6 November 2019, https://www.washingtonpost.com/technology/2019/10/22/ai-hiring-face-scanning-algorithm-increasingly-decides-whether-you-deserve-job/.

6   Reuters, 'Amazon ditched AI recruiting tool that favoured men for technical jobs', *Guardian*, 11 October 2018, https://www.theguardian.com/technology/2018/oct/10/amazon-hiring-ai-gender-bias-recruiting-engine.

7   Kuba Krys et al., 'Be Careful Where You Smile: Culture Shapes

Judgments of Intelligence and Honesty of Smiling Individuals', *Journal of Nonverbal Behavior* 40 (2016), 101–16, https://doi.org/10.1007/s10919-015-0226-4. these assumptions, reflected in proverbs and stereotypes, are now backed up by quantitative analysis of 44 countries.

8 The broad theory holds that in countries with more historical diversity – i.e. populated by a large proportion of immigrants who may not share languages or cultural norms – smiles are more expected and used as social currency; see Khazan, 'Why Americans smile so much', *The Atlantic*, 3 May 2017, https://www.theatlantic.com/science/archive/2017/05/why-americans-smile-so-much/524967/.

9 The retail giant's eventual closure of its German stores was related, analysts speculate, to its inability to adapt to different cultural expectations; Mark Landler and Michael Barbaro, 'Wal-Mart Finds That Its Formula Doesn't Fit Every Culture', *New York Times*, 2 August 2006, https://www.nytimes.com/2006/08/02/business/worldbusiness/02walmart.html; see also Khazan, 'Why Americans smile so much'.

10 Implied in this statement on its website under FAQ for interviewees: 'Customer-facing jobs, like a bank teller role, do require a degree of friendliness and attention to other people. A more technical job may not require the same degree of social interaction, and so factors such as whether you smile or make extended eye contact aren't likely to be a part of the assessment model for that job'; HireVue, https://www.hirevue.com/candidates/faq.

11 Stéphanie Thomson, 'Here's why you didn't get that job: your name', World Economic Forum, 23 May 2017, https://www.weforum.org/agenda/2017/05/job-applications-resume-cv-name-discrimination/.

12 Dave Gershgorn, 'AI is now so complex its creators can't trust why it makes decisions', *Quartz*, 7 December 2017, https://qz.com/1146753/ai-is-now-so-complex-its-creators-cant-trust-why-it-makes-decisions/.

13 Jordi Canals and Franz Heukamp, *The Future of Management in an AI World: Redesigning Purpose and Strategy in the Fourth Industrial Revolution* (Springer Nature, 2019), p.108.

14   Note that as well as the video interview, I had to 'play' a few psychometric 'games'. To what extent they were accounted for in this assessment was not made clear.

15   Terena Bell, 'This bot judges how much you smile during your job interview', *Fast Company*, 15 January 2019, https://www. fastcompany.com/90284772/this-bot-judges-how-much-you-smile-during-your-job-interview.

16   'Jane' is a composite character.

17   Cogito Corporation, https://www.cogitocorp.com.

18   'Jack' is also a composite character.

19   Ron Miller, 'New Firm Combines Wearables And Data To Improve Decision Making', *TechCrunch*, 24 February 2015, https:// techcrunch.com/2015/02/24/new-firm-combines-wearables-and-data-to-improve-decision-making/.

20   Jessica Bruder, 'These Workers Have a New Demand: Stop Watching Us', *The Nation*, 27 May 2015, https://www.thenation.com/article/archive/these-workers-have-new-demand-stop-watching-us/.

21   Ceylan Yeginsu, 'If Workers Slack Off, the Wristband Will Know. (And Amazon Has a Patent for It.)', *New York Times*, 1 February 2018, https://www.nytimes.com/2018/02/01/technology/amazon-wristband-tracking-privacy.html.

22   James Bloodworth, *Hired: Six Months Undercover in Low-Wage Britain* (Atlantic Books, 2018).

23   Luke Tredinnick and Claire Laybats, 'Workplace surveillance', *Business Information Review* 36, no. 2 (2019), 50–2, https://doi.org/10.1177/0266382119853890.

24   Ivan Manokha, 'New Means of Workplace Surveillance: From the Gaze of the Supervisor to the Digitalization of Employees', *Monthly Review*, 1 February 2019, https://monthlyreview.org/2019/02/01/new-means-of-workplace-surveillance/.

25   Zuboff, *The Age of Surveillance Capitalism*.

26   Olivia Solon, 'Big Brother isn't just watching: workplace surveillance can track your every move', *Guardian*, 6 November 2017, https://www.theguardian.com/world/2017/nov/06/workplace-surveillance-big-brother-technology.

27   Ibid.

28   Note that by 'sales' I am including trials. For example, one supplier

of such software, Hubstaff, reported that the number of companies trialling its time-tracking products nearly tripled as more and more employers required staff to work from home. Other companies said that interest in their products increased sixfold. Jessica Golden and Eric Chemi, 'Worker monitoring tools see surging growth as companies adjust to stay-at-home orders', CNBC, 13 May 2020, https://www.cnbc.com/2020/05/13/employee-monitoring-tools-see-uptick-as-more-people-work-from-home.html.

29 The app was made voluntary and then eliminated following a teacher strike. Jess Bidgood, '"I Live Paycheck to Paycheck": A West Virginia Teacher Explains Why She's on Strike', *New York Times*, 1 March 2018, https://www.nytimes.com/2018/03/01/us/west-virginia-teachers-strike.html?.

30 Bruder, 'These Workers Have a New Demand: Stop Watching Us'.

31 Padraig Belton, 'How does it feel to be watched at work all the time?', BBC News, 12 April 2019, https://www.bbc.com/news/business-47879798.

32 Ibid.

33 Ellen Ruppel Shell, 'The Employer-Surveillance State', *The Atlantic*, 15 October 2018, https://www.theatlantic.com/business/archive/2018/10/employee-surveillance/568159/.

34 Antti Oulasvirta et al., 'Long-term effects of ubiquitous surveillance in the home', Proceedings of the 2012 ACM Conference on Ubiquitous Computing (2012), https://doi.org/10.1145/2370216.2370224.

35 Shell, 'The Employer-Surveillance State'.

36 Although through-lines certainly exist between institutions of forced labour and today's workplace, I have chosen to focus on the 'workplace' in the post-industrial capitalist landscape. However, as many scholars have demonstrated, slavery, whether in the ancient world or in for example the US plantation system, furnishes many further examples of surveillance as a weapon of social control, dehumanisation and othering. For further reading on racialised surveillance, see for example Simone Browne, *Dark Matters: On the Surveillance of Blackness* (Duke University Press, 2015).

37 'Pinkerton National Detective Agency', *Encyclopaedia Britannica*, 25
    September 2017, https://www.britannica.com/topic/Pinkerton-
    National-Detective-Agency.

38 Ifeoma Ajunwa, Kate Crawford and Jason Schultz, 'Limitless
    Worker Surveillance', *California Law Review* 105, no. 3 (2017), 735–6.

39 Julie A. Flanagan, 'Restricting electronic monitoring in the private
    workplace', *Duke Law Journal* 43 (1993), 1256, https://scholarship.
    law.duke.edu/cgi/viewcontent.cgi?article=3255&context=dlj.

40 Even in the 1980s, scholars were sounding the alarm. See, for
    instance, Shoshana Zuboff, *In the Age of the Smart Machine: The
    Future of Work and Power* (Basic Books, 1988); Barbara Garson, *The
    Electronic Sweatshop: How Computers Are Turning the Office of the
    Future into the Factory of the Past* (Simon & Schuster, 1988); Michael
    Wallace, 'Brave New Workplace: Technology and Work in the
    New Economy', *Work and Occupations* 16, no. 4 (1989), 363–92.

41 Ivan Manokha, 'New Means of Workplace Surveillance: From the
    Gaze of the Supervisor to the Digitalization of Employees',
    Monthly Review, 1 February 2019, https://monthlyreview.
    org/2019/02/01/new-means-of-workplace-surveillance/.

42 In 1985, 30% of OECD workers were unionized; by 2019 this had
    fallen to 16%. Niall McCarthy, 'The State Of Global Trade Union
    Membership', Statista, 7 May 2019, https://www.statista.com/
    chart/9919/the-state-of-the-unions/.

43 Trade union membership has halved since the 1980s, pretty much
    all over the globe; Niall McCarthy, 'The State of Global Trade
    Union Membership', *Forbes*, 6 May 2019, https://www.forbes.com/
    sites/niallmccarthy/2019/05/06/the-state-of-global-trade-union-
    membership-infographic/); ONS, 'Trade Union Membership
    Statistics 2018', Department for Business, Energy and Industrial
    Strategy, https://assets.publishing.service.gov.uk/government/
    uploads/system/uploads/attachment_data/file/805268/trade-
    union-membership-2018-statistical-bulletin.pdf.

44 Richard Feloni, 'Employees at the world's largest hedge fund use
    iPads to rate each other's performance in real-time – see how it
    works', *Business Insider*, 6 September 2017, https://www.
    businessinsider.com/bridgewater-ray-dalio-radical-transparency-app-
    dots-2017-9?IR=T.

45 https://www.glassdoor.com/Reviews/Employee-Review-Bridgewater-Associates-RVW28623146.htm

46 https://www.glassdoor.com/Reviews/Employee-Review-Bridgewater-Associates-RVW25872721.htm

47 https://www.glassdoor.com/Reviews/Employee-Review-Bridgewater-Associates-RVW25450329.htm; Allana Akhtar, 'What it's like to work at the most successful hedge fund in the world, where 30% of new employees don't make it and those who do are considered "intellectual Navy SEALs"', *Business Insider*, 16 April 2019, https://www.businessinsider.com/what-its-like-to-work-at-ray-dalio-bridgewater-associates-2019-4.

48 Ibid.

49 Amir Anwar, 'How Marx predicted the worst effects of the gig economy more than 150 years ago', *New Statesman*, 8 August 2018, https://tech.newstatesman.com/guest-opinion/karl-marx-gig-economy.

50 Richard Partington, 'Gig economy in Britain doubles, accounting for 4.7 million workers', *Guardian*, 28 June 2019, https://www.theguardian.com/business/2019/jun/28/gig-economy-in-britain-doubles-accounting-for-47-million-workers; Siddharth Suri and Mary L. Gray, 'Spike in online gig work: flash in the pan or future of employment?', Ghost Work, November 2016, https://ghostwork.info/2016/11/spike-in-online-gig-work-flash-in-the-pan-or-future-of-employment/.

51 Thor Berger, Chinchih Chen, and Carl Frey, 'Drivers of disruption? Estimating the Uber effect', *European Economic Review* 110 (2018), 197–210, https://doi.org/10.1016/j.euroecorev.2018.05.006.

52 Professor Stephen Zoepf of MIT made a splash in March 2018 when he published findings that Uber drivers made an average of $3.37 per hour, a claim that Uber's chief economist then refuted by challenging Zoepf's methodology. However, after Zoepf acknowledged the validity of the criticism and recalculated his results, he came up with $8.55 instead – hardly a princely sum. See Lawrence Mishel, 'Uber and the labor market', *Economic Policy Institute*, 15 May 2018, https://www.epi.org/publication/uber-and-the-labor-market-uber-drivers-compensation-wages-and-the-scale-of-uber-and-the-gig-economy/.

53 This is of course in addition to the thousands of workers whose
    non-gig jobs also now depend heavily on customer ratings; when
    were you last asked to take a survey after getting off the phone
    with a customer-service representative? Their job might be on the
    line; Rob Brogle, 'How to Avoid the Evils Within Customer
    Satisfaction Surveys', ISIXIGMA.com, https://www.isixsigma.com/
    methodology/voc-customer-focus/how-to-avoid-the-evils-within-
    customer-satisfaction-surveys/. See especially user comments and
    personal anecdotes.

54 Will Knight, 'Is the Gig Economy Rigged?', *MIT Technology Review*,
    17 November 2016, https://www.technologyreview.com/s/602832/
    is-the-gig-economy-rigged/; Aniko Hannak et al., 'Bias in online
    freelance marketplaces: Evidence from Taskrabbit and Fiverr',
    *Proceedings of the 2017 ACM Conference on Computer Supported
    Cooperative Work and Social Computing* (2017), 13, http://
    claudiawagner.info/publications/cscw_bias_olm.pdf.

55 See, for instance, Lev Muchnik, Sinan Aral and Sean J. Taylor,
    'Social Influence Bias: A Randomized Experiment', *Science* 341, no.
    6146 (9 August 2013), 647–51; for more detail see Daniel Kahneman,
    Thinking, Fast and Slow (Penguin, 2011).

56 The platforms insist ratings are the only way to signal how
    trustworthy their 'Taskers' or 'walkers' or 'drivers' (never
    'contractors') are. Obviously it's not the *only* way. Before the gig
    economy emerged, informal and formal mechanisms such as client
    or employer references served this purpose. To offload ratings onto
    consumers may, however, be the only way of signalling how
    trustworthy masses of people are at scale, if the online platform is
    not willing to assume liability for the trustworthiness or standards
    of the people working for it.

57 Aaron Smith, 'Gig Work, Online Selling and Home Sharing', Pew
    Research Center, 17 November 2016, https://www.pewresearch.
    org/internet/2016/11/17/gig-work-online-selling-and-home-
    sharing/.

58 All this was something the rosy employment data in many
    countries of the late 2010s completely obscured. See for example
    Lawrence Mishel and Julia Wolfe, 'CEO compensation has grown
    940% since 1978', Economic Policy Institute, 14 August 2019,

https://www.epi.org/publication/ceo-compensation-2018/; Richard Partington, 'Four million British workers live in poverty, charity says', *Guardian*, 4 December 2018, https://www.theguardian.com/business/2018/dec/04/four-million-british-workers-live-in-poverty-charity-says; Anjum Klair, 'Zero-hours contracts are still rife – it's time to give all workers the rights they deserve', Trades Union Congress, 19 February 2019, https://www.tuc.org.uk/blogs/zero-hours-contracts-are-still-rife-its-time-give-all-workers-rights-they-deserve; Nassim Khadem, 'Australia has a high rate of casual work and many jobs face automation threats: OECD', ABC News, 25 April 2019, https://www.abc.net.au/news/2019-04-25/australia-sees-increase-in-casual-workers-ai-job-threats/11043772; Melisa R. Serrano, ed., *Between Flexibility and Security: The Rise of Non-Standard Employment in Selected ASEAN Countries* (ASETUC, 2014), https://library.fes.de/pdf-files/bueros/singapur/10792.pdf; Simon Roughneen, 'Nearly one billion Asians in vulnerable jobs, says ILO', *Nikkei Asian Review*, 23 January 2018, https://asia.nikkei.com/Economy/Nearly-one-billion-Asians-in-vulnerable-jobs-says-ILO; Bas ter Weel, 'The Rise of Temporary Work in Europe', *De Economist* 166 (2018), 397–401, https://doi.org/10.1007/s10645-018-9329-8; Yuki Noguchi, 'Freelanced: The Rise Of The Contract Workforce', NPR, 22 January 2018, https://www.npr.org/2018/01/22/578825135/rise-of-the-contract-workers-work-is-different-now?t=1576074901406; Jack Kelly, 'The Frightening Rise in Low-Quality, Low-Paying Jobs: Is This Really a Strong Job Market?', *Forbes*, 25 November 2019, https://www.forbes.com/sites/jackkelly/2019/11/25/the-frightening-rise-in-low-quality-low-paying-jobs-is-this-really-a-strong-job-market/; see also Martha Ross and Nicole Bateman, 'Meet the low-wage workforce', Brookings, 7 November 2019, https://www.brookings.edu/research/meet-the-low-wage-workforce/; Hanna Brooks Olsen, 'Here's how the stress of the gig economy can affect your mental health', *Healthline*, 3 June 2020, https://www.healthline.com/health/mental-health/gig-economy#6; Edison Research, 'Gig Economy', Marketplace–Edison Research Poll, December 2018, http://www.edisonresearch.com/wp-content/uploads/2019/01/Gig-Economy-2018-Marketplace-Edison-Research-Poll-FINAL.pdf.

59 See Karl Marx, 'Economic and Philosophical Manuscripts of 1844', in *Karl Marx, Friedrich Engels: Collected Works*, vol. 3 (London: Lawrence & Wishart, 1975), 229–347.

60 In the wake of the 2008 financial crisis, many businesses laid off full-time staff only to replace them with contract workers and unpaid interns whose terms of employment were more precarious and who received few if any benefits. See Katherine S. Newman, 'The Great Recession and the Pressure on Workplace Rights', *Chicago-Kent Law Review* 88, no. 2 (April 2013), https://scholarship. kentlaw.iit.edu/cklawreview/vol88/iss2/13.

61 See Michael Kearns and Aaron Roth, *The Ethical Algorithm* (Oxford University Press, 2019).

62 Joseph J. Lazzarotti and Maya Atrakchi, 'Illinois Leads the Way on AI Regulation in the Workplace', *SHRM*, 6 November 2019, https://www.shrm.org/resourcesandtools/legal-and-compliance/ state-and-local-updates/pages/illinois-leads-the-way-on-ai- regulation-in-the-workplace.aspx; Gerard Stegmaier, Stephanie Wilson, Alexis Cocco and Jim Barbuto, 'New Illinois employment law signals increased state focus on artificial intelligence in 2020', *Technology Law Dispatch*, 21 January 2020, https://www. technologylawdispatch.com/2020/01/privacy-data-protection/ new-illinois-employment-law-signals-increased-state-focus-on- artificial-intelligence-in-2020/.

63 This is especially the case outside of Europe, where the General Data Protection Regulation (GDPR) that entered into force in May 2018 goes some of the way to address the imbalance.

64 Radio-Frequency Identification, or RFID, is the technology embedded in almost all of the 'contactless' cards you'd use on a daily basis, from credit and debit cards to transit cards such as Oyster.

65 Maggie Astor, 'Microchip Implants for Employees? One Company Says Yes', *New York Times*, 25 July 2017, https://www.nytimes. com/2017/07/25/technology/microchips-wisconsin-company- employees.html. John Moritz, 'Rules on worker microchipping pass Arkansas House', *Arkansas Democrat Gazette*, 25 January 2019, https://www.arkansasonline.com/news/2019/jan/25/rules-on- worker-microchipping-passes-ho/. California, North Dakota and Wisconsin – Three Square Market's home state – already have

similar laws against forcible chipping, though these are not workplace-specific; a ban had also been proposed in Florida though it failed to pass. See Mary Colleen Charlotte Fowler, 'Chipping Away Employee Privacy: Legal Implications of RFID Microchip Implants for Employees', *National Law Review*, 10 October 2019, https://www.natlawreview.com/article/chipping-away-employee-privacy-legal-implications-rfid-microchip-implants-employees.

66 Joshua Z. Wasbin, 'Examining the Legality of Employee Microchipping Under the Lens of the Transhumanistic Proactionary Principle', *Washington University Jurisprudence Review* 11, no. 2 (2019), 401, https://openscholarship.wustl.edu/law_jurisprudence/vol11/iss2/10.

67 European Parliament, 'Gig economy: EU law to improve workers' rights (infographic)', 9 April 2019, https://www.europarl.europa.eu/news/en/headlines/society/20190404STO35070/gig-economy-eu-law-to-improve-workers-rights-infographic; Kate Conger and Noam Scheiber, 'California Bill Makes App-Based Companies Treat Workers as Employees', *New York Times*, 11 September 2019, https://www.nytimes.com/2019/09/11/technology/california-gig-economy-bill.html. In addition, in November 2019 the state of New Jersey served Uber a tax bill of $649 million in back taxes for allegedly misclassifying its drivers as contractors rather than employees. Matthew Haag and Patrick McGeehan, 'Uber Fined $649 Million for Saying Drivers Aren't Employees', *New York Times*, 14 November 2019, https://www.nytimes.com/2019/11/14/nyregion/uber-new-jersey-drivers.html.

68 State of California, 'Assembly Bill no. 5', published 19 September 2019, https://leginfo.legislature.ca.gov/faces/billTextClient.xhtml?bill_id=201920200AB5; 'ABC is not as easy as 1-2-3 – Which independent contractor classification test applies to whom after AB5?', Porter Simon, 19 December 2019, https://www.portersimon.com/abc-is-not-as-easy-as-1-2-3-which-independent-contractor-classification-test-applies-to-whom-after-ab5/.

69 Kate Conger, 'California Sues Uber and Lyft, Claiming Workers Are Misclassified', *New York Times*, 5 May 2020, https://www.nytimes.com/2020/05/05/technology/california-uber-lyft-lawsuit.html.

70   '3F reaches groundbreaking collective agreement with platform
     company Hilfr', Uni Global Union, 18 September 2018, https://
     www.uniglobalunion.org/news/3f-reaches-groundbreaking-
     collective-agreement-platform-company-hilfr.

71   GMB Union, 'Hermes and GMB in groundbreaking gig economy
     deal', 4 February 2019, https://www.gmb.org.uk/news/hermes-
     gmb-groundbreaking-gig-economy-deal; see also Robert Wright,
     'Hermes couriers awarded union recognition in gig economy first',
     Financial Times, 4 February 2019, https://www.ft.com/
     content/255950d2-264d-11e9-b329-c7e6ceb5ffdf.

72   Liz Alderman, 'Amazon Loses Appeal of French Order to Stop
     Selling Nonessential Items', *New York Times*, 24 April 2020, https://
     www.nytimes.com/2020/04/24/business/amazon-france-unions-
     coronavirus.html.

73   Even then, the kits took weeks to arrive, the ordering process was
     mired in bureaucracy, and the number of kits was limited. Arielle
     Pardes, 'Instacart Workers Are Still Waiting for Those Safety
     Supplies', *Wired*, 18 April 2020, https://www.wired.com/story/
     instacart-delivery-workers-still-waiting-safety-kits/.

74   Mark Muro, Robert Maxim, and Jacob Whiton, 'Automation and
     Artificial Intelligence: How machines are affecting people and
     places', Brookings, 24 January 2019, https://www.brookings.edu/
     research/automation-and-artificial-intelligence-how-machines-affect-
     people-and-places/; see also Tom Simonite, 'Robots Will Take Jobs
     From Men, the Young, and Minorities', *Wired*, 24 January 2019,
     https://www.wired.com/story/robots-will-take-jobs-from-men-
     young-minorities/.

75   Cate Cadell, 'At Alibaba's futuristic hotel, robots deliver towels and
     mix cocktails', Reuters, 22 January 2019, https://www.reuters.com/
     article/us-alibaba-hotels-robots/at-alibabas-futuristic-hotel-robots-
     deliver-towels-and-mix-cocktails-idUSKCN1PG21W.

76   The precise figure is 47%. Carl Benedikt Frey and Michael A.
     Osborne, 'The Future of Employment: How Susceptible are Jobs
     to Computerisation?', *Technological Forecasting and Social Change* 114
     (2017): 254–280, https://www.oxfordmartin.ox.ac.uk/downloads/
     academic/The_Future_of_Employment.pdf.

77   Carl Benedikt Frey, 'Covid-19 will only increase automation

anxiety', *Financial Times*, 21 April 2020, https://www.ft.com/
content/817228a2-82e1-11ea-b6e9-a94cffd1d9bf.

78 PA Media, 'Bosses speed up automation as virus keeps workers
    home', *Guardian*, 30 March 2020, https://www.theguardian.com/
    world/2020/mar/30/bosses-speed-up-automation-as-virus-keeps-
    workers-home; Peter Bluestone, Emmanuel Chike and Sally
    Wallace, 'The Future of Industry and Employment: COVID-19
    Effects Exacerbate the March of Artificial Intelligence', The Center
    for State and Local Finance, 28 April 2020, https://cslf.gsu.edu/
    download/covid-19-ai/?wpdmdl=6496041&refresh=5ea830a
    fd2a471588080815.

79 Andrew G. Haldane, 'Ideas and Institutions – A Growth Story',
    Bank of England, 23 May 2018, 13, https://www.bankofengland.co.
    uk/-/media/boe/files/speech/2018/ideas-and-institutions-a-growth-
    story-speech-by-andy-haldane; see also Table 1.

80 Daron Acemoglu and Pascual Restrepo, 'Robots and Jobs:
    Evidence from US Labor Markets', *Journal of Political Economy*
    128, no. 6 (June 2020), 2188–244, https://www.journals.uchicago.
    edu/doi/abs/10.1086/705716. Note that in 'commuting zones
    where robots were added to the workforce, each robot replaces
    about 6.6 jobs locally, the researchers found. However, in a
    subtle twist, adding robots in manufacturing benefits people in
    other industries and other areas of the country – by lowering
    the cost of goods, among other things. These national economic
    benefits are the reason the researchers calculated that adding
    one robot replaces 3.3 jobs for the country as a whole.' Peter
    Dizikes, 'How many jobs do robots really replace?', *MIT News*, 4
    May 2020, http://news.mit.edu/2020/how-many-jobs-robots-
    replace-0504.

81 As economist Henry Siu put it in 2015, 'The personal computer
    existed in the '80s, but you don't see any effect on office and
    administrative-support jobs until the 1990s, and then suddenly, in
    the last recession, it's huge. So today you've got checkout screens
    and the promise of driverless cars, flying drones, and little
    warehouse robots. We know that these tasks can be done by
    machines rather than people. But we may not see the effect until
    the next recession, or the recession after that.' Derek Thompson,

'When Will Robots Take All the Jobs?', *The Atlantic*, 31 October 2016, https://www.theatlantic.com/business/archive/2016/10/the-robot-paradox/505973/. Siu's instincts are supported by research showing that job listings significantly upskilled in the wake of the 2008 financial crisis: Brad Hershbein and Lisa B. Kahn, 'Do Recessions Accelerate Routine-Biased Technological Change? Evidence from Vacancy Postings', The National Bureau of Economic Research, October 2016 (revised in September 2017), https://www.nber.org/papers/w22762.

82 Yuan Yang and Xinning Lu, 'China's AI push raises fears over widespread job cuts', *Financial Times*, 30 August 2018, https://www.ft.com/content/1e2db400-ac2d-11e8-94bd-cba20d67390c.

83 June Javelosa and Kristin Houser, 'This company replaced 90% of its workforce with machines. Here's what happened', World Economic Forum, 16 February 2017, https://www.weforum.org/agenda/2017/02/after-replacing-90-of-employees-with-robots-this-companys-productivity-soared.

84 Brennan Hoban, 'Robots aren't taking the jobs, just the paychecks – and other new findings in economics', Brookings, 8 March 2018, https://www.brookings.edu/blog/brookings-now/2018/03/08/robots-arent-taking-the-jobs-just-the-paychecks-and-other-new-findings-in-economics/; David Autor and Anna Salomons, 'Is automation labor-displacing? Productivity growth, employment, and the labor share', Brookings, 8 March 2018, https://www.brookings.edu/bpea-articles/is-automation-labor-displacing-productivity-growth-employment-and-the-labor-share/.

85 Carl Benedikt Frey, 'The robot revolution is here. Prepare for workers to revolt', University of Oxford, 1 August 2019, https://www.oxfordmartin.ox.ac.uk/blog/the-robot-revolution-is-here-prepare-for-workers-to-revolt/.

86 Jenny Chan, 'Robots, not humans: Official policy in China', *New Internationalist*, 1 November 2017, https://newint.org/features/2017/11/01/industrial-robots-china.

87 Carl Benedikt Frey, Thor Berger and Chinchih Chen, 'Political Machinery: Automation Anxiety and the 2016 U.S. Presidential Election', University of Oxford, 23 July 2017, https://www.oxfordmartin.ox.ac.uk/downloads/academic/Political%20

Machinery-Automation%20Anxiety%20and%20the%202016%20
U_S_%20Presidential%20Election_230712.pdf.

88 Massimo Anelli, Italo Colantone, and Piero Stanig, 'We Were the
Robots: Automation and Voting Behavior in Western Europe', IZA
Institute of Labor Economics, July 2019, 24, http://ftp.iza.org/
dp12485.pdf.

89 'The Mini Bakery', Wilkinson Baking Company, https://www.
wilkinsonbaking.com/the-mini-bakery.

90 Mark Muro, Robert Maxim, and Jacob Whiton, 'The robots are
ready as the COVID-19 recession spreads', Brookings, 24 March
2020, https://www.brookings.edu/blog/the-avenue/2020/03/24/
the-robots-are-ready-as-the-covid-19-recession-spreads/?preview_
id=791044.

91 Barack Obama's Council for Economic Advisers estimated in 2016
that 83% of workers in occupations that paid less than $20 an
hour were at high risk of being replaced, while the corresponding
figure for works in occupations that paid more than $40 an hour
was only 4%. Jason Furman, 'How to Protect Workers from
Job-Stealing Robots', *The Atlantic*, 21 September 2016, https://
www.theatlantic.com/business/archive/2016/09/jason-
furman-ai/499682/.

92 Jaclyn Peiser, 'The Rise of the Robot Reporter', *New York Times*, 5
February 2019, https://www.nytimes.com/2019/02/05/business/
media/artificial-intelligence-journalism-robots.html.

93 Christ Baraniuk, 'China's Xinhua agency unveils AI news
presenter', BBC News, 8 November 2018, https://www.bbc.com/
news/technology-46136504.

94 Isabella Steger, 'Chinese state media's latest innovation is an AI
female news anchor', *Quartz*, 20 February 2019, https://qz.
com/1554471/chinas-xinhua-launches-worlds-first-ai-female-news-
anchor/.

95 Michelle Cheng, 'JPMorgan Chase has an AI copywriter that writes
better ads than humans can', *Quartz*, 7 August 2019, https://qz.
com/work/1682579/jpmorgan-chase-chooses-ai-copywriter-persado-
to-write-ads/.

96 James Gallagher, 'Artificial intelligence diagnoses lung cancer', BBC
News, 20 May 2019, https://www.bbc.com/news/health-48334649;

Sara Reardon, 'Rise of Robot Radiologists', *Nature*, 19 December 2019, https://www.nature.com/articles/d41586-019-03847-z; D. Douglas Miller and Eric W. Brown, 'Artificial Intelligence in Medical Practice: The Question to the Answer?', *American Journal of Medicine* 131, no. 2 (2018), 129–33, https://doi.org/10.1016/j.amjmed.2017.10.035.

97 'The Rise of the Robo-advisor: How Fintech Is Disrupting Retirement', *Knowledge@Wharton*, 14 June 2018, https://knowledge.wharton.upenn.edu/article/rise-robo-advisor-fintech-disrupting-retirement/; Charlie Wood, 'Robot analysts are better than humans at picking stocks, a new study found', *Business Insider*, 11 February 2020, https://www.businessinsider.com/robot-analysts-better-than-humans-at-picking-good-investments-study-2020-2?r=US&IR=T.

98 'Robotic reverend blesses worshippers in eight languages', BBC News, 30 May 2017, https://www.bbc.com/news/av/world-europe-40101661/robotic-reverend-blesses-worshippers-in-eight-languages.

99 This thought is inspired by a conversation with Gabrielle Rifkind, Oxford Research Group.

100 Daiga Kameräde et al., 'A shorter working week for everyone: How much paid work is needed for mental health and well-being?', *Social Science & Medicine* 241 (November 2019), 112353, https://doi.org/10.1016/j.socscimed.2019.06.006; 'One day of employment a week is all we need for mental health benefits', University of Cambridge, 18 June 2019, https://www.sciencedaily.com/releases/2019/06/190618192030.htm.

101 Kevin J. Delaney, 'The robot that takes your job should pay taxes, says Bill Gates', *Quartz*, 17 Debruary 2017, https://qz.com/911968/bill-gates-the-robot-that-takes-your-job-should-pay-taxes/.

102 David Rotman, 'Should we tax robots? A debate', *MIT Technology Review*, 12 June 2019, https://www.technologyreview.com/2019/06/12/134982/should-we-tax-robots-a-debate/.

103 House of Commons, Business – Energy and Industrial Strategy Committee, 'Oral evidence: Automation and the future of work, HC 1093', 15 May 2019, https://publications.parliament.uk/pa/cm201719/cmselect/cmbeis/1093/1093.pdf; House of Commons – Business, Energy and Industrial Strategy Committee, 'Automation

and the future of work – Twenty-Third Report of Session 2017-19',
9 September 2019, http://data.parliament.uk/writtenevidence/
committeeevidence.svc/evidencedocument/business-energy-and-
industrial-strategy-committee/automation-and-the-future-of-work/
oral/102291.html Q303.

104 Eduardo Porter, 'Don't Fight the Robots. Tax Them.', *New York
Times*, 23 February 2019, https://www.nytimes.com/2019/02/
23/sunday-review/tax-artificial-intelligence.html; 'Robot density
rises globally', International Federation of Robotics, 7 February
2018, https://ifr.org/ifr-press-releases/news/robot-density-rises-
globally.

CHAPTER NINE:
Sex, Love and Robots

1   'Gentle touch soothes the pain of social rejection', *UCL News*, 18
    October 2017, https://www.ucl.ac.uk/news/2017/oct/gentle-touch-
    soothes-pain-social-rejection.

2   Allison Marsh, 'Elektro the Moto-Man Had the Biggest Brain at
    the 1939 World's Fair', IEEE *Spectrum*, 28 September 2018, https://
    spectrum.ieee.org/tech-history/dawn-of-electronics/elektro-the-
    motoman-had-the-biggest-brain-at-the-1939-worlds-fair.

3   *Time*, 24 April 1939, 61, http://content.time.com/time/magazine/
    0,9263,7601390424,00.html.

4   H.R. Everett, *Unmanned Systems of Worlds War I and II* (MIT Press,
    2015), p.451; Justin Martin, 'Elektro?', *Discover* Magazine, 6 January
    2009, http://discovermagazine.com/2009/jan/06-whatever-
    happened-to-elektro; Despina Kakoudaki, *Anatomy of a Robot:
    Literature, Cinema and the Cultural Work of Artificial People* (Rutgers
    University Press, 2014), p.9.

5   Library of Congress, 'The Middleton Family at the New York
    World's Fair', https://www.youtube.com/watch?v=Q6TQEoDS-fQ.

6   Noel Sharkey, 'Elektro's return', *New Scientist*, 20 December 2008;
    Marsh 'Elektro the Moto-Man Had the Biggest Brain at the 1939
    World's Fair'.

7   Library of Congress, 'The Middleton Family at the New York
    World's Fair'.

8   Marsh, 'Electro the Moto-Man Had the Biggest Brain at the 1939 World's Fair'.

9   Ibid.

10   H.R. Everett, *Unmanned Systems of Worlds War I and II*, p.458.

11   Ibid.

12   J. Gilbert Baird, letter to *LIFE* Magazine, 22 September 1952.

13   Louise Moon, 'Chinese man buried in his car as dying wish is granted', *South China Morning Post*, 31 May 2018, https://www.scmp.com/news/china/society/article/2148677/chinese-man-buried-his-car-dying-wish-granted.

14   JaYoung Soung, Rebecca E. Grinter and Henrik I. Christensen, 'Domestic Robot Ecology: An Initial Framework to Unpack Long-Term Acceptance of Robots at Home', *International Journal of Social Robotics* 2 (July 2010), 425, https://doi.org/10.1007/s12369-010-0065-8.

15   Personal conversation, December 2018.

16   Neil Steinberg, 'Why some robots are created cute', *Mosaic Science*, 13 July 2016, https://mosaicscience.com/story/why-some-robots-are-created-cute/.

17   Julie Carpenter, *Culture and Human-Robot Interaction in Militarized Spaces: A War Story* (Ashgate, 2016).

18   Ibid.

19   'MARCbot', Exponent, https://www.exponent.com/experience/marcbot.

20   Paul J. Springer, *Outsourcing War to Machines: The Military Robotics Revolution* (Praeger Security International, 2018), p.93.

21   'Soldiers are developing relationships with their battlefield robots, naming them, assigning genders, and even holding funerals when they are destroyed', Reddit, 2014, https://www.reddit.com/r/Military/comments/1mn6y1/soldiers_are_developing_relationships_with_their/ccat8a7/.

22   Christian J.A.M. Willemse and Jan B.F. van Erp, 'Social Touch in Human-Robot Interaction: Robot Initiated Touches Can Induce Positive Responses Without Extensive Prior Bonding', *International Journal of Social Robotics* 11 (April 2019), 285–304, https://doi.org/10.1007/s12369-018-0500-9.

23   Note that the response was purely physiological.

24   'Value of social and entertainment robot market worldwide from

2015 to 2025 (in billion U.S. dollars)', Statista, May 2019, https://www.statista.com/statistics/755684/social-and-entertainment-robot-market-value-worldwide/; Public Relations Office: Government of Japan, https://www.gov-online.go.jp/cam/s5/eng/; Abishur Prakash, 'China Robot Market Likely to Continue Rising, Despite Trade Disputes,' *Robotics Business Review*, July 2018, https://www.roboticsbusinessreview.com/regional/china-robot-market-still-rising/; Kim Sang-mo, 'Policy Directions for S. Korea's Robot Industry,' *Business Korea*, August 2018, http://www.businesskorea.co.kr/news/articleView.html?idxno=24394; Tony Diver, 'Robot 'carers' to be funded by government scheme', *Telegraph*, 26 October 2016, https://www.telegraph.co.uk/politics/2019/10/26/robot-carers-funded-government-scheme/; 'Europe develops range of next-generation robots for the elderly', *Apolitical*, 30 January 2017, https://apolitical.co/en/solution_article/using-robots-ease-pain-old-age. During the Covid-19 crisis, robots were also swiftly mobilised to deliver food and sanitise surfaces in hospitals in China and then in India. 'Robots help combat COVID-19 in world, and maybe soon in India too', *Economic Times*, 30 March 2020, https://economictimes.indiatimes.com/news/science/robots-help-combat-covid-19-in-world-and-maybe-soon-in-india-too/.

25 'Sony's beloved robotic dog is back with a new bag of tricks', ABC News, 1 October 2018, https://www.nbcnews.com/mach/video/sony-s-beloved-robotic-dog-is-back-with-a-new-bag-of-tricks-1333791811671; Kate Baggaley, 'New companion robots can't do much but make us love them', NBC News, 23 June 2019, https://www.nbcnews.com/mach/science/new-companion-robots-can-t-do-much-make-us-love-ncna1015986.

26 A.J. Dellinger, 'Furhat Robots gives AI a face with its new social robot', Engadget, November 11 2018, https://www.engadget.com/2018/11/06/furhat-robotics-furhat-social-robot/.

27 Jamie Carter, 'Amazon could be set to redefine personal robots in 2019, as rumours fly at CES', *South China Morning Post*, 12 January 2019, https://www.scmp.com/lifestyle/gadgets/article/2181642/amazon-could-be-set-redefine-personal-robots-2019-rumours-fly-ces; Chris DeGraw, 'The robot invasion arrived at CES 2019 – and it was cuter than we expected', *Digital Trends*,

11 January 2019, https://www.digitaltrends.com/home/cutest-companion-robots-ces-2019/; 'Top Tech Themes from the Consumer Electronics Show: 2020', Acceleration Through Innovation, 3 February 2020, https://aticornwallinnovation.co.uk/knowledge-base/top-tech-themes-from-the-consumer-electronics-show-2020/.

28 Ibid.; Nick Summers, 'Groove X's Lovot is a fuzzy and utterly adorable robot', Engadget, 7 January 2019; https://www.engadget.com/2019/01/07/lovot-groove-x-robot-adorable.

29 Baggaley, 'New companion robots can't do much but make us love them'.

30 'Kiki: A Robot Pet That Grows With You', Zoetic AI, https://www.kiki.ai.

31 'Hi, I'm ElliQ', ElliQ, https://elliq.com.

32 28% of Japanese population is over age 65 as of 2019. World Bank, 'Population ages 65 and above,' The World Bank, 2019, https://data.worldbank.org/indicator/SP.POP.65UP.TO.ZS.

33 '19 prefectures to see 20% population drops by '35', Japan Times, 30 May 2007, https://www.japantimes.co.jp/news/2007/05/30/national/19-prefectures-to-see-20-population-drops-by-35/; 'Statistical Handbook of Japan', Statistics Bureau, Ministry of Internal Affairs and Communications: Statistics Japan, 2018, https://www.stat.go.jp/english/data/handbook/pdf/2018all.pdf.

34 'Japan is fighting back against loneliness among the elderly', Apolitical, 18 March 2019, https://apolitical.co/solution_article/japan-is-fighting-back-against-loneliness-among-the-elderly/; original statistics from Nobuyuki Izumida, 'Japan's Changing Societal Structure and Support by Families and Communities (Japanese National Institute of Population and Social Security Research, 2017). https://fpcj.jp/wp/wp-content/uploads/2018/09/a1b488733565199b8c9c8f9ac437b042.pdf.

35 Emiko Takagi, Merril Silverstein and Eileen Crimmins, 'Intergenerational Coresidence of Older Adults in Japan: Conditions for Cultural Plasticity', The Journals of Gerontology 62, no. 5 (September 2007), 330–9, https://doi.org/10.1093/geronb/62.5.S330; Mayumi Hayashi, 'The care of older people in Japan: myths and realities of family "care"', History and Policy, 3

June 2011, http://www.historyandpolicy.org/policy-papers/papers/
the-care-of-older-people-in-japan-myths-and-realities-of-family-care.
By 2040, Japan's National Institute of Population and Social
Security Research estimates that the number of elderly people
living alone will have increased by 43% from already-high 2015
numbers; 'Rising numbers of elderly people are living alone',
Japan Times, 3 May 2019, https://www.japantimes.co.jp/opinion/
2019/05/03/editorials/rising-numbers-elderly-people-living-alone/.

36 The age and years are all from an article published in summer 2019
so are relative to then.

37 'Robots perking up the lives of the lonely elderly across Japan',
Straits Times, 19 August 2019, https://www.straitstimes.com/asia/
east-asia/robots-perking-up-lives-of-the-lonely-elderly-across-japan;
Ikuko Mitsuda, 'Lonely? There's a bot for that', *Oregonian*, 18
August 2018, https://www.oregonlive.com/business/2019/08/
lonely-theres-a-bot-for-that.html; Martin Coulter, 'Will virtual
reality and AI help us to find love or make us lonelier', *Financial
Times*, 12 September 2019, https://www.ft.com/content/4fab7952-
b796-11e9-8a88-aa6628ac896c.

38 'Robots perking up the lives of the lonely elderly across Japan';
Ikuko Mitsuda, 'Lonely? There's a bot for that'.

39 Anne Tergesen and Miho Inada, 'It's Not A Stuffed Animal, It's a
$6,000 Medical Device', *Wall Street Journal*, 21 June 2010, https://
www.wsj.com/articles/.
SB10001424052748704463504575301051844937276.

40 Malcolm Foster, 'Ageing Japan: Robots' role in future of elder
care', *Reuters*, 28 March 2018, https://widerimage.reuters.com/
story/ageing-japan-robots-role-in-future-of-elder-care.

41 Personal conversation, June 2019; see also Shizuko Tanigaki,
Kensaku Kishida and Akihito Fujita, 'A preliminary study of the
effects of a smile-supplement robot on behavioral and psychological
symptoms of elderly people with mild impairment', Journal of
Humanities and Social Sciences 45 (2018), https://core.ac.uk/
reader/154410008.

42 Malcolm Foster, 'Ageing Japan: Robots' role in future of elder care'.

43 Note that as recently as 2011, rental programmes for robotic
hospital guides were scrapped due to low demand in Japan – so it's

also been a rapid turnaround in people's receptivity; 'Over 80% of Japanese Would Welcome Robot Caregivers', Nippon.com, 4 December 2018, https://www.nippon.com/en/features/h00342/over-80-of-japanese-would-welcome-robot-caregivers.html.

44 'Robot density rises globally', International Federation of Robotics, 7 February 2018, https://ifr.org/ifr-press-releases/news/robot-density-rises-globally.

45 Terry, 'Destroy All Monsters! Tokusatsu in America', Comic Art Community, 8 March 2013, http://comicartcommunity.com/comicart_news/destroy-all-monsters-tokusatsu-in-america/.

46 For more on Japan's 'techno-animism', see Casper Bruun Jensen and Anders Blok, 'Techno-animism in Japan: Shinto Cosmograms, Actor-network Theory, and the Enabling Powers of Non-human Agencies', *Theory, Culture and Society* 30, no. 2 (2013), 84–115, https://doi.org/10.1177/0263276412456564.

47 John Thornhill, 'Asia has learnt to love robots – the West should, too', *Financial Times*, 31 May 2018, https://www.ft.com/content/6e408f42-4145-11e8-803a-295c97e6fd0b.

48 Aaron Smith and Monica Anderson, '4. Americans' attitudes toward robot caregivers', Pew Research Center, 4 October 2017, https://www.pewinternet.org/2017/10/04/americans-attitudes-toward-robot-caregivers/.

49 Ibid.

50 'ElliQ beta users' testimonials', Intuition Robotics, Youtube, 6 January 2019, https://www.youtube.com/watch?v=emrqHpC8Bs8&feature=youtu.be.

51 This is according to their manufacturer. Maggie Jackson, 'Would You Let a Robot Take Care of Your Mother?', *New York Times,* 13 December 2019, https://www.nytimes.com/2019/12/13/opinion/robot-caregiver-aging.html.

52 'Amazon Alexa 'Sharing is caring' by Joint', Campaign US, 29 May 2019, https://www.campaignlive.com/article/amazon-alexa-sharing-caring-joint/1585979.

53 Alireza Taheri, Ali Meghdari, Minoo Alemi and Hamidreza Pouretema, 'Human-Robot Interaction in Autism Treatment: A Case Study on Three Autistic Children as Twins, Siblings and Classmates', *International Journal of Social Robotics* 10 (2018), 93–113,

https://doi.org/10.1007/s12369-017-0433-8; Hideki Kozima, Cocoro Nakagawa and Yuiko Yasuda, 'Children-robot interaction: a pilot study in autism therapy', *Progress in Brain Research* 164 (2007), 385–400, https://doi.org/10.1016/S0079-6123(07)64021-7; H. Kumuzaki et al., 'The impact of robotic intervention on joint attention in children with autism spectrum disorders', *Molecular Autism* 9, no. 46 (2018), https://doi.org/10.1186/s13229-018-0230-8.

54 Alyssa M. Alcorn, Eloise Ainger et al., 'Educators' Views on Using Humanoid Robots With Autistic Learners in Special Education Settings in England', *Frontiers in Robotics and AI* 6, no. 107 (November 2019), https://doi.org/10.3389/frobt.2019.00107.

55 Victoria Waldersee, 'One in five young Brits can imagine being friends with a robot', YouGov, 1 November 2018, https://yougov.co.uk/topics/technology/articles-reports/2018/11/01/one-five-young-brits-can-imagine-being-friends-rob; original data at 'Internal Robots and You', YouGov, 2018, https://d25d2506sfb94s.cloudfront.net/cumulus_uploads/document/opta4dnee1/YG-Archive-RobotsAndYouInternal-220818.pdf.

56 Elizabeth Foster, 'Young kids use smart speakers daily', *Kidscreen,* 28 March 2019, https://kidscreen.com/2019/03/28/young-kids-use-smart-speakers-daily-survey/.

57 Jacqueline M. Kory-Westlund, 'Kids' relationships and learning with social robots', MIT Media Lab, 21 February 2019, https://www.media.mit.edu/posts/kids-relationships-and-learning-with-social-robots/; Jacqueline Kory-Westlund, Hae Won Park, Randi Williams and Cynthia Breazeal, 'Measuring young children's long-term relationships with social robots', *Proceedings of the 17th ACM Conference on Interaction Design and Children* (June 2018), 207–18, https://doi.org/10.1145/3202185.3202732.

58 Jacqueline M. Kory-Westlund, 'Measuring kids' relationships with robots', MIT Media Lab, https://www.media.mit.edu/posts/measuring-kids-relationships-with-robots.

59 Ibid.

60 Natt Garun, 'One Year Later, Restaurants are Still Confused by Google Duplex', *The Verge,* 9 May 2019, https://www.theverge.com/2019/5/9/18538194/google-duplex-ai-restaurants-experiences-review-robocalls.

61 Ibid.

62 Hassan Ugail and Ahmad Al-dahoud, 'A genuine smile is indeed in the eyes – The computer aided non-invasive analysis of the exact weight distribution of human smiles across the face', *Advanced Engineering Informatics* 42 (October 2019), https://doi.org/10.1016/j.aei.2019.100967.

63 Erico Guizzo, 'How Aldebaran Robotics Built its Friendly Humanoid Robot, Pepper', *Spectrum*, 26 December 2014, https://spectrum.ieee.org/robotics/home-robots/how-aldebaran-robotics-built-its-friendly-humanoid-robot-pepper; Alderaban/SoftBank, 'Pepper Press Kit', https://cdn.shopify.com/s/files/1/0059/3932/files/SoftBank_Pepper_Robot_Overview_Robot_Center.pdf.

64 Ibid.

65 Yoko Wakatsuki and Emiko Jozuka, 'Robots to cheer coronavirus patients are also helping hotel staff to keep a safe distance', CNN, 1 May 2020, https://edition.cnn.com/world/live-news/coronavirus-pandemic-05-01-20-intl/h_6df7c15d1192ae720a504dc90ead353c; '"I'm cheering for you": Robot welcome at Tokyo quarantine', Barrons, 1 May 2020, https://www.barrons.com/news/i-m-cheering-for-you-robot-welcome-at-tokyo-quarantine-01588319705.

66 'Pepper Press Kit'.

67 Sharon Gaudin, 'Personal robot that shows emotions sells out in 1 minute', *Computer World*, 22 June 2015, https://www.computerworld.com/article/2938897/personal-robot-that-shows-emotions-sells-out-in-1-minute.html.

68 Simon Chandler, 'Tech's dangerous race to control our emotions', *Daily Dot*, 7 June 2019, https://www.dailydot.com/debug/emotional-manipulation-ai-technology/.

69 Email conversation with Professor Adrian Cheok, i-University, Tokyo.

70 Hayley Tsukayama, 'When your kid tries to say "Alexa" before "Mama"', *Washington Post*, 21 November 2017, https://www.washingtonpost.com/news/the-switch/wp/2017/11/21/when-your-kid-tries-to-say-alexa-before-mama/.

71 'How does sex feel with a RealDoll?', RealDoll, https://www.realdoll.com/knowledgebase/how-does-sex-feel-with-a-realdoll; 'How strong are the doll's joints?', RealDoll, https://www.realdoll.com/knowledgebase/how-strong-are-the-dolls-joints/.

72 'Michelle 4.0', RealDoll, https://www.realdoll.com/product/michelle-4-0/.

73 Allison P. Davis, 'Are We Ready for Robot Sex?', *The Cut,* https://www.thecut.com/2018/05/sex-robots-realbotix.html.

74 'Sex Robot Doll with Artificial Intelligence: Introducing Emma . . .', Smart Doll World, https://www.smartdollworld.com/ai-sex-robot-doll-emma; Emily Gaudette, 'There's a Heated Debate Over the Best Sex Doll Skin Material', *Inverse,* 9 August 2017, https://www.inverse.com/article/36055-best-sex-doll-robot-tpe-silicone.

75 'Sex Robot Doll with Artificial Intelligence: Introducing Emma . . .'.

76 See for example David G. Cowan, Eric J. Vanman and Mark Nielsen, 'Motivated empathy: The mechanics of the empathetic gaze', *Cognition and Emotion* 28, no. 8 (2014), 1522–30, https://doi.org/10.1080/02699931.2014.890563.

77 Jenna Owsianik, 'RealDoll Releasing Intimate AI App That Will Pair with Love Dolls', *Future of Sex,* https://futureofsex.net/robots/realdoll-releasing-intimate-ai-app-will-pair-love-dolls/.

78 Jenny Kleeman, 'The race to build the world's first sex robot', *Guardian,* 27 April 2017, https://www.theguardian.com/technology/2017/apr/27/race-to-build-world-first-sex-robot.

79 Andrea Morris, 'Meet The Man Who Test Drives Sex Robots', *Forbes,* 27 September 2018, https://www.forbes.com/sites/andreamorris/2018/09/27/meet-the-man-who-test-drives-sex-robots/#419c304c452d.

80 Katherine E. Powers et al., 'Social Connection Modulates Perceptions of Animacy', *Psychological Science* 25, no. 10 (October 2014), 1943–8, https://doi.org/10.1177%2F0956797614547706.

81 Philosopher John Danaher points out 'We have no way of getting inside our friends' heads to figure out their true interests and values' – and yet we still consider them friends. So wouldn't robots be able to be our friends? As discussed in John Danaher, 'The Philosophical Case for Robot Friendship', *Journal of Post Human Studies* 3, no. 1 (2019), 5–24, https://doi.org/10.5325/jpoststud.3.1.0005.

82 Aristotle, *Nicomachean Ethics,* Book 8, (Cambridge University Press, 2000).

83 'Drunken Kanagawa man arrested after kicking SoftBank robot',

Japan Times, 7 September 2015, https://www.japantimes.co.jp/news/2015/09/07/national/crime-legal/drunken-kanagawa-man-60-arrested-after-kicking-softbank-robot-in-fit-of-rage/#.XeLHii2cZeM.

84 Tomasz Frymorgen, 'Sex robot sent for repairs after being molested at tech fair', BBC, 29 September 2017, https://www.bbc.co.uk/bbcthree/article/610ec648-b348-423a-bd3c-04dc701b2985.

85 Hunter Walk, 'Amazon Echo Is Magical. It's Also Turning My Kid Into an Asshole', HunterWalk.com, 6 April 2016, https://hunterwalk.com/2016/04/06/amazon-echo-is-magical-its-also-turning-my-kid-into-an-asshole/.

86 Mark West, Rebecca Kraut and Han Ei Chew, 'The Rise of Gendered AI and Its Troubling Repercussions', in *I'd Blush If I Could: Closing Gender Divides in Digital Skills Through Education* (UNESCO / EQUALS Skills Coalition, 2019), 113, 104, 107.

87 Ibid. Note that Siri's response has now been changed following an outcry.

88 A major focus of these inquiries has been the proliferation of child-like sex dolls, which have been flagged by governments around the world, most notably by Australia, as risks to real children. See Rick Brown and Jane Shelling, 'Exploring the implications of child sex dolls', *Trends and Issues in Criminal Justice* (Australian Institute of Criminology, March 2019). See also Caitlin Roper, '"Better a robot than a real child": The spurious logic used to justify child sex dolls', ABC Religion and Ethics, 9 January 2020, https://www.abc.net.au/religion/spurious-logic-used-to-justify-child-sex-dolls/11856284.

89 Xanthe Mallett, 'No evidence that sexbots reduce harms to women and children', *The Conversation,* 5 June 2018, https://theconversation.com/no-evidence-that-sexbots-reduce-harms-to-women-and-children-97694. Kathleen Richardson, a professor at DeMontfort University and the founder of the Campaign Against Sex Robots, agrees, stressing that sex dolls and sex robots are fundamentally different from sex toys such as vibrators. As she says: 'In the mind of someone buying and using them – they *are* women and girls. They are designed deliberately to resemble women and girls because they want the man buying and using the dolls to believe it is a woman or girl. These are markedly different

things. Sex dolls and mechanical dolls in the form of women and girls play on the idea that women are orifices to be penetrated'. Terri Murray, 'Interview with Kathleen Richardson on Sex Robots', *Conatus News,* 25 October 2017, https://conatusnews.com/kathleen-richardson-sex-robots/.

90 Jessica Miley, 'Sex Robot Samantha Gets an Update to Say "No" if She Feels Disrespected or Bored', *Interesting Engineering,* 28 June 2018, https://interestingengineering.com/sex-robot-samantha-gets-an-update-to-say-no-if-she-feels-disrespected-or-bored.

91 'Amazon Alexa to reward kids who say: 'Please'', BBC News, 25 April 2018, https://www.bbc.com/news/technology-43897516.

92 'Studying Computers To Learn About Ourselves', NPR, 3 September 2010, https://www.npr.org/templates/story/story.php?storyId=129629756.

93 I appreciate of course that determining which categories of mechanical objects should be protected is not an insignificant challenge.

94 G.W.F. Hegel, *Phenomenology of Spirit*, trans. A.V. Miller with analysis of the text and foreword by J.N. Findlay (Clarendon Press, 1977); see for example III, paragraph 179.

95 Jacqueline M. Kory-Westlund, 'Robots, Gender, and the Design of Relational Technology', MIT Media Lab, 12 August 2019, https://www.media.mit.edu/posts/robots-gender-and-the-design-of-relational-technology/.

96 Nicholas A. Christakis, 'How AI Will Rewire Us', *The Atlantic,* April 2019, https://www.theatlantic.com/magazine/archive/2019/04/robots-human-relationships/583204/.

97 David Levy, *Love and Sex With Robots* (HarperCollins, 2007), p.132; Laurence Goasduff, 'Emotion AI Will Personalize Interactions', Smarter With Gartner, 22 January 2018, https://www.gartner.com/smarterwithgartner/emotion-ai-will-personalize-interactions/.

98 Anco Peeters and Pim Haselager, 'Designing Virtuous Sex Robots', *International Journal of Social Robotics* (2019), https://doi.org/10.1007/s12369-019-00592-1.

99 Brian Borzykowski, 'Truth be told, we're more honest with robots', BBC, 19 April 2016, https://www.bbc.com/worklife/article/20160412-truth-be-told-were-more-honest-with-robots.

100 Judith Shulevitz, 'Alexa, Should We Trust You?', *The Atlantic*, November 2018, https://www.theatlantic.com/magazine/archive/2018/11/alexa-how-will-you-change-us/570844/.

101 Adam Satariano, Elian Peltier and Dmitry Kostyukov, 'Meet Zora, the Robot Caregiver', *New York Times*, 23 November 2018, https://www.nytimes.com/interactive/2018/11/23/technology/robot-nurse-zora.html.

102 Kate Julian, 'Why Are Young People Having So Little Sex?', *The Atlantic*, December 2018, https://www.theatlantic.com/magazine/archive/2018/12/the-sex-recession/573949/.

103 Jean M. Twenge, 'Have Smartphones Destroyed a Generation?', *The Atlantic*, September 2017, https://www.theatlantic.com/magazine/archive/2017/09/has-the-smartphone-destroyed-a-generation/534198/.

104 'British people 'having less sex' than previously', BBC News, 8 May 2019, https://www.bbc.co.uk/news/health-48184848.

105 Klinenberg, *Going Solo*, p.15.

106 Chen Mengwei, 'Survey: Young, alone, no house and not much sex', *China Daily*, 5 May 2017, http://africa.chinadaily.com.cn/china/2017-05/05/content_29210757.htm.

107 'Meet Henry, The World's First Generation Of Male Sex Robots', Fight The New Drug, 27 September 2019, https://fightthenewdrug.org/meet-henry-the-worlds-first-generation-of-male-sex-robots/.

108 Gabby Jeffries, 'Transgender sex robots are a thing now and apparently they're very popular', *Pink News*, 9 April 2018, https://www.pinknews.co.uk/2018/04/09/transgender-sex-robots-are-a-thing-now-and-apparently-theyre-very-popular/.

109 'Meet Henry, The World's First Generation Of Male Sex Robots'.

110 Realbotix, https://realbotix.com.

111 Eve Herold, 'Meet Your Child's New Nanny: A Robot', *Leaps* magazine, 31 December 2018, https://leapsmag.com/meet-your-childrens-new-nanny-a-robot/.

CHAPTER TEN:
The Loneliness Economy

1   Lanre Bakare, 'Glastonbury tickets sell out in 34 minutes',
    Guardian, 6 October 2019, https://www.theguardian.com/music/
    2019/oct/06/glastonbury-tickets-sell-out-in-34-minutes; around 2
    million people registered to be eligible to purchase tickets.

2   David Doyle, '12 things I learned as a Glastonbury virgin', 4 News,
    23 June 2015, https://www.channel4.com/news/glastonbury-2015-
    festival-lessons-12-things-know-virgin.

3   Robyn Taylor-Stavely, 'Glastonbury Festival, the weird and the
    wonderful', *The Fair,* 23 July 2019, https://wearethefair.com/2019/
    07/23/glastonbury-festival-review/; Crispin Aubrey and John
    Shearlaw, *Glastonbury: An Oral History of the Music, Mud and Magic*
    (Ebury Press, 2005), p.220.

4   Jenny Stevens, 'Glastonbury's Healing Fields: festivalgoer wellbeing
    is not just for hippies', *Guardian,* 27 June 2015, https://www.
    theguardian.com/music/2015/jun/27/glastonbury-healing-green-
    fields-hippies-wellbeing.

5   See original tweets at https://twitter.com/CNDTradeUnions/
    status/482469314831085568; https://twitter.com/WI_Glasto_Cakes/
    status/600374352475992064.

6   Lisa O'Carroll and Hannah Ellis-Petersen, 'Michael Eavis laments
    muddiest ever Glastonbury festival', *Guardian,* 26 June 2016,
    https://www.theguardian.com/music/2016/jun/26/michael-eavis-
    laments-muddiest-ever-glastonbury-festival; Neil McCormick, 'A
    wonderful wet weekend', *Telegraph,* 27 June 2016.

7   'Working at the Festival', Glastonbury Festival, https://www.
    glastonburyfestivals.co.uk/information/jobs/.

8   Stevie Martin, 'Shit-Covered Tents And Used Tampons: What It's
    Really Like To Clean Up After Glastonbury', *Grazia,* 4 August 2018,
    https://graziadaily.co.uk/life/opinion/shit-covered-tents-used-
    tampons-s-really-like-clean-glastonbury/.

9   Hannah Ellis-Petersen, '15,000 at Glastonbury set for record human
    peace sign', *Guardian,* 23 June 2017, https://www.theguardian.com/
    music/2017/jun/22/glastonbury-weather-to-cool-after-heat-left-
    dozens-needing-a-medic.

10 Akanksha Singh, 'Biggest Music Festivals on the Planet', Far &
    Wide, 10 June 2019, https://www.farandwide.com/s/biggest-music-
    festivals-ca71f3346443426e.

11 Joey Gibbons, 'Why I Loved Coachella', *Gibbons Whistler*, 6 June
    2016, https://gibbonswhistler.com/why-i-loved-coachella/.

12 'The Largest Music Festivals in the World', Statista, 18 April 2019,
    https://www.statista.com/chart/17757/total-attendance-of-music-
    festivals/; for 2019 attendance at Donauinselfest, Rock in Rio, and
    Kostrzyn nad Odra, see, respectively, '2,7 Millionen Besucher beim
    Donauinselfest', *Die Presse*, 24 June 2019, https://www.diepresse.
    com/5648670/27-millionen-besucher-beim-donauinselfest; Mark
    Beaumont, 'Rock in Rio: Brazil's Totemic Event That Brings the
    Entire Country Together', *Independent*, 17 October 2019, https://
    www.independent.co.uk/arts-entertainment/music/features/rock-
    in-rio-festival-brazil-lineup-roberto-medina-2020-a9160101.html;
    'Record attendance and a global reach for the 18th edition of
    Mawazine', Mawazine Rabat, 30 June 2019, http://www.mawazine.
    ma/en/mawazine-2019-reussite-totale-et-historique-2/.

13 Simon Usborne, 'Get me out of here! Why escape rooms have
    become a global craze', *Guardian*, 1 April 2019, https://www.
    theguardian.com/games/2019/apr/01/get-out-how-escape-rooms-
    became-a-global-craze; Will Coldwell, 'Escape games: why the
    latest city-break craze is being locked in a room', *Guardian*,
    3 April 2015, https://www.theguardian.com/travel/2015/apr/03/
    room-escape-games-city-breaks-gaming.

14 Simon Usborne, 'Get me out of here! Why escape rooms have
    become a global craze'.

15 Malu Rocha, 'The rising appeal of board game cafés', *Nouse*, 21
    January 2020, https://nouse.co.uk/2020/01/21/the-rising-appeal-of-
    board-game-cafs-.

16 Tom Walker, '"Huge growth" in number of people doing group
    exercise', *Health Club Management*, 14 May 2018, https://www.
    healthclubmanagement.co.uk/health-club-management-news/
    Huge-growth-in-number-of-people-doing-group-exercise-/337501.

17 Vanessa Grigoriadis, 'Riding High', *Vanity Fair*, 15 August 2012,
    https://www.vanityfair.com/hollywood/2012/09/soul-cycle-
    celebrity-cult-following.

18 Tara Isabella Burton, "'CrossFit is my church'", *Vox,* 10 September 2018, https://www.vox.com/the-goods/2018/9/10/17801164/ crossfit-soulcycle-religion-church-millennials-casper-ter-kuile.

19 Tom Layman, 'CrossFit as Church? Examining How We Gather', Harvard Divinity School, 4 November 2015, https://hds.harvard. edu/news/2015/11/04/crossfit-church-examining-how-we-gather#; Tara Isabella Burton, "'CrossFit is my church'".

20 One study found that people who exercised on a stationary bicycle for 30 minutes with a partner experienced more calmness and positive psychological effects than those who exercised alone. Thomas Plante, Laura Coscarelli, and Marie Ford, 'Does Exercising with Another Enhance the Stress-Reducing Benefits of Exercise?' *International Journal of Stress Management* 8, no. 3 (July 2001), 201–13, https://www.psychologytoday.com/files/attachments/34033/ exercise-another.pdf.

21 Cynthia Kim, 'In daytime discos, South Korea's elderly find escape from anxiety', *Reuters,* 16 April 2018, https://af.reuters.com/article/ worldNews/idAFKBN1HN01F.

22 Émile Durkheim, *The Elementary Forms of the Religious Life,* trans. Carol Closman, ed. Mark Cladis (Oxford University Press, 2008). Whilst online communities can provide some degree of collective effervescence, it is of a much a weaker form. See for example Randall Collins, 'Interaction Rituals and the New Electronic Media', *The Sociological Eye,* 25 January 2015, https://sociological-eye. blogspot.com/2011/01/interaction-rituals-and-new-electronic.html.

23 Charles Walter Masters, *The Respectability of Late Victorian Workers: A Case Study of York, 1867–1914* (Cambridge Scholars Publishing, 2010).

24 National Museum of African American History & Culture, 'The Community Roles of the Barber Shop and Beauty Salon,' 2019, https://nmaahc.si.edu/blog/community-roles-barber-shop-and- beauty-salon.

25 Ray Oldenburg, *The Great Good Place* (Da Capo Press, 1999), p.22. Note that the 'universal' accessibility of such 'third places' is itself an idealistic assumption that does not necessarily take into account barriers that have been widely exposed since Oldenburg first wrote, such as the racism that has routinely rendered these same 'third places' uncomfortable and/or inaccessible to people of

colour. For a critique of Oldenburg along these lines, see F. Yuen and A.J. Johnson, 'Leisure spaces, community, and third places', *Leisure Sciences* 39, no. 2 (2017), 295–303.

26   'ANNOUNCING Mission Pie's 12th Annual PIE CONTEST', Mission Pie, 2018, https://missionpie.com/posts/12th-annual-community-pie-baking-contest-september-9-2018/; 'Join us on National Typewriter Day for typewriter art, poetry, stories, and letter writing – and of course, delicious pie!', Mission Pie, https://missionpie.com/posts/3rd-annual-type-in/.

27   'PAN in conversation with Karen Heisler', Pesticide Action Network, http://www.panna.org/PAN-conversation-Karen-Heisler.

28   Joe Eskenazi, 'Last meal: Mission Pie will soon close its doors', *Mission Local,* 17 June 2019, https://missionlocal.org/2019/06/last-meal-mission-pie-will-soon-close-its-doors/.

29   J.D. Esajian, 'Rent Report: Highest Rent In US 2020', *Fortune Builders,* https://www.fortunebuilders.com/top-10-u-s-cities-with-the-highest-rents/.

30   Nuala Sawyer Bishari, 'Can the Mission Save Itself from Commercial Gentrification?', *SF Weekly,* 13 February 2029, http://www.sfweekly.com/topstories/can-the-mission-save-itself-from-commercial-gentrification/; Kimberly Truong, 'Historically Latino district in San Francisco on track to lose half its Latino population', Mashable UK, 30 October 2015, https://mashable.com/2015/10/30/san-francisco-mission-latino-population/; Chris Colin, '36 Hours in San Francisco', *New York Times,* 11 September 2008, https://www.nytimes.com/2008/09/14/travel/14hours.html; Joyce E. Cutler, '"Twitter" Tax Break in San Francisco Ends Amid Push For New Funds', *Bloomberg Tax,* 15 May 2019, https://news.bloombergtax.com/daily-tax-report-state/twitter-tax-break-in-san-francisco-ends-amid-push-for-new-taxes.

31   Carolyn Alburger, 'As Twitter Tax Break Nears Its End, Mid-Market Restaurants Feel Glimmer of Hope', *Eater San Francisco,* 19 September 2018, https://sf.eater.com/2018/9/19/17862118/central-market-tax-exclusion-restaurants-post-mortem-future.

32   James Vincent, 'DoorDash promises to change controversial tipping policy after public outcry', *The Verge,* 24 July 2019, https://www.theverge.com/2019/7/24/20708212/doordash-delivery-tip-theft-

policy-change-tony-xu-tweets; Jaya Saxena, 'Delivery Apps Aren't Getting Any Better', *Eater*, 29 May 2019, https://www.eater.com/2019/5/29/18636255/delivery-apps-hurting-restaurants-grubhub-seamless-ubereats.

33 Joe Eskenazi, 'Last meal: Mission Pie will soon close its doors'.

34 Unfortunately this Facebook post is no longer available following Mission Pie's closure.

35 See original Facebook post at: https://www.facebook.com/131553526891752/photos/a.213721682008269/2380204862026596/?type=3&theater.

36 Melissa Harrison, 'We Must Be Brave by Francis Liardet review – a child in wartime', *Guardian*, 13 February 2019, https://www.theguardian.com/books/2019/feb/13/we-must-be-brave-frances-liardet-review.

37 'One Community One Book', Kett's Books, https://www.kettsbooks.co.uk/onecommunity/.

38 'Clarkes Bookshop Cape Town', Getaway.co.za, http://www.clarkesbooks.co.za/assets/docs/GW1214p69%202%20(3).pdf.

39 June McNicholas and Glyn M. Collis, 'Dogs as catalysts for social interactions: Robustness of the Effect', *British Journal of Psychology* 91, no. 1 (February 2000), 61–70, https://doi.org/10.1348/000712600161673.

40 Abha Bhattarai, 'Apple wants its stores to become "town squares." But skeptics are calling it a "branding fantasy"', *Washington Post,* 13 September 2017, https://www.washingtonpost.com/news/business/wp/2017/09/13/apple-wants-its-stores-to-become-town-squares-but-skeptics-call-it-a-branding-fantasy/.

41 Andrew Hill, 'Apple stores are not "town squares" and never should be', *Financial Times*, 17 September 2017, https://www.ft.com/content/8c5d4aec-988f-11e7-a652-cde3f882dd7b.

42 Julia Carrie Wong, 'Pepsi pulls Kendall Jenner ad ridiculed for co-opting protest movements', *Guardian,* 6 April 2017, https://www.theguardian.com/media/2017/apr/05/pepsi-kendall-jenner-pepsi-apology-ad-protest.

43 See original tweet at: https://twitter.com/BerniceKing/status/849656699464056832? s=20pepsi-kendall-jenner-pepsi-apology-ad-protest.

44 Wong, 'Pepsi pulls Kendall Jenner ad ridiculed for co-opting protest

movements'; as many critics pointed out, the framing of Jenner and the police officer seem to reference a striking image of Ieshia Evans, a black woman photographed standing still in a flowing dress while offering up her hands for arrest at a protest against police brutality in Louisiana. See photo by Jonathan Bachman, Reuters, at https://www.nytimes.com/slideshow/2017/02/13/blogs/the-worlds-best-photo/s/13-lens-WPress-slide-JSQ0.html.

45 Keiko Morris and Elliot Brown, 'WeWork Surpasses JPMorgan as Biggest Occupier of Manhattan Office Space,' *Wall Street Journal*, September 18 2018, https://www.wsj.com/articles/wework-surpasses-jpmorgan-as-biggest-occupier-of-manhattan-office-space-1537268401; 'WeWork Locations,' archived November 2017, https://www.wework.com/locations.

46 'The We Company', United States Securities and Exchange Commission, 14 August 2019, https://www.sec.gov/Archives/edgar/data/1533523/000119312519220499/d781982ds1.htm.

47 Rani Molla, '"Co-living" is the new "having roommates" – with an app', *Vox*, 29 May 2019, https://www.vox.com/recode/2019/5/29/18637898/coliving-shared-housing-welive-roommates-common-quarters.

48 Henny Sender, 'Investors embrace millennial co-living in Asia's megacities', *Financial Times*, 28 January 2020, https://www.ft.com/content/c57129f8-40d9-11ea-a047-eae9bd51ceba.

49 'Coliving is city living made better', Common, https://www.common.com; Society, http://oursociety.com; 'Join the global living movement', The Collective, https://thecollective.com; Winnie Agbonlahor, 'Co-living in London: Friendship, fines and frustration,' BBC, April 24, 2018, https://www.bbc.com/news/uk-england-london-43090849.

50 Common, https://www.common.com/why-common/; 'The 4 Co's of Coliving', Ollie, https://www.ollie.co/coliving.

51 Jessica Burdon, 'Norn: the offline social network reviving the art of conversation', *The Week*, 30 April 2018, https://www.theweek.co.uk/93266/norn-the-offline-social-network-reviving-the-art-of-conversation; Annabel Herrick, 'Norn rethinks co-living for a new generation of nomads', *The Spaces*, https://thespaces.com/introducing-norn-the-startup-taking-co-living-to-new-heights/.

52   See comment at: https://news.ycombinator.com/
     threads?id=rcconf.

53   See comment at: https://news.ycombinator.com/
     item?id=19783245.

54   Conversation with Daniel.

55   Agbonlahor, 'Co-living in London: Friendship, fines and frustration'.

56   Will Coldwell, '"Co-living": the end of urban loneliness –or cynical
     corporate dormitories?', *Guardian,* 3 September 2019, https://www.
     theguardian.com/cities/2019/sep/03/co-living-the-end-of-urban-
     loneliness-or-cynical-corporate-dormitories.

57   Peter Timko, 'Co-Living With Lefebvre: The Production of Space
     at The Collective Old Oak' (Radboud University, 2018), p.49,
     https://theses.ubn.ru.nl/bitstream/handle/123456789/7424/
     Timko%2C_Peter_1.pdf?sequence=1.

58   Agbonlahor, 'Co-living in London: Friendship, fines and frustration'.

59   Timko, 'Co-Living With Lefebvre'.

60   Ibid.

61   Coldwell, '"Co-living': the end of urban loneliness'.

62   'Berlin Coliving Meetup: How Can Coliving Foster Thriving
     Communities?', *Conscious Coliving,* 30 July 2019, https://www.
     consciouscoliving.com/2019/07/30/berlin-co-living-meet-up-how-
     can-coliving-foster-thriving-communities/.

63   Coldwell, '"Co-Living": The end of urban loneliness'.

64   Venn, '2019 Semi Annual Impact Report' (Venn, 2019), https://39q
     77k1dd7472q159r3hoq5p-wpengine.netdna-ssl.com/wp-content/
     uploads/2019/10/impactreport2019.pdf.

65   'Your Amenities', Nomadworks, https://nomadworks.com/
     amenities/.

66   Alessandro Gandini, 'The rise of coworking spaces: A literature
     review', *Ephemera* 15, no. 1 (February 2015), 193–205, http://www.
     ephemerajournal.org/contribution/rise-coworking-spaces-literature-
     review.

67   'Doing things together', Happy City, https://thehappycity.com/
     resources/happy-homes/doing-things-together-principle/.

68   Oliver Smith, 'Exclusive: Britain's Co-living King Has Raised $400m
     To Take On WeWork In America', *Forbes,* 27 March 2018, https://
     www.forbes.com/sites/oliversmith/2018/03/27/exclusive-britains-

co-living-king-has-raised-400m-to-take-on-wework-in-america/.

69 Brad Eisenberg, 'Why is WeWork so popular?', *Medium,* 15 July
2017, https://medium.com/@eisen.brad/why-is-wework-so-
popular-934b07736cae.

70 Hannah Foulds, 'Co-Living Spaces: Modern Utopia Or Over-
Organised Hell?', *The Londonist,* 12 April 2017, https://londonist.
com/london/housing/co-living-spaces-modern-utopia-or-over-
organised-hell.

71 Marisa Meltzer, 'Why Fitness Classes Are Making You Go Broke',
Racked, 10 June 2015, https://www.racked.com/2015/6/10/8748149/
fitness-class-costs.

72 Hillary Hoffower, 'Nearly one-third of millennials who went to a
music festival in the past year say they took on debt to afford it,
survey finds', *Business Insider,* 1 August 2019, https://www.business
insider.com/millennials-going-into-debt-music-festivals-coachella-
lollapalooza-bonnaroo-2019.

73 'City Reveals Selected Shared Housing Development Proposals',
NYC Housing Preservation and Development, https://www1.nyc.
gov/site/hpd/news/092-19/city-reveals-selected-shared-housing-
development-proposals#/o.

74 Jane Margolies, 'Co-Living Grows Up', *New York Times,* 14 January
2020, https://www.nytimes.com/2020/01/14/realestate/co-living-
grows-up.html; 'City Reveals Selected Shared Housing
Development Proposals'.

75 The Common Team, 'Common and L+M Development Partners
Win ShareNYC', Common, 8 October 2019, https://www.
common.com/blog/2019/10/common-announced-as-winner-of-
sharenyc-hpd/.

CHAPTER ELEVEN:
Coming Together in a World that's Pulling Apart

1 Even within individuals, loneliness can take several forms, as we've
seen. See too Fay Bound Alberti who describes loneliness as a
historically emergent 'emotion cluster'. Fay Bound Alberti, 'This
"Modern Epidemic": Loneliness as an Emotion Cluster and a
Neglected Subject in the History of Emotions,' *Emotion Review* 10,

no. 3 (July 2018), 242–54, https://doi.org/10.1177/1754073918768876; and for more detail, Fay Bound Alberti, *A Biography of Loneliness: The History of an Emotion* (Oxford University Press, 2019).

2   See for example Corinne Purtill, 'Loneliness costs the US almost $7 billion extra each year', *Quartz*, 28 October 2018, https://qz. com/1439200/loneliness-costs-the-us-almost-7-billion-extra-each-year/; 'The cost of loneliness to employers', Campaign to End Loneliness, https://www.campaigntoendloneliness.org/wp-content/uploads/cost-of-loneliness-2017.pdf.

3   I am including here too those who have written about the collapse of community. Conservatives taking this line include Roger Scruton and Mary Eberstadt; see, respectively, Roger Scruton, 'Identity, family, marriage: our core conservative values have been betrayed,' *Guardian*, 11 May 2013, https://www.theguardian.com/commentisfree/2013/may/11/identity-family-marriage-conservative-values-betrayed; Mary Eberstadt, *Primal Screams: How the Sexual Revolution Created Identity Politics* (Templeton Press, 2019). Jeremy Corbyn would be an example of a voice on the left who holds the all-responsibility-is-with-the-state point of view. As would political theorists such as Neil Vallelly.

Note too that there are thinkers on the 'left' like Alasdair MacIntyre (*After Virtue: A Study in Moral Theory* [University of Notre Dame Press, 1981]) or Christopher Lasch (*The True and Only Heaven: Progress and Its Critics* [W.W. Norton, 1991]) who have also written about the integral role the breakdown of the family has played in the collapse of community. So whilst the debate can be characterised along partisan lines, there are obvious exceptions.

4   For the authoritative view of modern inequality and its relationship to neoliberal capitalism, see Thomas Piketty, *Capital in the Twenty-First Century*, trans. Arthur Goldhammer (Cambridge, Mass.: Harvard University Press, 2014). On race and neoliberalism, see Darrick Hamilton and Kyle Strickland, 'The Racism of Neoliberalism', *Evonomics*, 22 February 2020, https://evonomics. com/racism-neoliberalism-darrick-hamilton/; or for more detail, see David Theo Goldberg, *The Threat of Race: Reflections on Racial Neoliberalism* (Wiley-Blackwell, 2008). On gender and neoliberalism

see for example Andrea Cornwall, Jasmine Gideon and Kalpana Wilson, 'Reclaiming Feminism: Gender and Neoliberalism', *Institute of Development Studies Bulletin* 39, no. 6 (December 2008), https://doi.org/10.1111/j.1759-5436.2008.tb00505.x; or more comprehensively, Nancy Fraser, *Fortunes of Feminism: From State-Managed Capitalism to Neoliberal Crisis* (Verso, 2013).

5   Adam Smith, *The Theory of Moral Sentiments*, ed. Ryan Patrick Hanley (Penguin Random House, 2010).

6   David J. Davis, 'Adam Smith, Communitarian', *The American Conservative*, 19 December 2013, https://www.theamericanconservative.com/articles/adam-smith-communitarian/; Jack Russell Weinstein, *Adam Smith's Pluralism,* (Yale University Press, 2013); Jesse Norman, 'How Adam Smith Would Fix Capitalism', *Financial Times,* 21 June 2018, https://www.ft.com/content/6795a1a0-7476-11e8-b6ad-3823e4384287.

7   This would amount to roughly $287 billion given the size of the US economy. OECD, 'Social Expenditure: Aggregated data', OECD Social and Welfare Statistics (database), https://doi.org/10.1787/data-00166-en (accessed 30 June 2020). socialexp/social-spending.htm.

8   'Fauci, Governors Get Highest Marks For Response To Coronavirus, Quinnipiac University National Poll Finds; Majority Say Trump's Response Not Aggressive Enough', Quinnipiac University, 8 April 2020, https://poll.qu.edu/national/release-detail?ReleaseID=3658.

9   Luke Savage, 'The Coronavirus Has Created Record Support for Medicare For All', *Jacobin,* 2 April 2020, https://www.jacobinmag.com/2020/04/coronavirus-pandemic-medicare-for-all-support; original poll at Yusra Murad, 'As Coronavirus Surges, 'Medicare For All' Support Hits 9-Month High', *Morning Consult,* 1 April 2020, https://morningconsult.com/2020/04/01/medicare-for-all-coronavirus-pandemic/.

10 Laura Gardiner, 'The shifting shape of social security: Charting the changing size and shape of the British welfare system', Resolution Foundation, November 2019, https://www.resolutionfoundation.org/app/uploads/2019/11/The-shifting-shape-of-social-security.pdf.

11 Phillip Inman, 'Rightwing thinktanks call time on age of austerity',

Guardian, 16 May 2020, https://www.theguardian.com/politics/2020/may/16/thatcherite-thinktanks-back-increase-public-spending-in-lockdown.

12 'A New Deal For The Arts', The National Archives, https://www.archives.gov/exhibits/new_deal_for_the_arts/index.html#.

13 Although some countries have considerably more leeway here than others.

14 Jonathan Nicholson, 'Tax "excess" profits of big money-making companies to fix coronavirus economy, scholar urges', MarketWatch, 30 April 2020, https://www.marketwatch.com/story/tax-excess-profits-of-big-money-making-companies-to-fix-coronavirus-economy-scholar-urges-2020-04-30.

15 Tommy Wilson, 'Budget wish list – look after those who look after others,' *New Zealand Herald,* 31 May 2019, https://www.nzherald.co.nz/premium/news/article.cfm?c_id=1504669&objectid=12235697.

16 'The Wellbeing Budget', Budget 2019 New Zealand, 30 May 2019, esp. 10, 18, https://treasury.govt.nz/sites/default/files/2019-05/b19-wellbeing-budget.pdf.

17 'Build Back Better', Wellbeing Economy Alliance, https://wellbeingeconomy.org.

18 Richard A. Easterlin, 'Well-Being, Front and Center: A Note on the Sarkozy Report', *Population and Development Review 36,* no. 1 (March 2010), 119–124, https://www.jstor.org/stable/25699039?seq=1#metadata_info_tab_contents; 'PM Speech on Wellbeing', Gov.uk, 25 November 2010, https://www.gov.uk/government/speeches/pm-speech-on-wellbeing; Emma Bryce, 'The flawed era of GDP is finally coming to an end', *Wired,* 3 August 2019, https://www.wired.co.uk/article/countries-gdp-gross-national-happiness.

19 Dan Button, 'The UK should stop obsessing over GDP. Wellbeing is more telling', *Guardian,* 10 June 2019, https://www.theguardian.com/commentisfree/2019/jun/10/uk-obsessing-gdp-wellbeing-new-zealand; for more on the legacy of the Sarkozy Commission, see Paul Allin and David J. Hand, *The Wellbeing of Nations: Meaning, Motive, and Measurement* (New York: Wiley, 2014).

20 Noreena Hertz, *The Silent Takeover* (Random House, 2002), 17–20.

21 See here too Diane Coyle's work in this area, e.g., *GDP: A Brief But Affectionate History* (Princeton University Press, 2014).

22 'Business Roundtable Members', Business Roundtable, https://
    www.businessroundtable.org/about-us/members.

23 Milton Friedman, 'The Social Responsibility of Business is to
    Increase Its Profits,' *New York Times* magazine, 13 September 1970.

24 'Business Roundtable Redefines the Purpose of a Corporation to
    Promote "An Economy That Serves All Americans"', Business
    Roundtable, 19 August 2019, https://www.businessroundtable.org/
    business-roundtable-redefines-the-purpose-of-a-corporation-to-
    promote-an-economy-that-serves-all-americans.

25 Julia Carrie Wong, 'Amazon execs labeled fired worker "not smart
    or articulate" in leaked PR notes', *Guardian*, 3 April 2020, https://
    www.theguardian.com/technology/2020/apr/02/amazon-chris-
    smalls-smart-articulate-leaked-memo.

26 Chris Smalls, 'Dear Jeff Bezos, instead of firing me, protect your
    workers from coronavirus', *Guardian*, 2 April 2020, https://www.
    theguardian.com/commentisfree/2020/apr/02/dear-jeff-bezos-
    amazon-instead-of-firing-me-protect-your-workers-from-coronavirus.

27 Julia Carrie Wong, 'Amazon execs labeled fired worker "not smart
    or articulate" in leaked PR notes'.

28 'AG James' Statement on Firing of Amazon Worker Who
    Organized Walkout', Office of the New York State Attorney
    General, https://ag.ny.gov/press-release/2020/ag-james-statement-
    firing-amazon-worker-who-organized-walkout.

29 Brad Smith, 'As we work to protect public health, we also need to
    protect the income of hourly workers who support our campus',
    Microsoft, 5 March 2020, https://blogs.microsoft.com/on-the-
    issues/2020/03/05/covid-19-microsoft-hourly-workers/.

30 See for example Republican Senator Josh Hawley's bill in July 2019
    to curb smartphone addiction by banning the 'infinite scroll' of
    social media feeds, and limiting an individual's social media usage
    to thirty minutes a day across all devices, Emily Stewart, 'Josh
    Hawley's bill to limit your Twitter time to 30 minutes a day,
    explained', *Vox*, 31 July 2019, https://www.vox.com/
    recode/2019/7/31/20748732/josh-hawley-smart-act-social-media-
    addiction); or EU industry chief Thierry Breton's warnings in
    February 2020 that should major tech platforms fail to adequately
    curb hate speech and disinformation, tougher rules and penalties

would be forthcoming ('EU threatens tougher hate-speech rules after Facebook meeting', *DW,* 17 February 2020, https://www.dw.com/en/eu-threatens-tougher-hate-speech-rules-after-facebook-meeting/a-52410851).

31 'Camden Council tackles the climate crisis', see video at: https://youtu.be/JzzWc5wMQ6s. Of course, there are limitations to participation; while participants received a £150 voucher in recognition of their time, I know this might not be a viable option for people in precarious work or who aren't guaranteed time off. But with childcare provided, and translators for those who weren't as comfortable in English, the council did start the process of opening up such community engagement to all.

32 These are due to be approved in summer 2020. 'Camden Climate Action Plan', Camden Council, https://consultations.wearecamden.org/supporting-communities/camden-climate-action-plan/.

33 Carl Miller, 'Taiwan is making democracy work again. It's time we paid attention', *Wired,* 26 November 2019, https://www.wired.co.uk/article/taiwan-democracy-social-media.

34 'VTaiwan: Using digital technology to write digital laws', The Gov Lab, https://congress.crowd.law/case-vtaiwan.html.

35 Liz Barry, 'VTaiwan: Public Participation Methods on the Cyberpunk Frontier of Democracy', Civic Hall, 11 August 2016, https://civichall.org/civicist/vtaiwan-democracy-frontier/.

36 Crucially, while anyone can post a standalone comment, the design of the process is such that direct replies are not permitted, meaning that trolls are not able to do their destructive work.

37 'Camden Council tackles the climate crisis', see video at: https://youtu.be/JzzWc5wMQ6s.

38 See Hélène Landemore's work on Democratic reason, for instance *Democratic Reason: Politics, Collective Intelligence, and the Rule of the Many* (Princeton University Press, 2012).

39 Note however that as we've seen, within our local geographies especially, inclusivity and diversity may be absent. And that some communities expressly define themselves by who it is they exclude.

40 Thomas F. Pettigrew and Linda R. Tropp, 'A Meta-Analytic Test of Intergroup Contact Theory', *Journal of Personality and Social*

Psychology 90, no. 5 (2006), 751–83; Bhikhu Parekh et al., 'The Commission on the Future of Multi-Ethnic Britain', The Runnymede Trust, 2000; Alejandro Portes and Julia Sensenbrenner, 'Embeddedness and Immigration: Notes on the Social Determinants of Economic Action', *American Journal of Sociology* 98, no. 6 (May 1993), 1320–50.

41　This is the cumulative total for registrations in 2017, 2018 and 2019, reported directly by *Die Zeit*. Christian Bangel et al., 'Start debating!', *Zeit Online*, 9 March 2018, https://www.zeit.de/gesellschaft/2018-03/germany-talks-match-debate-politics-english.

42　Shan Wang, 'In Germany, a news site is pairing up liberals and conservatives and actually getting them to (gasp) have a civil conversation', Nieman Lab, 8 August 2018, https://www.niemanlab.org/2018/08/in-germany-a-news-site-is-pairing-up-liberals-and-conservatives-and-actually-getting-them-to-gasp-have-a-civil-conversation/.

43　Bangel et al., 'Start debating!'

44　'"You Are Rejecting an Entire Religion"', *Zeit Online*, May 2018, https://www.zeit.de/gesellschaft/2018-04/germany-talks-experience-report-meeting/seite-2.

45　Jochen Wegner, 'There Is No Mirko Here', *Zeit Online*, 22 June 2017, https://www.zeit.de/gesellschaft/2017-06/germany-talks-dispute-political-contention-english.

46　Bangel et al., 'Start debating!', 2.

47　'Improving Social Cohesion, One Discussion at a Time', *Zeit Online*, August 2019, https://www.zeit.de/wissen/2019-08/armin-falk-germany-talks-behaviour-research-english/seite-2.

48　Ibid.

49　Elena Erdmann et al., 'The Issues Dividing Germany', *Zeit Online*, 18 November 2019, https://www.zeit.de/gesellschaft/2019-11/germany-talks-discussion-issues-democracy-english; Armin Falk, Lasse Stötzer and Sven Walter, 'Evaluation Deutschland Spricht', https://news.briq-institute.org/wp-content/uploads/2019/08/Technical_Report_Deutschland_Spricht.pdf. The humanising effect of different people coming together shouldn't be underestimated – indeed there's a significant body of research that supports this being so. See for example Thomas F. Pettigrew and Linda R. Tropp, 'A

Meta-Analytic Test of Intergroup Contact Theory', *Journal of Personality and Social Psychology* 90, no. 5 (June 2006), 751–83.

50 91 Ways, http://91ways.org/.

51 'Public Works', The Public Theater, https://publictheater.org/programs/publicworks/; Richard Halpern, 'Theater and Democratic Thought: Arendt to Rancière', *Critical Inquiry* 37, no. 3 (Spring 2011), 545–72, https://doi.org/10.1086/659358. In Ancient Athens, replacing fragmented tribe-specific performances with a unified public theatre festival brought the tribes together in a common experience.

52 'Public Works' *As You Like It*', The Public Theater, https://publictheater.org/productions/season/1920/sitp/as-you-like-it/.

53 Carl Worswick, 'Colombia's Farc guerillas turn to football as route back into society', *Guardian*, 11 October 2017, https://www.theguardian.com/football/2017/oct/11/colombia-football-farc-la-paz-fc.

54 'Who's Doing What in Italy', Refugees and Football, https://refugeesandfootball.org/whos-doing-what/in/italy.

55 Eytan Halon, 'Playing on the same team for a peaceful future', *Jerusalem Post*, 14 May 2019, https://www.jpost.com/israel-news/playing-on-the-same-team-for-a-peaceful-future-589575.

56 'Umuganda', Rwanda Governance Board, http://www.rgb.rw/index.php?id=37; Amy Yee, 'How Rwanda Tidied Up Its Streets (And The Rest Of The Country, Too)', NPR, 18 July 2018, https://www.npr.org/sections/goatsandsoda/2018/07/18/628364015/how-rwanda-tidied-up-its-streets-and-the-rest-of-the-country-too. Note that *Umuganda* has a dark side as well; the word *Umuganda* was hijacked by the extremist Hutu government during the 1994 genocide when, writes historian Penine Uwimbabazi, Umuganda 'did not involve planting trees but "clearing out the weeds" – a phrase used by the genocidaires to mean the killing of Tutsis' and moderate Hutus. For analysis and synthesis of this history, see Penine Uwimbabazi, 'An Analysis of *Umuganda*: The Policy and Practice of Community Work in Rwanda', University of KwaZulu-Natal, 2012, 47–9. For the history of *Umuganda* during Rwanda's post-genocide rebuilding, see, e.g., Timothy Longman, *Memory and Justice in Post-Genocide Rwanda* (Cambridge University Press, 2017).

57 'Umuganda', Rwanda Governance Board, http://www.rgb.rw/fileadmin/Key_documents/HGS/UMUGANDA_2017.pdf.

58 UNESCO, *Mapping Research and Innovation in the Republic of Rwanda*, ed. G.A. Lemarchand and A. Tash; GOSPIN Country Profiles in Science, *Technology and Innovation Policy* 4, (UNESCO, 2015), p.31.

59 Melanie Lidman, 'In once-torn Rwanda, fear of a fine molds a nation of do-gooders', *Times of Israel*, 27 March 2017, https://www.timesofisrael.com/in-rwanda-where-good-deeds-are-law/.

60 Ibid.

61 The community meeting is less common in the capital city of Kigali and larger towns.

62 Lidman, 'In once-torn Rwanda, fear of a fine molds a nation of do-gooders'.

63 Marie Anne Dushimimana and Joost Bastmeijer, 'Rwanda, part 4: The "reconciliation villages" where genocide survivor and perpetrator live side by side', *New Humanitarian*, 20 May 2019, https://www.thenewhumanitarian.org/special-report/2019/05/20/rwanda-reconciliation-villages-genocide-survivor-perpetrator.

64 Laura Eramian, 'Ethnic Boundaries in Contemporary Rwanda: Fixity, Flexibility and Their Limits', *Anthropologica* 57, no. 1, (2015), 93–104.

65 In this pilot case they were volunteers but the intention is that the scheme is compulsory.

66 Angelique Chrisafis, 'Macron's national service sparks criticism from French left', *Guardian,* 19 June 2019, https://www.theguardian.com/world/2019/jun/19/rollout-of-compulsory-civic-service-for-young-people-in-france-sparks-criticisms.

67 Ibid.; 'France begins trial of compulsory civic service for teens', *France 24,* 16 June 2019, https://www.france24.com/en/20190616-france-trial-macron-new-compulsory-national-service-teen-military.

68 George Makin, 'Small acts of kindness helping lives in lockdown', *Express and Star,* 30 April 2020, https://www.expressandstar.com/news/health/coronavirus-covid19/2020/04/30/small-acts-of-kindness-helping-lives-in-lockdown/.

69 Andy Devane, 'Acts of kindness: Italy helps the most fragile during crisis', Wanted In Milan, 14 March 2020, https://www.

wantedinmilan.com/news/acts-of-kindness-italy-helps-the-most-fragile-during-crisis.html.

70 The Learning Network, 'What Students Are Saying About Random Acts of Kindness, Internet Habits and Where They'd Like To Be Stranded', *New York Times*, 16 April 2020, https://www.nytimes.com/2020/04/16/learning/what-students-are-saying-about-acts-of-kindness-internet-habits-and-where-theyd-like-to-be-stranded.html.

Index